STAN: OECD Structural Analysis Statistics 2016

OECD

BETTER POLICIES FOR BETTER LIVES

This work is published under the responsibility of the Secretary-General of the OECD. The opinions expressed and arguments employed herein do not necessarily reflect the official views of OECD member countries.

This document and any map included herein are without prejudice to the status of or sovereignty over any territory, to the delimitation of international frontiers and boundaries and to the name of any territory, city or area.

Please cite this publication as:
OECD (2017), *STAN: OECD Structural Analysis Statistics 2016*, OECD Publishing.
http://dx.doi.org/10.1787/stan-2016-en

ISBN 978-92-64-27443-3 (print)
ISBN 978-92-64-22677-7 (PDF)

Annual: STAN: OECD Structural Analysis Statistics
ISSN 2225-2150 (print)
ISSN 2225-2169 (online)

The statistical data for Israel are supplied by and under the responsibility of the relevant Israeli authorities. The use of such data by the OECD is without prejudice to the status of the Golan Heights, East Jerusalem and Israeli settlements in the West Bank under the terms of international law.

Corrigenda to OECD publications may be found on line at: *www.oecd.org/about/publishing/corrigenda.htm*.

Table of contents

Country tables

Readers' guide

Main features

This publication includes data according to SNA08/ISIC Rev.4, for 18 OECD member economies as at January 2017.

STAN is primarily based on member countries' annual national accounts by economic activity tables compiled according to the recommendations of System of National Accounts 2008 (SNA08). Previous versions of STAN (from 2000) were based on SNA93 statistics. Missing detail is estimated using data from other sources such as results from national industrial surveys/censuses. Many data points in STAN are estimated and are flagged as such; they do not represent official member countries' submissions.

The data according to different versions of ISIC classification are published in the following database:

- OECD (2017), STAN: OECD Structural Analysis Statistics (database), *http://dx.doi.org/10.1787/stan-data-en*.

Signs and abbreviations

..	Not available
.	Decimal point
n.e.c.	not elsewhere classified

Sources and methods:

- Industry list (PDF): *www.oecd.org/sti/ind/2stan-indlist.pdf*.
- Coverage table (XLS): *http://stats.oecd.org/wbos/fileview2.aspx?IDFile=e63ecbb1-82eb-44db-a5f6-ac356f43da52*.

Contact details

- For any enquiries, please contact *oecdilibrary@oecd.org* or *stan.contact@oecd.org*.

Classification

- The International Standard Industrial Classification (ISIC) Rev. 4 is available online at *http://unstats.un.org/unsd/cr/registry/isic-4.asp*.

ISIC Rev. 4 classification

Section	Division	Description
A	**01-03**	**Agriculture, forestry and fishing**
B	**05-09**	**Mining and quarrying**
C	**10-33**	**Manufacturing**
	10-12	Manufacturing of food products, beverages and tobacco
	13-15	Manufacture of textiles, wearing apparel, leather and related products
	16-18	Manufacture of wood and paper products; printing and reproduction of recorded media
	19-23	Manufacture of chemicals, rubber, plastics, fuel and other non-metallic mineral products
	20-21	Manufacture of chemicals and pharmaceutical products
	22-23	Manufacture of rubber and plastics products and other non-metallic mineral products
	24-25	Manufacture of basic metals and fabricated metal products, except machinery and equipment
	241+2431	Manufacture and casting of basic iron and steel
	242+2432	Manufacture and casting of basic precious and other non-ferrous metals
	26-28	
	26	Manufacture of computer, electronic and optical products
	262	Manufacture of computers and peripheral equipment
	27	Manufacture of electrical equipment
	28	Manufacture of machinery and equipment n.e.c.
	29-30	
	29	Manufacture of motor vehicles, trailers and semi-trailers
	30	Manufacture of other transport equipment
	31-33	Manufacture of furniture; other manufacturing and repair and installation of machinery and equipment
	31-32	Manufacture of furniture and other manufacturing
	33	Repair and installation of machinery and equipment
D+E	**35-39**	
D	35	Electricity, gas, steam and air conditioning supply
E	36-39	Water supply; sewerage, waste, remediation activities
F	**41-43**	**Construction**
G-I	45-56	
G	**45-47**	**Wholesale and retail trade; repair of motor vehicles and motorcycle repairs**
H	**49-53**	**Transportation and storage**
I	**55-56**	**Accommodation and food service activities**
J	**58-63**	**Information and communication**
	58-60	Publishing, audio visual and broadcasting activities
	61	Telecommunications
	62-63	IT and other information services
K	**64-66**	**Financial and insurance activities**
L-N	**68-82**	
L	68	Real estate activities
M+N	69-82	
M	69-75	Professional, scientific and technical activities
	69-71	Legal and accounting activities; head offices; management consultancy; architecture and engineering activities; technical testing and analysis
	73-75	Advertising, market research; other professional, scientific and technical activities
N	77-82	Administrative and support service activities
O-U	84-99	
O-Q	84-88	
O	**84**	**Public administration and defence; compulsory social security**
P	**85**	**Education**
Q	**86-88**	**Human health and social work activities**
R-U	90-99	
R	**90-93**	**Arts, entertainment and recreation**
S	**94-96**	**Other service activities**
T	**97-98**	**Activities of households as employers; undifferentiated goods- and services-producing activities of households for own use**
B-E	**05-39**	**INDUSTRY INCLUDING ENERGY**
	24-33x	**Metal industry including repairs**
G-U	**45-99**	**TOTAL SERVICES**
G-N	**45-82**	**BUSINESS SECTOR SERVICES**
	45-82x	**BUSINESS SECTOR SERVICES excluding real estate**
	05-82x	**NON-AGRICULTURE BUSINESS SECTOR excluding real estate**
	ENERGYP	**Energy producing activities**

Country tables

AUSTRIA

Table 1. Production (gross output), current prices

ISIC Rev. 4

Million EUR

		2007	2008	2009	2010	2011	2012	2013	2014
	TOTAL	**516 584**	**546 557**	**520 436**	**543 978**	**578 347**	**595 245**	**605 227**	**613 284**
01-03	**AGRICULTURE, FORESTRY AND FISHING**	**8 719**	**8 878**	**7 902**	**8 686**	**9 867**	**9 934**	**9 747**	**9 596**
05-09	**MINING AND QUARRYING**	**2 071**	**2 443**	**2 111**	**2 289**	**2 660**	**2 718**	**2 645**	**2 581**
10-33	**MANUFACTURING**	**152 179**	**159 865**	**138 053**	**151 215**	**169 446**	**173 893**	**174 407**	**174 328**
10-12	Food products, beverages and tobacco	16 041	17 409	16 712	17 088	18 305	19 483	20 212	20 445
13-14	Textiles and wearing apparel	2 728	2 509	2 161	2 289	2 408	2 250	2 275	2 302
15	Leather and related products	636	771	616	694	766	783	853	886
16	Wood, wood and cork products	8 072	7 734	6 681	7 369	8 098	8 006	8 036	8 043
17	Paper and paper products	5 855	5 988	5 219	5 932	6 291	6 305	6 247	6 298
18	Printing and reproduction of recorded media	3 026	3 106	2 832	2 943	2 929	2 777	2 687	2 537
19-23	Chemical, rubber, plastics, non-metallic products	26 928	29 209	25 378	32 320	35 717	36 851	37 018	36 758
20	Chemicals and chemical products	6 707	7 423	6 599	12 323	13 172	13 674	13 946	13 793
21	Pharmaceutical products	3 123	3 051	3 452	3 606	3 797	3 886	4 098	4 251
22-23	Rubber, plastic, non-metallic mineral products	12 070	12 622	11 099	11 485	12 456	12 271	12 479	12 815
24	Basic metals	14 169	15 476	11 953	13 160	16 445	16 539	15 121	15 074
25	Metal products, except machinery and equipment	13 439	13 699	12 107	11 835	13 442	14 170	14 219	14 190
26-28	Machinery and equipment	33 747	35 961	31 102	31 380	35 864	37 692	37 348	37 738
26	Computer, electronic and optical products	5 879	5 725	5 032	4 835	5 429	5 640	5 822	6 103
27	Electrical equipment	10 057	10 871	10 149	9 791	10 556	10 851	10 119	10 237
28	Machinery and equipment n.e.c.	17 811	19 365	15 921	16 754	19 879	21 201	21 407	21 398
29-30	Transport equipment	18 362	16 991	12 444	13 976	15 831	16 024	16 782	17 162
29	Motor vehicles, trailers and semi-trailers	15 770	13 864	9 805	11 642	13 450	13 709	14 236	14 681
30	Other transport equipment	2 591	3 126	2 640	2 334	2 381	2 314	2 546	2 481
31-33	Furniture; repair, installation of machinery and equipment	9 177	11 011	10 848	12 228	13 351	13 014	13 609	12 897
31-32	Furniture, other manufacturing	6 154	7 177	7 155	7 111	8 192	7 431	7 475	6 718
33	Repair and installation of machinery and equipment	3 022	3 834	3 693	5 118	5 159	5 582	6 135	6 180
35-39	**ELECTRICITY, GAS, WATER AND WASTE MANAGEMENT**	**25 131**	**30 037**	**29 202**	**29 117**	**27 844**	**29 374**	**29 487**	**27 507**
35	Electricity, gas, steam and air conditioning supply	19 462	23 985	23 221	22 717	21 184	22 228	22 074	19 894
36-39	Water supply; sewerage, waste, remediation activities	5 669	6 051	5 980	6 400	6 660	7 146	7 413	7 614
41-43	**CONSTRUCTION**	**40 603**	**45 137**	**43 928**	**43 654**	**44 931**	**46 814**	**47 257**	**48 248**
45-56	Distribution; transportation, accommodation, food service	102 256	106 469	104 585	108 559	114 186	117 257	118 708	122 362
45-47	**Wholesale and retail trade; motor vehicle and motorcycle repairs**	**54 632**	**56 173**	**55 565**	**58 235**	**61 392**	**62 425**	**62 293**	**64 327**
49-53	**Transportation and storage**	**29 185**	**30 707**	**29 123**	**29 921**	**31 276**	**32 336**	**33 042**	**33 788**
55-56	**Accommodation and food service activities**	**18 439**	**19 589**	**19 897**	**20 403**	**21 517**	**22 496**	**23 374**	**24 247**
58-63	**Information and communication**	**19 047**	**19 343**	**19 109**	**19 254**	**20 651**	**21 301**	**22 036**	**22 819**
58-60	Publishing, audiovisual and broadcasting activities	4 536	4 772	4 680	4 876	5 110	5 406	5 632	5 628
61	Telecommunications	7 496	7 382	7 044	6 787	6 519	6 385	6 082	5 916
62-63	IT and other information services	7 016	7 190	7 385	7 592	9 022	9 510	10 322	11 275
64-66	**Financial and insurance activities**	**24 574**	**24 400**	**22 816**	**23 753**	**25 140**	**24 541**	**25 862**	**26 614**
68	**Real estate activities**	**32 791**	**33 644**	**34 514**	**36 052**	**37 924**	**39 662**	**41 724**	**42 717**
69-82	**Professional, scientific, technical, admin., support activities**	**40 526**	**43 595**	**42 273**	**43 632**	**46 383**	**48 112**	**49 761**	**50 838**
69-75	Professional, scientific and technical activities	25 219	26 687	25 962	26 608	28 171	29 238	30 410	30 958
69-71	Legal, accounting activities; mgt consultancy; engineering	18 229	19 416	19 118	19 516	20 645	21 570	22 336	22 722
73-75	Advertising, market research; other prof., scientific, tech.	6 084	5 969	5 514	5 660	5 986	6 020	6 108	6 242
77-82	Administrative and support service activities	15 307	16 908	16 311	17 024	18 212	18 873	19 351	19 880
84-88	**Public administration, defence; social security; education; health**	**57 920**	**61 390**	**64 432**	**66 041**	**67 323**	**69 314**	**70 898**	**72 514**
84	**Public administration, defence; compulsory social security**	**19 304**	**20 540**	**21 719**	**21 908**	**22 026**	**22 541**	**22 688**	**22 998**
85	**Education**	**15 615**	**16 549**	**17 321**	**17 840**	**18 275**	**18 741**	**19 184**	**19 525**
86-88	**Human health and social work activities**	**23 001**	**24 301**	**25 392**	**26 293**	**27 023**	**28 032**	**29 026**	**29 992**
90-99	**Arts, entertainment, household goods repairs, other**	**10 765**	**11 355**	**11 513**	**11 726**	**11 992**	**12 326**	**12 694**	**13 159**
90-93	**Arts, entertainment and recreation**	**4 490**	**4 941**	**4 912**	**5 024**	**5 216**	**5 353**	**5 501**	**5 722**
94-96	**Other service activities**	**6 109**	**6 245**	**6 423**	**6 526**	**6 604**	**6 803**	**7 012**	**7 264**
97-98	**Activities of households as employers and for own use**	**165**	**169**	**178**	**177**	**173**	**171**	**181**	**173**
05-39	**INDUSTRY INCLUDING ENERGY**	**179 381**	**192 345**	**169 366**	**182 621**	**199 950**	**205 986**	**206 538**	**204 417**
45-99	**TOTAL SERVICES**	**287 881**	**300 197**	**299 241**	**309 017**	**323 599**	**332 512**	**341 684**	**351 023**
45-82	**BUSINESS SECTOR SERVICES**	**219 195**	**227 452**	**223 296**	**231 250**	**244 284**	**250 872**	**258 092**	**265 350**
45-82x	**BUSINESS SECTOR SERVICES excluding real estate**	**186 404**	**193 808**	**188 782**	**195 198**	**206 360**	**211 210**	**216 368**	**222 633**
05-82x	**NON-AGRICULTURE BUSINESS SECTOR excluding real estate**	..	..	..	..	..	..	..	..

.. Not available

Note: Detailed metadata at: http://metalinks.oecd.org/stan/20170410/1c43.

Information on data for Israel: http://oe.cd/israel-disclaimer.

Disclaimer: http://oe.cd/disclaimer

AUSTRIA

Table 2. Value added, current prices

ISIC Rev. 4

Million EUR

		2007	2008	2009	2010	2011	2012	2013	2014
	TOTAL	**251 926**	**260 533**	**254 763**	**262 311**	**274 852**	**281 956**	**287 195**	**294 443**
01-03	**AGRICULTURE, FORESTRY AND FISHING**	**4 030**	**3 947**	**3 306**	**3 762**	**4 428**	**4 330**	**4 124**	**4 034**
05-09	**MINING AND QUARRYING**	**987**	**1 345**	**1 076**	**1 179**	**1 503**	**1 516**	**1 483**	**1 453**
10-33	**MANUFACTURING**	**51 524**	**51 052**	**47 034**	**48 983**	**51 581**	**53 382**	**53 554**	**54 582**
10-12	Food products, beverages and tobacco	4 931	4 705	4 967	5 107	4 918	5 394	5 177	5 195
13-14	Textiles and wearing apparel	1 014	886	798	838	862	799	809	831
15	Leather and related products	185	226	221	259	239	231	194	202
16	Wood, wood and cork products	2 340	2 125	1 893	2 055	2 091	2 042	2 066	2 084
17	Paper and paper products	1 784	1 634	1 659	1 705	1 748	1 796	1 742	1 866
18	Printing and reproduction of recorded media	1 223	1 249	1 158	1 119	1 100	1 073	984	960
19-23	Chemical, rubber, plastics, non-metallic products	9 330	8 596	8 378	8 456	8 938	8 717	8 974	9 372
20	Chemicals and chemical products	2 065	2 005	1 922	1 953	2 145	1 873	2 187	2 369
21	Pharmaceutical products	1 808	1 468	1 724	1 797	1 877	1 975	1 979	2 051
22-23	Rubber, plastic, non-metallic mineral products	4 930	4 673	4 216	4 426	4 682	4 598	4 768	4 914
24	Basic metals	3 951	4 011	3 004	3 388	3 606	3 795	3 488	3 557
25	Metal products, except machinery and equipment	5 084	4 922	4 761	4 677	4 968	5 205	5 472	5 455
26-28	Machinery and equipment	12 829	13 735	12 610	13 142	14 417	15 130	15 137	15 225
26	Computer, electronic and optical products	2 585	2 487	2 294	2 314	2 723	2 751	2 896	2 890
27	Electrical equipment	3 913	4 586	4 562	4 662	4 361	4 902	4 548	4 583
28	Machinery and equipment n.e.c.	6 332	6 662	5 754	6 166	7 333	7 477	7 694	7 752
29-30	Transport equipment	4 809	4 745	3 836	3 863	4 230	4 442	4 553	4 752
29	Motor vehicles, trailers and semi-trailers	3 945	3 765	3 103	3 140	3 425	3 855	3 719	3 922
30	Other transport equipment	864	980	732	723	805	588	834	830
31-33	Furniture; repair, installation of machinery and equipment	4 044	4 218	3 750	4 374	4 464	4 756	4 959	5 082
31-32	Furniture, other manufacturing	2 742	2 621	2 311	2 457	2 496	2 535	2 582	2 616
33	Repair and installation of machinery and equipment	1 302	1 598	1 439	1 918	1 968	2 221	2 378	2 466
35-39	**ELECTRICITY, GAS, WATER AND WASTE MANAGEMENT**	**7 711**	**7 938**	**8 098**	**7 970**	**7 875**	**8 250**	**8 502**	**8 212**
35	Electricity, gas, steam and air conditioning supply	4 968	5 318	5 433	5 222	5 034	5 228	5 448	5 021
36-39	Water supply; sewerage, waste, remediation activities	2 743	2 620	2 665	2 749	2 841	3 022	3 054	3 191
41-43	**CONSTRUCTION**	**17 436**	**18 163**	**17 462**	**17 122**	**17 465**	**18 015**	**18 554**	**19 003**
45-56	Distribution; transportation, accommodation, food service	57 232	59 705	59 015	61 288	64 481	65 694	65 708	67 729
45-47	**Wholesale and retail trade; motor vehicle and motorcycle repairs**	**31 633**	**32 685**	**32 187**	**34 025**	**35 917**	**36 111**	**35 179**	**36 151**
49-53	**Transportation and storage**	**14 279**	**14 907**	**14 469**	**14 601**	**15 314**	**15 656**	**16 150**	**16 632**
55-56	**Accommodation and food service activities**	**11 319**	**12 113**	**12 359**	**12 662**	**13 250**	**13 927**	**14 378**	**14 946**
58-63	**Information and communication**	**8 443**	**8 574**	**8 338**	**8 424**	**9 137**	**9 333**	**9 752**	**10 357**
58-60	Publishing, audiovisual and broadcasting activities	1 767	1 748	1 691	1 773	1 892	2 067	2 221	2 181
61	Telecommunications	3 161	3 122	2 960	2 864	2 704	2 531	2 401	2 601
62-63	IT and other information services	3 514	3 704	3 687	3 788	4 540	4 734	5 130	5 575
64-66	**Financial and insurance activities**	**12 858**	**12 926**	**11 887**	**11 921**	**12 716**	**12 054**	**12 645**	**12 826**
68	**Real estate activities**	**22 169**	**22 806**	**23 011**	**24 077**	**25 332**	**26 341**	**27 759**	**28 890**
69-82	**Professional, scientific, technical, admin., support activities**	**21 299**	**23 166**	**22 447**	**23 256**	**24 860**	**25 979**	**26 998**	**27 799**
69-75	Professional, scientific and technical activities	11 378	12 361	12 195	12 529	13 356	14 112	14 786	15 052
69-71	Legal, accounting activities; mgt consultancy; engineering	9 217	9 917	9 868	10 215	10 758	11 352	11 776	12 148
73-75	Advertising, market research; other prof., scientific, tech.	1 714	1 806	1 698	1 692	1 846	1 984	2 008	2 011
77-82	Administrative and support service activities	9 921	10 805	10 252	10 727	11 504	11 867	12 212	12 747
84-88	**Public administration, defence; social security; education; health**	**41 420**	**43 746**	**45 699**	**46 787**	**47 707**	**49 104**	**49 987**	**51 181**
84	**Public administration, defence; compulsory social security**	**12 904**	**13 591**	**14 151**	**14 332**	**14 467**	**14 817**	**14 896**	**15 161**
85	**Education**	**13 147**	**13 833**	**14 442**	**14 851**	**15 156**	**15 547**	**15 656**	**15 947**
86-88	**Human health and social work activities**	**15 369**	**16 323**	**17 107**	**17 604**	**18 084**	**18 739**	**19 436**	**20 073**
90-99	**Arts, entertainment, household goods repairs, other**	**6 818**	**7 165**	**7 388**	**7 541**	**7 769**	**7 957**	**8 129**	**8 379**
90-93	**Arts, entertainment and recreation**	**2 967**	**3 219**	**3 255**	**3 330**	**3 460**	**3 544**	**3 575**	**3 697**
94-96	**Other service activities**	**3 685**	**3 777**	**3 956**	**4 034**	**4 136**	**4 242**	**4 373**	**4 509**
97-98	**Activities of households as employers and for own use**	**165**	**169**	**178**	**177**	**173**	**171**	**181**	**173**
05-39	**INDUSTRY INCLUDING ENERGY**	**60 222**	**60 335**	**56 208**	**58 133**	**60 958**	**63 148**	**63 539**	**64 246**
45-99	**TOTAL SERVICES**	**170 239**	**178 088**	**177 786**	**183 295**	**192 001**	**196 462**	**200 978**	**207 160**
45-82	**BUSINESS SECTOR SERVICES**	**122 001**	**127 177**	**124 699**	**128 967**	**136 526**	**139 401**	**142 862**	**147 600**
45-82x	**BUSINESS SECTOR SERVICES excluding real estate**	**99 832**	**104 371**	**101 688**	**104 889**	**111 193**	**113 059**	**115 103**	**118 710**
05-82x	**NON-AGRICULTURE BUSINESS SECTOR excluding real estate**	..	..	..	..	..	..	..	..

.. Not available

Note: Detailed metadata at: http://metalinks.oecd.org/stan/20170410/1c43.
Information on data for Israel: http://oe.cd/israel-disclaimer.

Disclaimer: http://oe.cd/disclaimer

AUSTRIA

Table 3. Value added, volumes

ISIC Rev. 4

Million 2010 EUR

		2007	2008	2009	2010	2011	2012	2013	2014
	TOTAL	**263 927**	**268 491**	**257 126**	**262 311**	**270 538**	**272 166**	**272 885**	**274 731**
01-03	**AGRICULTURE, FORESTRY AND FISHING**	**3 968**	**4 239**	**3 950**	**3 762**	**4 322**	**3 979**	**3 883**	**3 971**
05-09	**MINING AND QUARRYING**	**1 154**	**1 381**	**1 185**	**1 179**	**1 384**	**1 340**	**1 330**	**1 340**
10-33	**MANUFACTURING**	**52 655**	**53 132**	**45 314**	**48 983**	**52 187**	**53 461**	**53 630**	**54 467**
10-12	Food products, beverages and tobacco	5 813	5 048	4 818	5 107	4 876	5 319	4 957	4 936
13-14	Textiles and wearing apparel	1 040	917	784	838	826	742	729	747
15	Leather and related products	169	205	191	259	251	249	213	251
16	Wood, wood and cork products	2 465	2 236	1 899	2 055	2 267	2 117	2 123	2 173
17	Paper and paper products	1 797	1 653	1 538	1 705	1 838	1 905	1 939	2 154
18	Printing and reproduction of recorded media	1 162	1 169	1 095	1 119	1 171	1 160	1 074	1 015
19-23	Chemical, rubber, plastics, non-metallic products	8 168	8 018	8 313	8 456	9 103	8 848	9 316	9 922
20	Chemicals and chemical products	2 132	1 921	2 001	1 953	1 950	1 761	2 240	2 582
21	Pharmaceutical products	1 871	1 440	1 733	1 797	1 969	2 097	2 101	2 237
22-23	Rubber, plastic, non-metallic mineral products	5 355	5 072	3 969	4 426	4 647	4 498	4 704	4 853
24	Basic metals	6 155	6 447	2 700	3 388	3 418	3 728	3 634	3 674
25	Metal products, except machinery and equipment	5 389	5 372	4 427	4 677	5 091	5 245	5 482	5 426
26-28	Machinery and equipment	12 883	14 143	12 227	13 142	14 611	15 210	14 984	14 833
26	Computer, electronic and optical products	2 431	2 436	2 260	2 314	2 748	2 783	2 964	2 927
27	Electrical equipment	3 878	4 741	4 388	4 662	4 491	4 987	4 566	4 570
28	Machinery and equipment n.e.c.	6 591	6 985	5 581	6 166	7 371	7 448	7 457	7 341
29-30	Transport equipment	4 865	5 013	3 740	3 863	4 357	4 452	4 496	4 645
29	Motor vehicles, trailers and semi-trailers	3 980	3 976	3 006	3 140	3 551	3 915	3 721	3 877
30	Other transport equipment	885	1 039	735	723	805	546	766	761
31-33	Furniture; repair, installation of machinery and equipment	4 193	4 345	3 631	4 374	4 379	4 453	4 646	4 695
31-32	Furniture, other manufacturing	2 787	2 702	2 222	2 457	2 403	2 296	2 398	2 410
33	Repair and installation of machinery and equipment	1 393	1 640	1 405	1 918	1 975	2 163	2 255	2 291
35-39	**ELECTRICITY, GAS, WATER AND WASTE MANAGEMENT**	**8 685**	**7 968**	**8 336**	**7 970**	**7 465**	**7 784**	**8 241**	**8 056**
35	Electricity, gas, steam and air conditioning supply	5 807	5 252	5 645	5 222	4 816	4 965	5 295	4 977
36-39	Water supply; sewerage, waste, remediation activities	2 900	2 729	2 696	2 749	2 648	2 817	2 945	3 077
41-43	**CONSTRUCTION**	**19 937**	**19 686**	**17 815**	**17 122**	**16 965**	**16 863**	**16 681**	**16 367**
45-56	Distribution; transportation, accommodation, food service	61 383	61 523	60 299	61 288	62 990	62 627	61 884	62 638
45-47	**Wholesale and retail trade; motor vehicle and motorcycle repairs**	**33 499**	**32 919**	**33 172**	**34 025**	**35 240**	**34 659**	**33 922**	**34 593**
49-53	**Transportation and storage**	**15 728**	**15 987**	**14 640**	**14 601**	**14 990**	**14 968**	**14 915**	**14 982**
55-56	**Accommodation and food service activities**	**12 196**	**12 672**	**12 481**	**12 662**	**12 760**	**12 994**	**13 035**	**13 064**
58-63	**Information and communication**	**8 958**	**8 933**	**8 556**	**8 424**	**9 065**	**9 011**	**9 201**	**9 384**
58-60	Publishing, audiovisual and broadcasting activities	2 115	2 020	1 833	1 773	1 864	1 940	2 007	1 945
61	Telecommunications	3 204	3 150	3 037	2 864	2 690	2 466	2 264	2 161
62-63	IT and other information services	3 668	3 782	3 692	3 788	4 511	4 603	4 929	5 285
64-66	**Financial and insurance activities**	**10 499**	**11 051**	**11 884**	**11 921**	**12 073**	**12 048**	**11 736**	**11 408**
68	**Real estate activities**	**23 081**	**23 973**	**23 584**	**24 077**	**24 880**	**25 207**	**25 733**	**26 196**
69-82	**Professional, scientific, technical, admin., support activities**	**22 361**	**23 670**	**22 469**	**23 256**	**24 459**	**24 985**	**25 617**	**25 885**
69-75	Professional, scientific and technical activities	12 201	12 663	12 220	12 529	13 187	13 716	14 110	14 026
69-71	Legal, accounting activities; mgt consultancy; engineering	10 000	10 268	9 943	10 215	10 594	10 965	11 161	11 203
73-75	Advertising, market research; other prof., scientific, tech.	1 755	1 766	1 666	1 692	1 859	2 017	2 013	2 015
77-82	Administrative and support service activities	10 170	11 005	10 249	10 727	11 272	11 272	11 511	11 860
84-88	**Public administration, defence; social security; education; health**	**44 584**	**45 950**	**46 474**	**46 787**	**47 111**	**47 272**	**47 376**	**47 437**
84	**Public administration, defence; compulsory social security**	**13 842**	**14 213**	**14 334**	**14 332**	**14 285**	**14 265**	**14 195**	**14 209**
85	**Education**	**14 030**	**14 452**	**14 611**	**14 851**	**14 996**	**15 082**	**15 065**	**15 095**
86-88	**Human health and social work activities**	**16 712**	**17 285**	**17 531**	**17 604**	**17 830**	**17 925**	**18 115**	**18 131**
90-99	**Arts, entertainment, household goods repairs, other**	**7 412**	**7 545**	**7 466**	**7 541**	**7 638**	**7 621**	**7 603**	**7 656**
90-93	**Arts, entertainment and recreation**	**3 234**	**3 395**	**3 280**	**3 330**	**3 389**	**3 392**	**3 356**	**3 404**
94-96	**Other service activities**	**3 990**	**3 969**	**4 002**	**4 034**	**4 082**	**4 072**	**4 089**	**4 107**
97-98	**Activities of households as employers and for own use**	**188**	**181**	**185**	**177**	**167**	**157**	**158**	**147**
05-39	**INDUSTRY INCLUDING ENERGY**	**62 330**	**62 355**	**54 773**	**58 133**	**61 036**	**62 587**	**63 222**	**63 875**
45-99	**TOTAL SERVICES**	**177 993**	**182 464**	**180 727**	**183 295**	**188 215**	**188 766**	**189 153**	**190 605**
45-82	**BUSINESS SECTOR SERVICES**	**125 957**	**128 936**	**126 786**	**128 967**	**133 467**	**133 873**	**134 174**	**135 509**
45-82x	**BUSINESS SECTOR SERVICES excluding real estate**	**102 871**	**104 962**	**103 201**	**104 889**	**108 587**	**108 667**	**108 440**	**109 309**
05-82x	**NON-AGRICULTURE BUSINESS SECTOR excluding real estate**	..	..	..	..	..	..	..	..

.. Not available

Note: Detailed metadata at: http://metalinks.oecd.org/stan/20170410/1c43.

Information on data for Israel: http://oe.cd/israel-disclaimer.

Disclaimer: http://oe.cd/disclaimer

AUSTRIA

Table 4. Gross fixed capital formation, current prices

ISIC Rev. 4

Million EUR

		2007	2008	2009	2010	2011	2012	2013	2014
	TOTAL	**64 934**	**68 247**	**64 342**	**63 764**	**69 418**	**71 925**	**74 624**	**75 133**
01-03	**AGRICULTURE, FORESTRY AND FISHING**	**1 970**	**2 241**	**2 249**	**2 287**	**2 314**	**2 528**	**2 351**	**2 040**
05-09	**MINING AND QUARRYING**	**419**	**512**	**431**	**434**	**356**	**328**	**550**	**640**
10-33	**MANUFACTURING**	**10 352**	**10 506**	**10 113**	**9 864**	**10 536**	**12 273**	**13 512**	**13 206**
10-12	Food products, beverages and tobacco	672	749	703	750	765	934	885	1 108
13-14	Textiles and wearing apparel	112	112	86	91	100	134	119	121
15	Leather and related products	16	19	17	21	30	35	22	26
16	Wood, wood and cork products	413	394	279	269	367	352	325	363
17	Paper and paper products	285	242	249	220	278	438	382	236
18	Printing and reproduction of recorded media	251	185	228	205	159	161	153	115
19-23	Chemical, rubber, plastics, non-metallic products	2 442	2 419	1 923	2 050	2 278	2 469	2 797	2 504
20	Chemicals and chemical products	578	715	532	574	675	691	827	594
21	Pharmaceutical products	588	493	452	424	472	696	700	653
22-23	Rubber, plastic, non-metallic mineral products	957	972	778	888	942	963	1 120	1 102
24	Basic metals	951	903	966	706	642	823	1 103	1 200
25	Metal products, except machinery and equipment	862	836	806	749	815	914	1 065	1 024
26-28	Machinery and equipment	2 719	3 030	3 214	3 227	3 378	3 823	4 335	4 303
26	Computer, electronic and optical products	725	630	574	629	864	996	984	1 038
27	Electrical equipment	875	1 252	1 534	1 510	1 164	1 293	1 543	1 553
28	Machinery and equipment n.e.c.	1 119	1 148	1 106	1 088	1 350	1 535	1 809	1 712
29-30	Transport equipment	1 121	1 181	1 159	1 073	1 175	1 473	1 604	1 546
29	Motor vehicles, trailers and semi-trailers	921	995	1 026	885	1 007	1 284	1 378	1 347
30	Other transport equipment	200	186	133	188	169	189	226	199
31-33	Furniture; repair, installation of machinery and equipment	508	435	482	502	548	716	722	660
31-32	Furniture, other manufacturing	370	353	326	364	365	405	440	426
33	Repair and installation of machinery and equipment	137	83	156	138	183	311	282	233
35-39	**ELECTRICITY, GAS, WATER AND WASTE MANAGEMENT**	**2 759**	**2 895**	**3 148**	**2 781**	**3 624**	**3 887**	**3 227**	**3 343**
35	Electricity, gas, steam and air conditioning supply	1 599	1 822	2 311	1 966	2 721	2 936	2 290	2 345
36-39	Water supply; sewerage, waste, remediation activities	1 160	1 073	838	815	903	950	937	999
41-43	**CONSTRUCTION**	**1 705**	**1 122**	**1 061**	**1 317**	**1 160**	**1 308**	**1 409**	**1 414**
45-56	Distribution; transportation, accommodation, food service	9 952	10 712	10 090	9 872	10 845	10 360	10 767	11 844
45-47	**Wholesale and retail trade; motor vehicle and motorcycle repairs**	**3 225**	**3 243**	**2 895**	**3 010**	**3 663**	**3 707**	**3 837**	**4 281**
49-53	**Transportation and storage**	**5 570**	**6 317**	**6 056**	**5 787**	**6 086**	**5 355**	**5 458**	**6 164**
55-56	**Accommodation and food service activities**	**1 156**	**1 152**	**1 139**	**1 075**	**1 097**	**1 297**	**1 472**	**1 399**
58-63	**Information and communication**	**2 408**	**2 553**	**2 329**	**1 532**	**2 478**	**2 487**	**2 877**	**3 035**
58-60	Publishing, audiovisual and broadcasting activities	315	337	279	317	336	402	381	370
61	Telecommunications	1 331	1 590	1 400	448	1 214	1 108	1 209	1 362
62-63	IT and other information services	763	626	649	768	928	976	1 287	1 304
64-66	**Financial and insurance activities**	**1 488**	**1 438**	**1 545**	**1 446**	**1 924**	**1 965**	**2 237**	**2 283**
68	**Real estate activities**	**19 278**	**20 210**	**19 445**	**19 589**	**20 564**	**21 099**	**21 671**	**21 108**
69-82	**Professional, scientific, technical, admin., support activities**	**6 866**	**7 416**	**5 632**	**6 586**	**7 404**	**7 090**	**7 071**	**6 653**
69-75	Professional, scientific and technical activities	1 746	2 023	1 585	1 835	2 186	2 216	2 160	2 170
69-71	Legal, accounting activities; mgt consultancy; engineering	1 359	1 613	1 166	1 261	1 507	1 553	1 478	1 487
73-75	Advertising, market research; other prof., scientific, tech.	186	153	142	170	178	175	192	207
77-82	Administrative and support service activities	5 120	5 393	4 047	4 751	5 218	4 874	4 911	4 483
84-88	**Public administration, defence; social security; education; health**	**6 648**	**7 437**	**7 090**	**6 878**	**7 015**	**7 245**	**7 527**	**7 908**
84	**Public administration, defence; compulsory social security**	**2 651**	**3 099**	**2 390**	**2 003**	**1 976**	**2 030**	**2 137**	**2 320**
85	**Education**	**1 776**	**1 942**	**2 195**	**2 255**	**2 284**	**2 237**	**2 448**	**2 530**
86-88	**Human health and social work activities**	**2 220**	**2 396**	**2 504**	**2 619**	**2 756**	**2 978**	**2 942**	**3 059**
90-99	**Arts, entertainment, household goods repairs, other**	**1 090**	**1 206**	**1 211**	**1 178**	**1 197**	**1 355**	**1 425**	**1 659**
90-93	**Arts, entertainment and recreation**	**595**	**650**	**667**	**639**	**614**	**704**	**746**	**869**
94-96	**Other service activities**	**495**	**557**	**543**	**539**	**583**	**650**	**679**	**790**
97-98	**Activities of households as employers and for own use**	**0**	**0**	**0**	**0**	**0**	**0**	**0**	**0**
05-39	**INDUSTRY INCLUDING ENERGY**	**13 530**	**13 912**	**13 692**	**13 079**	**14 516**	**16 487**	**17 289**	**17 189**
45-99	**TOTAL SERVICES**	**47 729**	**50 973**	**47 341**	**47 081**	**51 427**	**51 601**	**53 575**	**54 490**
45-82	**BUSINESS SECTOR SERVICES**	**39 992**	**42 329**	**39 040**	**39 026**	**43 215**	**43 001**	**44 623**	**44 923**
45-82x	**BUSINESS SECTOR SERVICES excluding real estate**	**20 714**	**22 119**	**19 595**	**19 437**	**22 651**	**21 902**	**22 952**	**23 815**
05-82x	**NON-AGRICULTURE BUSINESS SECTOR excluding real estate**	..	..	..	..	..	..	..	..

.. Not available

Note: Detailed metadata at: http://metalinks.oecd.org/stan/20170410/1c43.
Information on data for Israel: http://oe.cd/israel-disclaimer.

Disclaimer: http://oe.cd/disclaimer

Table 5. Number of persons engaged, total employment

ISIC Rev. 4

Thousands

		2007	2008	2009	2010	2011	2012	2013	2014
	TOTAL	**4 014**	**4 090**	**4 073**	**4 102**	**4 166**	**4 210**	**4 224**	**4 263**
01-03	**AGRICULTURE, FORESTRY AND FISHING**	**209**	**206**	**202**	**199**	**196**	**185**	**182**	**188**
05-09	**MINING AND QUARRYING**	**6**	**7**	**6**	**6**	**6**	**6**	**6**	**6**
10-33	**MANUFACTURING**	**645**	**651**	**625**	**612**	**623**	**631**	**627**	**628**
10-12	Food products, beverages and tobacco	84	81	81	81	81	81	81	82
13-14	Textiles and wearing apparel	21	20	18	18	17	17	16	16
15	Leather and related products	5	5	4	4	4	4	4	4
16	Wood, wood and cork products	37	37	34	34	34	34	33	33
17	Paper and paper products	19	19	18	17	17	17	17	17
18	Printing and reproduction of recorded media	18	17	16	14	14	14	13	12
19-23	Chemical, rubber, plastics, non-metallic products	96	97	93	92	94	95	95	95
20	Chemicals and chemical products	18	18	17	17	18	18	18	17
21	Pharmaceutical products	11	11	12	12	13	13	14	15
22-23	Rubber, plastic, non-metallic mineral products	66	66	63	61	63	63	62	62
24	Basic metals	35	36	35	34	34	35	35	36
25	Metal products, except machinery and equipment	74	76	73	71	73	75	75	75
26-28	Machinery and equipment	140	146	142	135	138	143	144	145
26	Computer, electronic and optical products	24	25	25	21	21	22	22	23
27	Electrical equipment	42	44	43	42	44	44	42	42
28	Machinery and equipment n.e.c.	73	76	74	72	74	77	79	80
29-30	Transport equipment	42	43	39	36	37	38	37	38
29	Motor vehicles, trailers and semi-trailers	35	35	31	30	31	32	31	31
30	Other transport equipment	7	8	8	6	6	6	6	7
31-33	Furniture; repair, installation of machinery and equipment	74	75	73	77	77	77	76	75
31-32	Furniture, other manufacturing	52	52	50	49	49	48	47	46
33	Repair and installation of machinery and equipment	22	23	23	28	28	29	30	29
35-39	**ELECTRICITY, GAS, WATER AND WASTE MANAGEMENT**	**47**	**48**	**49**	**49**	**50**	**50**	**51**	**51**
35	Electricity, gas, steam and air conditioning supply	26	27	27	27	27	27	27	27
36-39	Water supply; sewerage, waste, remediation activities	21	21	22	22	23	23	24	24
41-43	**CONSTRUCTION**	**278**	**286**	**287**	**289**	**295**	**297**	**295**	**297**
45-56	Distribution; transportation, accommodation, food service	1 099	1 113	1 105	1 113	1 131	1 145	1 145	1 158
45-47	**Wholesale and retail trade; motor vehicle and motorcycle repairs**	**633**	**637**	**631**	**637**	**650**	**660**	**658**	**663**
49-53	**Transportation and storage**	**214**	**216**	**211**	**207**	**208**	**207**	**205**	**207**
55-56	**Accommodation and food service activities**	**252**	**259**	**262**	**269**	**272**	**278**	**282**	**287**
58-63	**Information and communication**	**94**	**95**	**96**	**97**	**102**	**105**	**106**	**110**
58-60	Publishing, audiovisual and broadcasting activities	24	25	25	25	26	26	27	27
61	Telecommunications	20	20	18	18	18	17	17	16
62-63	IT and other information services	50	51	52	54	59	61	63	66
64-66	**Financial and insurance activities**	**135**	**138**	**137**	**135**	**135**	**134**	**131**	**129**
68	**Real estate activities**	**52**	**52**	**52**	**53**	**54**	**54**	**56**	**56**
69-82	**Professional, scientific, technical, admin., support activities**	**408**	**428**	**423**	**438**	**458**	**474**	**484**	**490**
69-75	Professional, scientific and technical activities	217	225	234	239	245	254	262	262
69-71	Legal, accounting activities; mgt consultancy; engineering	161	166	174	178	180	188	195	195
73-75	Advertising, market research; other prof., scientific, tech.	46	47	46	47	50	52	51	52
77-82	Administrative and support service activities	191	202	190	199	213	220	223	228
84-88	**Public administration, defence; social security; education; health**	**861**	**884**	**903**	**918**	**923**	**930**	**940**	**948**
84	**Public administration, defence; compulsory social security**	**252**	**254**	**254**	**255**	**252**	**252**	**253**	**253**
85	**Education**	**234**	**241**	**245**	**250**	**251**	**254**	**253**	**254**
86-88	**Human health and social work activities**	**375**	**389**	**403**	**413**	**420**	**425**	**434**	**441**
90-99	**Arts, entertainment, household goods repairs, other**	**179**	**183**	**188**	**191**	**194**	**197**	**199**	**203**
90-93	**Arts, entertainment and recreation**	**56**	**58**	**60**	**60**	**61**	**63**	**63**	**63**
94-96	**Other service activities**	**112**	**114**	**117**	**119**	**121**	**123**	**126**	**129**
97-98	**Activities of households as employers and for own use**	**11**	**11**	**12**	**12**	**12**	**11**	**11**	**11**
05-39	**INDUSTRY INCLUDING ENERGY**	**699**	**706**	**680**	**668**	**679**	**688**	**684**	**685**
45-99	**TOTAL SERVICES**	**2 829**	**2 893**	**2 904**	**2 946**	**2 996**	**3 040**	**3 062**	**3 093**
45-82	**BUSINESS SECTOR SERVICES**	**1 788**	**1 826**	**1 813**	**1 837**	**1 880**	**1 912**	**1 923**	**1 943**
45-82x	**BUSINESS SECTOR SERVICES excluding real estate**	**1 736**	**1 774**	**1 761**	**1 784**	**1 826**	**1 858**	**1 866**	**1 887**
05-82x	**NON-AGRICULTURE BUSINESS SECTOR excluding real estate**	..	..	..	..	..	..	..	..

.. Not available

Note: Detailed metadata at: http://metalinks.oecd.org/stan/20170410/1c43.

Information on data for Israel: http://oe.cd/israel-disclaimer.

Disclaimer: http://oe.cd/disclaimer

AUSTRIA

Table 6. Labour costs (compensation of employees), current prices

ISIC Rev. 4

Million EUR

		2007	2008	2009	2010	2011	2012	2013	2014
	TOTAL	**128 190**	**134 961**	**136 224**	**138 905**	**144 343**	**150 342**	**154 502**	**158 686**
01-03	**AGRICULTURE, FORESTRY AND FISHING**	**489**	**480**	**492**	**511**	**551**	**587**	**621**	**658**
05-09	**MINING AND QUARRYING**	**291**	**305**	**324**	**325**	**329**	**338**	**345**	**368**
10-33	**MANUFACTURING**	**25 671**	**27 243**	**25 796**	**25 959**	**27 364**	**28 824**	**29 590**	**30 311**
10-12	Food products, beverages and tobacco	2 537	2 549	2 530	2 578	2 560	2 658	2 750	2 859
13-14	Textiles and wearing apparel	568	573	516	518	530	528	536	533
15	Leather and related products	127	125	116	117	115	121	131	136
16	Wood, wood and cork products	1 123	1 192	1 077	1 114	1 174	1 211	1 221	1 232
17	Paper and paper products	938	951	877	876	897	962	953	994
18	Printing and reproduction of recorded media	681	681	626	612	608	600	576	560
19-23	Chemical, rubber, plastics, non-metallic products	4 212	4 421	4 272	4 350	4 541	4 840	4 919	5 157
20	Chemicals and chemical products	882	938	899	990	1 051	1 124	1 130	1 138
21	Pharmaceutical products	561	593	620	649	683	800	848	930
22-23	Rubber, plastic, non-metallic mineral products	2 627	2 737	2 604	2 564	2 675	2 790	2 821	2 963
24	Basic metals	1 645	1 810	1 719	1 683	1 853	1 953	2 069	2 079
25	Metal products, except machinery and equipment	2 711	2 947	2 803	2 814	3 016	3 192	3 308	3 372
26-28	Machinery and equipment	6 673	7 281	6 904	6 737	7 237	7 646	7 974	8 156
26	Computer, electronic and optical products	1 295	1 320	1 282	1 070	1 132	1 210	1 278	1 325
27	Electrical equipment	2 036	2 281	2 224	2 164	2 289	2 314	2 354	2 372
28	Machinery and equipment n.e.c.	3 342	3 679	3 397	3 502	3 816	4 122	4 342	4 458
29-30	Transport equipment	2 001	2 117	1 882	1 797	1 964	2 133	2 048	2 115
29	Motor vehicles, trailers and semi-trailers	1 558	1 610	1 427	1 476	1 620	1 767	1 657	1 701
30	Other transport equipment	444	508	454	322	345	366	391	414
31-33	Furniture; repair, installation of machinery and equipment	2 456	2 596	2 476	2 763	2 868	2 981	3 105	3 119
31-32	Furniture, other manufacturing	1 435	1 488	1 452	1 445	1 483	1 504	1 519	1 529
33	Repair and installation of machinery and equipment	1 021	1 109	1 023	1 318	1 385	1 476	1 586	1 590
35-39	**ELECTRICITY, GAS, WATER AND WASTE MANAGEMENT**	**2 561**	**2 720**	**2 879**	**2 868**	**2 986**	**3 241**	**3 369**	**3 375**
35	Electricity, gas, steam and air conditioning supply	1 777	1 878	1 945	1 916	1 989	2 194	2 302	2 264
36-39	Water supply; sewerage, waste, remediation activities	784	843	934	952	997	1 047	1 067	1 111
41-43	**CONSTRUCTION**	**9 317**	**9 583**	**9 901**	**9 900**	**10 239**	**10 670**	**10 913**	**11 229**
45-56	Distribution; transportation, accommodation, food service	29 390	30 945	31 285	31 775	32 940	34 309	35 426	36 692
45-47	**Wholesale and retail trade; motor vehicle and motorcycle repairs**	**16 721**	**17 544**	**17 808**	**18 103**	**18 960**	**19 924**	**20 504**	**21 174**
49-53	**Transportation and storage**	**7 534**	**7 975**	**7 923**	**7 944**	**7 968**	**8 092**	**8 211**	**8 532**
55-56	**Accommodation and food service activities**	**5 135**	**5 427**	**5 554**	**5 728**	**6 012**	**6 293**	**6 711**	**6 986**
58-63	**Information and communication**	**4 232**	**4 393**	**4 522**	**4 549**	**4 966**	**5 331**	**5 466**	**5 689**
58-60	Publishing, audiovisual and broadcasting activities	1 027	1 053	1 085	1 105	1 149	1 212	1 272	1 292
61	Telecommunications	1 039	1 063	1 030	989	1 005	1 071	1 075	1 056
62-63	IT and other information services	2 167	2 277	2 407	2 455	2 813	3 049	3 119	3 341
64-66	**Financial and insurance activities**	**7 364**	**7 702**	**7 780**	**7 911**	**8 140**	**8 091**	**8 363**	**8 334**
68	**Real estate activities**	**1 327**	**1 387**	**1 373**	**1 453**	**1 538**	**1 666**	**1 819**	**1 879**
69-82	**Professional, scientific, technical, admin., support activities**	**11 016**	**11 817**	**11 752**	**12 441**	**13 318**	**14 104**	**14 695**	**15 147**
69-75	Professional, scientific and technical activities	6 359	6 713	6 979	7 271	7 584	8 071	8 542	8 691
69-71	Legal, accounting activities; mgt consultancy; engineering	5 059	5 300	5 540	5 779	5 962	6 373	6 713	6 836
73-75	Advertising, market research; other prof., scientific, tech.	856	861	859	877	948	990	1 005	1 015
77-82	Administrative and support service activities	4 658	5 105	4 773	5 171	5 734	6 034	6 153	6 456
84-88	**Public administration, defence; social security; education; health**	**32 680**	**34 370**	**35 803**	**36 768**	**37 414**	**38 469**	**39 093**	**40 067**
84	**Public administration, defence; compulsory social security**	**10 495**	**10 884**	**11 249**	**11 379**	**11 472**	**11 787**	**11 885**	**12 136**
85	**Education**	**10 594**	**11 170**	**11 713**	**12 031**	**12 248**	**12 552**	**12 688**	**12 917**
86-88	**Human health and social work activities**	**11 591**	**12 317**	**12 841**	**13 358**	**13 694**	**14 129**	**14 519**	**15 014**
90-99	**Arts, entertainment, household goods repairs, other**	**3 853**	**4 014**	**4 317**	**4 445**	**4 557**	**4 711**	**4 802**	**4 937**
90-93	**Arts, entertainment and recreation**	**1 505**	**1 578**	**1 715**	**1 789**	**1 851**	**1 910**	**1 928**	**1 966**
94-96	**Other service activities**	**2 182**	**2 267**	**2 424**	**2 479**	**2 533**	**2 629**	**2 693**	**2 798**
97-98	**Activities of households as employers and for own use**	**165**	**169**	**178**	**177**	**173**	**171**	**181**	**173**
05-39	**INDUSTRY INCLUDING ENERGY**	**28 523**	**30 269**	**28 999**	**29 152**	**30 679**	**32 403**	**33 304**	**34 054**
45-99	**TOTAL SERVICES**	**89 861**	**94 629**	**96 831**	**99 342**	**102 874**	**106 682**	**109 664**	**112 745**
45-82	**BUSINESS SECTOR SERVICES**	**53 329**	**56 245**	**56 711**	**58 129**	**60 903**	**63 502**	**65 769**	**67 742**
45-82x	**BUSINESS SECTOR SERVICES excluding real estate**	**52 002**	**54 857**	**55 339**	**56 676**	**59 364**	**61 836**	**63 950**	**65 862**
05-82x	**NON-AGRICULTURE BUSINESS SECTOR excluding real estate**	..	..	..	..	..	..	..	..

.. Not available

Note: Detailed metadata at: http://metalinks.oecd.org/stan/20170410/1c43.
Information on data for Israel: http://oe.cd/israel-disclaimer.

Disclaimer: http://oe.cd/disclaimer

BELGIUM

Table 1. Production (gross output), current prices

ISIC Rev. 4

Million EUR

		2007	2008	2009	2010	2011	2012	2013	2014
	TOTAL	**714 865**	**750 193**	**697 458**	**751 109**	**809 645**	**823 010**	**819 905**	**830 458**
01-03	**AGRICULTURE, FORESTRY AND FISHING**	**8 257**	**8 482**	**7 972**	**8 981**	**9 322**	**10 243**	**10 154**	**9 733**
05-09	**MINING AND QUARRYING**	**906**	**1 006**	**624**	**671**	**707**	**637**	**619**	**723**
10-33	**MANUFACTURING**	**212 435**	**219 438**	**176 319**	**201 771**	**229 112**	**229 384**	**223 128**	**220 536**
10-12	Food products, beverages and tobacco	29 702	32 622	32 237	32 845	36 793	37 908	38 740	39 044
13-14	Textiles and wearing apparel	7 078	6 355	5 075	5 127	5 008	4 650	4 707	4 625
15	Leather and related products	274	256	219	353	379	377	276	454
16	Wood, wood and cork products	3 703	3 340	2 857	3 092	3 186	3 074	3 008	3 151
17	Paper and paper products	4 058	4 182	3 410	3 627	4 236	4 352	4 418	4 743
18	Printing and reproduction of recorded media	3 738	3 690	3 393	3 339	3 439	3 342	3 149	3 126
19-23	Chemical, rubber, plastics, non-metallic products	82 699	89 663	68 640	83 354	95 113	98 293	96 205	93 045
20	Chemicals and chemical products	28 753	31 410	24 768	29 593	33 309	33 780	33 132	31 584
21	Pharmaceutical products	9 067	9 413	10 091	12 096	11 610	12 688	14 486	15 145
22-23	Rubber, plastic, non-metallic mineral products	14 225	13 890	12 042	12 527	13 689	13 151	12 560	12 575
24	Basic metals	24 868	22 647	14 887	20 016	24 023	21 685	18 692	18 179
25	Metal products, except machinery and equipment	13 826	14 515	10 667	10 991	12 511	11 998	11 444	11 222
26-28	Machinery and equipment	18 293	18 664	14 938	16 041	17 595	17 464	16 393	16 573
26	Computer, electronic and optical products	4 509	4 161	2 641	3 058	3 254	3 442	3 159	3 278
27	Electrical equipment	3 654	4 018	4 461	4 474	4 599	4 234	3 909	3 798
28	Machinery and equipment n.e.c.	10 130	10 486	7 836	8 509	9 742	9 788	9 324	9 497
29-30	Transport equipment	19 334	18 332	13 333	16 077	19 376	18 777	18 613	18 664
29	Motor vehicles, trailers and semi-trailers	17 776	16 740	11 923	14 647	17 628	16 759	16 595	16 548
30	Other transport equipment	1 558	1 592	1 410	1 430	1 747	2 018	2 019	2 116
31-33	Furniture; repair, installation of machinery and equipment	4 863	5 174	6 663	6 911	7 454	7 463	7 484	7 710
31-32	Furniture, other manufacturing	3 567	3 794	3 371	3 615	3 854	3 781	3 561	3 742
33	Repair and installation of machinery and equipment	1 297	1 379	3 292	3 296	3 600	3 682	3 923	3 968
35-39	**ELECTRICITY, GAS, WATER AND WASTE MANAGEMENT**	**18 256**	**19 594**	**20 981**	**22 966**	**24 554**	**24 301**	**24 468**	**22 862**
35	Electricity, gas, steam and air conditioning supply	10 846	11 944	12 500	13 197	13 831	13 203	13 681	11 837
36-39	Water supply; sewerage, waste, remediation activities	7 410	7 650	8 481	9 769	10 723	11 098	10 787	11 025
41-43	**CONSTRUCTION**	**53 227**	**58 141**	**58 062**	**59 531**	**66 014**	**65 947**	**65 250**	**67 286**
45-56	Distribution; transportation, accommodation, food service	146 003	152 246	133 495	145 943	154 814	155 898	151 888	157 028
45-47	**Wholesale and retail trade; motor vehicle and motorcycle repairs**	**82 957**	**84 542**	**72 674**	**81 184**	**86 681**	**87 107**	**85 497**	**88 333**
49-53	**Transportation and storage**	**49 952**	**53 822**	**47 748**	**50 998**	**53 717**	**54 129**	**51 276**	**52 718**
55-56	**Accommodation and food service activities**	**13 094**	**13 882**	**13 072**	**13 760**	**14 415**	**14 662**	**15 116**	**15 977**
58-63	**Information and communication**	**25 247**	**26 251**	**30 039**	**30 823**	**31 613**	**32 699**	**32 339**	**32 675**
58-60	Publishing, audiovisual and broadcasting activities	5 749	6 006	6 471	6 727	6 862	7 048	7 054	7 165
61	Telecommunications	10 665	10 851	12 304	12 466	11 889	12 323	11 992	11 403
62-63	IT and other information services	8 834	9 393	11 265	11 630	12 862	13 328	13 293	14 107
64-66	**Financial and insurance activities**	**34 559**	**35 818**	**37 601**	**40 549**	**42 267**	**42 381**	**43 069**	**45 981**
68	**Real estate activities**	**34 765**	**36 535**	**39 056**	**40 285**	**41 858**	**43 774**	**44 696**	**43 152**
69-82	**Professional, scientific, technical, admin., support activities**	**81 657**	**86 323**	**81 010**	**83 829**	**88 834**	**92 044**	**94 997**	**98 469**
69-75	Professional, scientific and technical activities	55 777	59 489	57 357	58 626	61 278	63 669	66 355	69 097
69-71	Legal, accounting activities; mgt consultancy; engineering	45 482	48 443	47 035	48 053	50 610	53 107	55 449	56 559
73-75	Advertising, market research; other prof., scientific, tech.	9 249	9 722	8 030	8 317	8 253	8 001	8 076	8 210
77-82	Administrative and support service activities	25 880	26 834	23 654	25 203	27 556	28 375	28 642	29 372
84-88	**Public administration, defence; social security; education; health**	**86 971**	**93 010**	**97 382**	**100 485**	**104 881**	**109 297**	**112 697**	**114 952**
84	**Public administration, defence; compulsory social security**	**30 701**	**32 617**	**33 297**	**33 892**	**35 296**	**36 732**	**38 120**	**38 348**
85	**Education**	**22 527**	**24 094**	**24 868**	**25 668**	**27 074**	**28 215**	**29 013**	**29 534**
86-88	**Human health and social work activities**	**33 743**	**36 300**	**39 217**	**40 925**	**42 511**	**44 350**	**45 564**	**47 070**
90-99	**Arts, entertainment, household goods repairs, other**	**12 582**	**13 350**	**14 917**	**15 277**	**15 670**	**16 407**	**16 599**	**17 061**
90-93	**Arts, entertainment and recreation**	**4 660**	**4 901**	**4 239**	**4 552**	**4 915**	**5 192**	**5 424**	**5 756**
94-96	**Other service activities**	**7 392**	**7 930**	**10 179**	**10 277**	**10 319**	**10 749**	**10 767**	**10 891**
97-98	**Activities of households as employers and for own use**	**530**	**519**	**499**	**449**	**436**	**466**	**408**	**414**
05-39	**INDUSTRY INCLUDING ENERGY**	**231 597**	**240 038**	**197 924**	**225 407**	**254 373**	**254 321**	**248 215**	**244 122**
45-99	**TOTAL SERVICES**	**421 784**	**443 533**	**433 501**	**457 190**	**479 937**	**492 500**	**496 285**	**509 317**
45-82	**BUSINESS SECTOR SERVICES**	**322 231**	**337 173**	**321 202**	**341 428**	**359 385**	**366 796**	**366 989**	**377 305**
45-82x	**BUSINESS SECTOR SERVICES excluding real estate**	**287 466**	**300 638**	**282 146**	**301 144**	**317 528**	**323 022**	**322 293**	**334 153**
05-82x	**NON-AGRICULTURE BUSINESS SECTOR excluding real estate**	..	..	..	..	..	..	..	..

.. Not available

Note: Detailed metadata at: http://metalinks.oecd.org/stan/20170410/1c43.
Information on data for Israel: http://oe.cd/israel-disclaimer.

Disclaimer: http://oe.cd/disclaimer

BELGIUM

Table 2. Value added, current prices

ISIC Rev. 4

Million EUR

		2007	2008	2009	2010	2011	2012	2013	2014
	TOTAL	**307 960**	**317 009**	**312 596**	**326 534**	**339 644**	**346 698**	**350 217**	**358 478**
01-03	**AGRICULTURE, FORESTRY AND FISHING**	**3 051**	**2 507**	**2 265**	**2 784**	**2 441**	**3 040**	**2 699**	**2 565**
05-09	**MINING AND QUARRYING**	**330**	**340**	**254**	**249**	**272**	**244**	**225**	**279**
10-33	**MANUFACTURING**	**52 039**	**50 300**	**44 651**	**48 069**	**48 401**	**48 810**	**49 033**	**50 151**
10-12	Food products, beverages and tobacco	6 580	6 676	7 209	6 921	6 893	7 227	7 573	7 814
13-14	Textiles and wearing apparel	2 034	1 776	1 440	1 503	1 378	1 307	1 291	1 318
15	Leather and related products	97	104	76	72	82	87	98	111
16	Wood, wood and cork products	1 014	907	827	820	836	779	712	720
17	Paper and paper products	1 126	1 078	969	906	958	1 008	979	1 056
18	Printing and reproduction of recorded media	1 301	1 285	1 174	1 162	1 173	1 132	1 055	1 039
19-23	Chemical, rubber, plastics, non-metallic products	18 777	18 188	16 376	18 704	17 822	18 457	18 742	19 172
20	Chemicals and chemical products	7 396	6 936	6 798	7 425	7 635	7 602	7 616	8 005
21	Pharmaceutical products	4 701	4 974	4 759	5 807	4 985	5 407	6 061	6 051
22-23	Rubber, plastic, non-metallic mineral products	4 718	4 561	4 269	4 234	4 413	4 215	4 105	4 173
24	Basic metals	4 329	3 493	2 210	2 724	2 730	2 384	2 477	2 505
25	Metal products, except machinery and equipment	4 359	4 424	3 492	3 555	3 819	3 864	3 678	3 592
26-28	Machinery and equipment	6 886	6 897	5 410	5 922	6 418	6 243	6 055	6 345
26	Computer, electronic and optical products	1 870	1 653	966	1 080	1 171	1 223	1 199	1 305
27	Electrical equipment	1 450	1 607	1 637	1 735	1 674	1 469	1 425	1 418
28	Machinery and equipment n.e.c.	3 566	3 637	2 807	3 107	3 573	3 550	3 431	3 621
29-30	Transport equipment	3 699	3 595	2 879	3 198	3 504	3 595	3 585	3 622
29	Motor vehicles, trailers and semi-trailers	3 118	3 024	2 356	2 643	2 739	2 733	2 816	2 779
30	Other transport equipment	581	571	523	556	765	862	769	844
31-33	Furniture; repair, installation of machinery and equipment	1 837	1 877	2 589	2 583	2 789	2 728	2 788	2 858
31-32	Furniture, other manufacturing	1 290	1 337	1 288	1 265	1 321	1 282	1 254	1 293
33	Repair and installation of machinery and equipment	547	540	1 300	1 318	1 468	1 446	1 534	1 565
35-39	**ELECTRICITY, GAS, WATER AND WASTE MANAGEMENT**	**7 813**	**8 371**	**8 687**	**9 231**	**10 022**	**9 153**	**9 167**	**8 678**
35	Electricity, gas, steam and air conditioning supply	5 460	6 047	5 969	6 178	6 815	5 724	5 812	5 235
36-39	Water supply; sewerage, waste, remediation activities	2 353	2 324	2 717	3 053	3 207	3 428	3 355	3 443
41-43	**CONSTRUCTION**	**16 711**	**18 057**	**17 938**	**18 129**	**19 456**	**19 633**	**19 481**	**19 716**
45-56	Distribution; transportation, accommodation, food service	65 155	67 269	64 195	66 678	68 751	69 282	69 220	70 711
45-47	**Wholesale and retail trade; motor vehicle and motorcycle repairs**	**41 029**	**41 928**	**39 650**	**41 487**	**42 758**	**43 194**	**43 257**	**44 199**
49-53	**Transportation and storage**	**18 774**	**19 623**	**19 080**	**19 353**	**19 844**	**19 885**	**19 541**	**19 736**
55-56	**Accommodation and food service activities**	**5 352**	**5 717**	**5 465**	**5 838**	**6 149**	**6 203**	**6 422**	**6 775**
58-63	**Information and communication**	**12 479**	**12 890**	**13 418**	**13 942**	**14 316**	**14 977**	**14 552**	**14 606**
58-60	Publishing, audiovisual and broadcasting activities	2 352	2 469	2 629	2 743	2 838	2 904	2 983	3 011
61	Telecommunications	5 452	5 401	5 587	5 714	5 442	5 504	5 105	4 834
62-63	IT and other information services	4 676	5 020	5 202	5 485	6 035	6 569	6 464	6 761
64-66	**Financial and insurance activities**	**15 780**	**15 086**	**17 851**	**20 098**	**21 396**	**21 896**	**21 512**	**22 883**
68	**Real estate activities**	**28 117**	**29 126**	**28 467**	**28 796**	**29 628**	**30 059**	**29 962**	**30 442**
69-82	**Professional, scientific, technical, admin., support activities**	**37 626**	**39 967**	**39 179**	**40 721**	**43 584**	**44 645**	**47 011**	**48 937**
69-75	Professional, scientific and technical activities	24 771	26 550	27 633	28 272	30 005	30 705	32 645	33 782
69-71	Legal, accounting activities; mgt consultancy; engineering	21 439	22 973	24 235	24 887	26 560	27 212	28 932	29 819
73-75	Advertising, market research; other prof., scientific, tech.	2 474	2 582	2 190	2 196	2 231	2 237	2 310	2 400
77-82	Administrative and support service activities	12 855	13 418	11 546	12 449	13 578	13 940	14 366	15 155
84-88	**Public administration, defence; social security; education; health**	**62 187**	**66 159**	**68 689**	**70 682**	**73 886**	**77 239**	**79 476**	**81 310**
84	**Public administration, defence; compulsory social security**	**22 657**	**23 738**	**24 461**	**25 140**	**26 133**	**27 191**	**28 086**	**28 666**
85	**Education**	**19 407**	**20 760**	**21 321**	**22 008**	**23 183**	**24 188**	**24 771**	**25 180**
86-88	**Human health and social work activities**	**20 123**	**21 661**	**22 907**	**23 535**	**24 571**	**25 859**	**26 619**	**27 464**
90-99	**Arts, entertainment, household goods repairs, other**	**6 672**	**6 937**	**7 003**	**7 155**	**7 491**	**7 723**	**7 880**	**8 201**
90-93	**Arts, entertainment and recreation**	**2 049**	**2 146**	**1 993**	**2 060**	**2 232**	**2 348**	**2 331**	**2 454**
94-96	**Other service activities**	**4 093**	**4 273**	**4 511**	**4 647**	**4 822**	**4 909**	**5 141**	**5 333**
97-98	**Activities of households as employers and for own use**	**530**	**519**	**499**	**449**	**436**	**466**	**408**	**414**
05-39	**INDUSTRY INCLUDING ENERGY**	**60 182**	**59 012**	**53 592**	**57 549**	**58 695**	**58 206**	**58 425**	**59 107**
45-99	**TOTAL SERVICES**	**228 016**	**237 434**	**238 801**	**248 072**	**259 052**	**265 820**	**269 612**	**277 089**
45-82	**BUSINESS SECTOR SERVICES**	**159 157**	**164 337**	**163 109**	**170 235**	**177 676**	**180 858**	**182 257**	**187 579**
45-82x	**BUSINESS SECTOR SERVICES excluding real estate**	**131 040**	**135 212**	**134 642**	**141 438**	**148 047**	**150 800**	**152 295**	**157 137**
05-82x	**NON-AGRICULTURE BUSINESS SECTOR excluding real estate**	..	..	..	..	..	..	..	..

.. Not available

Note: Detailed metadata at: http://metalinks.oecd.org/stan/20170410/1c43.

Information on data for Israel: http://oe.cd/israel-disclaimer.

Disclaimer: http://oe.cd/disclaimer

BELGIUM

Table 3. Value added, volumes

ISIC Rev. 4

Million 2010 EUR

		2007	2008	2009	2010	2011	2012	2013	2014
	TOTAL	**321 979**	**325 997**	**318 537**	**326 534**	**333 533**	**333 819**	**333 336**	**338 907**
01-03	**AGRICULTURE, FORESTRY AND FISHING**	**2 815**	**2 832**	**2 581**	**2 784**	**2 807**	**2 786**	**2 380**	**2 346**
05-09	**MINING AND QUARRYING**	**258**	**315**	**245**	**249**	**281**	**250**	**228**	**270**
10-33	**MANUFACTURING**	**51 201**	**50 510**	**45 173**	**48 069**	**48 946**	**49 023**	**49 837**	**51 741**
10-12	Food products, beverages and tobacco	6 423	6 785	6 885	6 921	7 426	8 092	7 740	8 068
13-14	Textiles and wearing apparel	..	..	..	..	..	..	..	..
15	Leather and related products	..	..	..	..	..	..	..	..
16	Wood, wood and cork products	913	837	874	820	837	796	715	677
17	Paper and paper products	1 042	1 083	960	906	958	1 049	1 027	1 155
18	Printing and reproduction of recorded media	1 394	1 364	1 153	1 162	1 217	1 134	1 016	955
19-23	Chemical, rubber, plastics, non-metallic products	17 386	17 281	16 495	18 704	18 402	18 162	19 318	19 572
20	Chemicals and chemical products	6 515	6 105	6 959	7 425	7 494	6 882	6 591	6 786
21	Pharmaceutical products	4 913	5 027	4 662	5 807	5 067	5 447	6 199	6 287
22-23	Rubber, plastic, non-metallic mineral products	4 734	4 728	4 260	4 234	4 509	4 507	4 466	4 350
24	Basic metals	3 866	3 214	2 264	2 724	2 915	3 374	3 885	5 142
25	Metal products, except machinery and equipment	4 132	4 267	3 602	3 555	3 749	3 882	3 963	3 971
26-28	Machinery and equipment	7 666	7 459	5 661	5 922	6 066	5 649	5 240	5 319
26	Computer, electronic and optical products	2 017	1 851	982	1 080	1 071	1 105	1 049	1 109
27	Electrical equipment	1 709	1 865	1 743	1 735	1 559	1 330	1 225	1 189
28	Machinery and equipment n.e.c.	3 924	3 743	2 940	3 107	3 436	3 213	2 964	3 020
29-30	Transport equipment	4 291	4 141	2 986	3 198	3 209	3 020	3 150	3 383
29	Motor vehicles, trailers and semi-trailers	3 681	3 547	2 438	2 643	2 464	2 243	2 425	2 576
30	Other transport equipment	626	609	548	556	745	784	723	807
31-33	Furniture; repair, installation of machinery and equipment	1 955	1 993	2 647	2 583	2 763	2 657	2 710	2 764
31-32	Furniture, other manufacturing	1 377	1 395	1 288	1 265	1 316	1 254	1 219	1 250
33	Repair and installation of machinery and equipment	563	583	1 359	1 318	1 447	1 403	1 490	1 513
35-39	**ELECTRICITY, GAS, WATER AND WASTE MANAGEMENT**	**7 993**	**7 911**	**8 830**	**9 231**	**9 131**	**8 288**	**7 902**	**8 194**
35	Electricity, gas, steam and air conditioning supply	5 434	5 479	5 986	6 178	5 955	4 977	4 740	5 186
36-39	Water supply; sewerage, waste, remediation activities	2 547	2 412	2 840	3 053	3 176	3 368	3 217	3 018
41-43	**CONSTRUCTION**	**17 886**	**18 081**	**18 086**	**18 129**	**19 220**	**19 381**	**19 059**	**19 338**
45-56	Distribution; transportation, accommodation, food service	67 326	68 071	65 256	66 678	67 300	66 760	65 327	65 852
45-47	**Wholesale and retail trade; motor vehicle and motorcycle repairs**	**42 027**	**42 103**	**40 476**	**41 487**	**41 494**	**41 130**	**40 406**	**40 953**
49-53	**Transportation and storage**	**18 943**	**19 469**	**18 937**	**19 353**	**20 000**	**19 807**	**19 000**	**18 945**
55-56	**Accommodation and food service activities**	**6 418**	**6 568**	**5 850**	**5 838**	**5 807**	**5 820**	**5 898**	**5 924**
58-63	**Information and communication**	**12 796**	**13 106**	**13 737**	**13 942**	**14 252**	**14 502**	**13 952**	**13 970**
58-60	Publishing, audiovisual and broadcasting activities	2 469	2 591	2 689	2 743	2 834	2 774	2 790	2 789
61	Telecommunications	5 407	5 362	5 726	5 714	5 481	5 448	5 049	4 856
62-63	IT and other information services	4 915	5 157	5 322	5 485	5 937	6 275	6 101	6 304
64-66	**Financial and insurance activities**	**19 490**	**19 784**	**19 110**	**20 098**	**21 115**	**22 116**	**21 985**	**22 091**
68	**Real estate activities**	**27 054**	**27 558**	**28 242**	**28 796**	**29 326**	**29 402**	**29 175**	**29 170**
69-82	**Professional, scientific, technical, admin., support activities**	**39 499**	**40 858**	**39 671**	**40 721**	**42 727**	**41 402**	**43 020**	**44 485**
69-75	Professional, scientific and technical activities	25 995	27 001	28 010	28 272	29 422	28 435	29 812	30 812
69-71	Legal, accounting activities; mgt consultancy; engineering	22 642	23 445	24 645	24 887	26 004	25 085	26 252	26 969
73-75	Advertising, market research; other prof., scientific, tech.	2 431	2 522	2 151	2 196	2 222	2 137	2 229	2 426
77-82	Administrative and support service activities	13 538	13 892	11 663	12 449	13 305	12 967	13 208	13 672
84-88	**Public administration, defence; social security; education; health**	**68 581**	**69 741**	**70 468**	**70 682**	**71 061**	**72 441**	**72 968**	**73 945**
84	**Public administration, defence; compulsory social security**	**24 440**	**24 838**	**24 725**	**25 140**	**25 351**	**25 678**	**25 960**	**26 119**
85	**Education**	**21 838**	**22 180**	**22 073**	**22 008**	**21 984**	**22 170**	**22 546**	**23 471**
86-88	**Human health and social work activities**	**22 315**	**22 736**	**23 678**	**23 535**	**23 726**	**24 597**	**24 457**	**24 343**
90-99	**Arts, entertainment, household goods repairs, other**	**7 087**	**7 320**	**7 115**	**7 155**	**7 368**	**7 518**	**7 531**	**7 545**
90-93	**Arts, entertainment and recreation**	**2 156**	**2 300**	**2 045**	**2 060**	**2 190**	**2 288**	**2 244**	**2 268**
94-96	**Other service activities**	**4 356**	**4 481**	**4 561**	**4 647**	**4 746**	**4 776**	**4 906**	**4 909**
97-98	**Activities of households as employers and for own use**	**582**	**544**	**510**	**449**	**432**	**454**	**381**	**368**
05-39	**INDUSTRY INCLUDING ENERGY**	**59 338**	**58 638**	**54 248**	**57 549**	**58 358**	**57 484**	**57 842**	**60 073**
45-99	**TOTAL SERVICES**	**241 722**	**246 335**	**243 618**	**248 072**	**253 148**	**254 151**	**254 059**	**257 219**
45-82	**BUSINESS SECTOR SERVICES**	**166 037**	**169 250**	**166 043**	**170 235**	**174 719**	**174 168**	**173 522**	**175 686**
45-82x	**BUSINESS SECTOR SERVICES excluding real estate**	**139 107**	**141 821**	**137 796**	**141 438**	**145 393**	**144 767**	**144 346**	**146 506**
05-82x	**NON-AGRICULTURE BUSINESS SECTOR excluding real estate**	..	..	..	..	..	..	..	..

.. Not available

Note: Detailed metadata at: http://metalinks.oecd.org/stan/20170410/1c43.

Information on data for Israel: http://oe.cd/israel-disclaimer.

Disclaimer: http://oe.cd/disclaimer

Table 4. Gross fixed capital formation, current prices

ISIC Rev. 4

Million EUR

		2007	2008	2009	2010	2011	2012	2013	2014
	TOTAL	**80 096**	**84 890**	**78 782**	**79 665**	**85 612**	**87 674**	**86 967**	**91 760**
01-03	**AGRICULTURE, FORESTRY AND FISHING**	**823**	**966**	**1 042**	**975**	**1 142**	**1 169**	**1 150**	**1 163**
05-09	**MINING AND QUARRYING**	**98**	**108**	**73**	**59**	**46**	**44**	**48**	**57**
10-33	**MANUFACTURING**	**12 932**	**12 703**	**10 672**	**10 555**	**11 797**	**12 142**	**11 761**	**11 846**
10-12	Food products, beverages and tobacco	1 550	1 468	1 385	1 363	1 490	1 517	1 694	1 792
13-14	Textiles and wearing apparel	298	268	200	173	241	198	208	213
15	Leather and related products	12	11	7	68	18	13	21	26
16	Wood, wood and cork products	224	227	149	167	167	177	165	226
17	Paper and paper products	222	239	176	177	159	173	153	141
18	Printing and reproduction of recorded media	352	337	321	230	227	224	173	187
19-23	Chemical, rubber, plastics, non-metallic products	6 217	6 182	5 106	5 085	5 804	5 970	5 949	5 817
20	Chemicals and chemical products	1 939	1 681	1 387	1 301	1 592	1 567	1 631	1 831
21	Pharmaceutical products	2 889	3 015	2 578	2 644	3 131	3 290	3 176	2 628
22-23	Rubber, plastic, non-metallic mineral products	987	1 040	837	832	887	919	848	837
24	Basic metals	714	781	598	475	558	645	499	512
25	Metal products, except machinery and equipment	698	689	544	566	621	616	512	555
26-28	Machinery and equipment	1 565	1 483	1 225	1 269	1 358	1 267	1 249	1 280
26	Computer, electronic and optical products	663	632	411	442	446	444	448	477
27	Electrical equipment	221	236	346	329	332	220	216	229
28	Machinery and equipment n.e.c.	681	616	469	498	580	604	586	574
29-30	Transport equipment	766	665	592	598	734	965	812	778
29	Motor vehicles, trailers and semi-trailers	619	514	445	417	453	686	563	533
30	Other transport equipment	147	152	147	180	281	279	250	245
31-33	Furniture; repair, installation of machinery and equipment	316	352	369	384	420	376	328	320
31-32	Furniture, other manufacturing	223	259	248	238	271	235	202	204
33	Repair and installation of machinery and equipment	93	93	121	146	150	141	127	116
35-39	**ELECTRICITY, GAS, WATER AND WASTE MANAGEMENT**	**2 964**	**3 575**	**4 162**	**4 044**	**4 045**	**4 447**	**4 302**	**3 553**
35	Electricity, gas, steam and air conditioning supply	1 752	2 338	2 629	2 550	2 400	2 748	2 815	2 117
36-39	Water supply; sewerage, waste, remediation activities	1 213	1 237	1 533	1 494	1 645	1 699	1 487	1 436
41-43	**CONSTRUCTION**	**3 260**	**3 566**	**3 151**	**2 747**	**3 512**	**3 119**	**3 096**	**3 621**
45-56	Distribution; transportation, accommodation, food service	13 591	13 874	13 553	12 985	14 196	13 973	13 886	14 572
45-47	**Wholesale and retail trade; motor vehicle and motorcycle repairs**	**6 242**	**6 240**	**5 665**	**5 768**	**6 708**	**6 496**	**6 404**	**6 521**
49-53	**Transportation and storage**	**6 344**	**6 575**	**6 831**	**6 276**	**6 461**	**6 408**	**6 585**	**7 041**
55-56	**Accommodation and food service activities**	**1 005**	**1 059**	**1 057**	**941**	**1 027**	**1 069**	**896**	**1 011**
58-63	**Information and communication**	**2 893**	**3 222**	**3 323**	**3 619**	**3 685**	**3 951**	**4 319**	**4 589**
58-60	Publishing, audiovisual and broadcasting activities	623	655	739	770	825	901	1 005	978
61	Telecommunications	1 304	1 395	1 499	1 566	1 586	1 566	1 647	1 801
62-63	IT and other information services	966	1 172	1 085	1 284	1 274	1 484	1 668	1 810
64-66	**Financial and insurance activities**	**2 804**	**3 128**	**3 193**	**2 758**	**3 042**	**2 657**	**2 534**	**2 864**
68	**Real estate activities**	**23 418**	**25 147**	**22 969**	**23 546**	**23 847**	**25 171**	**25 125**	**26 349**
69-82	**Professional, scientific, technical, admin., support activities**	**7 785**	**8 822**	**6 510**	**7 316**	**8 606**	**8 345**	**8 266**	**10 355**
69-75	Professional, scientific and technical activities	3 981	4 571	4 115	4 624	4 688	4 888	5 121	7 026
69-71	Legal, accounting activities; mgt consultancy; engineering	3 134	3 567	2 910	3 416	3 384	3 692	3 934	3 972
73-75	Advertising, market research; other prof., scientific, tech.	436	485	526	524	508	475	422	488
77-82	Administrative and support service activities	3 804	4 252	2 395	2 691	3 918	3 457	3 146	3 329
84-88	**Public administration, defence; social security; education; health**	**8 297**	**8 589**	**8 982**	**9 862**	**10 404**	**11 269**	**11 202**	**11 340**
84	**Public administration, defence; compulsory social security**	**3 456**	**3 550**	**3 668**	**3 703**	**4 176**	**4 489**	**4 079**	**4 346**
85	**Education**	**1 858**	**2 105**	**2 339**	**2 532**	**2 793**	**2 793**	**2 927**	**2 921**
86-88	**Human health and social work activities**	**2 983**	**2 934**	**2 976**	**3 627**	**3 435**	**3 987**	**4 196**	**4 072**
90-99	**Arts, entertainment, household goods repairs, other**	**1 231**	**1 189**	**1 152**	**1 200**	**1 291**	**1 389**	**1 278**	**1 450**
90-93	**Arts, entertainment and recreation**	**644**	**597**	**508**	**512**	**601**	**632**	**591**	**721**
94-96	**Other service activities**	**587**	**592**	**644**	**687**	**689**	**757**	**687**	**729**
97-98	**Activities of households as employers and for own use**	**0**	**0**	**0**	**0**	**0**	**0**	**0**	**0**
05-39	**INDUSTRY INCLUDING ENERGY**	15 995	16 387	14 907	14 658	15 888	16 632	16 111	15 457
45-99	**TOTAL SERVICES**	60 018	63 972	59 681	61 285	65 070	66 754	66 610	71 518
45-82	**BUSINESS SECTOR SERVICES**	50 490	54 193	49 547	50 224	53 376	54 096	54 130	58 729
45-82x	**BUSINESS SECTOR SERVICES excluding real estate**	27 072	29 046	26 579	26 678	29 529	28 925	29 005	32 380
05-82x	**NON-AGRICULTURE BUSINESS SECTOR excluding real estate**	..	..	..	..	..	..	..	..

.. Not available

Note: Detailed metadata at: http://metalinks.oecd.org/stan/20170410/1c43.
Information on data for Israel: http://oe.cd/israel-disclaimer.

Disclaimer: http://oe.cd/disclaimer

Table 5. Number of persons engaged, total employment

ISIC Rev. 4

Thousands

		2007	2008	2009	2010	2011	2012	2013	2014
	TOTAL	**4 374**	**4 453**	**4 446**	**4 474**	**4 535**	**4 555**	**4 540**	**4 559**
01-03	**AGRICULTURE, FORESTRY AND FISHING**	**71**	**69**	**68**	**64**	**62**	**61**	**60**	**60**
05-09	**MINING AND QUARRYING**	**3**	**3**	**3**	**3**	**3**	**3**	**3**	**3**
10-33	**MANUFACTURING**	**593**	**592**	**560**	**542**	**543**	**535**	**523**	**509**
10-12	Food products, beverages and tobacco	99	99	99	97	97	96	96	95
13-14	Textiles and wearing apparel	38	36	31	29	27	25	24	23
15	Leather and related products	2	2	2	1	1	1	1	1
16	Wood, wood and cork products	15	15	14	14	14	14	13	13
17	Paper and paper products	14	14	13	12	12	12	12	12
18	Printing and reproduction of recorded media	21	21	20	19	19	19	18	17
19-23	Chemical, rubber, plastics, non-metallic products	132	132	128	126	127	126	124	122
20	Chemicals and chemical products	48	48	46	46	46	45	44	44
21	Pharmaceutical products	23	23	21	21	22	23	23	23
22-23	Rubber, plastic, non-metallic mineral products	56	57	56	54	55	54	52	51
24	Basic metals	36	36	33	31	31	30	28	26
25	Metal products, except machinery and equipment	73	74	65	63	63	62	59	56
26-28	Machinery and equipment	74	76	68	65	66	64	62	60
26	Computer, electronic and optical products	16	15	11	11	11	11	11	11
27	Electrical equipment	19	20	21	20	19	18	17	17
28	Machinery and equipment n.e.c.	39	40	36	35	36	35	34	32
29-30	Transport equipment	55	53	45	42	44	44	44	43
29	Motor vehicles, trailers and semi-trailers	49	46	38	36	37	38	38	36
30	Other transport equipment	7	7	7	6	6	6	7	7
31-33	Furniture; repair, installation of machinery and equipment	36	36	44	43	43	43	43	43
31-32	Furniture, other manufacturing	27	27	25	24	24	23	22	22
33	Repair and installation of machinery and equipment	9	9	19	19	19	19	20	21
35-39	**ELECTRICITY, GAS, WATER AND WASTE MANAGEMENT**	**40**	**42**	**49**	**50**	**51**	**51**	**51**	**51**
35	Electricity, gas, steam and air conditioning supply	18	19	18	19	20	20	20	19
36-39	Water supply; sewerage, waste, remediation activities	22	22	31	31	31	32	32	32
41-43	**CONSTRUCTION**	**262**	**268**	**268**	**270**	**275**	**276**	**272**	**268**
45-56	Distribution; transportation, accommodation, food service	996	1 005	997	995	995	990	976	971
45-47	**Wholesale and retail trade; motor vehicle and motorcycle repairs**	**593**	**597**	**585**	**585**	**585**	**586**	**581**	**577**
49-53	**Transportation and storage**	**256**	**259**	**265**	**261**	**259**	**254**	**248**	**244**
55-56	**Accommodation and food service activities**	**148**	**149**	**147**	**150**	**151**	**150**	**148**	**150**
58-63	**Information and communication**	**100**	**103**	**108**	**108**	**110**	**110**	**110**	**111**
58-60	Publishing, audiovisual and broadcasting activities	25	25	25	24	24	23	23	23
61	Telecommunications	28	28	28	29	28	28	27	26
62-63	IT and other information services	47	50	55	55	57	59	59	62
64-66	**Financial and insurance activities**	**135**	**134**	**132**	**130**	**130**	**129**	**127**	**126**
68	**Real estate activities**	**20**	**21**	**24**	**24**	**25**	**25**	**25**	**25**
69-82	**Professional, scientific, technical, admin., support activities**	**701**	**738**	**738**	**768**	**799**	**813**	**824**	**849**
69-75	Professional, scientific and technical activities	389	408	416	422	433	445	454	460
69-71	Legal, accounting activities; mgt consultancy; engineering	346	363	372	378	388	400	408	412
73-75	Advertising, market research; other prof., scientific, tech.	35	37	35	35	35	35	35	36
77-82	Administrative and support service activities	312	329	322	346	366	367	370	389
84-88	**Public administration, defence; social security; education; health**	**1 253**	**1 276**	**1 300**	**1 326**	**1 349**	**1 364**	**1 376**	**1 392**
84	**Public administration, defence; compulsory social security**	**429**	**433**	**431**	**434**	**432**	**432**	**431**	**431**
85	**Education**	**339**	**346**	**355**	**360**	**367**	**370**	**374**	**381**
86-88	**Human health and social work activities**	**484**	**497**	**514**	**532**	**550**	**562**	**571**	**581**
90-99	**Arts, entertainment, household goods repairs, other**	**201**	**203**	**200**	**195**	**196**	**200**	**194**	**194**
90-93	**Arts, entertainment and recreation**	**40**	**41**	**38**	**38**	**39**	**39**	**40**	**41**
94-96	**Other service activities**	**109**	**112**	**114**	**115**	**117**	**117**	**118**	**118**
97-98	**Activities of households as employers and for own use**	**53**	**50**	**48**	**42**	**41**	**43**	**36**	**36**
05-39	**INDUSTRY INCLUDING ENERGY**	**636**	**637**	**612**	**594**	**597**	**589**	**577**	**563**
45-99	**TOTAL SERVICES**	**3 406**	**3 479**	**3 499**	**3 546**	**3 603**	**3 629**	**3 631**	**3 668**
45-82	**BUSINESS SECTOR SERVICES**	**1 952**	**2 000**	**1 999**	**2 025**	**2 057**	**2 066**	**2 061**	**2 082**
45-82x	**BUSINESS SECTOR SERVICES excluding real estate**	**1 932**	**1 979**	**1 975**	**2 001**	**2 033**	**2 041**	**2 036**	**2 057**
05-82x	**NON-AGRICULTURE BUSINESS SECTOR excluding real estate**	..	..	..	..	..	..	..	..

.. Not available

Note: Detailed metadata at: http://metalinks.oecd.org/stan/20170410/1c43.

Information on data for Israel: http://oe.cd/israel-disclaimer.

Disclaimer: http://oe.cd/disclaimer

BELGIUM

Table 6. Labour costs (compensation of employees), current prices

ISIC Rev. 4

Million EUR

		2007	2008	2009	2010	2011	2012	2013	2014
	TOTAL	**168 895**	**178 361**	**179 623**	**183 229**	**191 626**	**198 306**	**202 110**	**204 832**
01-03	**AGRICULTURE, FORESTRY AND FISHING**	**342**	**358**	**393**	**411**	**455**	**482**	**500**	**531**
05-09	**MINING AND QUARRYING**	**159**	**161**	**133**	**130**	**139**	**135**	**132**	**165**
10-33	**MANUFACTURING**	**30 555**	**31 205**	**29 051**	**29 063**	**30 227**	**30 928**	**31 198**	**31 200**
10-12	Food products, beverages and tobacco	3 785	3 915	4 066	4 040	4 216	4 431	4 585	4 630
13-14	Textiles and wearing apparel	1 327	1 287	1 087	1 051	984	957	929	898
15	Leather and related products	58	59	53	52	50	52	54	59
16	Wood, wood and cork products	532	523	519	523	529	530	520	523
17	Paper and paper products	713	728	664	652	658	680	684	683
18	Printing and reproduction of recorded media	807	840	801	777	784	788	757	725
19-23	Chemical, rubber, plastics, non-metallic products	8 990	9 459	9 139	9 168	9 599	9 864	10 048	9 939
20	Chemicals and chemical products	3 716	3 863	3 733	3 830	3 965	4 070	4 096	4 145
21	Pharmaceutical products	1 804	1 999	1 837	1 798	1 937	2 048	2 201	2 102
22-23	Rubber, plastic, non-metallic mineral products	2 880	2 970	2 912	2 923	3 083	3 127	3 087	3 052
24	Basic metals	2 398	2 479	2 140	2 164	2 210	2 259	2 207	2 143
25	Metal products, except machinery and equipment	2 988	3 141	2 607	2 629	2 768	2 818	2 735	2 620
26-28	Machinery and equipment	4 163	4 454	3 755	3 728	3 950	3 949	3 899	3 915
26	Computer, electronic and optical products	1 075	1 063	707	699	764	806	769	758
27	Electrical equipment	1 027	1 126	1 151	1 116	1 081	1 052	1 037	1 008
28	Machinery and equipment n.e.c.	2 061	2 266	1 897	1 913	2 105	2 090	2 094	2 149
29-30	Transport equipment	3 510	2 969	2 306	2 402	2 518	2 598	2 745	2 964
29	Motor vehicles, trailers and semi-trailers	3 107	2 544	1 904	2 016	2 114	2 159	2 285	2 485
30	Other transport equipment	404	425	402	386	404	440	460	478
31-33	Furniture; repair, installation of machinery and equipment	1 285	1 350	1 915	1 878	1 962	2 001	2 037	2 103
31-32	Furniture, other manufacturing	826	857	826	824	852	861	832	856
33	Repair and installation of machinery and equipment	459	493	1 089	1 054	1 110	1 140	1 205	1 247
35-39	**ELECTRICITY, GAS, WATER AND WASTE MANAGEMENT**	**3 118**	**3 354**	**3 510**	**3 616**	**3 855**	**3 972**	**4 022**	**4 056**
35	Electricity, gas, steam and air conditioning supply	1 956	2 084	1 838	1 899	2 073	2 061	2 056	2 034
36-39	Water supply; sewerage, waste, remediation activities	1 162	1 270	1 672	1 716	1 782	1 911	1 966	2 022
41-43	**CONSTRUCTION**	**8 561**	**9 146**	**9 292**	**9 301**	**9 996**	**10 222**	**10 140**	**10 238**
45-56	Distribution; transportation, accommodation, food service	35 259	37 343	38 132	38 972	39 833	41 180	41 515	41 697
45-47	**Wholesale and retail trade; motor vehicle and motorcycle repairs**	**21 142**	**22 383**	**22 615**	**23 241**	**23 713**	**24 690**	**24 923**	**25 028**
49-53	**Transportation and storage**	**11 392**	**12 053**	**12 524**	**12 609**	**12 776**	**12 979**	**12 961**	**12 863**
55-56	**Accommodation and food service activities**	**2 725**	**2 908**	**2 993**	**3 122**	**3 345**	**3 511**	**3 631**	**3 806**
58-63	**Information and communication**	**6 103**	**6 587**	**7 133**	**7 083**	**7 345**	**7 549**	**7 729**	**7 772**
58-60	Publishing, audiovisual and broadcasting activities	1 343	1 397	1 435	1 442	1 471	1 476	1 491	1 542
61	Telecommunications	1 856	1 897	1 935	1 980	1 916	1 980	2 056	1 854
62-63	IT and other information services	2 903	3 293	3 763	3 661	3 958	4 092	4 183	4 376
64-66	**Financial and insurance activities**	**9 103**	**9 515**	**9 489**	**9 306**	**9 718**	**9 877**	**9 968**	**9 993**
68	**Real estate activities**	**679**	**733**	**813**	**827**	**866**	**897**	**938**	**939**
69-82	**Professional, scientific, technical, admin., support activities**	**18 105**	**19 410**	**18 614**	**19 462**	**20 997**	**21 783**	**22 362**	**23 332**
69-75	Professional, scientific and technical activities	8 841	9 447	9 210	9 278	9 767	10 185	10 593	10 971
69-71	Legal, accounting activities; mgt consultancy; engineering	7 122	7 547	7 402	7 463	7 900	8 279	8 582	8 761
73-75	Advertising, market research; other prof., scientific, tech.	1 066	1 204	1 014	984	1 009	1 023	1 038	1 060
77-82	Administrative and support service activities	9 264	9 963	9 404	10 184	11 231	11 598	11 769	12 361
84-88	**Public administration, defence; social security; education; health**	**52 864**	**56 197**	**58 490**	**60 419**	**63 454**	**66 291**	**68 503**	**69 763**
84	**Public administration, defence; compulsory social security**	**20 443**	**21 417**	**22 159**	**22 731**	**23 550**	**24 489**	**25 349**	**25 898**
85	**Education**	**17 103**	**18 348**	**18 943**	**19 520**	**20 561**	**21 423**	**21 952**	**22 289**
86-88	**Human health and social work activities**	**15 318**	**16 432**	**17 388**	**18 169**	**19 343**	**20 378**	**21 203**	**21 575**
90-99	**Arts, entertainment, household goods repairs, other**	**4 048**	**4 353**	**4 575**	**4 640**	**4 743**	**4 991**	**5 102**	**5 147**
90-93	**Arts, entertainment and recreation**	**1 044**	**1 175**	**1 110**	**1 150**	**1 195**	**1 297**	**1 345**	**1 358**
94-96	**Other service activities**	**2 475**	**2 660**	**2 966**	**3 042**	**3 112**	**3 227**	**3 350**	**3 375**
97-98	**Activities of households as employers and for own use**	**530**	**519**	**499**	**449**	**436**	**466**	**408**	**414**
05-39	**INDUSTRY INCLUDING ENERGY**	**33 832**	**34 720**	**32 693**	**32 808**	**34 221**	**35 035**	**35 352**	**35 421**
45-99	**TOTAL SERVICES**	**126 161**	**134 137**	**137 246**	**140 709**	**146 955**	**152 567**	**156 117**	**158 642**
45-82	**BUSINESS SECTOR SERVICES**	**69 249**	**73 587**	**74 181**	**75 650**	**78 759**	**81 285**	**82 512**	**83 733**
45-82x	**BUSINESS SECTOR SERVICES excluding real estate**	**68 570**	**72 854**	**73 368**	**74 823**	**77 893**	**80 388**	**81 574**	**82 794**
05-82x	**NON-AGRICULTURE BUSINESS SECTOR excluding real estate**	..	..	..	..	..	..	..	..

.. Not available

Note: Detailed metadata at: http://metalinks.oecd.org/stan/20170410/1c43.

Information on data for Israel: http://oe.cd/israel-disclaimer.

Disclaimer: http://oe.cd/disclaimer

CZECH REPUBLIC

Table 1. Production (gross output), current prices

ISIC Rev. 4

Million CZK

		2007	2008	2009	2010	2011	2012	2013	2014
	TOTAL	9 223 289	9 603 919	8 849 287	9 258 166	9 685 836	9 620 603	9 645 911	10 178 269
01-03	AGRICULTURE, FORESTRY AND FISHING	195 750	202 495	175 216	175 264	230 859	239 916	249 759	260 220
05-09	MINING AND QUARRYING	91 514	103 653	86 859	88 832	93 048	88 743	77 642	74 264
10-33	MANUFACTURING	3 494 260	3 501 598	2 943 456	3 247 096	3 533 960	3 580 181	3 602 915	3 995 275
10-12	Food products, beverages and tobacco	341 966	352 584	332 798	317 921	331 728	336 923	341 256	347 953
13-14	Textiles and wearing apparel	75 285	69 421	59 656	55 855	60 759	60 025	61 723	67 854
15	Leather and related products	6 982	6 930	6 860	5 399	5 508	5 516	5 655	5 620
16	Wood, wood and cork products	95 685	94 865	83 775	80 774	84 780	80 842	80 235	85 425
17	Paper and paper products	62 484	57 305	50 663	56 813	58 428	58 955	60 886	67 046
18	Printing and reproduction of recorded media	53 359	55 599	43 304	43 953	41 244	37 314	36 619	40 378
19-23	Chemical, rubber, plastics, non-metallic products	658 082	688 279	544 468	606 913	667 877	689 329	672 466	737 916
20	Chemicals and chemical products	134 677	147 400	114 062	135 807	149 865	160 342	155 840	171 531
21	Pharmaceutical products	35 804	34 767	34 813	37 553	38 889	38 896	39 554	42 405
22-23	Rubber, plastic, non-metallic mineral products	389 282	382 369	316 530	326 455	356 734	353 473	353 652	387 600
24	Basic metals	237 112	242 928	144 862	182 649	209 614	188 684	183 536	194 417
25	Metal products, except machinery and equipment	293 057	306 515	237 947	262 489	290 792	299 322	301 651	329 066
26-28	Machinery and equipment	782 989	777 583	636 685	708 975	758 370	801 590	794 134	876 515
26	Computer, electronic and optical products	295 213	298 269	243 744	270 270	254 314	285 729	263 054	290 911
27	Electrical equipment	194 330	187 123	160 988	188 019	226 754	224 917	231 528	262 857
28	Machinery and equipment n.e.c.	293 446	292 191	231 953	250 686	277 302	290 944	299 552	322 747
29-30	Transport equipment	700 785	660 384	633 977	753 419	844 857	837 405	877 962	1 043 142
29	Motor vehicles, trailers and semi-trailers	662 847	616 687	586 191	705 555	791 384	782 812	824 236	980 884
30	Other transport equipment	37 938	43 697	47 786	47 864	53 473	54 593	53 726	62 258
31-33	Furniture; repair, installation of machinery and equipment	186 474	189 205	168 461	171 936	180 003	184 276	186 792	199 943
31-32	Furniture, other manufacturing	89 090	89 073	84 765	86 308	86 895	89 447	90 968	98 011
33	Repair and installation of machinery and equipment	97 384	100 132	83 696	85 628	93 108	94 829	95 824	101 932
35-39	ELECTRICITY, GAS, WATER AND WASTE MANAGEMENT	450 822	496 111	485 432	492 430	541 536	547 368	542 530	488 437
35	Electricity, gas, steam and air conditioning supply	353 308	390 655	386 020	382 707	421 425	430 167	428 903	370 932
36-39	Water supply; sewerage, waste, remediation activities	97 514	105 456	99 412	109 723	120 111	117 201	113 627	117 505
41-43	CONSTRUCTION	889 077	914 816	846 548	836 486	799 468	728 037	698 338	719 369
45-56	Distribution; transportation, accommodation, food service	1 484 021	1 544 506	1 453 290	1 529 040	1 571 388	1 548 702	1 553 619	1 636 552
45-47	Wholesale and retail trade; motor vehicle and motorcycle repairs	759 953	797 352	759 658	817 506	851 522	830 635	839 330	890 039
49-53	Transportation and storage	548 652	571 351	527 202	555 293	560 605	561 379	558 271	590 069
55-56	Accommodation and food service activities	175 416	175 803	166 430	156 241	159 261	156 688	156 018	156 444
58-63	Information and communication	340 478	350 676	359 127	354 741	357 891	353 533	352 366	361 132
58-60	Publishing, audiovisual and broadcasting activities	78 615	77 212	79 643	79 759	78 393	80 438	83 414	85 792
61	Telecommunications	142 731	143 576	138 823	130 283	121 377	115 107	107 540	107 347
62-63	IT and other information services	119 132	129 888	140 661	144 699	158 121	157 988	161 412	167 993
64-66	Financial and insurance activities	272 743	291 003	296 834	315 162	313 131	310 910	316 397	319 727
68	Real estate activities	484 516	565 692	577 620	608 797	617 507	618 992	612 859	624 896
69-82	Professional, scientific, technical, admin., support activities	612 094	676 297	636 930	623 123	635 209	626 244	641 407	665 614
69-75	Professional, scientific and technical activities	437 509	488 192	455 632	458 800	462 899	456 420	459 800	480 684
69-71	Legal, accounting activities; mgt consultancy; engineering	255 600	289 932	289 214	284 733	287 812	279 342	273 914	279 423
73-75	Advertising, market research; other prof., scientific, tech.	157 516	172 267	140 127	148 048	144 418	144 938	150 282	160 947
77-82	Administrative and support service activities	174 585	188 105	181 298	164 323	172 310	169 824	181 607	184 930
84-88	Public administration, defence; social security; education; health	739 364	783 826	818 440	818 211	817 911	808 992	827 267	856 870
84	Public administration, defence; compulsory social security	346 803	365 249	375 213	371 350	354 953	342 762	351 159	360 423
85	Education	183 464	192 681	200 193	201 332	206 087	205 056	210 902	217 808
86-88	Human health and social work activities	209 097	225 896	243 034	245 529	256 871	261 174	265 206	278 639
90-99	Arts, entertainment, household goods repairs, other	168 650	173 246	169 535	168 984	173 928	168 985	170 812	175 913
90-93	Arts, entertainment and recreation	92 095	97 775	96 718	93 102	96 105	92 118	93 274	96 141
94-96	Other service activities	74 882	73 326	70 046	73 261	75 253	73 999	74 387	76 438
97-98	Activities of households as employers and for own use	1 673	2 145	2 771	2 621	2 570	2 868	3 151	3 334
05-39	INDUSTRY INCLUDING ENERGY	4 036 596	4 101 362	3 515 747	3 828 358	4 168 544	4 216 292	4 223 087	4 557 976
45-99	TOTAL SERVICES	4 101 866	4 385 246	4 311 776	4 418 058	4 486 965	4 436 358	4 474 727	4 640 704
45-82	BUSINESS SECTOR SERVICES	3 193 852	3 428 174	3 323 801	3 430 863	3 495 126	3 458 381	3 476 648	3 607 921
45-82x	BUSINESS SECTOR SERVICES excluding real estate	2 709 336	2 862 482	2 746 181	2 822 066	2 877 619	2 839 389	2 863 789	2 983 025
05-82x	NON-AGRICULTURE BUSINESS SECTOR excluding real estate	..	..	..	..	..	..	..	..

.. Not available

Note: Detailed metadata at: http://metalinks.oecd.org/stan/20170410/1c43.

Information on data for Israel: http://oe.cd/israel-disclaimer.

Disclaimer: http://oe.cd/disclaimer

CZECH REPUBLIC

Table 2. Value added, current prices

ISIC Rev. 4

Million CZK

		2007	2008	2009	2010	2011	2012	2013	2014
	TOTAL	**3 473 464**	**3 647 113**	**3 553 172**	**3 582 869**	**3 640 335**	**3 648 512**	**3 668 332**	**3 898 599**
01-03	**AGRICULTURE, FORESTRY AND FISHING**	**75 389**	**77 800**	**64 525**	**60 217**	**86 632**	**95 396**	**98 504**	**106 720**
05-09	**MINING AND QUARRYING**	**44 822**	**50 933**	**43 669**	**45 029**	**48 181**	**42 979**	**31 957**	**39 274**
10-33	**MANUFACTURING**	**901 750**	**894 785**	**812 564**	**840 146**	**889 814**	**902 251**	**911 016**	**1 043 300**
10-12	Food products, beverages and tobacco	79 711	81 386	88 053	83 442	84 034	82 250	81 390	87 330
13-14	Textiles and wearing apparel	24 954	26 264	24 027	19 239	19 640	19 507	20 357	22 684
15	Leather and related products	2 439	2 667	2 595	2 120	2 137	2 135	2 261	2 210
16	Wood, wood and cork products	26 655	27 833	23 898	22 719	22 440	21 647	20 777	23 206
17	Paper and paper products	17 699	15 533	14 084	14 920	13 703	13 709	13 661	16 285
18	Printing and reproduction of recorded media	16 327	17 194	15 593	15 270	14 343	12 732	12 508	13 528
19-23	Chemical, rubber, plastics, non-metallic products	165 538	167 043	149 855	149 628	155 417	157 014	157 024	189 037
20	Chemicals and chemical products	30 172	29 722	22 643	28 159	29 861	31 324	29 255	39 127
21	Pharmaceutical products	14 634	13 960	14 910	16 266	15 829	16 388	16 469	18 551
22-23	Rubber, plastic, non-metallic mineral products	114 762	115 380	110 643	103 844	108 465	106 671	109 073	124 927
24	Basic metals	52 196	44 987	27 011	24 114	32 582	29 087	31 533	39 811
25	Metal products, except machinery and equipment	91 474	95 064	82 186	87 906	92 911	97 995	99 862	114 360
26-28	Machinery and equipment	196 782	190 584	172 553	187 962	201 380	217 223	219 611	241 769
26	Computer, electronic and optical products	50 032	46 904	42 070	47 000	47 082	57 779	54 269	59 394
27	Electrical equipment	59 112	55 673	52 575	59 354	69 844	69 802	71 243	80 958
28	Machinery and equipment n.e.c.	87 638	88 007	77 908	81 608	84 454	89 642	94 099	101 417
29-30	Transport equipment	156 028	154 016	143 916	166 486	181 759	177 049	178 998	217 632
29	Motor vehicles, trailers and semi-trailers	143 415	140 323	128 266	150 347	162 075	157 327	159 269	195 098
30	Other transport equipment	12 613	13 693	15 650	16 139	19 684	19 722	19 729	22 534
31-33	Furniture; repair, installation of machinery and equipment	71 947	72 214	68 793	66 340	69 468	71 903	73 034	75 448
31-32	Furniture, other manufacturing	33 512	33 276	32 574	31 537	31 697	32 369	32 841	34 261
33	Repair and installation of machinery and equipment	38 435	38 938	36 219	34 803	37 771	39 534	40 193	41 187
35-39	**ELECTRICITY, GAS, WATER AND WASTE MANAGEMENT**	**155 893**	**189 699**	**211 119**	**186 559**	**184 897**	**187 584**	**192 400**	**180 092**
35	Electricity, gas, steam and air conditioning supply	119 048	150 002	170 668	145 885	142 695	145 347	151 770	137 258
36-39	Water supply; sewerage, waste, remediation activities	36 845	39 697	40 451	40 674	42 202	42 237	40 630	42 834
41-43	**CONSTRUCTION**	**225 677**	**239 307**	**239 190**	**246 127**	**224 114**	**213 612**	**210 879**	**214 628**
45-56	Distribution; transportation, accommodation, food service	681 478	697 975	646 419	668 181	662 448	666 399	658 940	694 386
45-47	**Wholesale and retail trade; motor vehicle and motorcycle repairs**	**381 854**	**394 309**	**357 448**	**375 160**	**376 540**	**383 154**	**377 535**	**403 612**
49-53	**Transportation and storage**	**224 039**	**227 157**	**215 561**	**220 918**	**212 741**	**211 471**	**209 301**	**217 799**
55-56	**Accommodation and food service activities**	**75 585**	**76 509**	**73 410**	**72 103**	**73 167**	**71 774**	**72 104**	**72 975**
58-63	**Information and communication**	**181 555**	**188 081**	**188 617**	**183 752**	**187 848**	**186 241**	**184 493**	**195 666**
58-60	Publishing, audiovisual and broadcasting activities	35 125	34 768	33 479	33 345	33 634	35 746	35 748	39 525
61	Telecommunications	81 481	79 990	77 504	73 221	67 334	61 510	56 871	56 151
62-63	IT and other information services	64 949	73 323	77 634	77 186	86 880	88 985	91 874	99 990
64-66	**Financial and insurance activities**	**126 764**	**149 991**	**159 791**	**169 583**	**168 816**	**164 197**	**170 694**	**168 093**
68	**Real estate activities**	**274 534**	**305 997**	**321 451**	**322 254**	**320 048**	**319 377**	**321 564**	**333 741**
69-82	**Professional, scientific, technical, admin., support activities**	**231 416**	**253 509**	**243 664**	**237 179**	**238 413**	**237 032**	**246 524**	**253 363**
69-75	Professional, scientific and technical activities	167 071	181 794	178 563	175 951	176 205	176 967	181 900	188 301
69-71	Legal, accounting activities; mgt consultancy; engineering	112 639	121 837	121 679	119 103	116 499	115 674	116 661	119 093
73-75	Advertising, market research; other prof., scientific, tech.	36 487	41 441	37 723	38 645	39 169	38 949	41 959	41 962
77-82	Administrative and support service activities	64 345	71 715	65 101	61 228	62 208	60 065	64 624	65 062
84-88	**Public administration, defence; social security; education; health**	**490 122**	**517 059**	**540 583**	**542 896**	**543 625**	**550 579**	**559 227**	**583 938**
84	**Public administration, defence; compulsory social security**	**227 441**	**235 559**	**244 096**	**244 630**	**232 773**	**232 889**	**235 930**	**244 185**
85	**Education**	**139 641**	**146 165**	**151 454**	**151 520**	**155 772**	**157 831**	**161 565**	**167 684**
86-88	**Human health and social work activities**	**123 040**	**135 335**	**145 033**	**146 746**	**155 080**	**159 859**	**161 732**	**172 069**
90-99	**Arts, entertainment, household goods repairs, other**	**84 064**	**81 977**	**81 580**	**80 946**	**84 899**	**82 865**	**82 134**	**85 398**
90-93	**Arts, entertainment and recreation**	**40 457**	**41 139**	**40 768**	**38 248**	**40 308**	**36 925**	**36 521**	**38 818**
94-96	**Other service activities**	**41 934**	**38 693**	**38 041**	**40 077**	**42 021**	**43 072**	**42 462**	**43 246**
97-98	**Activities of households as employers and for own use**	**1 673**	**2 145**	**2 771**	**2 621**	**2 570**	**2 868**	**3 151**	**3 334**
05-39	**INDUSTRY INCLUDING ENERGY**	**1 102 465**	**1 135 417**	**1 067 352**	**1 071 734**	**1 122 892**	**1 132 814**	**1 135 373**	**1 262 666**
45-99	**TOTAL SERVICES**	**2 069 933**	**2 194 589**	**2 182 105**	**2 204 791**	**2 206 097**	**2 206 690**	**2 223 576**	**2 314 585**
45-82	**BUSINESS SECTOR SERVICES**	**1 495 747**	**1 595 553**	**1 559 942**	**1 580 949**	**1 577 573**	**1 573 246**	**1 582 215**	**1 645 249**
45-82x	**BUSINESS SECTOR SERVICES excluding real estate**	**1 221 213**	**1 289 556**	**1 238 491**	**1 258 695**	**1 257 525**	**1 253 869**	**1 260 651**	**1 311 508**
05-82x	**NON-AGRICULTURE BUSINESS SECTOR excluding real estate**	..	..	..	..	..	..	..	..

.. Not available

Note: Detailed metadata at: http://metalinks.oecd.org/stan/20170410/1c43.

Information on data for Israel: http://oe.cd/israel-disclaimer.

Disclaimer: http://oe.cd/disclaimer

CZECH REPUBLIC

Table 3. Value added, volumes

ISIC Rev. 4

Million 2010 CZK

		2007	2008	2009	2010	2011	2012	2013	2014
	TOTAL	**3 557 780**	**3 685 359**	**3 482 957**	**3 582 869**	**3 655 028**	**3 624 215**	**3 606 414**	**3 729 050**
01-03	**AGRICULTURE, FORESTRY AND FISHING**	**54 657**	**59 555**	**71 916**	**60 217**	**61 372**	**63 900**	**62 339**	**67 368**
05-09	**MINING AND QUARRYING**	**58 118**	**51 541**	**46 808**	**45 029**	**42 547**	**41 897**	**33 704**	**44 153**
10-33	**MANUFACTURING**	**792 864**	**859 425**	**755 781**	**840 146**	**924 958**	**895 200**	**870 703**	**924 555**
10-12	Food products, beverages and tobacco	87 116	82 859	80 956	83 442	89 238	84 036	78 928	80 000
13-14	Textiles and wearing apparel	24 600	30 341	24 351	19 239	18 864	17 904	17 796	17 771
15	Leather and related products	3 037	2 990	3 091	2 120	1 958	1 815	1 796	1 719
16	Wood, wood and cork products	21 943	25 217	21 307	22 719	21 635	21 181	17 815	17 469
17	Paper and paper products	14 251	14 427	14 303	14 920	13 913	13 902	13 070	14 334
18	Printing and reproduction of recorded media	13 808	14 828	13 143	15 270	15 018	13 464	13 277	14 540
19-23	Chemical, rubber, plastics, non-metallic products	136 036	157 280	156 348	149 628	153 200	147 394	146 651	163 366
20	Chemicals and chemical products	24 241	28 762	27 954	28 159	25 040	25 194	22 788	28 294
21	Pharmaceutical products	14 244	14 734	14 819	16 266	17 517	17 392	18 393	19 708
22-23	Rubber, plastic, non-metallic mineral products	98 784	108 146	102 093	103 844	110 460	102 320	102 102	106 857
24	Basic metals	35 205	25 715	23 750	24 114	28 225	26 465	29 823	30 662
25	Metal products, except machinery and equipment	86 112	87 908	74 518	87 906	91 464	93 940	95 579	104 947
26-28	Machinery and equipment	169 542	183 606	151 143	187 962	213 237	218 013	207 081	224 066
26	Computer, electronic and optical products	36 931	37 528	31 785	47 000	48 997	53 353	46 186	51 873
27	Electrical equipment	53 921	56 311	50 120	59 354	72 036	70 009	68 429	77 429
28	Machinery and equipment n.e.c.	80 057	91 837	70 551	81 608	92 204	94 703	93 061	95 000
29-30	Transport equipment	133 972	165 167	130 068	166 486	208 029	182 514	173 447	179 114
29	Motor vehicles, trailers and semi-trailers	118 290	148 759	115 429	150 347	186 900	163 125	153 507	155 419
30	Other transport equipment	17 090	16 264	14 733	16 139	21 129	19 330	19 801	23 681
31-33	Furniture; repair, installation of machinery and equipment	76 039	78 225	68 249	66 340	70 177	72 787	72 749	73 573
31-32	Furniture, other manufacturing	33 638	36 235	31 630	31 537	33 147	34 357	34 461	34 200
33	Repair and installation of machinery and equipment	42 605	42 029	36 653	34 803	37 030	38 429	38 297	39 322
35-39	**ELECTRICITY, GAS, WATER AND WASTE MANAGEMENT**	**203 167**	**229 314**	**206 775**	**186 559**	**174 672**	**172 550**	**156 129**	**149 639**
35	Electricity, gas, steam and air conditioning supply	157 432	183 732	156 626	145 885	134 071	134 890	123 891	116 454
36-39	Water supply; sewerage, waste, remediation activities	47 768	47 995	52 209	40 674	40 601	37 601	32 260	33 144
41-43	**CONSTRUCTION**	**245 535**	**245 359**	**236 748**	**246 127**	**229 718**	**222 536**	**225 395**	**229 821**
45-56	Distribution; transportation, accommodation, food service	710 426	701 532	640 160	668 181	672 679	672 016	668 290	690 941
45-47	**Wholesale and retail trade; motor vehicle and motorcycle repairs**	**373 885**	**374 044**	**345 781**	**375 160**	**390 442**	**401 289**	**401 125**	**435 429**
49-53	**Transportation and storage**	**251 306**	**244 475**	**220 048**	**220 918**	**206 676**	**199 934**	**197 391**	**190 114**
55-56	**Accommodation and food service activities**	**87 588**	**84 571**	**75 097**	**72 103**	**75 561**	**71 250**	**70 409**	**68 224**
58-63	**Information and communication**	**180 949**	**185 854**	**184 241**	**183 752**	**187 263**	**182 843**	**188 944**	**204 999**
58-60	Publishing, audiovisual and broadcasting activities	34 464	35 086	32 719	33 345	32 725	32 775	29 985	34 099
61	Telecommunications	76 835	74 822	75 573	73 221	67 357	62 472	70 696	78 459
62-63	IT and other information services	69 194	76 036	75 944	77 186	87 181	87 580	88 723	93 094
64-66	**Financial and insurance activities**	**139 309**	**154 782**	**168 996**	**169 583**	**173 576**	**174 368**	**190 465**	**187 786**
68	**Real estate activities**	**316 956**	**326 347**	**317 743**	**322 254**	**328 681**	**334 140**	**340 642**	**351 481**
69-82	**Professional, scientific, technical, admin., support activities**	**249 556**	**257 242**	**238 553**	**237 179**	**241 694**	**244 324**	**251 613**	**254 750**
69-75	Professional, scientific and technical activities	180 380	183 948	174 267	175 951	175 223	178 102	180 407	183 591
69-71	Legal, accounting activities; mgt consultancy; engineering	119 562	121 735	119 652	119 103	117 041	117 684	118 302	116 812
73-75	Advertising, market research; other prof., scientific, tech.	43 252	44 394	35 878	38 645	37 489	38 278	39 350	40 297
77-82	Administrative and support service activities	69 260	73 374	64 318	61 228	66 471	66 149	71 416	71 263
84-88	**Public administration, defence; social security; education; health**	**526 137**	**535 843**	**538 616**	**542 896**	**533 143**	**534 736**	**537 242**	**541 343**
84	**Public administration, defence; compulsory social security**	**228 097**	**235 077**	**238 431**	**244 630**	**235 014**	**236 909**	**235 498**	**234 381**
85	**Education**	**150 111**	**152 098**	**151 504**	**151 520**	**156 619**	**156 007**	**159 068**	**162 532**
86-88	**Human health and social work activities**	**148 712**	**148 993**	**148 867**	**146 746**	**141 510**	**141 835**	**142 608**	**144 256**
90-99	**Arts, entertainment, household goods repairs, other**	**95 018**	**86 534**	**82 218**	**80 946**	**84 725**	**83 887**	**82 943**	**84 171**
90-93	**Arts, entertainment and recreation**	**45 848**	**43 594**	**40 291**	**38 248**	**40 367**	**39 169**	**39 469**	**40 871**
94-96	**Other service activities**	**47 325**	**40 709**	**39 056**	**40 077**	**41 836**	**41 985**	**40 564**	**40 324**
97-98	**Activities of households as employers and for own use**	**1 823**	**2 199**	**2 813**	**2 621**	**2 522**	**2 724**	**2 955**	**3 114**
05-39	**INDUSTRY INCLUDING ENERGY**	**1 052 248**	**1 138 810**	**1 007 187**	**1 071 734**	**1 142 177**	**1 110 025**	**1 060 103**	**1 114 496**
45-99	**TOTAL SERVICES**	**2 219 918**	**2 249 161**	**2 170 432**	**2 204 791**	**2 221 761**	**2 226 169**	**2 259 070**	**2 314 336**
45-82	**BUSINESS SECTOR SERVICES**	**1 599 008**	**1 626 515**	**1 549 647**	**1 580 949**	**1 603 893**	**1 607 546**	**1 639 185**	**1 689 860**
45-82x	**BUSINESS SECTOR SERVICES excluding real estate**	**1 281 300**	**1 299 763**	**1 231 893**	**1 258 695**	**1 275 212**	**1 273 465**	**1 298 602**	**1 338 448**
05-82x	**NON-AGRICULTURE BUSINESS SECTOR excluding real estate**	..	..	..	..	..	..	..	..

.. Not available

Note: Detailed metadata at: http://metalinks.oecd.org/stan/20170410/1c43.

Information on data for Israel: http://oe.cd/israel-disclaimer.

Disclaimer: http://oe.cd/disclaimer

Table 4. Gross fixed capital formation, current prices

ISIC Rev. 4

Million CZK

		2007	2008	2009	2010	2011	2012	2013	2014
	TOTAL	**1 132 392**	**1 165 332**	**1 063 472**	**1 066 005**	**1 067 017**	**1 051 943**	**1 027 089**	**1 084 075**
01-03	**AGRICULTURE, FORESTRY AND FISHING**	**28 093**	**25 976**	**21 257**	**24 660**	**28 969**	**39 493**	**37 075**	**37 320**
05-09	**MINING AND QUARRYING**	**12 008**	**15 177**	**15 368**	**13 863**	**16 840**	**15 224**	**18 156**	**13 338**
10-33	**MANUFACTURING**	**280 989**	**266 023**	**202 576**	**188 576**	**219 000**	**236 071**	**239 120**	**265 280**
10-12	Food products, beverages and tobacco	22 399	17 112	17 396	14 164	14 953	15 551	14 355	17 652
13-14	Textiles and wearing apparel	5 904	4 606	2 619	2 553	4 080	3 398	3 681	4 691
15	Leather and related products	292	167	187	261	346	551	258	608
16	Wood, wood and cork products	8 285	7 276	4 669	5 183	4 801	3 655	5 272	5 914
17	Paper and paper products	5 143	4 902	3 734	4 957	4 112	4 424	5 590	6 034
18	Printing and reproduction of recorded media	4 473	3 794	3 033	2 789	3 793	2 272	4 472	3 747
19-23	Chemical, rubber, plastics, non-metallic products	52 235	46 434	35 039	27 871	33 250	34 357	40 237	41 394
20	Chemicals and chemical products	11 816	10 185	7 568	7 837	7 690	6 428	7 746	8 851
21	Pharmaceutical products	4 620	3 710	4 146	3 333	3 762	4 132	3 644	3 428
22-23	Rubber, plastic, non-metallic mineral products	33 206	30 817	20 732	15 070	20 816	22 756	26 357	28 476
24	Basic metals	11 275	10 215	7 486	5 618	5 611	6 609	7 829	8 968
25	Metal products, except machinery and equipment	24 771	31 743	17 327	18 781	20 131	17 781	19 711	22 314
26-28	Machinery and equipment	74 844	70 481	55 455	55 480	62 597	66 374	59 183	71 690
26	Computer, electronic and optical products	34 066	30 481	23 852	26 376	24 882	27 349	20 546	29 488
27	Electrical equipment	14 561	13 369	12 575	12 264	15 972	17 132	14 355	16 931
28	Machinery and equipment n.e.c.	26 217	26 631	19 028	16 840	21 743	21 893	24 282	25 271
29-30	Transport equipment	57 050	56 264	44 068	36 306	51 530	66 127	65 487	68 220
29	Motor vehicles, trailers and semi-trailers	53 037	51 461	39 076	31 461	45 605	60 390	58 910	61 450
30	Other transport equipment	4 013	4 803	4 992	4 845	5 925	5 737	6 577	6 770
31-33	Furniture; repair, installation of machinery and equipment	14 318	13 029	11 563	14 613	13 796	14 972	13 045	14 048
31-32	Furniture, other manufacturing	5 824	5 580	4 753	5 980	6 619	7 568	5 901	7 808
33	Repair and installation of machinery and equipment	8 494	7 449	6 810	8 633	7 177	7 404	7 144	6 240
35-39	**ELECTRICITY, GAS, WATER AND WASTE MANAGEMENT**	**64 468**	**69 700**	**81 111**	**105 216**	**96 561**	**84 397**	**82 504**	**76 916**
35	Electricity, gas, steam and air conditioning supply	48 798	53 287	63 894	90 844	82 298	69 355	67 840	63 505
36-39	Water supply; sewerage, waste, remediation activities	15 670	16 413	17 217	14 372	14 263	15 042	14 664	13 411
41-43	**CONSTRUCTION**	**35 087**	**42 630**	**34 859**	**40 311**	**33 256**	**31 458**	**27 082**	**33 963**
45-56	Distribution; transportation, accommodation, food service	216 308	229 534	202 241	186 878	180 361	153 662	146 173	150 360
45-47	**Wholesale and retail trade; motor vehicle and motorcycle repairs**	**77 889**	**79 672**	**68 098**	**69 548**	**67 935**	**65 269**	**58 982**	**59 910**
49-53	**Transportation and storage**	**125 676**	**139 612**	**125 125**	**110 225**	**101 625**	**78 002**	**76 976**	**81 220**
55-56	**Accommodation and food service activities**	**12 743**	**10 250**	**9 018**	**7 105**	**10 801**	**10 391**	**10 215**	**9 230**
58-63	**Information and communication**	**56 692**	**49 788**	**56 607**	**53 794**	**52 188**	**51 691**	**57 742**	**62 008**
58-60	Publishing, audiovisual and broadcasting activities	14 541	14 924	11 998	11 061	10 844	9 876	12 728	12 799
61	Telecommunications	26 992	18 823	25 562	25 695	17 511	16 113	22 853	22 679
62-63	IT and other information services	15 159	16 041	19 047	17 038	23 833	25 702	22 161	26 530
64-66	**Financial and insurance activities**	**27 523**	**34 040**	**26 195**	**26 978**	**28 195**	**28 629**	**26 511**	**27 454**
68	**Real estate activities**	**221 518**	**221 253**	**197 570**	**210 861**	**200 569**	**195 963**	**197 920**	**202 736**
69-82	**Professional, scientific, technical, admin., support activities**	**55 415**	**68 683**	**56 939**	**59 416**	**61 372**	**65 541**	**59 022**	**57 386**
69-75	Professional, scientific and technical activities	33 981	43 654	40 851	44 443	43 258	45 731	42 469	42 760
69-71	Legal, accounting activities; mgt consultancy; engineering	17 624	26 105	23 465	26 289	22 702	25 353	20 123	15 837
73-75	Advertising, market research; other prof., scientific, tech.	4 991	6 561	6 167	7 552	8 330	6 772	6 887	7 999
77-82	Administrative and support service activities	21 434	25 029	16 088	14 973	18 114	19 810	16 553	14 626
84-88	**Public administration, defence; social security; education; health**	**114 915**	**121 848**	**147 041**	**138 377**	**131 087**	**131 979**	**119 782**	**141 285**
84	**Public administration, defence; compulsory social security**	**67 802**	**71 432**	**91 168**	**83 522**	**74 067**	**76 949**	**67 133**	**85 751**
85	**Education**	**27 709**	**29 326**	**28 605**	**28 467**	**32 449**	**33 151**	**34 183**	**36 085**
86-88	**Human health and social work activities**	**19 404**	**21 090**	**27 268**	**26 388**	**24 571**	**21 879**	**18 466**	**19 449**
90-99	**Arts, entertainment, household goods repairs, other**	**19 376**	**20 680**	**21 708**	**17 075**	**18 619**	**17 835**	**16 002**	**16 029**
90-93	**Arts, entertainment and recreation**	**13 380**	**15 108**	**15 636**	**11 854**	**13 496**	**11 688**	**11 648**	**10 810**
94-96	**Other service activities**	**5 996**	**5 572**	**6 072**	**5 221**	**5 123**	**6 147**	**4 354**	**5 219**
97-98	**Activities of households as employers and for own use**	**0**	**0**	**0**	**0**	**0**	**0**	**0**	**0**
05-39	**INDUSTRY INCLUDING ENERGY**	**357 465**	**350 900**	**299 055**	**307 655**	**332 401**	**335 692**	**339 780**	**355 534**
45-99	**TOTAL SERVICES**	**711 747**	**745 826**	**708 301**	**693 379**	**672 391**	**645 300**	**623 152**	**657 258**
45-82	**BUSINESS SECTOR SERVICES**	**577 456**	**603 298**	**539 552**	**537 927**	**522 685**	**495 486**	**487 368**	**499 944**
45-82x	**BUSINESS SECTOR SERVICES excluding real estate**	**355 938**	**382 045**	**341 982**	**327 066**	**322 116**	**299 523**	**289 448**	**297 208**
05-82x	**NON-AGRICULTURE BUSINESS SECTOR excluding real estate**	..	..	..	..	..	..	..	..

.. Not available

Note: Detailed metadata at: http://metalinks.oecd.org/stan/20170410/1c43.
Information on data for Israel: http://oe.cd/israel-disclaimer.

Disclaimer: http://oe.cd/disclaimer

CZECH REPUBLIC

Table 5. Number of persons engaged, total employment

ISIC Rev. 4

Thousands

		2007	2008	2009	2010	2011	2012	2013	2014
	TOTAL	5 093	5 204	5 110	5 057	5 043	5 065	5 081	5 109
01-03	**AGRICULTURE, FORESTRY AND FISHING**	170	168	168	159	163	165	167	166
05-09	**MINING AND QUARRYING**	42	45	39	36	35	35	34	36
10-33	**MANUFACTURING**	1 393	1 401	1 293	1 252	1 298	1 310	1 308	1 325
10-12	Food products, beverages and tobacco	129	131	134	127	126	128	127	125
13-14	Textiles and wearing apparel	74	68	59	55	54	54	54	53
15	Leather and related products	9	8	7	7	7	7	7	6
16	Wood, wood and cork products	69	70	66	66	63	63	60	59
17	Paper and paper products	22	20	21	20	20	20	20	20
18	Printing and reproduction of recorded media	30	32	30	28	27	26	26	25
19-23	Chemical, rubber, plastics, non-metallic products	205	210	191	179	187	187	187	191
20	Chemicals and chemical products	30	30	31	30	30	30	30	30
21	Pharmaceutical products	11	11	12	11	11	11	12	12
22-23	Rubber, plastic, non-metallic mineral products	160	166	146	135	143	143	144	147
24	Basic metals	59	53	49	46	50	46	47	48
25	Metal products, except machinery and equipment	180	189	172	172	181	185	189	194
26-28	Machinery and equipment	307	306	265	255	269	280	281	283
26	Computer, electronic and optical products	54	56	47	42	42	48	46	45
27	Electrical equipment	103	101	92	93	101	100	104	107
28	Machinery and equipment n.e.c.	150	150	126	120	126	131	132	132
29-30	Transport equipment	176	179	164	164	183	181	179	187
29	Motor vehicles, trailers and semi-trailers	158	160	143	144	161	159	156	162
30	Other transport equipment	18	18	20	19	21	23	23	25
31-33	Furniture; repair, installation of machinery and equipment	134	136	136	134	132	133	132	133
31-32	Furniture, other manufacturing	81	81	81	81	78	78	78	78
33	Repair and installation of machinery and equipment	53	54	55	53	54	55	54	55
35-39	**ELECTRICITY, GAS, WATER AND WASTE MANAGEMENT**	89	90	91	90	91	91	92	93
35	Electricity, gas, steam and air conditioning supply	33	33	33	32	33	33	33	34
36-39	Water supply; sewerage, waste, remediation activities	56	57	58	58	58	58	59	59
41-43	**CONSTRUCTION**	434	444	463	471	447	442	431	411
45-56	Distribution; transportation, accommodation, food service	1 196	1 234	1 244	1 240	1 237	1 231	1 236	1 233
45-47	**Wholesale and retail trade; motor vehicle and motorcycle repairs**	687	716	714	723	722	722	727	731
49-53	**Transportation and storage**	320	321	320	312	311	306	308	310
55-56	**Accommodation and food service activities**	189	197	210	205	204	202	201	192
58-63	**Information and communication**	117	126	134	130	125	127	129	133
58-60	Publishing, audiovisual and broadcasting activities	32	32	33	31	29	29	29	29
61	Telecommunications	23	23	23	21	21	20	20	19
62-63	IT and other information services	61	71	78	78	75	78	81	85
64-66	**Financial and insurance activities**	87	90	90	87	89	95	96	97
68	**Real estate activities**	92	100	101	103	90	95	96	96
69-82	**Professional, scientific, technical, admin., support activities**	416	423	423	419	405	414	422	432
69-75	Professional, scientific and technical activities	271	272	275	277	264	272	276	284
69-71	Legal, accounting activities; mgt consultancy; engineering	188	179	181	181	172	176	178	180
73-75	Advertising, market research; other prof., scientific, tech.	64	72	73	75	70	73	73	77
77-82	Administrative and support service activities	144	152	147	142	141	142	146	148
84-88	**Public administration, defence; social security; education; health**	896	920	899	900	889	879	890	905
84	**Public administration, defence; compulsory social security**	315	315	310	317	295	280	283	286
85	**Education**	301	301	288	282	288	289	295	299
86-88	**Human health and social work activities**	280	304	301	300	306	310	312	320
90-99	**Arts, entertainment, household goods repairs, other**	160	165	166	169	174	180	180	183
90-93	**Arts, entertainment and recreation**	64	67	68	67	69	71	72	72
94-96	**Other service activities**	90	91	91	95	98	101	100	102
97-98	**Activities of households as employers and for own use**	6	7	7	7	7	8	8	8
05-39	**INDUSTRY INCLUDING ENERGY**	1 524	1 536	1 422	1 379	1 424	1 437	1 434	1 454
45-99	**TOTAL SERVICES**	2 965	3 057	3 057	3 048	3 009	3 021	3 049	3 078
45-82	**BUSINESS SECTOR SERVICES**	1 908	1 972	1 992	1 980	1 946	1 962	1 978	1 991
45-82x	**BUSINESS SECTOR SERVICES excluding real estate**	1 816	1 873	1 890	1 876	1 856	1 867	1 883	1 895
05-82x	**NON-AGRICULTURE BUSINESS SECTOR excluding real estate**	..	..	..	..	..	..	..	..

.. Not available

Note: Detailed metadata at: http://metalinks.oecd.org/stan/20170410/1c43.

Information on data for Israel: http://oe.cd/israel-disclaimer.

Disclaimer: http://oe.cd/disclaimer

CZECH REPUBLIC

Table 6. Labour costs (compensation of employees), current prices

ISIC Rev. 4

Million CZK

		2007	2008	2009	2010	2011	2012	2013	2014
	TOTAL	1 513 254	1 616 849	1 568 561	1 589 052	1 626 392	1 664 701	1 676 183	1 734 660
01-03	AGRICULTURE, FORESTRY AND FISHING	36 741	38 517	35 799	33 292	34 492	36 113	37 390	38 683
05-09	MINING AND QUARRYING	20 532	22 186	19 180	18 919	20 034	20 245	19 476	19 937
10-33	MANUFACTURING	427 082	450 320	407 107	409 185	437 150	450 215	454 084	476 514
10-12	Food products, beverages and tobacco	37 642	38 972	39 292	38 977	38 279	39 008	38 324	38 815
13-14	Textiles and wearing apparel	15 098	14 370	12 029	11 479	11 462	11 290	11 483	11 950
15	Leather and related products	1 758	1 617	1 449	1 450	1 498	1 466	1 394	1 311
16	Wood, wood and cork products	11 825	12 197	10 786	10 531	10 096	9 998	9 635	9 685
17	Paper and paper products	7 448	7 307	7 288	7 412	7 260	7 453	7 388	7 480
18	Printing and reproduction of recorded media	7 616	8 137	7 346	7 297	7 124	6 864	6 678	6 518
19-23	Chemical, rubber, plastics, non-metallic products	72 310	76 586	68 836	67 238	70 957	73 051	73 200	76 511
20	Chemicals and chemical products	12 084	13 119	13 186	13 079	12 677	13 274	13 044	13 681
21	Pharmaceutical products	4 709	4 674	5 499	5 394	5 265	5 097	5 083	5 078
22-23	Rubber, plastic, non-metallic mineral products	54 135	56 924	48 628	47 272	51 591	53 031	53 642	56 232
24	Basic metals	22 036	21 966	19 776	18 824	20 923	20 362	20 664	21 722
25	Metal products, except machinery and equipment	47 947	51 874	45 202	47 457	52 073	54 839	55 856	59 481
26-28	Machinery and equipment	98 533	104 120	90 016	89 826	99 586	106 633	109 101	113 842
26	Computer, electronic and optical products	18 126	19 484	16 606	15 111	15 940	18 947	17 876	18 259
27	Electrical equipment	30 861	31 191	27 185	29 668	34 854	35 791	37 413	39 854
28	Machinery and equipment n.e.c.	49 546	53 445	46 225	45 047	48 792	51 895	53 812	55 729
29-30	Transport equipment	67 732	72 932	65 985	69 859	78 651	79 318	80 579	88 506
29	Motor vehicles, trailers and semi-trailers	60 561	65 470	57 657	61 795	69 830	69 615	70 634	77 422
30	Other transport equipment	7 171	7 462	8 328	8 064	8 821	9 703	9 945	11 084
31-33	Furniture; repair, installation of machinery and equipment	37 137	40 242	39 102	38 835	39 241	39 933	39 782	40 693
31-32	Furniture, other manufacturing	17 437	18 301	17 400	17 781	17 612	18 107	18 600	19 267
33	Repair and installation of machinery and equipment	19 700	21 941	21 702	21 054	21 629	21 826	21 182	21 426
35-39	ELECTRICITY, GAS, WATER AND WASTE MANAGEMENT	37 486	38 338	39 086	38 640	42 206	43 360	43 611	43 792
35	Electricity, gas, steam and air conditioning supply	19 252	19 303	19 133	19 037	21 186	22 067	22 090	21 901
36-39	Water supply; sewerage, waste, remediation activities	18 234	19 035	19 953	19 603	21 020	21 293	21 521	21 891
41-43	CONSTRUCTION	98 820	106 266	102 435	102 355	98 866	95 828	88 993	86 820
45-56	Distribution; transportation, accommodation, food service	307 060	330 790	318 628	329 098	334 722	337 266	337 534	346 584
45-47	Wholesale and retail trade; motor vehicle and motorcycle repairs	174 499	192 079	180 678	193 559	197 067	199 301	199 383	205 488
49-53	Transportation and storage	101 274	107 312	107 693	105 166	105 580	104 432	103 964	106 376
55-56	Accommodation and food service activities	31 287	31 399	30 257	30 373	32 075	33 533	34 187	34 720
58-63	Information and communication	62 329	70 004	72 370	72 115	71 991	74 892	77 572	82 153
58-60	Publishing, audiovisual and broadcasting activities	12 940	13 616	14 081	13 014	11 806	12 118	12 407	12 636
61	Telecommunications	15 424	15 972	15 749	15 829	15 624	15 295	14 680	15 056
62-63	IT and other information services	33 965	40 416	42 540	43 272	44 561	47 479	50 485	54 461
64-66	Financial and insurance activities	50 919	54 195	52 174	53 243	56 253	61 096	59 301	62 133
68	Real estate activities	14 242	17 150	17 254	17 470	16 125	18 347	19 647	19 268
69-82	Professional, scientific, technical, admin., support activities	101 193	112 168	114 229	119 961	118 168	122 638	124 271	127 749
69-75	Professional, scientific and technical activities	71 117	78 756	80 130	84 245	82 393	86 718	87 279	90 284
69-71	Legal, accounting activities; mgt consultancy; engineering	48 581	51 577	53 233	56 027	55 833	58 359	59 343	61 077
73-75	Advertising, market research; other prof., scientific, tech.	14 164	18 520	17 674	19 109	16 055	16 940	16 049	16 310
77-82	Administrative and support service activities	30 076	33 412	34 099	35 716	35 775	35 920	36 992	37 465
84-88	Public administration, defence; social security; education; health	327 031	344 420	356 870	360 160	360 497	368 239	376 697	392 343
84	Public administration, defence; compulsory social security	142 702	147 711	152 201	150 415	138 860	139 364	142 524	148 871
85	Education	99 560	102 050	107 209	107 170	110 677	113 171	115 823	118 896
86-88	Human health and social work activities	84 769	94 659	97 460	102 575	110 960	115 704	118 350	124 576
90-99	Arts, entertainment, household goods repairs, other	29 819	32 495	33 429	34 614	35 888	36 462	37 607	38 684
90-93	Arts, entertainment and recreation	15 638	16 548	16 997	17 209	17 386	18 098	18 466	18 963
94-96	Other service activities	12 784	14 331	14 609	15 743	16 502	16 405	16 913	17 373
97-98	Activities of households as employers and for own use	1 397	1 616	1 823	1 662	2 000	1 959	2 228	2 348
05-39	INDUSTRY INCLUDING ENERGY	485 100	510 844	465 373	466 744	499 390	513 820	517 171	540 243
45-99	TOTAL SERVICES	892 593	961 222	964 954	986 661	993 644	1 018 940	1 032 629	1 068 914
45-82	BUSINESS SECTOR SERVICES	535 743	584 307	574 655	591 887	597 259	614 239	618 325	637 887
45-82x	BUSINESS SECTOR SERVICES excluding real estate	521 501	567 157	557 401	574 417	581 134	595 892	598 678	618 619
05-82x	NON-AGRICULTURE BUSINESS SECTOR excluding real estate	..	..	..	..	..	..	..	..

.. Not available

Note: Detailed metadata at: http://metalinks.oecd.org/stan/20170410/1c43.
Information on data for Israel: http://oe.cd/israel-disclaimer.

Disclaimer: http://oe.cd/disclaimer

Table 1. Production (gross output), current prices

ISIC Rev. 4

Million DKK

		2007	2008	2009	2010	2011	2012	2013	2014
	TOTAL	**3 093 079**	**3 263 452**	**3 002 408**	**3 120 573**	**3 257 067**	**3 365 521**	**3 384 439**	**3 458 998**
01-03	**AGRICULTURE, FORESTRY AND FISHING**	**67 408**	**68 250**	**65 419**	**72 909**	**80 298**	**88 913**	**84 450**	**85 170**
05-09	**MINING AND QUARRYING**	**65 385**	**74 416**	**50 394**	**55 646**	**63 864**	**65 784**	**55 525**	**47 199**
10-33	**MANUFACTURING**	**633 711**	**670 203**	**567 176**	**577 899**	**625 510**	**655 332**	**650 135**	**656 624**
10-12	Food products, beverages and tobacco	137 742	145 761	133 713	132 532	139 876	141 548	145 794	137 105
13-14	Textiles and wearing apparel	10 549	9 834	8 317	8 150	8 416	7 743	8 595	..
15	Leather and related products	420	455	528	781	794	751	998	..
16	Wood, wood and cork products	16 708	15 145	11 433	11 253	11 183	11 499	10 572	11 199
17	Paper and paper products	9 923	9 746	8 566	8 701	9 516	8 978	8 916	9 123
18	Printing and reproduction of recorded media	12 488	13 861	11 381	10 295	9 593	9 641	8 993	9 133
19-23	Chemical, rubber, plastics, non-metallic products	154 340	162 939	139 478	157 147	172 190	190 886	191 754	199 949
20	Chemicals and chemical products	27 422	30 238	27 962	30 454	30 220	33 714	36 108	37 407
21	Pharmaceutical products	44 151	48 604	49 829	61 327	64 301	73 252	78 055	87 759
22-23	Rubber, plastic, non-metallic mineral products	51 920	47 806	37 024	34 858	39 975	39 871	40 244	40 426
24	Basic metals	13 150	12 449	6 851	7 772	9 490	8 673	8 509	9 344
25	Metal products, except machinery and equipment	48 975	51 976	41 107	38 327	42 564	43 251	43 097	46 121
26-28	Machinery and equipment	166 724	184 469	151 206	148 356	163 015	172 000	160 386	158 711
26	Computer, electronic and optical products	34 285	30 488	26 665	28 781	29 967	30 749	29 943	27 991
27	Electrical equipment	18 540	20 615	15 548	17 067	19 209	18 356	15 971	17 690
28	Machinery and equipment n.e.c.	113 899	133 366	108 993	102 508	113 839	122 895	114 472	113 030
29-30	Transport equipment	16 881	16 878	12 776	12 799	12 926	11 049	10 287	11 179
29	Motor vehicles, trailers and semi-trailers	8 244	7 929	5 150	6 533	7 354	7 060	6 396	7 249
30	Other transport equipment	8 637	8 949	7 626	6 266	5 572	3 989	3 891	3 930
31-33	Furniture; repair, installation of machinery and equipment	45 812	46 691	41 819	41 787	45 948	49 313	52 234	55 068
31-32	Furniture, other manufacturing	33 666	32 813	30 551	31 592	33 699	34 058	36 618	39 300
33	Repair and installation of machinery and equipment	12 146	13 878	11 268	10 195	12 249	15 255	15 616	15 768
35-39	**ELECTRICITY, GAS, WATER AND WASTE MANAGEMENT**	**79 602**	**92 267**	**84 452**	**93 715**	**94 471**	**93 546**	**95 216**	**89 140**
35	Electricity, gas, steam and air conditioning supply	52 326	61 971	53 031	60 290	58 887	57 582	58 322	51 746
36-39	Water supply; sewerage, waste, remediation activities	27 276	30 296	31 421	33 425	35 584	35 964	36 894	37 394
41-43	**CONSTRUCTION**	**239 662**	**242 098**	**202 865**	**191 242**	**204 102**	**205 612**	**204 880**	**211 205**
45-56	Distribution; transportation, accommodation, food service	733 237	761 288	664 490	720 903	765 120	793 628	812 717	842 211
45-47	**Wholesale and retail trade; motor vehicle and motorcycle repairs**	**355 762**	**369 001**	**342 702**	**348 689**	**371 585**	**384 117**	**396 477**	**414 849**
49-53	**Transportation and storage**	**325 676**	**337 968**	**270 072**	**321 106**	**339 615**	**353 726**	**356 902**	**365 778**
55-56	**Accommodation and food service activities**	**51 800**	**54 318**	**51 715**	**51 107**	**53 921**	**55 785**	**59 338**	**61 584**
58-63	**Information and communication**	**151 305**	**157 456**	**156 822**	**158 108**	**157 511**	**155 878**	**156 421**	**157 970**
58-60	Publishing, audiovisual and broadcasting activities	46 834	47 013	44 959	44 763	45 040	44 807	44 936	46 812
61	Telecommunications	47 635	48 606	47 571	45 609	46 362	44 679	42 228	39 350
62-63	IT and other information services	56 836	61 837	64 292	67 736	66 109	66 392	69 257	71 808
64-66	**Financial and insurance activities**	**137 616**	**146 980**	**148 985**	**160 248**	**159 276**	**167 115**	**162 790**	**170 390**
68	**Real estate activities**	**204 823**	**208 934**	**212 037**	**225 736**	**234 033**	**243 191**	**249 606**	**255 434**
69-82	**Professional, scientific, technical, admin., support activities**	**245 429**	**269 252**	**243 608**	**242 319**	**256 510**	**262 418**	**274 522**	**288 818**
69-75	Professional, scientific and technical activities	156 858	177 579	162 661	156 774	157 533	160 663	168 740	177 996
69-71	Legal, accounting activities; mgt consultancy; engineering	104 901	115 147	105 262	100 147	102 273	105 746	113 729	115 967
73-75	Advertising, market research; other prof., scientific, tech.	37 919	40 052	35 270	34 437	35 553	34 697	34 027	36 133
77-82	Administrative and support service activities	88 571	91 673	80 947	85 545	98 977	101 755	105 782	110 822
84-88	**Public administration, defence; social security; education; health**	**455 672**	**489 735**	**521 923**	**536 245**	**528 892**	**544 871**	**547 787**	**561 461**
84	**Public administration, defence; compulsory social security**	**125 204**	**135 069**	**142 761**	**145 456**	**140 115**	**144 613**	**141 234**	**142 871**
85	**Education**	**112 341**	**121 818**	**130 290**	**136 787**	**138 081**	**143 770**	**145 506**	**152 751**
86-88	**Human health and social work activities**	**218 128**	**232 849**	**248 871**	**254 003**	**250 697**	**256 488**	**261 047**	**265 839**
90-99	**Arts, entertainment, household goods repairs, other**	**79 230**	**82 575**	**84 236**	**85 606**	**87 481**	**89 233**	**90 389**	**93 377**
90-93	**Arts, entertainment and recreation**	**36 128**	**38 361**	**38 623**	**39 346**	**40 231**	**41 852**	**43 066**	**44 344**
94-96	**Other service activities**	**39 559**	**40 453**	**41 497**	**41 896**	**42 571**	**42 757**	**42 425**	**44 087**
97-98	**Activities of households as employers and for own use**	**3 543**	**3 761**	**4 116**	**4 364**	**4 679**	**4 624**	**4 898**	**4 946**
05-39	**INDUSTRY INCLUDING ENERGY**	**778 698**	**836 886**	**702 022**	**727 260**	**783 845**	**814 662**	**800 876**	**792 963**
45-99	**TOTAL SERVICES**	**2 007 311**	**2 116 219**	**2 032 102**	**2 129 163**	**2 188 822**	**2 256 334**	**2 294 233**	**2 369 660**
45-82	**BUSINESS SECTOR SERVICES**	**1 472 409**	**1 543 909**	**1 425 943**	**1 507 312**	**1 572 449**	**1 622 230**	**1 656 056**	**1 714 823**
45-82x	**BUSINESS SECTOR SERVICES excluding real estate**	**1 267 586**	**1 334 975**	**1 213 906**	**1 281 577**	**1 338 416**	**1 379 039**	**1 406 450**	**1 459 389**
05-82x	**NON-AGRICULTURE BUSINESS SECTOR excluding real estate**	..	..	..	..	..	..	..	..

.. Not available

Note: Detailed metadata at: http://metalinks.oecd.org/stan/20170410/1c43.

Information on data for Israel: http://oe.cd/israel-disclaimer.

Disclaimer: http://oe.cd/disclaimer

DENMARK

Table 2. Value added, current prices

ISIC Rev. 4

Million DKK

		2007	2008	2009	2010	2011	2012	2013	2014
	TOTAL	**1 475 015**	**1 545 452**	**1 484 941**	**1 562 743**	**1 593 742**	**1 636 086**	**1 669 456**	**1 715 195**
01-03	**AGRICULTURE, FORESTRY AND FISHING**	**20 421**	**15 453**	**14 356**	**21 766**	**24 234**	**31 356**	**25 127**	**27 086**
05-09	**MINING AND QUARRYING**	**58 493**	**65 210**	**41 413**	**48 384**	**56 446**	**56 646**	**47 366**	**39 986**
10-33	**MANUFACTURING**	**207 818**	**211 183**	**191 244**	**198 003**	**203 956**	**216 674**	**227 310**	**232 718**
10-12	Food products, beverages and tobacco	31 087	30 700	30 890	29 414	27 699	26 510	27 796	25 782
13-14	Textiles and wearing apparel	3 182	3 050	2 503	2 280	2 363	2 175	2 503	..
15	Leather and related products	117	94	110	114	106	54	165	..
16	Wood, wood and cork products	5 934	5 308	3 853	3 898	3 981	3 994	3 872	3 965
17	Paper and paper products	3 355	3 181	3 045	2 868	3 025	2 824	2 720	2 693
18	Printing and reproduction of recorded media	5 081	5 635	4 567	3 910	3 861	3 333	3 265	3 365
19-23	Chemical, rubber, plastics, non-metallic products	52 522	53 407	52 403	60 566	61 172	74 356	76 876	84 874
20	Chemicals and chemical products	9 005	10 269	11 051	12 040	11 685	14 445	14 046	13 932
21	Pharmaceutical products	20 450	22 987	25 726	34 235	36 734	44 627	48 734	55 479
22-23	Rubber, plastic, non-metallic mineral products	21 667	19 356	15 238	13 962	13 681	14 489	14 330	15 111
24	Basic metals	3 587	3 362	1 851	1 755	2 177	2 179	2 252	2 597
25	Metal products, except machinery and equipment	17 901	19 476	16 786	15 292	14 025	15 293	17 426	18 579
26-28	Machinery and equipment	62 824	62 611	53 570	54 779	59 877	59 362	64 018	59 459
26	Computer, electronic and optical products	16 896	14 346	13 371	14 757	15 227	15 509	15 820	14 227
27	Electrical equipment	6 718	8 130	6 093	6 696	6 983	6 684	6 090	6 773
28	Machinery and equipment n.e.c.	39 210	40 135	34 106	33 326	37 667	37 169	42 108	38 459
29-30	Transport equipment	4 439	5 145	3 401	4 157	4 700	3 819	3 371	3 389
29	Motor vehicles, trailers and semi-trailers	2 905	3 080	1 966	2 395	2 774	2 432	2 140	2 186
30	Other transport equipment	1 534	2 065	1 435	1 762	1 926	1 387	1 231	1 203
31-33	Furniture; repair, installation of machinery and equipment	17 789	19 214	18 265	18 970	20 971	22 775	23 046	25 203
31-32	Furniture, other manufacturing	13 445	13 771	13 625	14 694	16 062	16 551	17 308	19 175
33	Repair and installation of machinery and equipment	4 344	5 443	4 640	4 276	4 909	6 224	5 738	6 028
35-39	**ELECTRICITY, GAS, WATER AND WASTE MANAGEMENT**	**34 497**	**37 271**	**34 713**	**41 459**	**39 893**	**38 690**	**36 791**	**33 842**
35	Electricity, gas, steam and air conditioning supply	24 515	25 774	23 204	28 848	26 686	25 068	23 239	20 376
36-39	Water supply; sewerage, waste, remediation activities	9 982	11 497	11 509	12 611	13 207	13 622	13 552	13 466
41-43	**CONSTRUCTION**	**84 636**	**93 359**	**76 199**	**68 993**	**73 782**	**74 530**	**75 662**	**79 350**
45-56	Distribution; transportation, accommodation, food service	304 183	305 112	277 017	304 453	309 279	314 410	336 368	353 834
45-47	**Wholesale and retail trade; motor vehicle and motorcycle repairs**	**190 829**	**195 460**	**184 573**	**191 951**	**204 729**	**208 782**	**214 401**	**224 779**
49-53	**Transportation and storage**	**90 830**	**86 517**	**70 711**	**91 511**	**81 648**	**81 890**	**96 375**	**102 223**
55-56	**Accommodation and food service activities**	**22 524**	**23 135**	**21 733**	**20 991**	**22 902**	**23 738**	**25 592**	**26 832**
58-63	**Information and communication**	**64 001**	**69 963**	**72 573**	**74 120**	**73 521**	**73 194**	**78 298**	**77 681**
58-60	Publishing, audiovisual and broadcasting activities	18 189	20 286	18 876	20 464	20 914	21 239	22 222	23 692
61	Telecommunications	20 409	21 238	20 967	18 529	20 660	19 757	20 960	18 154
62-63	IT and other information services	25 403	28 439	32 730	35 127	31 947	32 198	35 116	35 835
64-66	**Financial and insurance activities**	**82 084**	**91 893**	**93 102**	**96 658**	**94 140**	**102 419**	**98 821**	**106 741**
68	**Real estate activities**	**136 901**	**138 324**	**145 697**	**155 198**	**164 389**	**164 888**	**168 068**	**170 310**
69-82	**Professional, scientific, technical, admin., support activities**	**114 014**	**126 180**	**123 551**	**124 530**	**126 633**	**128 238**	**137 477**	**145 258**
69-75	Professional, scientific and technical activities	72 336	84 215	84 334	85 015	83 853	82 949	89 044	93 746
69-71	Legal, accounting activities; mgt consultancy; engineering	52 174	57 381	57 834	59 173	61 116	62 260	66 220	67 222
73-75	Advertising, market research; other prof., scientific, tech.	13 140	15 055	13 634	12 913	13 198	12 558	12 949	13 975
77-82	Administrative and support service activities	41 678	41 965	39 217	39 515	42 780	45 289	48 433	51 512
84-88	**Public administration, defence; social security; education; health**	**319 222**	**340 091**	**362 128**	**375 161**	**371 651**	**378 873**	**381 394**	**389 713**
84	**Public administration, defence; compulsory social security**	**81 439**	**86 383**	**90 129**	**93 157**	**91 029**	**92 301**	**90 693**	**90 791**
85	**Education**	**84 975**	**91 870**	**97 225**	**101 559**	**102 247**	**105 618**	**106 282**	**112 359**
86-88	**Human health and social work activities**	**152 808**	**161 838**	**174 774**	**180 445**	**178 375**	**180 954**	**184 419**	**186 563**
90-99	**Arts, entertainment, household goods repairs, other**	**48 743**	**51 413**	**52 946**	**54 017**	**55 819**	**56 168**	**56 772**	**58 677**
90-93	**Arts, entertainment and recreation**	**21 446**	**23 634**	**23 486**	**23 718**	**24 692**	**25 008**	**25 732**	**26 382**
94-96	**Other service activities**	**23 754**	**24 018**	**25 344**	**25 935**	**26 448**	**26 536**	**26 142**	**27 349**
97-98	**Activities of households as employers and for own use**	**3 543**	**3 761**	**4 116**	**4 364**	**4 679**	**4 624**	**4 898**	**4 946**
05-39	**INDUSTRY INCLUDING ENERGY**	**300 808**	**313 664**	**267 370**	**287 846**	**300 295**	**312 010**	**311 467**	**306 546**
45-99	**TOTAL SERVICES**	**1 069 149**	**1 122 976**	**1 127 016**	**1 184 138**	**1 195 431**	**1 218 190**	**1 257 200**	**1 302 213**
45-82	**BUSINESS SECTOR SERVICES**	**701 184**	**731 472**	**711 941**	**754 959**	**767 962**	**783 149**	**819 033**	**853 824**
45-82x	**BUSINESS SECTOR SERVICES excluding real estate**	**564 283**	**593 148**	**566 244**	**599 761**	**603 572**	**618 261**	**650 965**	**683 514**
05-82x	**NON-AGRICULTURE BUSINESS SECTOR excluding real estate**	..	..	..	..	..	..	..	..

.. Not available

Note: Detailed metadata at: http://metalinks.oecd.org/stan/20170410/1c43.

Information on data for Israel: http://oe.cd/israel-disclaimer.

Disclaimer: http://oe.cd/disclaimer

DENMARK

Table 3. Value added, volumes

ISIC Rev. 4

Million 2010 DKK

		2007	2008	2009	2010	2011	2012	2013	2014
	TOTAL	**1 605 066**	**1 605 941**	**1 534 518**	**1 562 743**	**1 586 910**	**1 590 374**	**1 604 992**	**1 632 486**
01-03	**AGRICULTURE, FORESTRY AND FISHING**	**22 967**	**17 307**	**16 715**	**21 766**	**19 430**	**21 655**	**20 651**	**24 103**
05-09	**MINING AND QUARRYING**	**62 709**	**55 436**	**49 704**	**48 384**	**44 529**	**40 626**	**34 005**	**30 568**
10-33	**MANUFACTURING**	**217 902**	**216 551**	**190 786**	**198 003**	**210 380**	**218 966**	**225 068**	**228 832**
10-12	Food products, beverages and tobacco	32 073	30 091	29 548	29 414	29 191	28 466	28 824	26 165
13-14	Textiles and wearing apparel	3 039	2 933	2 397	2 280	2 205	2 019	2 316	..
15	Leather and related products	139	69	70	114	103	71	235	..
16	Wood, wood and cork products	6 542	5 489	3 821	3 898	3 829	3 830	3 644	3 808
17	Paper and paper products	3 320	3 373	2 731	2 868	2 881	2 364	2 345	2 411
18	Printing and reproduction of recorded media	5 109	5 604	4 743	3 910	4 201	3 652	3 602	3 796
19-23	Chemical, rubber, plastics, non-metallic products	57 313	57 834	54 842	60 566	65 279	77 080	77 295	82 444
20	Chemicals and chemical products	9 168	11 143	11 356	12 040	12 207	15 003	13 928	14 205
21	Pharmaceutical products	24 063	26 238	28 132	34 235	38 178	46 711	48 544	50 935
22-23	Rubber, plastic, non-metallic mineral products	21 361	19 069	14 357	13 962	13 330	13 655	13 249	14 173
24	Basic metals	2 889	2 887	1 925	1 755	2 156	2 013	2 115	2 424
25	Metal products, except machinery and equipment	19 354	20 010	16 498	15 292	14 029	14 794	16 637	17 753
26-28	Machinery and equipment	64 811	63 811	52 143	54 779	60 934	59 160	62 765	59 675
26	Computer, electronic and optical products	15 850	14 159	13 088	14 757	15 229	15 392	15 951	14 528
27	Electrical equipment	6 911	8 495	6 218	6 696	7 343	6 654	5 748	6 518
28	Machinery and equipment n.e.c.	41 973	41 217	32 812	33 326	38 362	37 088	41 043	38 552
29-30	Transport equipment	4 171	3 990	3 521	4 157	4 924	3 813	3 281	3 536
29	Motor vehicles, trailers and semi-trailers	3 046	3 169	1 905	2 395	2 811	2 389	1 974	2 303
30	Other transport equipment	1 577	1 258	1 638	1 762	2 113	1 406	1 294	1 195
31-33	Furniture; repair, installation of machinery and equipment	18 656	20 011	18 368	18 970	20 648	22 042	22 250	24 306
31-32	Furniture, other manufacturing	14 100	14 331	13 773	14 694	15 547	15 603	16 239	17 987
33	Repair and installation of machinery and equipment	4 548	5 670	4 585	4 276	5 101	6 512	6 031	6 311
35-39	**ELECTRICITY, GAS, WATER AND WASTE MANAGEMENT**	**38 967**	**40 631**	**38 011**	**41 459**	**40 413**	**41 359**	**38 068**	**35 391**
35	Electricity, gas, steam and air conditioning supply	27 463	28 052	26 382	28 848	27 656	29 259	26 205	22 918
36-39	Water supply; sewerage, waste, remediation activities	11 482	12 572	11 621	12 611	12 757	12 165	11 752	12 037
41-43	**CONSTRUCTION**	**84 473**	**86 768**	**78 688**	**68 993**	**71 361**	**73 019**	**74 463**	**78 416**
45-56	Distribution; transportation, accommodation, food service	335 859	316 871	291 201	304 453	315 476	311 241	321 340	328 921
45-47	**Wholesale and retail trade; motor vehicle and motorcycle repairs**	**197 989**	**191 393**	**180 767**	**191 951**	**193 994**	**190 385**	**191 462**	**198 317**
49-53	**Transportation and storage**	**117 771**	**104 109**	**89 461**	**91 511**	**98 243**	**98 164**	**108 380**	**107 277**
55-56	**Accommodation and food service activities**	**23 424**	**23 109**	**21 418**	**20 991**	**23 240**	**22 957**	**23 439**	**24 576**
58-63	**Information and communication**	**60 641**	**68 665**	**70 681**	**74 120**	**76 198**	**77 674**	**85 200**	**89 404**
58-60	Publishing, audiovisual and broadcasting activities	19 448	20 892	19 497	20 464	20 622	20 872	22 410	23 582
61	Telecommunications	14 401	17 679	18 125	18 529	23 888	25 051	28 310	29 351
62-63	IT and other information services	27 300	29 957	32 983	35 127	31 688	31 851	34 776	36 688
64-66	**Financial and insurance activities**	**95 799**	**105 590**	**100 236**	**96 658**	**91 264**	**90 370**	**88 885**	**88 503**
68	**Real estate activities**	**146 662**	**144 257**	**150 318**	**155 198**	**159 922**	**157 497**	**155 051**	**152 959**
69-82	**Professional, scientific, technical, admin., support activities**	**131 604**	**134 849**	**125 464**	**124 530**	**126 559**	**126 647**	**134 543**	**141 814**
69-75	Professional, scientific and technical activities	83 868	89 460	85 512	85 015	83 414	80 842	86 689	91 933
69-71	Legal, accounting activities; mgt consultancy; engineering	61 733	61 371	58 520	59 173	61 003	60 778	65 140	65 730
73-75	Advertising, market research; other prof., scientific, tech.	14 850	16 238	13 875	12 913	13 323	12 632	12 650	14 032
77-82	Administrative and support service activities	47 742	45 436	39 953	39 515	43 145	45 841	47 861	49 880
84-88	**Public administration, defence; social security; education; health**	**352 031**	**361 593**	**367 838**	**375 161**	**377 450**	**377 519**	**377 166**	**383 340**
84	**Public administration, defence; compulsory social security**	**92 331**	**92 443**	**93 480**	**93 157**	**90 643**	**90 288**	**87 069**	**88 126**
85	**Education**	**96 026**	**100 577**	**102 028**	**101 559**	**100 903**	**100 304**	**100 876**	**102 119**
86-88	**Human health and social work activities**	**163 966**	**168 842**	**172 578**	**180 445**	**185 905**	**186 979**	**189 391**	**193 327**
90-99	**Arts, entertainment, household goods repairs, other**	**54 304**	**55 686**	**54 797**	**54 017**	**53 929**	**54 571**	**55 155**	**56 294**
90-93	**Arts, entertainment and recreation**	**23 833**	**25 601**	**24 361**	**23 718**	**23 261**	**24 174**	**25 396**	**25 338**
94-96	**Other service activities**	**26 659**	**26 131**	**26 220**	**25 935**	**26 067**	**25 875**	**24 998**	**25 780**
97-98	**Activities of households as employers and for own use**	**3 834**	**3 964**	**4 219**	**4 364**	**4 601**	**4 492**	**4 723**	**5 121**
05-39	**INDUSTRY INCLUDING ENERGY**	**319 317**	**312 312**	**278 186**	**287 846**	**295 321**	**299 561**	**293 539**	**290 172**
45-99	**TOTAL SERVICES**	**1 175 905**	**1 187 053**	**1 160 375**	**1 184 138**	**1 200 798**	**1 195 452**	**1 216 345**	**1 239 521**
45-82	**BUSINESS SECTOR SERVICES**	**769 356**	**769 604**	**737 734**	**754 959**	**769 419**	**763 353**	**783 865**	**799 693**
45-82x	**BUSINESS SECTOR SERVICES excluding real estate**	**622 768**	**625 494**	**587 423**	**599 761**	**609 497**	**605 900**	**629 033**	**647 205**
05-82x	**NON-AGRICULTURE BUSINESS SECTOR excluding real estate**	..	..	..	..	..	..	..	..

.. Not available

Note: Detailed metadata at: http://metalinks.oecd.org/stan/20170410/1c43.

Information on data for Israel: http://oe.cd/israel-disclaimer.

Disclaimer: http://oe.cd/disclaimer

Table 4. Gross fixed capital formation, current prices

ISIC Rev. 4

Million DKK

		2007	2008	2009	2010	2011	2012	2013	2014
	TOTAL	**408 862**	**413 328**	**347 337**	**328 025**	**335 356**	**355 838**	**367 650**	**378 789**
01-03	**AGRICULTURE, FORESTRY AND FISHING**	**17 065**	**16 627**	**10 063**	**8 624**	**8 060**	**9 219**	**10 726**	**12 480**
05-09	**MINING AND QUARRYING**	**7 669**	**8 354**	**9 093**	**5 476**	**6 298**	**8 202**	**9 333**	**8 954**
10-33	**MANUFACTURING**	**47 605**	**56 870**	**53 998**	**43 823**	**52 990**	**57 568**	**56 262**	**56 561**
10-12	Food products, beverages and tobacco	7 405	9 355	8 735	4 733	5 554	7 359	6 648	7 151
13-14	Textiles and wearing apparel	553	496	278	210	283	..	..	..
15	Leather and related products	18	9	6	16	10	..	..	..
16	Wood, wood and cork products	690	768	538	311	419	499	701	715
17	Paper and paper products	533	549	456	475	450	385	495	492
18	Printing and reproduction of recorded media	912	918	843	474	471	414	328	351
19-23	Chemical, rubber, plastics, non-metallic products	17 749	22 974	24 146	21 933	22 733	26 217	26 893	26 632
20	Chemicals and chemical products	3 602	3 710	3 129	3 174	3 852	3 905	4 873	4 984
21	Pharmaceutical products	8 987	14 060	16 441	15 939	15 637	18 855	18 393	18 250
22-23	Rubber, plastic, non-metallic mineral products	4 152	4 284	4 174	2 205	2 505	3 037	3 299	3 106
24	Basic metals	677	841	384	462	248	1 196	325	348
25	Metal products, except machinery and equipment	2 546	3 815	2 574	1 575	1 687	1 611	2 158	2 102
26-28	Machinery and equipment	13 469	13 900	12 343	10 619	17 475	15 520	13 920	14 054
26	Computer, electronic and optical products	4 335	4 643	4 321	4 179	4 172	4 583	4 619	4 793
27	Electrical equipment	761	1 399	969	1 108	1 434	1 124	972	969
28	Machinery and equipment n.e.c.	8 373	7 858	7 053	5 332	11 869	9 813	8 329	8 292
29-30	Transport equipment	761	778	630	575	543	587	480	453
29	Motor vehicles, trailers and semi-trailers	531	528	428	413	398	411	297	263
30	Other transport equipment	230	250	202	162	145	176	183	190
31-33	Furniture; repair, installation of machinery and equipment	2 292	2 467	3 065	2 440	3 117	3 477	4 010	3 983
31-32	Furniture, other manufacturing	1 747	2 017	2 724	2 183	2 634	2 982	3 574	3 521
33	Repair and installation of machinery and equipment	545	450	341	257	483	495	436	462
35-39	**ELECTRICITY, GAS, WATER AND WASTE MANAGEMENT**	**14 630**	**15 610**	**16 609**	**18 696**	**16 189**	**20 183**	**29 163**	**18 584**
35	Electricity, gas, steam and air conditioning supply	8 643	8 538	10 617	10 139	8 449	11 343	20 121	11 935
36-39	Water supply; sewerage, waste, remediation activities	5 987	7 072	5 992	8 557	7 740	8 840	9 042	6 649
41-43	**CONSTRUCTION**	**8 029**	**7 113**	**4 693**	**5 005**	**5 473**	**5 664**	**6 103**	**6 735**
45-56	Distribution; transportation, accommodation, food service	66 297	63 870	56 261	49 014	39 423	46 821	56 914	64 811
45-47	**Wholesale and retail trade; motor vehicle and motorcycle repairs**	**24 426**	**24 191**	**16 180**	**18 220**	**16 793**	**17 262**	**17 114**	**19 694**
49-53	**Transportation and storage**	**38 705**	**37 225**	**38 209**	**29 157**	**20 530**	**27 707**	**37 355**	**42 995**
55-56	**Accommodation and food service activities**	**3 167**	**2 454**	**1 872**	**1 637**	**2 100**	**1 852**	**2 445**	**2 122**
58-63	**Information and communication**	**21 343**	**25 963**	**22 436**	**23 506**	**22 541**	**20 885**	**20 808**	**20 007**
58-60	Publishing, audiovisual and broadcasting activities	5 597	8 343	6 755	6 127	5 701	6 093	5 929	5 464
61	Telecommunications	8 198	10 165	8 744	8 624	8 130	8 439	8 009	7 563
62-63	IT and other information services	7 548	7 455	6 937	8 755	8 710	6 353	6 870	6 981
64-66	**Financial and insurance activities**	**8 396**	**8 818**	**10 627**	**10 691**	**10 822**	**15 457**	**10 767**	**10 701**
68	**Real estate activities**	**134 039**	**120 758**	**86 965**	**77 629**	**88 843**	**80 453**	**76 481**	**83 349**
69-82	**Professional, scientific, technical, admin., support activities**	**23 284**	**26 270**	**17 328**	**21 575**	**20 122**	**18 608**	**19 265**	**19 998**
69-75	Professional, scientific and technical activities	12 534	15 058	11 253	14 834	11 817	10 078	10 359	10 499
69-71	Legal, accounting activities; mgt consultancy; engineering	6 662	7 830	5 972	4 583	4 431	5 514	5 771	5 610
73-75	Advertising, market research; other prof., scientific, tech.	1 589	1 393	833	867	816	1 004	1 021	1 044
77-82	Administrative and support service activities	10 750	11 212	6 075	6 741	8 305	8 530	8 906	9 500
84-88	**Public administration, defence; social security; education; health**	**45 623**	**50 210**	**48 544**	**53 844**	**54 973**	**62 379**	**61 720**	**66 103**
84	**Public administration, defence; compulsory social security**	**20 554**	**19 478**	**16 537**	**18 281**	**19 205**	**21 315**	**20 055**	**21 269**
85	**Education**	**14 311**	**17 406**	**18 560**	**22 005**	**19 512**	**23 137**	**24 722**	**26 746**
86-88	**Human health and social work activities**	**10 758**	**13 326**	**13 447**	**13 558**	**16 256**	**17 927**	**16 942**	**18 088**
90-99	**Arts, entertainment, household goods repairs, other**	**14 884**	**12 866**	**10 721**	**10 142**	**9 621**	**10 397**	**10 107**	**10 506**
90-93	**Arts, entertainment and recreation**	**8 175**	**6 909**	**6 302**	**5 993**	**6 024**	**6 669**	**6 634**	**6 807**
94-96	**Other service activities**	**6 709**	**5 957**	**4 419**	**4 149**	**3 597**	**3 728**	**3 473**	**3 699**
97-98	**Activities of households as employers and for own use**	**0**	**0**	**0**	**0**	**0**	**0**	**0**	**0**
05-39	**INDUSTRY INCLUDING ENERGY**	**69 903**	**80 834**	**79 700**	**67 995**	**75 477**	**85 953**	**94 759**	**84 099**
45-99	**TOTAL SERVICES**	**313 865**	**308 755**	**252 881**	**246 401**	**246 346**	**255 001**	**256 062**	**275 475**
45-82	**BUSINESS SECTOR SERVICES**	**253 359**	**245 679**	**193 616**	**182 415**	**181 752**	**182 225**	**184 236**	**198 866**
45-82x	**BUSINESS SECTOR SERVICES excluding real estate**	**119 320**	**124 920**	**106 652**	**104 786**	**92 908**	**101 772**	**107 755**	**115 517**
05-82x	**NON-AGRICULTURE BUSINESS SECTOR excluding real estate**	..	..	..	..	..	..	..	..

.. Not available

Note: Detailed metadata at: http://metalinks.oecd.org/stan/20170410/1c43.
Information on data for Israel: http://oe.cd/israel-disclaimer.

Disclaimer: http://oe.cd/disclaimer

Table 5. Number of persons engaged, total employment

ISIC Rev. 4

Thousands

		2007	2008	2009	2010	2011	2012	2013	2014
	TOTAL	**2 912**	**2 947**	**2 854**	**2 788**	**2 787**	**2 767**	**2 766**	**2 794**
01-03	**AGRICULTURE, FORESTRY AND FISHING**	**73**	**74**	**72**	**71**	**70**	**69**	**69**	**69**
05-09	**MINING AND QUARRYING**	**4**	**4**	**5**	**5**	**5**	**6**	**4**	**4**
10-33	**MANUFACTURING**	**362**	**364**	**317**	**289**	**289**	**283**	**278**	**280**
10-12	Food products, beverages and tobacco	63	63	59	55	53	51	50	49
13-14	Textiles and wearing apparel	8	8	6	6	6	5	5	..
15	Leather and related products	0	0	0	0	0	0	0	..
16	Wood, wood and cork products	13	13	10	9	9	8	8	8
17	Paper and paper products	7	7	6	5	5	5	5	5
18	Printing and reproduction of recorded media	12	12	11	9	8	8	7	7
19-23	Chemical, rubber, plastics, non-metallic products	64	65	58	54	55	55	55	57
20	Chemicals and chemical products	12	13	12	11	11	11	11	11
21	Pharmaceutical products	16	17	18	18	18	19	19	21
22-23	Rubber, plastic, non-metallic mineral products	35	34	28	25	25	25	25	25
24	Basic metals	6	6	4	4	4	4	4	5
25	Metal products, except machinery and equipment	43	43	37	33	33	33	34	34
26-28	Machinery and equipment	99	101	87	79	80	78	76	75
26	Computer, electronic and optical products	19	19	17	16	16	16	15	15
27	Electrical equipment	12	13	11	10	10	10	9	9
28	Machinery and equipment n.e.c.	67	69	58	53	54	53	51	51
29-30	Transport equipment	10	10	8	7	7	6	6	6
29	Motor vehicles, trailers and semi-trailers	7	7	5	4	5	4	4	3
30	Other transport equipment	3	4	3	3	3	2	2	2
31-33	Furniture; repair, installation of machinery and equipment	37	36	31	27	29	29	29	29
31-32	Furniture, other manufacturing	26	25	21	17	18	18	18	18
33	Repair and installation of machinery and equipment	11	11	10	9	11	12	11	11
35-39	**ELECTRICITY, GAS, WATER AND WASTE MANAGEMENT**	**22**	**24**	**24**	**22**	**22**	**22**	**21**	**22**
35	Electricity, gas, steam and air conditioning supply	10	11	12	11	10	10	10	10
36-39	Water supply; sewerage, waste, remediation activities	12	12	12	11	11	11	11	11
41-43	**CONSTRUCTION**	**206**	**206**	**184**	**168**	**167**	**165**	**163**	**167**
45-56	Distribution; transportation, accommodation, food service	728	747	707	691	705	702	705	712
45-47	**Wholesale and retail trade; motor vehicle and motorcycle repairs**	**471**	**485**	**458**	**445**	**452**	**450**	**449**	**452**
49-53	**Transportation and storage**	**155**	**157**	**147**	**145**	**147**	**144**	**143**	**142**
55-56	**Accommodation and food service activities**	**103**	**105**	**102**	**101**	**106**	**108**	**114**	**117**
58-63	**Information and communication**	**98**	**99**	**99**	**98**	**96**	**96**	**97**	**98**
58-60	Publishing, audiovisual and broadcasting activities	38	36	35	35	34	35	35	36
61	Telecommunications	18	17	17	16	16	15	14	13
62-63	IT and other information services	42	46	48	48	46	47	48	49
64-66	**Financial and insurance activities**	**84**	**86**	**90**	**83**	**83**	**80**	**77**	**78**
68	**Real estate activities**	**41**	**42**	**41**	**44**	**45**	**44**	**45**	**45**
69-82	**Professional, scientific, technical, admin., support activities**	**281**	**281**	**270**	**261**	**262**	**266**	**276**	**284**
69-75	Professional, scientific and technical activities	151	157	156	149	145	148	152	153
69-71	Legal, accounting activities; mgt consultancy; engineering	93	99	99	97	98	101	105	105
73-75	Advertising, market research; other prof., scientific, tech.	44	46	45	37	34	33	34	33
77-82	Administrative and support service activities	130	125	113	112	117	119	124	130
84-88	**Public administration, defence; social security; education; health**	**865**	**870**	**895**	**904**	**889**	**881**	**881**	**884**
84	**Public administration, defence; compulsory social security**	**157**	**157**	**161**	**165**	**159**	**157**	**152**	**150**
85	**Education**	**201**	**207**	**214**	**216**	**217**	**217**	**218**	**225**
86-88	**Human health and social work activities**	**507**	**506**	**520**	**523**	**513**	**507**	**511**	**509**
90-99	**Arts, entertainment, household goods repairs, other**	**147**	**149**	**150**	**152**	**154**	**152**	**151**	**152**
90-93	**Arts, entertainment and recreation**	**53**	**54**	**55**	**55**	**55**	**56**	**55**	**57**
94-96	**Other service activities**	**70**	**71**	**70**	**71**	**71**	**70**	**69**	**69**
97-98	**Activities of households as employers and for own use**	**24**	**24**	**25**	**26**	**28**	**26**	**27**	**26**
05-39	**INDUSTRY INCLUDING ENERGY**	**388**	**392**	**346**	**316**	**315**	**311**	**303**	**306**
45-99	**TOTAL SERVICES**	**2 244**	**2 276**	**2 252**	**2 233**	**2 234**	**2 221**	**2 232**	**2 251**
45-82	**BUSINESS SECTOR SERVICES**	**1 232**	**1 257**	**1 207**	**1 178**	**1 191**	**1 189**	**1 200**	**1 216**
45-82x	**BUSINESS SECTOR SERVICES excluding real estate**	**1 191**	**1 214**	**1 166**	**1 134**	**1 147**	**1 144**	**1 155**	**1 171**
05-82x	**NON-AGRICULTURE BUSINESS SECTOR excluding real estate**	..	..	..	..	..	..	..	..

.. Not available

Note: Detailed metadata at: http://metalinks.oecd.org/stan/20170410/1c43.
Information on data for Israel: http://oe.cd/israel-disclaimer.

Disclaimer: http://oe.cd/disclaimer

Table 6. Labour costs (compensation of employees), current prices

ISIC Rev. 4

Million DKK

		2007	2008	2009	2010	2011	2012	2013	2014
	TOTAL	**902 639**	**949 819**	**945 677**	**953 668**	**966 474**	**977 516**	**993 804**	**1 019 230**
01-03	**AGRICULTURE, FORESTRY AND FISHING**	**7 613**	**8 163**	**8 191**	**8 777**	**8 903**	**9 048**	**9 346**	**9 571**
05-09	**MINING AND QUARRYING**	**2 329**	**2 592**	**3 007**	**3 170**	**3 600**	**4 089**	**3 588**	**3 484**
10-33	**MANUFACTURING**	**135 153**	**139 549**	**125 585**	**120 844**	**124 074**	**123 974**	**123 709**	**127 031**
10-12	Food products, beverages and tobacco	21 316	21 729	20 676	20 426	19 645	19 207	18 798	18 998
13-14	Textiles and wearing apparel	2 353	2 313	1 933	1 770	1 787	1 609	1 749	..
15	Leather and related products	99	91	88	84	75	38	49	..
16	Wood, wood and cork products	4 484	4 276	3 374	3 086	2 996	2 970	2 798	2 819
17	Paper and paper products	2 736	2 697	2 426	2 294	2 119	2 116	2 060	2 075
18	Printing and reproduction of recorded media	4 190	4 327	3 795	3 267	3 111	2 876	2 698	2 745
19-23	Chemical, rubber, plastics, non-metallic products	27 768	28 959	27 144	27 053	28 392	28 988	30 078	31 929
20	Chemicals and chemical products	5 670	6 074	5 606	5 661	5 729	5 598	5 763	5 995
21	Pharmaceutical products	8 585	9 132	10 158	10 917	11 627	12 187	13 132	14 492
22-23	Rubber, plastic, non-metallic mineral products	12 958	13 183	10 974	10 056	10 571	10 720	10 604	10 905
24	Basic metals	2 102	2 128	1 661	1 593	1 763	1 844	1 818	1 952
25	Metal products, except machinery and equipment	14 828	15 514	13 401	12 554	12 753	12 952	13 211	13 637
26-28	Machinery and equipment	39 333	41 609	37 028	36 157	37 418	37 374	36 573	36 935
26	Computer, electronic and optical products	7 910	8 284	7 703	7 650	7 764	7 693	7 802	7 505
27	Electrical equipment	4 649	5 034	4 375	4 163	4 390	4 293	4 057	4 304
28	Machinery and equipment n.e.c.	26 774	28 291	24 950	24 344	25 264	25 388	24 714	25 126
29-30	Transport equipment	3 778	3 813	3 162	2 894	3 178	2 632	2 359	2 446
29	Motor vehicles, trailers and semi-trailers	2 433	2 363	1 728	1 686	1 818	1 665	1 472	1 444
30	Other transport equipment	1 345	1 450	1 434	1 208	1 360	967	887	1 002
31-33	Furniture; repair, installation of machinery and equipment	12 166	12 093	10 897	9 666	10 837	11 368	11 518	11 663
31-32	Furniture, other manufacturing	8 621	8 381	7 435	6 450	6 855	6 978	7 077	7 269
33	Repair and installation of machinery and equipment	3 545	3 712	3 462	3 216	3 982	4 390	4 441	4 394
35-39	**ELECTRICITY, GAS, WATER AND WASTE MANAGEMENT**	**9 130**	**10 019**	**10 565**	**10 040**	**9 966**	**10 324**	**9 866**	**10 533**
35	Electricity, gas, steam and air conditioning supply	4 831	5 442	6 057	5 660	5 437	5 842	5 664	5 995
36-39	Water supply; sewerage, waste, remediation activities	4 299	4 577	4 508	4 380	4 529	4 482	4 202	4 538
41-43	**CONSTRUCTION**	**62 666**	**65 157**	**58 239**	**54 349**	**55 858**	**56 314**	**55 714**	**58 287**
45-56	Distribution; transportation, accommodation, food service	196 713	207 916	200 029	201 286	207 121	209 524	211 424	216 034
45-47	**Wholesale and retail trade; motor vehicle and motorcycle repairs**	**130 059**	**136 202**	**130 626**	**131 785**	**136 644**	**139 067**	**140 288**	**143 047**
49-53	**Transportation and storage**	**51 219**	**55 063**	**53 281**	**53 526**	**53 383**	**52 875**	**52 936**	**53 992**
55-56	**Accommodation and food service activities**	**15 435**	**16 651**	**16 122**	**15 975**	**17 095**	**17 582**	**18 200**	**18 996**
58-63	**Information and communication**	**43 001**	**45 336**	**46 006**	**46 900**	**46 231**	**46 021**	**46 064**	**47 115**
58-60	Publishing, audiovisual and broadcasting activities	13 355	13 383	13 215	13 218	13 283	13 092	13 279	14 067
61	Telecommunications	8 210	8 424	8 338	8 124	8 165	7 696	7 521	7 227
62-63	IT and other information services	21 436	23 529	24 453	25 558	24 783	25 233	25 264	25 821
64-66	**Financial and insurance activities**	**45 643**	**46 840**	**50 534**	**49 958**	**50 856**	**49 762**	**49 891**	**50 845**
68	**Real estate activities**	**12 015**	**12 661**	**12 057**	**12 549**	**12 831**	**13 057**	**13 307**	**13 615**
69-82	**Professional, scientific, technical, admin., support activities**	**86 929**	**91 716**	**88 895**	**90 804**	**94 298**	**97 664**	**103 600**	**108 258**
69-75	Professional, scientific and technical activities	54 756	57 785	57 684	59 486	60 853	62 651	65 968	68 060
69-71	Legal, accounting activities; mgt consultancy; engineering	38 177	41 599	41 118	42 581	43 891	45 803	48 546	49 719
73-75	Advertising, market research; other prof., scientific, tech.	9 852	10 227	9 858	9 485	9 568	9 489	9 472	9 744
77-82	Administrative and support service activities	32 173	33 931	31 211	31 318	33 445	35 013	37 632	40 198
84-88	**Public administration, defence; social security; education; health**	**268 319**	**285 107**	**306 675**	**317 899**	**314 764**	**319 248**	**328 935**	**335 868**
84	**Public administration, defence; compulsory social security**	**61 271**	**64 761**	**68 901**	**71 821**	**70 205**	**70 785**	**69 931**	**70 219**
85	**Education**	**70 727**	**76 618**	**82 068**	**85 486**	**86 005**	**87 964**	**88 109**	**93 177**
86-88	**Human health and social work activities**	**136 320**	**143 728**	**155 706**	**160 592**	**158 555**	**160 499**	**170 895**	**172 472**
90-99	**Arts, entertainment, household goods repairs, other**	**33 127**	**34 763**	**35 895**	**37 092**	**37 973**	**38 492**	**38 362**	**38 590**
90-93	**Arts, entertainment and recreation**	**12 685**	**13 467**	**13 916**	**14 071**	**14 209**	**14 723**	**14 482**	**14 852**
94-96	**Other service activities**	**16 899**	**17 535**	**17 863**	**18 657**	**19 085**	**19 145**	**18 982**	**18 792**
97-98	**Activities of households as employers and for own use**	**3 543**	**3 761**	**4 116**	**4 364**	**4 679**	**4 624**	**4 898**	**4 946**
05-39	**INDUSTRY INCLUDING ENERGY**	**146 612**	**152 160**	**139 157**	**134 054**	**137 640**	**138 387**	**137 162**	**141 048**
45-99	**TOTAL SERVICES**	**685 748**	**724 339**	**740 090**	**756 488**	**764 074**	**773 767**	**791 582**	**810 325**
45-82	**BUSINESS SECTOR SERVICES**	**384 302**	**404 469**	**397 521**	**401 497**	**411 337**	**416 028**	**424 285**	**435 867**
45-82x	**BUSINESS SECTOR SERVICES excluding real estate**	**372 287**	**391 808**	**385 464**	**388 948**	**398 506**	**402 971**	**410 978**	**422 252**
05-82x	**NON-AGRICULTURE BUSINESS SECTOR excluding real estate**	..	..	..	..	..	..	..	..

.. Not available

Note: Detailed metadata at: http://metalinks.oecd.org/stan/20170410/1c43.

Information on data for Israel: http://oe.cd/israel-disclaimer.

Disclaimer: http://oe.cd/disclaimer

FINLAND

Table 1. Production (gross output), current prices

ISIC Rev. 4

Million EUR

		2007	2008	2009	2010	2011	2012	2013	2014
	TOTAL	**359 087**	**378 348**	**338 774**	**355 324**	**380 370**	**386 115**	**385 715**	**387 355**
01-03	**AGRICULTURE, FORESTRY AND FISHING**	**8 879**	**8 572**	**7 903**	**8 533**	**9 266**	**9 533**	**9 976**	**9 717**
05-09	**MINING AND QUARRYING**	**1 438**	**1 658**	**1 533**	**1 979**	**2 179**	**2 164**	**1 891**	**1 796**
10-33	**MANUFACTURING**	**128 660**	**134 491**	**101 838**	**108 998**	**119 260**	**116 633**	**112 391**	**110 299**
10-12	Food products, beverages and tobacco	9 662	10 646	10 258	10 387	11 392	11 728	11 484	11 284
13-14	Textiles and wearing apparel	1 210	1 165	994	1 046	1 113	1 044	994	1 004
15	Leather and related products	209	203	173	191	220	221	214	206
16	Wood, wood and cork products	7 332	6 191	4 529	5 498	5 636	5 510	5 745	5 778
17	Paper and paper products	15 095	14 647	11 100	13 474	13 637	13 422	13 283	13 068
18	Printing and reproduction of recorded media	1 863	1 793	1 560	1 525	1 519	1 487	1 362	1 278
19-23	Chemical, rubber, plastics, non-metallic products	21 797	24 443	18 825	20 087	25 620	26 401	26 356	24 847
20	Chemicals and chemical products	6 451	7 171	5 856	5 275	6 370	7 019	7 530	7 524
21	Pharmaceutical products	1 150	1 222	1 290	1 390	1 493	1 746	1 702	1 834
22-23	Rubber, plastic, non-metallic mineral products	6 533	6 675	5 085	5 530	6 543	6 327	5 970	6 014
24	Basic metals	10 960	9 562	5 365	8 500	9 253	8 543	8 138	9 147
25	Metal products, except machinery and equipment	8 376	9 003	6 285	6 086	7 042	7 135	6 677	6 687
26-28	Machinery and equipment	42 986	47 599	35 467	35 079	36 253	33 328	30 522	29 417
26	Computer, electronic and optical products	23 624	25 453	18 366	17 678	16 533	13 302	11 546	10 563
27	Electrical equipment	4 181	4 973	3 833	4 114	4 444	4 540	4 338	4 572
28	Machinery and equipment n.e.c.	15 181	17 173	13 268	13 287	15 276	15 486	14 638	14 282
29-30	Transport equipment	4 160	4 066	2 924	2 686	2 733	2 945	3 104	3 099
29	Motor vehicles, trailers and semi-trailers	1 677	1 671	1 075	1 196	1 463	1 399	1 412	1 521
30	Other transport equipment	2 483	2 395	1 849	1 490	1 270	1 546	1 692	1 578
31-33	Furniture; repair, installation of machinery and equipment	5 010	5 173	4 358	4 439	4 842	4 869	4 512	4 484
31-32	Furniture, other manufacturing	2 318	2 101	1 693	1 743	1 866	1 842	1 680	1 638
33	Repair and installation of machinery and equipment	2 692	3 072	2 665	2 696	2 976	3 027	2 832	2 846
35-39	**ELECTRICITY, GAS, WATER AND WASTE MANAGEMENT**	**8 498**	**9 878**	**9 777**	**11 621**	**11 201**	**12 017**	**12 235**	**12 497**
35	Electricity, gas, steam and air conditioning supply	6 143	7 203	7 182	8 612	8 034	8 577	8 779	8 898
36-39	Water supply; sewerage, waste, remediation activities	2 355	2 675	2 595	3 009	3 167	3 440	3 456	3 599
41-43	**CONSTRUCTION**	**29 703**	**31 819**	**27 570**	**27 998**	**30 130**	**30 303**	**29 728**	**28 794**
45-56	Distribution; transportation, accommodation, food service	58 133	60 163	55 118	56 800	61 081	62 741	62 411	62 322
45-47	**Wholesale and retail trade; motor vehicle and motorcycle repairs**	**30 762**	**31 215**	**28 974**	**29 285**	**31 370**	**32 005**	**31 969**	**31 753**
49-53	**Transportation and storage**	**21 609**	**22 554**	**19 859**	**21 103**	**22 918**	**23 572**	**23 261**	**23 376**
55-56	**Accommodation and food service activities**	**5 762**	**6 394**	**6 285**	**6 412**	**6 793**	**7 164**	**7 181**	**7 193**
58-63	**Information and communication**	**15 615**	**16 281**	**15 990**	**16 200**	**17 204**	**17 221**	**17 705**	**19 159**
58-60	Publishing, audiovisual and broadcasting activities	4 590	4 812	4 870	4 973	5 138	5 111	4 969	4 854
61	Telecommunications	4 818	4 757	4 702	4 697	4 699	4 254	4 161	4 295
62-63	IT and other information services	6 207	6 712	6 418	6 530	7 367	7 856	8 575	10 010
64-66	**Financial and insurance activities**	**8 500**	**8 440**	**8 557**	**8 535**	**8 989**	**9 490**	**9 825**	**10 911**
68	**Real estate activities**	**23 566**	**24 670**	**26 132**	**27 262**	**28 464**	**29 744**	**30 923**	**32 061**
69-82	**Professional, scientific, technical, admin., support activities**	**20 460**	**22 434**	**21 433**	**22 198**	**24 526**	**25 393**	**25 951**	**26 222**
69-75	Professional, scientific and technical activities	12 997	13 789	12 941	13 290	14 826	15 229	15 874	15 867
69-71	Legal, accounting activities; mgt consultancy; engineering	8 787	9 501	8 661	8 924	10 128	10 420	10 949	10 937
73-75	Advertising, market research; other prof., scientific, tech.	2 562	2 403	2 369	2 367	2 561	2 562	2 621	2 695
77-82	Administrative and support service activities	7 463	8 645	8 492	8 908	9 700	10 164	10 077	10 355
84-88	**Public administration, defence; social security; education; health**	**47 151**	**50 889**	**53 613**	**55 494**	**57 776**	**60 302**	**61 937**	**62 549**
84	**Public administration, defence; compulsory social security**	**16 468**	**17 615**	**18 362**	**18 765**	**19 093**	**19 588**	**20 117**	**20 088**
85	**Education**	**11 312**	**12 061**	**12 612**	**13 010**	**13 504**	**13 929**	**14 021**	**14 152**
86-88	**Human health and social work activities**	**19 371**	**21 213**	**22 639**	**23 719**	**25 179**	**26 785**	**27 799**	**28 309**
90-99	**Arts, entertainment, household goods repairs, other**	**8 484**	**9 053**	**9 310**	**9 706**	**10 294**	**10 574**	**10 742**	**11 028**
90-93	**Arts, entertainment and recreation**	**3 712**	**3 939**	**4 034**	**4 210**	**4 522**	**4 691**	**4 744**	**4 864**
94-96	**Other service activities**	**4 644**	**4 965**	**5 114**	**5 328**	**5 597**	**5 708**	**5 804**	**5 921**
97-98	**Activities of households as employers and for own use**	**128**	**149**	**162**	**168**	**175**	**175**	**194**	**243**
05-39	**INDUSTRY INCLUDING ENERGY**	**138 596**	**146 027**	**113 148**	**122 598**	**132 640**	**130 814**	**126 517**	**124 592**
45-99	**TOTAL SERVICES**	**181 909**	**191 930**	**190 153**	**196 195**	**208 334**	**215 465**	**219 494**	**224 252**
45-82	**BUSINESS SECTOR SERVICES**	**126 274**	**131 988**	**127 230**	**130 995**	**140 264**	**144 589**	**146 815**	**150 675**
45-82x	**BUSINESS SECTOR SERVICES excluding real estate**	**102 708**	**107 318**	**101 098**	**103 733**	**111 800**	**114 845**	**115 892**	**118 614**
05-82x	**NON-AGRICULTURE BUSINESS SECTOR excluding real estate**	..	..	..	..	..	..	..	..

.. Not available

Note: Detailed metadata at: http://metalinks.oecd.org/stan/20170410/1c43.

Information on data for Israel: http://oe.cd/israel-disclaimer.

Disclaimer: http://oe.cd/disclaimer

FINLAND

Table 2. Value added, current prices

ISIC Rev. 4

Million EUR

		2007	2008	2009	2010	2011	2012	2013	2014
	TOTAL	**163 654**	**170 386**	**158 348**	**163 620**	**170 454**	**172 417**	**175 002**	**176 877**
01-03	**AGRICULTURE, FORESTRY AND FISHING**	**4 391**	**4 198**	**4 028**	**4 468**	**4 649**	**4 713**	**5 222**	**4 934**
05-09	**MINING AND QUARRYING**	**559**	**661**	**616**	**811**	**810**	**804**	**593**	**552**
10-33	**MANUFACTURING**	**41 398**	**40 384**	**30 292**	**31 948**	**32 164**	**29 067**	**29 641**	**29 858**
10-12	Food products, beverages and tobacco	2 499	2 549	2 815	2 617	2 589	2 683	2 688	2 644
13-14	Textiles and wearing apparel	444	456	395	380	371	356	319	298
15	Leather and related products	87	94	76	82	88	93	84	78
16	Wood, wood and cork products	1 785	1 302	883	1 235	1 150	1 076	1 162	1 199
17	Paper and paper products	3 890	3 270	2 122	3 063	3 064	2 813	2 751	2 877
18	Printing and reproduction of recorded media	765	760	657	648	601	604	533	503
19-23	Chemical, rubber, plastics, non-metallic products	6 024	5 824	5 005	5 171	5 928	5 814	5 636	5 531
20	Chemicals and chemical products	1 860	1 804	1 545	1 692	2 023	1 622	1 797	1 775
21	Pharmaceutical products	800	868	918	983	1 027	1 231	1 153	1 317
22-23	Rubber, plastic, non-metallic mineral products	2 533	2 486	1 922	1 972	2 214	2 176	2 044	2 020
24	Basic metals	2 439	2 275	808	1 221	1 290	1 115	1 266	1 229
25	Metal products, except machinery and equipment	3 160	3 357	2 458	2 276	2 553	2 629	2 478	2 387
26-28	Machinery and equipment	17 009	17 139	12 279	12 522	11 631	8 973	9 883	10 315
26	Computer, electronic and optical products	11 193	10 584	6 852	6 601	5 401	2 633	3 960	4 183
27	Electrical equipment	1 469	1 836	1 455	1 642	1 639	1 763	1 618	1 769
28	Machinery and equipment n.e.c.	4 347	4 719	3 972	4 279	4 591	4 577	4 305	4 363
29-30	Transport equipment	1 039	1 092	779	784	895	871	907	881
29	Motor vehicles, trailers and semi-trailers	542	517	353	383	463	414	411	451
30	Other transport equipment	497	575	426	401	432	457	496	430
31-33	Furniture; repair, installation of machinery and equipment	2 257	2 266	2 015	1 949	2 004	2 040	1 934	1 916
31-32	Furniture, other manufacturing	928	801	667	661	680	669	618	594
33	Repair and installation of machinery and equipment	1 329	1 465	1 348	1 288	1 324	1 371	1 316	1 322
35-39	**ELECTRICITY, GAS, WATER AND WASTE MANAGEMENT**	**4 372**	**4 551**	**4 985**	**5 736**	**5 366**	**5 415**	**5 749**	**5 833**
35	Electricity, gas, steam and air conditioning supply	3 271	3 337	3 693	4 208	3 812	3 828	4 105	4 110
36-39	Water supply; sewerage, waste, remediation activities	1 101	1 214	1 292	1 528	1 554	1 587	1 644	1 723
41-43	**CONSTRUCTION**	**11 037**	**11 817**	**10 724**	**10 548**	**10 905**	**11 336**	**11 300**	**11 067**
45-56	Distribution; transportation, accommodation, food service	26 502	28 139	25 898	26 394	28 260	29 350	28 888	28 483
45-47	**Wholesale and retail trade; motor vehicle and motorcycle repairs**	**15 284**	**16 611**	**15 151**	**15 313**	**16 737**	**17 436**	**17 222**	**16 845**
49-53	**Transportation and storage**	**8 650**	**8 852**	**8 183**	**8 420**	**8 715**	**8 947**	**8 873**	**8 779**
55-56	**Accommodation and food service activities**	**2 568**	**2 676**	**2 564**	**2 661**	**2 808**	**2 967**	**2 793**	**2 859**
58-63	**Information and communication**	**7 931**	**8 215**	**8 039**	**8 168**	**8 593**	**8 961**	**9 253**	**9 825**
58-60	Publishing, audiovisual and broadcasting activities	2 059	2 233	2 318	2 371	2 410	2 374	2 246	2 262
61	Telecommunications	2 213	2 212	2 255	2 219	2 157	2 159	2 224	2 136
62-63	IT and other information services	3 659	3 770	3 466	3 578	4 026	4 428	4 783	5 427
64-66	**Financial and insurance activities**	**4 859**	**4 649**	**4 563**	**4 234**	**4 565**	**4 635**	**4 332**	**5 230**
68	**Real estate activities**	**15 997**	**17 359**	**17 789**	**18 325**	**19 414**	**20 079**	**20 967**	**21 663**
69-82	**Professional, scientific, technical, admin., support activities**	**11 571**	**12 935**	**12 536**	**12 947**	**13 914**	**14 523**	**14 735**	**14 832**
69-75	Professional, scientific and technical activities	7 139	7 645	7 509	7 674	8 316	8 745	8 934	8 904
69-71	Legal, accounting activities; mgt consultancy; engineering	4 939	5 166	5 013	5 099	5 573	5 903	6 023	6 076
73-75	Advertising, market research; other prof., scientific, tech.	1 113	1 144	1 121	1 152	1 207	1 221	1 225	1 222
77-82	Administrative and support service activities	4 432	5 290	5 027	5 273	5 598	5 778	5 801	5 928
84-88	**Public administration, defence; social security; education; health**	**30 691**	**32 800**	**33 992**	**34 964**	**36 523**	**38 142**	**38 839**	**39 054**
84	**Public administration, defence; compulsory social security**	**9 420**	**9 971**	**10 160**	**10 292**	**10 626**	**10 923**	**11 178**	**11 145**
85	**Education**	**8 204**	**8 703**	**9 042**	**9 409**	**9 746**	**10 105**	**10 201**	**10 252**
86-88	**Human health and social work activities**	**13 067**	**14 126**	**14 790**	**15 263**	**16 151**	**17 114**	**17 460**	**17 657**
90-99	**Arts, entertainment, household goods repairs, other**	**4 346**	**4 678**	**4 886**	**5 077**	**5 291**	**5 392**	**5 483**	**5 546**
90-93	**Arts, entertainment and recreation**	**1 785**	**1 987**	**1 997**	**2 065**	**2 219**	**2 258**	**2 297**	**2 273**
94-96	**Other service activities**	**2 433**	**2 542**	**2 727**	**2 844**	**2 897**	**2 959**	**2 992**	**3 030**
97-98	**Activities of households as employers and for own use**	**128**	**149**	**162**	**168**	**175**	**175**	**194**	**243**
05-39	**INDUSTRY INCLUDING ENERGY**	**46 329**	**45 596**	**35 893**	**38 495**	**38 340**	**35 286**	**35 983**	**36 243**
45-99	**TOTAL SERVICES**	**101 897**	**108 775**	**107 703**	**110 109**	**116 560**	**121 082**	**122 497**	**124 633**
45-82	**BUSINESS SECTOR SERVICES**	**66 860**	**71 297**	**68 825**	**70 068**	**74 746**	**77 548**	**78 175**	**80 033**
45-82x	**BUSINESS SECTOR SERVICES excluding real estate**	**50 863**	**53 938**	**51 036**	**51 743**	**55 332**	**57 469**	**57 208**	**58 370**
05-82x	**NON-AGRICULTURE BUSINESS SECTOR excluding real estate**	..	..	..	..	..	..	..	..

.. Not available

Note: Detailed metadata at: http://metalinks.oecd.org/stan/20170410/1c43.

Information on data for Israel: http://oe.cd/israel-disclaimer.

Disclaimer: http://oe.cd/disclaimer

FINLAND

Table 3. Value added, volumes

ISIC Rev. 4

Million 2010 EUR

		2007	2008	2009	2010	2011	2012	2013	2014
	TOTAL	**172 668**	**174 162**	**158 790**	**163 620**	**166 820**	**163 585**	**162 132**	**160 904**
01-03	**AGRICULTURE, FORESTRY AND FISHING**	**4 153**	**4 138**	**4 444**	**4 468**	**4 663**	**4 547**	**4 925**	**4 803**
05-09	**MINING AND QUARRYING**	**552**	**646**	**671**	**811**	**800**	**852**	**697**	**608**
10-33	**MANUFACTURING**	**39 686**	**38 649**	**29 670**	**31 948**	**31 912**	**28 258**	**28 497**	**28 118**
10-12	Food products, beverages and tobacco	3 004	2 789	2 651	2 617	2 624	2 521	2 336	2 198
13-14	Textiles and wearing apparel	444	441	387	380	370	342	306	278
15	Leather and related products	86	89	71	82	87	87	77	68
16	Wood, wood and cork products	1 668	1 317	969	1 235	1 221	1 186	1 245	1 133
17	Paper and paper products	3 855	3 677	2 087	3 063	2 888	2 912	3 041	3 113
18	Printing and reproduction of recorded media	838	773	655	648	638	654	551	501
19-23	Chemical, rubber, plastics, non-metallic products	5 411	5 110	4 978	5 171	6 085	5 515	5 678	5 443
20	Chemicals and chemical products	1 699	1 477	1 609	1 692	1 928	1 632	1 942	1 801
21	Pharmaceutical products	729	874	913	983	1 049	1 234	1 163	1 411
22-23	Rubber, plastic, non-metallic mineral products	2 520	2 461	1 820	1 972	2 229	2 114	1 893	1 849
24	Basic metals	2 237	1 195	765	1 221	960	1 031	1 212	1 280
25	Metal products, except machinery and equipment	3 069	3 122	2 344	2 276	2 490	2 328	2 152	2 022
26-28	Machinery and equipment	15 508	16 658	11 965	12 522	11 626	8 835	9 321	9 626
26	Computer, electronic and optical products	8 587	9 240	6 477	6 601	5 206	2 547	3 760	3 972
27	Electrical equipment	1 677	1 970	1 401	1 642	1 585	1 646	1 434	1 543
28	Machinery and equipment n.e.c.	5 191	5 374	4 083	4 279	4 835	4 734	4 181	4 159
29-30	Transport equipment	1 176	1 135	800	784	946	894	876	818
29	Motor vehicles, trailers and semi-trailers	600	529	345	383	501	436	406	424
30	Other transport equipment	579	611	460	401	445	456	467	393
31-33	Furniture; repair, installation of machinery and equipment	2 448	2 341	1 978	1 949	1 977	1 884	1 668	1 616
31-32	Furniture, other manufacturing	1 022	855	650	661	675	622	544	518
33	Repair and installation of machinery and equipment	1 434	1 490	1 328	1 288	1 302	1 262	1 124	1 097
35-39	**ELECTRICITY, GAS, WATER AND WASTE MANAGEMENT**	**5 857**	**5 572**	**5 592**	**5 736**	**5 564**	**5 956**	**5 840**	**6 132**
35	Electricity, gas, steam and air conditioning supply	4 469	4 143	4 222	4 208	4 099	4 525	4 402	4 662
36-39	Water supply; sewerage, waste, remediation activities	1 401	1 433	1 379	1 528	1 465	1 448	1 447	1 486
41-43	**CONSTRUCTION**	**10 703**	**10 427**	**9 602**	**10 548**	**10 671**	**10 102**	**9 897**	**9 531**
45-56	Distribution; transportation, accommodation, food service	27 611	29 014	25 620	26 394	27 451	27 942	26 958	26 370
45-47	**Wholesale and retail trade; motor vehicle and motorcycle repairs**	**15 517**	**16 870**	**14 934**	**15 313**	**15 766**	**16 071**	**15 432**	**15 262**
49-53	**Transportation and storage**	**9 031**	**9 099**	**7 930**	**8 420**	**8 956**	**9 088**	**9 099**	**8 708**
55-56	**Accommodation and food service activities**	**3 125**	**3 060**	**2 779**	**2 661**	**2 729**	**2 781**	**2 453**	**2 400**
58-63	**Information and communication**	**7 804**	**7 958**	**7 849**	**8 168**	**8 740**	**9 258**	**9 518**	**9 960**
58-60	Publishing, audiovisual and broadcasting activities	2 159	2 317	2 353	2 371	2 398	2 333	2 145	2 103
61	Telecommunications	1 867	1 869	2 046	2 219	2 389	2 646	2 905	2 865
62-63	IT and other information services	3 817	3 821	3 460	3 578	3 953	4 289	4 514	4 990
64-66	**Financial and insurance activities**	**4 329**	**4 376**	**4 154**	**4 234**	**4 211**	**4 116**	**3 731**	**4 122**
68	**Real estate activities**	**18 033**	**18 957**	**18 526**	**18 325**	**19 076**	**19 006**	**19 040**	**19 018**
69-82	**Professional, scientific, technical, admin., support activities**	**13 204**	**13 761**	**12 833**	**12 947**	**13 591**	**13 752**	**13 546**	**13 349**
69-75	Professional, scientific and technical activities	8 307	8 139	7 672	7 674	8 087	8 223	8 203	8 077
69-71	Legal, accounting activities; mgt consultancy; engineering	5 797	5 470	5 104	5 099	5 446	5 615	5 640	5 633
73-75	Advertising, market research; other prof., scientific, tech.	1 263	1 232	1 160	1 152	1 158	1 102	1 044	1 027
77-82	Administrative and support service activities	4 920	5 621	5 161	5 273	5 504	5 529	5 340	5 270
84-88	**Public administration, defence; social security; education; health**	**35 274**	**35 271**	**35 019**	**34 964**	**34 964**	**34 739**	**34 557**	**34 074**
84	**Public administration, defence; compulsory social security**	**10 543**	**10 538**	**10 482**	**10 292**	**10 215**	**10 055**	**10 163**	**10 015**
85	**Education**	**9 425**	**9 189**	**9 080**	**9 409**	**9 289**	**9 264**	**9 140**	**9 122**
86-88	**Human health and social work activities**	**15 311**	**15 555**	**15 469**	**15 263**	**15 460**	**15 419**	**15 256**	**14 941**
90-99	**Arts, entertainment, household goods repairs, other**	**4 849**	**4 911**	**4 982**	**5 077**	**5 177**	**5 054**	**4 968**	**4 907**
90-93	**Arts, entertainment and recreation**	**1 984**	**2 077**	**2 040**	**2 065**	**2 160**	**2 089**	**2 057**	**1 979**
94-96	**Other service activities**	**2 693**	**2 654**	**2 781**	**2 844**	**2 843**	**2 796**	**2 726**	**2 703**
97-98	**Activities of households as employers and for own use**	**175**	**183**	**161**	**168**	**174**	**169**	**185**	**228**
05-39	**INDUSTRY INCLUDING ENERGY**	**46 363**	**45 162**	**35 911**	**38 495**	**38 276**	**35 029**	**35 023**	**34 846**
45-99	**TOTAL SERVICES**	**111 091**	**114 271**	**108 941**	**110 109**	**113 210**	**113 835**	**112 249**	**111 702**
45-82	**BUSINESS SECTOR SERVICES**	**71 006**	**74 047**	**68 951**	**70 068**	**73 069**	**74 051**	**72 717**	**72 731**
45-82x	**BUSINESS SECTOR SERVICES excluding real estate**	**52 928**	**55 055**	**50 450**	**51 743**	**53 993**	**55 043**	**53 670**	**53 708**
05-82x	**NON-AGRICULTURE BUSINESS SECTOR excluding real estate**	..	..	..	..	..	..	..	..

.. Not available

Note: Detailed metadata at: http://metalinks.oecd.org/stan/20170410/1c43.

Information on data for Israel: http://oe.cd/israel-disclaimer.

Disclaimer: http://oe.cd/disclaimer

FINLAND

Table 4. Gross fixed capital formation, current prices

ISIC Rev. 4

Million EUR

		2007	2008	2009	2010	2011	2012	2013	2014
	TOTAL	**45 103**	**47 245**	**41 187**	**40 933**	**43 779**	**44 610**	**43 083**	**42 247**
01-03	**AGRICULTURE, FORESTRY AND FISHING**	**1 720**	**1 680**	**1 646**	**1 534**	**1 621**	**1 593**	**1 594**	**1 745**
05-09	**MINING AND QUARRYING**	**383**	**735**	**369**	**325**	**495**	**464**	**344**	**309**
10-33	**MANUFACTURING**	**8 627**	**8 942**	**7 854**	**7 246**	**7 203**	**6 845**	**6 321**	**6 274**
10-12	Food products, beverages and tobacco	492	496	422	366	405	459	470	539
13-14	Textiles and wearing apparel	46	36	17	19	20	24	14	19
15	Leather and related products	6	6	7	2	7	10	4	7
16	Wood, wood and cork products	259	254	150	146	224	171	119	170
17	Paper and paper products	802	861	358	399	392	497	573	362
18	Printing and reproduction of recorded media	95	111	65	50	46	45	43	32
19-23	Chemical, rubber, plastics, non-metallic products	1 859	1 192	1 258	929	934	1 074	1 198	1 054
20	Chemicals and chemical products	485	457	503	282	326	349	428	299
21	Pharmaceutical products	202	210	218	202	196	283	339	305
22-23	Rubber, plastic, non-metallic mineral products	322	349	307	238	293	261	247	257
24	Basic metals	296	385	364	393	363	594	240	295
25	Metal products, except machinery and equipment	376	436	439	227	243	320	185	243
26-28	Machinery and equipment	3 938	4 865	4 517	4 480	4 297	3 354	3 194	3 352
26	Computer, electronic and optical products	3 153	3 749	3 411	3 492	3 246	2 167	2 111	2 107
27	Electrical equipment	261	354	339	378	354	389	304	381
28	Machinery and equipment n.e.c.	524	762	767	610	697	798	779	864
29-30	Transport equipment	110	129	142	112	145	173	184	96
29	Motor vehicles, trailers and semi-trailers	52	54	66	63	94	88	148	77
30	Other transport equipment	58	75	76	49	51	85	36	19
31-33	Furniture; repair, installation of machinery and equipment	348	171	115	123	127	124	97	105
31-32	Furniture, other manufacturing	149	83	68	60	59	67	53	44
33	Repair and installation of machinery and equipment	199	88	47	63	68	57	44	61
35-39	**ELECTRICITY, GAS, WATER AND WASTE MANAGEMENT**	**1 679**	**2 130**	**2 309**	**2 139**	**2 174**	**2 289**	**2 362**	**2 522**
35	Electricity, gas, steam and air conditioning supply	1 110	1 513	1 698	1 458	1 573	1 684	1 779	1 938
36-39	Water supply; sewerage, waste, remediation activities	569	617	611	681	601	605	583	584
41-43	**CONSTRUCTION**	**844**	**959**	**719**	**755**	**813**	**887**	**798**	**810**
45-56	Distribution; transportation, accommodation, food service	3 350	3 256	3 274	2 780	3 144	3 530	3 223	3 059
45-47	**Wholesale and retail trade; motor vehicle and motorcycle repairs**	**1 455**	**1 536**	**1 373**	**1 299**	**1 436**	**1 868**	**1 588**	**1 630**
49-53	**Transportation and storage**	**1 689**	**1 501**	**1 699**	**1 275**	**1 516**	**1 437**	**1 467**	**1 245**
55-56	**Accommodation and food service activities**	**206**	**219**	**202**	**206**	**192**	**225**	**168**	**184**
58-63	**Information and communication**	**1 632**	**1 608**	**1 424**	**1 615**	**1 700**	**1 781**	**1 921**	**2 254**
58-60	Publishing, audiovisual and broadcasting activities	402	366	374	452	511	520	476	425
61	Telecommunications	533	593	549	609	597	562	609	571
62-63	IT and other information services	697	649	501	554	592	699	836	1 258
64-66	**Financial and insurance activities**	**556**	**560**	**497**	**323**	**356**	**418**	**396**	**412**
68	**Real estate activities**	**17 721**	**18 144**	**14 111**	**15 377**	**16 936**	**16 844**	**16 151**	**14 695**
69-82	**Professional, scientific, technical, admin., support activities**	**1 870**	**1 997**	**1 637**	**1 832**	**1 995**	**1 926**	**1 812**	**1 846**
69-75	Professional, scientific and technical activities	1 264	1 269	1 123	1 291	1 395	1 308	1 226	1 225
69-71	Legal, accounting activities; mgt consultancy; engineering	496	484	338	488	547	432	378	421
73-75	Advertising, market research; other prof., scientific, tech.	81	100	75	78	84	78	58	82
77-82	Administrative and support service activities	606	728	514	541	600	618	586	621
84-88	**Public administration, defence; social security; education; health**	**5 938**	**6 422**	**6 560**	**6 234**	**6 589**	**7 204**	**7 361**	**7 522**
84	**Public administration, defence; compulsory social security**	**2 940**	**3 264**	**3 315**	**2 897**	**3 096**	**3 621**	**3 693**	**3 798**
85	**Education**	**1 916**	**2 001**	**2 023**	**2 214**	**2 330**	**2 204**	**2 218**	**2 306**
86-88	**Human health and social work activities**	**1 082**	**1 157**	**1 222**	**1 123**	**1 163**	**1 379**	**1 450**	**1 418**
90-99	**Arts, entertainment, household goods repairs, other**	**783**	**812**	**787**	**773**	**753**	**829**	**800**	**799**
90-93	**Arts, entertainment and recreation**	**545**	**533**	**507**	**488**	**498**	**583**	**571**	**572**
94-96	**Other service activities**	**238**	**279**	**280**	**285**	**255**	**246**	**229**	**227**
97-98	**Activities of households as employers and for own use**	**0**	**0**	**0**	**0**	**0**	**0**	**0**	**0**
05-39	**INDUSTRY INCLUDING ENERGY**	**10 689**	**11 807**	**10 532**	**9 710**	**9 872**	**9 598**	**9 027**	**9 105**
45-99	**TOTAL SERVICES**	**31 850**	**32 799**	**28 290**	**28 934**	**31 473**	**32 532**	**31 664**	**30 587**
45-82	**BUSINESS SECTOR SERVICES**	**25 129**	**25 565**	**20 943**	**21 927**	**24 131**	**24 499**	**23 503**	**22 266**
45-82x	**BUSINESS SECTOR SERVICES excluding real estate**	**7 408**	**7 421**	**6 832**	**6 550**	**7 195**	**7 655**	**7 352**	**7 571**
05-82x	**NON-AGRICULTURE BUSINESS SECTOR excluding real estate**	..	..	..	..	..	..	..	..

.. Not available

Note: Detailed metadata at: http://metalinks.oecd.org/stan/20170410/1c43.
Information on data for Israel: http://oe.cd/israel-disclaimer.

Disclaimer: http://oe.cd/disclaimer

FINLAND

Table 5. Number of persons engaged, total employment

ISIC Rev. 4

Thousands

		2007	2008	2009	2010	2011	2012	2013	2014
	TOTAL	**2 507**	**2 563**	**2 501**	**2 484**	**2 516**	**2 538**	**2 520**	**2 507**
01-03	**AGRICULTURE, FORESTRY AND FISHING**	**123**	**122**	**121**	**120**	**115**	**115**	**112**	**111**
05-09	**MINING AND QUARRYING**	**6**	**6**	**6**	**6**	**7**	**7**	**6**	**7**
10-33	**MANUFACTURING**	**421**	**426**	**383**	**365**	**369**	**368**	**354**	**344**
10-12	Food products, beverages and tobacco	39	39	37	36	36	37	38	38
13-14	Textiles and wearing apparel	12	12	11	10	11	10	9	8
15	Leather and related products	2	2	3	3	3	2	2	2
16	Wood, wood and cork products	30	30	26	26	26	24	24	22
17	Paper and paper products	29	28	24	23	22	21	21	20
18	Printing and reproduction of recorded media	14	13	12	12	12	12	11	10
19-23	Chemical, rubber, plastics, non-metallic products	55	56	51	50	52	51	50	48
20	Chemicals and chemical products	14	15	13	13	13	13	13	13
21	Pharmaceutical products	4	4	4	4	4	5	5	5
22-23	Rubber, plastic, non-metallic mineral products	34	34	31	31	32	31	29	28
24	Basic metals	17	17	16	16	16	15	15	14
25	Metal products, except machinery and equipment	52	54	46	42	45	47	45	44
26-28	Machinery and equipment	112	114	103	97	94	97	91	89
26	Computer, electronic and optical products	44	41	37	34	31	32	27	25
27	Electrical equipment	16	20	18	17	17	17	17	17
28	Machinery and equipment n.e.c.	52	53	48	45	47	48	47	47
29-30	Transport equipment	20	20	17	15	14	15	15	14
29	Motor vehicles, trailers and semi-trailers	9	9	8	7	7	7	7	7
30	Other transport equipment	11	11	9	8	7	8	8	7
31-33	Furniture; repair, installation of machinery and equipment	40	41	38	37	38	37	35	33
31-32	Furniture, other manufacturing	19	18	16	16	16	16	15	14
33	Repair and installation of machinery and equipment	21	23	22	21	21	21	20	19
35-39	**ELECTRICITY, GAS, WATER AND WASTE MANAGEMENT**	**24**	**24**	**26**	**26**	**25**	**26**	**26**	**26**
35	Electricity, gas, steam and air conditioning supply	13	13	13	13	13	13	14	13
36-39	Water supply; sewerage, waste, remediation activities	11	12	13	12	12	13	13	13
41-43	**CONSTRUCTION**	**192**	**199**	**187**	**189**	**194**	**193**	**190**	**188**
45-56	Distribution; transportation, accommodation, food service	547	551	538	525	529	538	533	532
45-47	**Wholesale and retail trade; motor vehicle and motorcycle repairs**	**314**	**313**	**303**	**294**	**297**	**305**	**302**	**301**
49-53	**Transportation and storage**	**154**	**157**	**155**	**154**	**155**	**153**	**150**	**149**
55-56	**Accommodation and food service activities**	**79**	**82**	**80**	**77**	**78**	**80**	**81**	**82**
58-63	**Information and communication**	**93**	**96**	**94**	**94**	**95**	**96**	**99**	**98**
58-60	Publishing, audiovisual and broadcasting activities	28	29	30	30	29	29	28	27
61	Telecommunications	17	15	14	13	13	13	13	12
62-63	IT and other information services	48	52	50	51	53	55	58	59
64-66	**Financial and insurance activities**	**45**	**47**	**46**	**47**	**47**	**47**	**46**	**45**
68	**Real estate activities**	**23**	**23**	**24**	**24**	**24**	**24**	**24**	**24**
69-82	**Professional, scientific, technical, admin., support activities**	**236**	**256**	**254**	**261**	**271**	**277**	**277**	**285**
69-75	Professional, scientific and technical activities	126	135	133	137	141	145	145	146
69-71	Legal, accounting activities; mgt consultancy; engineering	80	87	86	90	93	97	97	98
73-75	Advertising, market research; other prof., scientific, tech.	31	33	31	32	31	32	32	32
77-82	Administrative and support service activities	109	120	121	124	130	132	133	139
84-88	**Public administration, defence; social security; education; health**	**682**	**695**	**702**	**704**	**713**	**717**	**719**	**714**
84	**Public administration, defence; compulsory social security**	**178**	**177**	**177**	**175**	**174**	**169**	**170**	**165**
85	**Education**	**160**	**162**	**163**	**165**	**165**	**165**	**164**	**163**
86-88	**Human health and social work activities**	**344**	**355**	**362**	**364**	**373**	**383**	**385**	**386**
90-99	**Arts, entertainment, household goods repairs, other**	**116**	**118**	**121**	**124**	**127**	**131**	**133**	**136**
90-93	**Arts, entertainment and recreation**	**42**	**43**	**45**	**46**	**47**	**48**	**48**	**49**
94-96	**Other service activities**	**66**	**66**	**67**	**69**	**70**	**73**	**74**	**74**
97-98	**Activities of households as employers and for own use**	**8**	**9**	**9**	**9**	**9**	**10**	**11**	**13**
05-39	**INDUSTRY INCLUDING ENERGY**	**450**	**457**	**415**	**396**	**401**	**400**	**386**	**376**
45-99	**TOTAL SERVICES**	**1 742**	**1 785**	**1 778**	**1 779**	**1 806**	**1 830**	**1 831**	**1 832**
45-82	**BUSINESS SECTOR SERVICES**	**944**	**972**	**956**	**951**	**966**	**982**	**979**	**983**
45-82x	**BUSINESS SECTOR SERVICES excluding real estate**	**921**	**949**	**931**	**927**	**942**	**958**	**955**	**959**
05-82x	**NON-AGRICULTURE BUSINESS SECTOR excluding real estate**	..	..	..	..	..	..	..	..

.. Not available

Note: Detailed metadata at: http://metalinks.oecd.org/stan/20170410/1c43.

Information on data for Israel: http://oe.cd/israel-disclaimer.

Disclaimer: http://oe.cd/disclaimer

FINLAND

Table 6. Labour costs (compensation of employees), current prices

ISIC Rev. 4

Million EUR

		2007	2008	2009	2010	2011	2012	2013	2014
	TOTAL	**86 299**	**91 983**	**90 940**	**92 404**	**96 828**	**100 288**	**101 169**	**101 410**
01-03	**AGRICULTURE, FORESTRY AND FISHING**	**980**	**1 003**	**1 038**	**1 125**	**1 121**	**1 163**	**1 169**	**1 175**
05-09	**MINING AND QUARRYING**	**234**	**247**	**237**	**236**	**271**	**304**	**296**	**304**
10-33	**MANUFACTURING**	**18 612**	**18 908**	**17 052**	**16 561**	**17 216**	**17 543**	**16 994**	**16 786**
10-12	Food products, beverages and tobacco	1 496	1 533	1 472	1 496	1 548	1 614	1 644	1 659
13-14	Textiles and wearing apparel	300	298	246	236	244	241	221	208
15	Leather and related products	55	54	53	49	54	52	51	47
16	Wood, wood and cork products	1 035	993	859	888	931	892	874	845
17	Paper and paper products	1 740	1 658	1 449	1 406	1 436	1 356	1 366	1 340
18	Printing and reproduction of recorded media	501	496	460	431	437	428	403	381
19-23	Chemical, rubber, plastics, non-metallic products	2 564	2 576	2 321	2 386	2 524	2 555	2 508	2 493
20	Chemicals and chemical products	774	778	710	735	765	768	765	759
21	Pharmaceutical products	184	220	208	201	227	243	257	264
22-23	Rubber, plastic, non-metallic mineral products	1 431	1 415	1 233	1 280	1 366	1 369	1 307	1 278
24	Basic metals	871	848	728	773	843	796	766	758
25	Metal products, except machinery and equipment	1 860	1 959	1 688	1 572	1 682	1 780	1 729	1 738
26-28	Machinery and equipment	5 895	6 099	5 597	5 292	5 409	5 638	5 280	5 243
26	Computer, electronic and optical products	2 700	2 660	2 520	2 302	2 172	2 197	1 868	1 754
27	Electrical equipment	717	851	783	761	789	846	836	869
28	Machinery and equipment n.e.c.	2 478	2 588	2 294	2 229	2 448	2 595	2 576	2 620
29-30	Transport equipment	804	841	712	638	627	683	689	669
29	Motor vehicles, trailers and semi-trailers	346	345	289	272	285	289	294	300
30	Other transport equipment	458	496	423	366	342	394	395	369
31-33	Furniture; repair, installation of machinery and equipment	1 491	1 553	1 467	1 394	1 481	1 508	1 463	1 405
31-32	Furniture, other manufacturing	554	525	473	459	479	477	462	445
33	Repair and installation of machinery and equipment	937	1 028	994	935	1 002	1 031	1 001	960
35-39	**ELECTRICITY, GAS, WATER AND WASTE MANAGEMENT**	**1 111**	**1 133**	**1 219**	**1 239**	**1 300**	**1 367**	**1 380**	**1 359**
35	Electricity, gas, steam and air conditioning supply	719	708	746	770	805	843	847	812
36-39	Water supply; sewerage, waste, remediation activities	392	425	473	469	495	524	533	547
41-43	**CONSTRUCTION**	**6 557**	**7 391**	**6 892**	**7 179**	**7 616**	**7 820**	**7 893**	**7 780**
45-56	Distribution; transportation, accommodation, food service	15 918	17 145	16 992	16 837	17 716	18 411	18 639	18 682
45-47	**Wholesale and retail trade; motor vehicle and motorcycle repairs**	**9 201**	**9 907**	**9 762**	**9 552**	**10 101**	**10 597**	**10 780**	**10 789**
49-53	**Transportation and storage**	**5 012**	**5 388**	**5 370**	**5 408**	**5 629**	**5 718**	**5 710**	**5 691**
55-56	**Accommodation and food service activities**	**1 705**	**1 850**	**1 860**	**1 877**	**1 986**	**2 096**	**2 149**	**2 202**
58-63	**Information and communication**	**4 281**	**4 654**	**4 647**	**4 714**	**4 982**	**5 149**	**5 459**	**5 475**
58-60	Publishing, audiovisual and broadcasting activities	1 213	1 257	1 334	1 382	1 410	1 430	1 420	1 405
61	Telecommunications	752	751	728	689	695	738	735	710
62-63	IT and other information services	2 316	2 646	2 585	2 643	2 877	2 981	3 304	3 360
64-66	**Financial and insurance activities**	**2 388**	**2 510**	**2 595**	**2 628**	**2 768**	**2 830**	**2 897**	**2 833**
68	**Real estate activities**	**801**	**835**	**895**	**874**	**901**	**934**	**929**	**930**
69-82	**Professional, scientific, technical, admin., support activities**	**7 685**	**8 587**	**8 648**	**9 191**	**9 822**	**10 294**	**10 445**	**10 766**
69-75	Professional, scientific and technical activities	4 579	5 024	5 103	5 414	5 737	5 988	6 096	6 192
69-71	Legal, accounting activities; mgt consultancy; engineering	3 146	3 485	3 536	3 755	3 991	4 190	4 269	4 399
73-75	Advertising, market research; other prof., scientific, tech.	692	750	732	800	839	860	874	872
77-82	Administrative and support service activities	3 106	3 563	3 545	3 777	4 085	4 306	4 349	4 574
84-88	**Public administration, defence; social security; education; health**	**24 679**	**26 329**	**27 393**	**28 332**	**29 503**	**30 775**	**31 293**	**31 441**
84	**Public administration, defence; compulsory social security**	**6 719**	**7 095**	**7 280**	**7 366**	**7 555**	**7 702**	**7 831**	**7 791**
85	**Education**	**6 501**	**6 887**	**7 177**	**7 513**	**7 722**	**7 966**	**8 028**	**8 040**
86-88	**Human health and social work activities**	**11 459**	**12 347**	**12 936**	**13 453**	**14 226**	**15 107**	**15 434**	**15 610**
90-99	**Arts, entertainment, household goods repairs, other**	**3 053**	**3 241**	**3 332**	**3 488**	**3 612**	**3 698**	**3 775**	**3 879**
90-93	**Arts, entertainment and recreation**	**1 193**	**1 286**	**1 315**	**1 366**	**1 436**	**1 475**	**1 501**	**1 529**
94-96	**Other service activities**	**1 732**	**1 806**	**1 855**	**1 954**	**2 001**	**2 048**	**2 080**	**2 107**
97-98	**Activities of households as employers and for own use**	**128**	**149**	**162**	**168**	**175**	**175**	**194**	**243**
05-39	**INDUSTRY INCLUDING ENERGY**	19 957	20 288	18 508	18 036	18 787	19 214	18 670	18 449
45-99	**TOTAL SERVICES**	**58 805**	**63 301**	**64 502**	**66 064**	**69 304**	**72 091**	**73 437**	**74 006**
45-82	**BUSINESS SECTOR SERVICES**	31 073	33 731	33 777	34 244	36 189	37 618	38 369	38 686
45-82x	**BUSINESS SECTOR SERVICES excluding real estate**	**30 272**	**32 896**	**32 882**	**33 370**	**35 288**	**36 684**	**37 440**	**37 756**
05-82x	**NON-AGRICULTURE BUSINESS SECTOR excluding real estate**	..	..	..	..	..	..	..	..

.. Not available

Note: Detailed metadata at: http://metalinks.oecd.org/stan/20170410/1c43.
Information on data for Israel: http://oe.cd/israel-disclaimer.

Disclaimer: http://oe.cd/disclaimer

FRANCE

Table 1. Production (gross output), current prices

ISIC Rev. 4

Million EUR

		2007	2008	2009	2010	2011	2012	2013	2014
	TOTAL	3 465 666	3 570 702	3 385 374	3 542 833	3 685 378	3 741 061	3 760 699	3 781 399
01-03	AGRICULTURE, FORESTRY AND FISHING	77 611	79 252	73 137	78 779	84 990	87 792	85 955	87 634
05-09	MINING AND QUARRYING	6 228	6 024	5 315	5 377	5 715	5 633	5 594	5 457
10-33	MANUFACTURING	773 991	787 617	665 088	709 971	765 733	758 201	745 223	741 029
10-12	Food products, beverages and tobacco	143 918	151 426	141 660	141 235	153 325	155 050	158 133	158 944
13-14	Textiles and wearing apparel	18 078	16 790	12 666	13 022	13 286	12 991	12 668	12 721
15	Leather and related products	3 300	3 241	2 364	2 818	3 243	3 384	3 232	3 419
16	Wood, wood and cork products	12 072	11 803	9 726	9 939	10 948	10 417	10 231	10 381
17	Paper and paper products	18 863	18 516	15 757	17 138	17 512	16 590	16 296	16 091
18	Printing and reproduction of recorded media	12 348	12 147	10 759	10 574	10 432	9 735	9 292	9 225
19-23	Chemical, rubber, plastics, non-metallic products	197 177	209 771	165 807	184 691	209 591	207 653	198 015	191 367
20	Chemicals and chemical products	61 490	65 406	53 292	60 660	68 452	67 725	66 068	66 335
21	Pharmaceutical products	24 872	25 328	25 298	25 583	24 522	24 583	25 479	24 727
22-23	Rubber, plastic, non-metallic mineral products	61 763	60 342	49 753	51 727	56 907	54 647	52 242	51 602
24	Basic metals	40 623	40 512	28 147	34 130	37 401	33 541	31 622	31 282
25	Metal products, except machinery and equipment	53 667	52 798	46 749	49 610	52 118	51 167	50 316	49 404
26-28	Machinery and equipment	95 976	95 051	76 701	80 595	84 706	82 836	80 672	79 667
26	Computer, electronic and optical products	29 280	27 757	22 733	25 818	24 588	23 417	23 007	21 908
27	Electrical equipment	23 617	23 536	19 928	21 282	22 553	21 487	20 906	20 098
28	Machinery and equipment n.e.c.	43 079	43 757	34 040	33 495	37 565	37 932	36 759	37 661
29-30	Transport equipment	114 356	110 727	91 150	103 105	106 844	108 137	108 538	111 216
29	Motor vehicles, trailers and semi-trailers	73 121	66 484	48 427	58 263	60 865	55 266	51 432	53 199
30	Other transport equipment	41 236	44 243	42 723	44 842	45 979	52 871	57 106	58 017
31-33	Furniture; repair, installation of machinery and equipment	63 613	64 835	63 602	63 114	66 327	66 700	66 208	67 312
31-32	Furniture, other manufacturing	17 823	17 820	16 187	16 200	16 498	16 171	16 051	16 049
33	Repair and installation of machinery and equipment	45 790	47 015	47 415	46 914	49 829	50 529	50 157	51 263
35-39	ELECTRICITY, GAS, WATER AND WASTE MANAGEMENT	123 897	129 327	127 579	138 461	140 605	147 379	147 396	140 036
35	Electricity, gas, steam and air conditioning supply	89 770	94 816	95 986	102 222	103 144	109 706	110 991	104 019
36-39	Water supply; sewerage, waste, remediation activities	34 127	34 511	31 593	36 239	37 461	37 673	36 405	36 017
41-43	CONSTRUCTION	270 093	283 736	264 335	264 969	279 230	279 221	282 417	275 235
45-56	Distribution; transportation, accommodation, food service	619 059	639 421	606 608	631 845	651 146	664 774	672 360	678 068
45-47	Wholesale and retail trade; motor vehicle and motorcycle repairs	362 392	376 604	357 688	365 386	374 925	382 990	386 995	391 474
49-53	Transportation and storage	174 359	179 316	164 716	175 440	181 573	185 355	187 409	187 337
55-56	Accommodation and food service activities	82 309	83 501	84 204	91 019	94 648	96 429	97 956	99 257
58-63	Information and communication	168 740	177 734	174 824	182 466	185 804	186 984	179 607	180 285
58-60	Publishing, audiovisual and broadcasting activities	49 033	50 807	48 891	49 673	50 715	50 906	50 777	51 825
61	Telecommunications	59 256	62 333	63 675	66 347	65 617	64 762	56 921	55 043
62-63	IT and other information services	60 451	64 594	62 258	66 446	69 472	71 316	71 909	73 417
64-66	Financial and insurance activities	182 998	181 779	184 938	200 531	196 295	200 094	206 192	214 874
68	Real estate activities	265 698	272 507	275 397	281 726	284 301	292 317	296 186	301 194
69-82	Professional, scientific, technical, admin., support activities	418 000	436 726	411 259	433 980	461 650	472 584	477 263	484 500
69-75	Professional, scientific and technical activities	250 759	263 112	252 535	270 029	288 988	297 973	303 630	307 804
69-71	Legal, accounting activities; mgt consultancy; engineering	170 715	180 356	171 911	185 992	201 588	208 088	212 604	216 166
73-75	Advertising, market research; other prof., scientific, tech.	30 724	31 381	27 607	28 885	30 156	31 318	30 319	30 595
77-82	Administrative and support service activities	167 241	173 613	158 724	163 951	172 662	174 611	173 633	176 696
84-88	Public administration, defence; social security; education; health	474 772	491 259	510 423	524 931	539 924	554 360	568 124	576 972
84	Public administration, defence; compulsory social security	183 133	188 140	196 483	200 235	204 980	210 513	214 311	214 540
85	Education	108 032	112 651	115 032	118 491	121 011	123 497	125 904	128 586
86-88	Human health and social work activities	183 607	190 468	198 908	206 205	213 933	220 350	227 909	233 846
90-99	Arts, entertainment, household goods repairs, other	84 578	85 321	86 472	89 797	89 985	91 722	94 382	96 114
90-93	Arts, entertainment and recreation	40 010	40 985	42 161	44 615	45 541	46 014	47 683	48 593
94-96	Other service activities	39 836	40 289	40 328	41 192	40 506	41 858	43 014	43 919
97-98	Activities of households as employers and for own use	4 733	4 047	3 983	3 990	3 938	3 850	3 685	3 602
05-39	INDUSTRY INCLUDING ENERGY	904 115	922 969	797 982	853 809	912 053	911 213	898 213	886 522
45-99	TOTAL SERVICES	2 213 846	2 284 745	2 249 921	2 345 276	2 409 105	2 462 835	2 494 114	2 532 007
45-82	BUSINESS SECTOR SERVICES	1 654 495	1 708 166	1 653 026	1 730 548	1 779 196	1 816 753	1 831 608	1 858 921
45-82x	BUSINESS SECTOR SERVICES excluding real estate	1 388 797	1 435 659	1 377 629	1 448 822	1 494 895	1 524 436	1 535 422	1 557 727
05-82x	NON-AGRICULTURE BUSINESS SECTOR excluding real estate	..	..	..	..	..	..	..	..

.. Not available

Note: Detailed metadata at: http://metalinks.oecd.org/stan/20170410/1c43.

Information on data for Israel: http://oe.cd/israel-disclaimer.

Disclaimer: http://oe.cd/disclaimer

FRANCE

Table 2. Value added, current prices

ISIC Rev. 4

Million EUR

		2007	2008	2009	2010	2011	2012	2013	2014
	TOTAL	**1 746 821**	**1 796 275**	**1 752 722**	**1 800 982**	**1 849 498**	**1 873 450**	**1 897 908**	**1 917 675**
01-03	**AGRICULTURE, FORESTRY AND FISHING**	**31 448**	**30 298**	**25 669**	**32 092**	**34 044**	**34 078**	**30 882**	**33 193**
05-09	**MINING AND QUARRYING**	**2 462**	**2 429**	**2 238**	**2 297**	**2 287**	**2 255**	**2 150**	**2 162**
10-33	**MANUFACTURING**	**221 488**	**217 208**	**201 691**	**202 620**	**210 379**	**212 245**	**215 361**	**213 677**
10-12	Food products, beverages and tobacco	40 985	40 617	39 733	39 079	41 293	41 853	43 624	44 529
13-14	Textiles and wearing apparel	4 762	4 430	3 646	3 358	3 503	3 602	3 498	3 339
15	Leather and related products	1 207	1 219	1 163	1 279	1 460	1 551	1 476	1 559
16	Wood, wood and cork products	3 128	3 243	2 952	2 652	3 050	2 940	2 950	2 823
17	Paper and paper products	4 866	4 581	4 276	4 036	4 310	4 388	4 162	4 098
18	Printing and reproduction of recorded media	5 038	4 907	4 453	4 336	4 314	4 158	4 106	4 006
19-23	Chemical, rubber, plastics, non-metallic products	51 906	49 564	46 032	44 886	47 548	47 342	48 945	49 165
20	Chemicals and chemical products	14 144	14 623	14 174	13 981	15 191	15 298	16 955	17 484
21	Pharmaceutical products	13 257	12 495	12 016	11 865	12 047	11 821	12 040	11 530
22-23	Rubber, plastic, non-metallic mineral products	21 892	20 575	18 506	17 448	18 398	18 084	17 928	17 939
24	Basic metals	7 290	7 596	5 721	5 874	6 787	5 435	5 500	5 562
25	Metal products, except machinery and equipment	20 443	20 010	18 720	19 588	20 115	20 154	20 273	19 615
26-28	Machinery and equipment	33 714	32 826	28 428	28 954	29 541	29 646	29 346	28 978
26	Computer, electronic and optical products	12 900	12 059	10 580	11 214	10 837	10 720	10 881	10 130
27	Electrical equipment	7 143	7 073	6 570	6 494	6 354	6 474	6 471	6 291
28	Machinery and equipment n.e.c.	13 671	13 694	11 278	11 246	12 350	12 451	11 993	12 558
29-30	Transport equipment	22 371	22 244	20 010	21 693	20 550	22 276	22 652	20 088
29	Motor vehicles, trailers and semi-trailers	12 089	11 097	9 340	10 755	10 540	9 546	9 412	9 784
30	Other transport equipment	10 282	11 147	10 669	10 938	10 010	12 729	13 240	10 304
31-33	Furniture; repair, installation of machinery and equipment	25 777	25 969	26 557	26 885	27 908	28 899	28 829	29 915
31-32	Furniture, other manufacturing	6 918	6 766	6 670	6 557	6 645	6 478	6 626	6 717
33	Repair and installation of machinery and equipment	18 859	19 203	19 887	20 329	21 263	22 421	22 202	23 197
35-39	**ELECTRICITY, GAS, WATER AND WASTE MANAGEMENT**	**37 775**	**36 999**	**37 618**	**38 863**	**41 398**	**43 967**	**46 256**	**48 361**
35	Electricity, gas, steam and air conditioning supply	25 907	24 874	25 695	25 525	27 464	30 342	32 543	34 718
36-39	Water supply; sewerage, waste, remediation activities	11 868	12 124	11 923	13 338	13 934	13 626	13 713	13 643
41-43	**CONSTRUCTION**	**106 204**	**114 750**	**109 755**	**109 247**	**112 731**	**110 445**	**112 759**	**111 079**
45-56	Distribution; transportation, accommodation, food service	311 545	326 552	317 373	322 391	328 763	333 591	335 065	335 908
45-47	**Wholesale and retail trade; motor vehicle and motorcycle repairs**	**184 536**	**195 741**	**190 306**	**187 338**	**191 871**	**193 976**	**194 475**	**194 801**
49-53	**Transportation and storage**	**80 902**	**84 154**	**80 932**	**85 686**	**85 219**	**87 200**	**87 313**	**87 576**
55-56	**Accommodation and food service activities**	**46 107**	**46 657**	**46 135**	**49 366**	**51 673**	**52 415**	**53 276**	**53 531**
58-63	**Information and communication**	**92 305**	**94 690**	**92 329**	**93 018**	**94 189**	**94 172**	**93 791**	**92 998**
58-60	Publishing, audiovisual and broadcasting activities	21 481	21 516	21 099	21 961	23 032	23 141	23 289	23 917
61	Telecommunications	30 615	31 261	31 081	29 736	28 584	26 854	25 704	23 303
62-63	IT and other information services	40 209	41 913	40 149	41 321	42 572	44 178	44 798	45 778
64-66	**Financial and insurance activities**	**67 325**	**64 143**	**69 261**	**81 796**	**78 971**	**79 347**	**83 951**	**87 577**
68	**Real estate activities**	**229 808**	**239 045**	**229 279**	**230 483**	**235 771**	**240 716**	**243 084**	**246 258**
69-82	**Professional, scientific, technical, admin., support activities**	**223 788**	**233 441**	**218 484**	**227 712**	**239 052**	**240 147**	**241 597**	**244 979**
69-75	Professional, scientific and technical activities	124 329	130 640	126 080	131 285	137 752	139 756	141 009	142 402
69-71	Legal, accounting activities; mgt consultancy; engineering	82 201	87 445	82 811	86 652	91 232	92 238	93 086	94 104
73-75	Advertising, market research; other prof., scientific, tech.	15 135	15 292	14 279	14 453	15 428	15 693	14 881	14 870
77-82	Administrative and support service activities	99 459	102 802	92 404	96 427	101 300	100 391	100 588	102 577
84-88	**Public administration, defence; social security; education; health**	**369 966**	**383 448**	**395 784**	**405 702**	**416 899**	**426 353**	**435 623**	**443 417**
84	**Public administration, defence; compulsory social security**	**136 197**	**139 383**	**144 161**	**147 173**	**150 618**	**154 017**	**156 765**	**158 140**
85	**Education**	**89 272**	**93 319**	**95 472**	**97 706**	**99 628**	**101 188**	**102 683**	**104 911**
86-88	**Human health and social work activities**	**144 498**	**150 746**	**156 151**	**160 823**	**166 653**	**171 148**	**176 175**	**180 366**
90-99	**Arts, entertainment, household goods repairs, other**	**52 706**	**53 272**	**53 240**	**54 761**	**55 014**	**56 134**	**57 391**	**58 066**
90-93	**Arts, entertainment and recreation**	**21 511**	**22 213**	**22 532**	**23 514**	**24 102**	**24 537**	**25 608**	**25 853**
94-96	**Other service activities**	**26 463**	**27 013**	**26 725**	**27 257**	**26 974**	**27 747**	**28 098**	**28 610**
97-98	**Activities of households as employers and for own use**	**4 733**	**4 047**	**3 983**	**3 990**	**3 938**	**3 850**	**3 685**	**3 602**
05-39	**INDUSTRY INCLUDING ENERGY**	**261 725**	**256 636**	**241 546**	**243 780**	**254 065**	**258 467**	**263 767**	**264 201**
45-99	**TOTAL SERVICES**	**1 347 443**	**1 394 591**	**1 375 751**	**1 415 863**	**1 448 659**	**1 470 460**	**1 490 501**	**1 509 202**
45-82	**BUSINESS SECTOR SERVICES**	**924 771**	**957 871**	**926 727**	**955 400**	**976 746**	**987 973**	**997 487**	**1 007 719**
45-82x	**BUSINESS SECTOR SERVICES excluding real estate**	**694 963**	**718 826**	**697 448**	**724 917**	**740 975**	**747 257**	**754 403**	**761 461**
05-82x	**NON-AGRICULTURE BUSINESS SECTOR excluding real estate**	..	..	..	..	..	..	..	..

.. Not available

Note: Detailed metadata at: http://metalinks.oecd.org/stan/20170410/1c43.

Information on data for Israel: http://oe.cd/israel-disclaimer.

Disclaimer: http://oe.cd/disclaimer

Table 3. Value added, volumes

ISIC Rev. 4

Million 2010 EUR

		2007	2008	2009	2010	2011	2012	2013	2014
	TOTAL	**1 810 863**	**1 818 946**	**1 769 818**	**1 800 982**	**1 839 021**	**1 846 727**	**1 858 169**	**1 873 440**
01-03	**AGRICULTURE, FORESTRY AND FISHING**	**29 925**	**31 238**	**33 209**	**32 092**	**33 342**	**30 467**	**29 884**	**33 837**
05-09	**MINING AND QUARRYING**	**2 818**	**2 613**	**2 364**	**2 297**	**2 284**	**2 146**	**1 944**	**1 908**
10-33	**MANUFACTURING**	**216 868**	**209 970**	**197 772**	**202 620**	**210 602**	**209 754**	**210 060**	**209 568**
10-12	Food products, beverages and tobacco	40 263	36 945	37 321	39 079	40 700	40 120	40 109	40 423
13-14	Textiles and wearing apparel	4 529	4 319	3 518	3 358	3 851	3 794	3 656	3 697
15	Leather and related products	1 641	1 615	1 291	1 279	1 442	1 545	1 375	1 386
16	Wood, wood and cork products	2 650	2 920	2 732	2 652	2 887	2 769	2 871	2 857
17	Paper and paper products	4 018	3 896	4 264	4 036	4 188	4 372	4 278	4 264
18	Printing and reproduction of recorded media	4 321	4 488	4 213	4 336	4 666	4 655	4 678	4 741
19-23	Chemical, rubber, plastics, non-metallic products	51 237	48 897	46 305	44 886	47 922	47 462	48 111	50 060
20	Chemicals and chemical products	15 037	14 031	14 715	13 981	14 629	14 869	16 823	17 295
21	Pharmaceutical products	12 134	12 260	11 874	11 865	12 282	12 643	12 262	12 272
22-23	Rubber, plastic, non-metallic mineral products	20 803	20 312	17 962	17 448	19 501	18 729	17 803	17 672
24	Basic metals	5 015	4 963	6 469	5 874	5 858	5 529	6 423	6 223
25	Metal products, except machinery and equipment	21 826	21 172	18 290	19 588	19 777	19 562	20 001	19 710
26-28	Machinery and equipment	31 327	31 328	26 567	28 954	30 362	30 412	31 277	31 157
26	Computer, electronic and optical products	9 589	9 893	9 186	11 214	11 675	12 154	13 353	13 041
27	Electrical equipment	7 767	7 519	6 397	6 494	6 199	6 084	5 979	5 801
28	Machinery and equipment n.e.c.	14 537	14 345	11 129	11 246	12 488	12 206	12 106	12 443
29-30	Transport equipment	23 965	23 218	19 868	21 693	21 404	21 767	20 896	18 566
29	Motor vehicles, trailers and semi-trailers	13 593	12 417	9 354	10 755	11 308	9 964	8 690	8 819
30	Other transport equipment	10 611	10 971	10 506	10 938	10 096	11 711	12 014	9 595
31-33	Furniture; repair, installation of machinery and equipment	27 977	27 940	27 246	26 885	27 546	27 834	26 542	26 724
31-32	Furniture, other manufacturing	7 190	6 810	6 586	6 557	6 501	6 267	6 047	6 004
33	Repair and installation of machinery and equipment	20 763	21 128	20 663	20 329	21 044	21 571	20 498	20 725
35-39	**ELECTRICITY, GAS, WATER AND WASTE MANAGEMENT**	**44 721**	**42 114**	**39 082**	**38 863**	**37 566**	**39 757**	**41 983**	**41 606**
35	Electricity, gas, steam and air conditioning supply	31 924	29 548	26 185	25 525	24 386	26 924	29 008	28 780
36-39	Water supply; sewerage, waste, remediation activities	12 991	12 692	12 867	13 338	13 179	12 761	12 867	12 716
41-43	**CONSTRUCTION**	**120 931**	**118 978**	**111 849**	**109 247**	**107 098**	**101 453**	**101 913**	**99 521**
45-56	Distribution; transportation, accommodation, food service	327 266	332 189	314 133	322 391	332 557	333 698	333 964	335 932
45-47	**Wholesale and retail trade; motor vehicle and motorcycle repairs**	**193 800**	**198 986**	**187 438**	**187 338**	**193 075**	**193 017**	**194 935**	**197 527**
49-53	**Transportation and storage**	**84 837**	**84 492**	**79 073**	**85 686**	**87 501**	**88 944**	**86 902**	**86 218**
55-56	**Accommodation and food service activities**	**48 591**	**48 671**	**47 637**	**49 366**	**51 982**	**51 761**	**52 096**	**52 170**
58-63	**Information and communication**	**90 433**	**93 477**	**89 587**	**93 018**	**98 787**	**103 102**	**102 576**	**105 315**
58-60	Publishing, audiovisual and broadcasting activities	23 254	22 921	21 116	21 961	23 165	22 351	21 959	22 258
61	Telecommunications	28 658	29 400	28 624	29 736	33 408	36 827	36 959	38 030
62-63	IT and other information services	38 721	41 246	39 848	41 321	42 213	44 195	44 024	45 442
64-66	**Financial and insurance activities**	**75 561**	**76 494**	**81 450**	**81 796**	**87 107**	**88 928**	**88 943**	**90 537**
68	**Real estate activities**	**225 340**	**224 997**	**226 774**	**230 483**	**229 181**	**232 605**	**236 396**	**238 741**
69-82	**Professional, scientific, technical, admin., support activities**	**232 739**	**236 628**	**219 311**	**227 712**	**235 316**	**234 462**	**235 252**	**237 425**
69-75	Professional, scientific and technical activities	126 478	129 565	125 197	131 285	135 898	138 846	140 898	142 489
69-71	Legal, accounting activities; mgt consultancy; engineering	85 039	86 533	82 007	86 652	89 588	91 182	92 395	93 565
73-75	Advertising, market research; other prof., scientific, tech.	13 902	14 095	13 824	14 453	15 427	16 036	15 843	15 896
77-82	Administrative and support service activities	106 636	107 393	94 146	96 427	99 418	95 633	94 436	95 038
84-88	**Public administration, defence; social security; education; health**	**392 688**	**396 818**	**401 906**	**405 702**	**411 324**	**416 996**	**421 553**	**425 934**
84	**Public administration, defence; compulsory social security**	**142 714**	**142 882**	**146 398**	**147 173**	**147 735**	**149 243**	**150 744**	**151 800**
85	**Education**	**100 303**	**99 422**	**97 855**	**97 706**	**98 316**	**99 598**	**100 021**	**101 106**
86-88	**Human health and social work activities**	**149 953**	**154 639**	**157 672**	**160 823**	**165 273**	**168 162**	**170 795**	**173 039**
90-99	**Arts, entertainment, household goods repairs, other**	**51 783**	**53 408**	**53 182**	**54 761**	**53 856**	**53 759**	**53 770**	**53 736**
90-93	**Arts, entertainment and recreation**	**21 634**	**22 544**	**22 799**	**23 514**	**23 466**	**23 310**	**23 754**	**23 796**
94-96	**Other service activities**	**26 264**	**26 864**	**26 406**	**27 257**	**26 511**	**26 704**	**26 439**	**26 471**
97-98	**Activities of households as employers and for own use**	**3 874**	**3 994**	**3 977**	**3 990**	**3 879**	**3 746**	**3 570**	**3 458**
05-39	**INDUSTRY INCLUDING ENERGY**	**264 054**	**254 544**	**239 157**	**243 780**	**250 452**	**251 861**	**254 354**	**253 429**
45-99	**TOTAL SERVICES**	**1 396 274**	**1 414 469**	**1 386 031**	**1 415 863**	**1 448 128**	**1 463 320**	**1 472 477**	**1 487 413**
45-82	**BUSINESS SECTOR SERVICES**	**951 571**	**963 933**	**930 997**	**955 400**	**982 948**	**992 556**	**997 108**	**1 007 732**
45-82x	**BUSINESS SECTOR SERVICES excluding real estate**	**726 873**	**739 805**	**704 177**	**724 917**	**753 767**	**759 897**	**760 514**	**768 797**
05-82x	**NON-AGRICULTURE BUSINESS SECTOR excluding real estate**	..	..	..	..	..	..	..	..

.. Not available

Note: Detailed metadata at: http://metalinks.oecd.org/stan/20170410/1c43.

Information on data for Israel: http://oe.cd/israel-disclaimer.

Disclaimer: http://oe.cd/disclaimer

FRANCE

Table 4. Gross fixed capital formation, current prices

ISIC Rev. 4

Million EUR

		2007	2008	2009	2010	2011	2012	2013	2014
	TOTAL	**450 059**	**470 123**	**427 320**	**441 067**	**461 566**	**469 104**	**466 666**	**465 902**
01-03	**AGRICULTURE, FORESTRY AND FISHING**	**11 401**	**12 302**	**10 907**	**10 676**	**12 073**	**13 210**	**12 935**	**12 004**
05-09	**MINING AND QUARRYING**	**985**	**862**	**701**	**1 235**	**782**	**1 020**	**847**	**873**
10-33	**MANUFACTURING**	**56 040**	**56 947**	**48 862**	**50 351**	**54 031**	**54 230**	**54 424**	**55 529**
10-12	Food products, beverages and tobacco	5 813	6 048	5 244	4 999	5 008	5 044	5 385	5 462
13-14	Textiles and wearing apparel	..	..	..	..	..	..	..	..
15	Leather and related products	..	..	..	..	..	..	..	..
16	Wood, wood and cork products	..	..	..	..	..	..	..	..
17	Paper and paper products	..	..	..	..	..	..	..	..
18	Printing and reproduction of recorded media	..	..	..	..	..	..	..	..
19-23	Chemical, rubber, plastics, non-metallic products	12 484	13 222	11 387	12 145	14 147	13 334	13 552	13 785
20	Chemicals and chemical products	4 055	4 353	3 511	4 239	5 401	4 733	5 240	5 308
21	Pharmaceutical products	4 294	4 685	4 547	4 450	4 450	4 222	4 316	4 387
22-23	Rubber, plastic, non-metallic mineral products	3 565	3 507	2 903	3 008	3 799	3 379	3 323	3 414
24	Basic metals	156	163	93	114	129	120	112	115
25	Metal products, except machinery and equipment	5 647	5 549	4 041	4 588	4 792	4 961	4 748	4 881
26-28	Machinery and equipment	12 535	12 610	11 143	11 448	12 161	12 333	12 467	12 694
26	Computer, electronic and optical products	8 383	8 266	7 414	7 794	7 932	8 107	8 221	8 395
27	Electrical equipment	1 645	1 721	1 622	1 590	1 681	1 757	1 822	1 837
28	Machinery and equipment n.e.c.	2 507	2 624	2 107	2 063	2 548	2 469	2 425	2 463
29-30	Transport equipment	13 030	12 880	11 304	11 096	11 592	12 355	12 033	12 333
29	Motor vehicles, trailers and semi-trailers	10 447	10 152	7 696	6 998	8 492	8 714	8 470	8 993
30	Other transport equipment	2 583	2 728	3 608	4 098	3 101	3 641	3 563	3 340
31-33	Furniture; repair, installation of machinery and equipment	3 343	3 492	3 405	3 382	3 680	3 665	3 909	3 984
31-32	Furniture, other manufacturing	652	682	599	624	602	622	633	639
33	Repair and installation of machinery and equipment	2 691	2 809	2 806	2 757	3 078	3 042	3 276	3 345
35-39	**ELECTRICITY, GAS, WATER AND WASTE MANAGEMENT**	**17 701**	**18 202**	**17 113**	**20 634**	**20 857**	**20 824**	**20 871**	**21 299**
35	Electricity, gas, steam and air conditioning supply	11 505	11 961	11 085	13 779	14 749	14 835	14 677	15 195
36-39	Water supply; sewerage, waste, remediation activities	6 196	6 241	6 028	6 854	6 108	5 989	6 194	6 104
41-43	**CONSTRUCTION**	**9 330**	**9 464**	**7 613**	**7 287**	**8 500**	**7 831**	**7 155**	**7 333**
45-56	Distribution; transportation, accommodation, food service	40 584	42 614	36 265	37 800	40 506	41 631	43 601	44 284
45-47	**Wholesale and retail trade; motor vehicle and motorcycle repairs**	**16 438**	**17 373**	**15 163**	**15 162**	**15 559**	**16 340**	**16 550**	**16 866**
49-53	**Transportation and storage**	**19 245**	**20 169**	**16 657**	**18 036**	**20 466**	**20 238**	**21 466**	**21 902**
55-56	**Accommodation and food service activities**	**4 900**	**5 072**	**4 446**	**4 602**	**4 481**	**5 053**	**5 585**	**5 516**
58-63	**Information and communication**	**23 237**	**25 207**	**24 010**	**25 141**	**26 351**	**27 410**	**28 187**	**28 856**
58-60	Publishing, audiovisual and broadcasting activities	7 960	8 438	8 036	8 070	8 690	8 982	9 102	9 247
61	Telecommunications	6 328	6 700	6 283	6 640	6 822	6 999	7 421	7 598
62-63	IT and other information services	8 949	10 069	9 692	10 430	10 838	11 430	11 665	12 011
64-66	**Financial and insurance activities**	**12 879**	**14 332**	**12 567**	**11 629**	**13 760**	**15 933**	**13 115**	**15 581**
68	**Real estate activities**	**159 365**	**166 373**	**149 613**	**154 112**	**160 112**	**157 641**	**156 098**	**153 985**
69-82	**Professional, scientific, technical, admin., support activities**	**45 964**	**49 028**	**42 803**	**44 926**	**48 606**	**49 426**	**49 606**	**50 420**
69-75	Professional, scientific and technical activities	27 490	29 400	28 790	30 196	32 637	32 693	33 710	33 880
69-71	Legal, accounting activities; mgt consultancy; engineering	11 589	12 620	11 337	11 823	12 811	13 948	14 520	14 988
73-75	Advertising, market research; other prof., scientific, tech.	1 880	1 981	1 626	1 690	2 195	1 857	1 868	1 875
77-82	Administrative and support service activities	18 474	19 628	14 013	14 729	15 968	16 733	15 896	16 540
84-88	**Public administration, defence; social security; education; health**	**63 084**	**65 100**	**67 314**	**67 892**	**66 204**	**69 258**	**68 271**	**64 911**
84	**Public administration, defence; compulsory social security**	**39 691**	**40 527**	**42 376**	**42 165**	**39 167**	**42 193**	**42 354**	**38 965**
85	**Education**	**10 620**	**10 818**	**11 261**	**11 224**	**10 820**	**10 778**	**10 554**	**10 140**
86-88	**Human health and social work activities**	**12 773**	**13 755**	**13 677**	**14 503**	**16 216**	**16 287**	**15 362**	**15 806**
90-99	**Arts, entertainment, household goods repairs, other**	**9 490**	**9 691**	**9 552**	**9 384**	**9 785**	**10 691**	**11 556**	**10 827**
90-93	**Arts, entertainment and recreation**	**7 279**	**7 396**	**7 466**	**7 276**	**7 637**	**8 466**	**9 283**	**8 492**
94-96	**Other service activities**	**2 211**	**2 295**	**2 086**	**2 109**	**2 148**	**2 225**	**2 273**	**2 334**
97-98	**Activities of households as employers and for own use**	**0**	**0**	**0**	**0**	**0**	**0**	**0**	**0**
05-39	**INDUSTRY INCLUDING ENERGY**	**74 725**	**76 010**	**66 676**	**72 220**	**75 670**	**76 074**	**76 141**	**77 701**
45-99	**TOTAL SERVICES**	**354 602**	**372 346**	**342 124**	**350 884**	**365 324**	**371 989**	**370 434**	**368 864**
45-82	**BUSINESS SECTOR SERVICES**	**282 028**	**297 555**	**265 258**	**273 607**	**289 335**	**292 040**	**290 608**	**293 126**
45-82x	**BUSINESS SECTOR SERVICES excluding real estate**	**122 663**	**131 182**	**115 645**	**119 495**	**129 223**	**134 399**	**134 510**	**139 141**
05-82x	**NON-AGRICULTURE BUSINESS SECTOR excluding real estate**	..	..	..	..	..	..	..	..

.. Not available

Note: Detailed metadata at: http://metalinks.oecd.org/stan/20170410/1c43.
Information on data for Israel: http://oe.cd/israel-disclaimer.

Disclaimer: http://oe.cd/disclaimer

Table 5. Number of persons engaged, total employment

ISIC Rev. 4

Thousands

		2007	2008	2009	2010	2011	2012	2013	2014
	TOTAL	27 042	27 168	26 863	26 896	27 107	27 196	27 267	27 394
01-03	AGRICULTURE, FORESTRY AND FISHING	826	801	782	766	760	760	758	761
05-09	MINING AND QUARRYING	21	22	21	20	20	20	19	19
10-33	MANUFACTURING	3 113	3 075	2 933	2 804	2 778	2 760	2 736	2 710
10-12	Food products, beverages and tobacco	637	634	623	619	626	629	632	634
13-14	Textiles and wearing apparel	124	116	102	94	93	90	88	87
15	Leather and related products	26	26	23	23	23	23	23	23
16	Wood, wood and cork products	76	76	73	70	70	68	68	66
17	Paper and paper products	76	74	67	65	65	63	62	61
18	Printing and reproduction of recorded media	101	97	91	86	82	78	77	74
19-23	Chemical, rubber, plastics, non-metallic products	523	516	477	454	454	450	444	438
20	Chemicals and chemical products	128	126	120	115	119	120	119	119
21	Pharmaceutical products	56	56	53	50	46	46	47	47
22-23	Rubber, plastic, non-metallic mineral products	328	325	295	280	280	275	269	264
24	Basic metals	101	98	90	85	88	87	85	84
25	Metal products, except machinery and equipment	353	351	346	324	320	318	319	319
26-28	Machinery and equipment	407	405	368	347	335	334	327	320
26	Computer, electronic and optical products	113	111	97	94	87	83	83	83
27	Electrical equipment	93	94	89	87	85	85	84	82
28	Machinery and equipment n.e.c.	200	201	182	165	163	166	161	155
29-30	Transport equipment	251	244	228	215	205	206	204	200
29	Motor vehicles, trailers and semi-trailers	169	162	150	139	131	128	126	122
30	Other transport equipment	82	82	78	76	74	78	78	78
31-33	Furniture; repair, installation of machinery and equipment	439	438	444	420	419	414	406	404
31-32	Furniture, other manufacturing	158	156	149	138	136	132	127	126
33	Repair and installation of machinery and equipment	281	282	295	282	283	282	279	278
35-39	ELECTRICITY, GAS, WATER AND WASTE MANAGEMENT	270	265	279	287	288	291	296	297
35	Electricity, gas, steam and air conditioning supply	131	126	133	133	133	135	137	138
36-39	Water supply; sewerage, waste, remediation activities	139	139	146	154	155	156	159	159
41-43	CONSTRUCTION	1 834	1 886	1 892	1 867	1 866	1 858	1 856	1 831
45-56	Distribution; transportation, accommodation, food service	6 103	6 144	6 093	6 142	6 183	6 224	6 182	6 194
45-47	Wholesale and retail trade; motor vehicle and motorcycle repairs	3 651	3 667	3 658	3 672	3 672	3 704	3 671	3 677
49-53	Transportation and storage	1 393	1 407	1 365	1 363	1 383	1 376	1 368	1 364
55-56	Accommodation and food service activities	1 059	1 069	1 070	1 107	1 129	1 144	1 144	1 153
58-63	Information and communication	783	800	791	789	798	816	824	827
58-60	Publishing, audiovisual and broadcasting activities	213	217	215	210	213	212	213	214
61	Telecommunications	152	148	146	140	136	139	135	130
62-63	IT and other information services	418	435	429	440	449	466	475	482
64-66	Financial and insurance activities	766	762	768	763	775	781	781	785
68	Real estate activities	381	381	351	349	357	356	357	354
69-82	Professional, scientific, technical, admin., support activities	3 762	3 790	3 636	3 720	3 883	3 905	3 928	3 983
69-75	Professional, scientific and technical activities	1 713	1 746	1 771	1 762	1 843	1 888	1 917	1 942
69-71	Legal, accounting activities; mgt consultancy; engineering	1 023	1 051	1 067	1 062	1 122	1 154	1 178	1 200
73-75	Advertising, market research; other prof., scientific, tech.	272	274	261	262	278	288	287	291
77-82	Administrative and support service activities	2 049	2 043	1 865	1 958	2 040	2 017	2 011	2 041
84-88	Public administration, defence; social security; education; health	7 814	7 847	7 884	7 916	7 912	7 928	8 017	8 106
84	Public administration, defence; compulsory social security	2 504	2 483	2 464	2 425	2 387	2 375	2 396	2 404
85	Education	1 870	1 876	1 868	1 882	1 849	1 835	1 845	1 874
86-88	Human health and social work activities	3 440	3 487	3 552	3 608	3 676	3 719	3 776	3 828
90-99	Arts, entertainment, household goods repairs, other	1 369	1 395	1 434	1 473	1 486	1 496	1 514	1 526
90-93	Arts, entertainment and recreation	522	532	545	566	570	570	584	595
94-96	Other service activities	679	690	712	731	749	764	777	785
97-98	Activities of households as employers and for own use	169	173	177	176	168	163	153	146
05-39	INDUSTRY INCLUDING ENERGY	3 404	3 361	3 233	3 111	3 086	3 071	3 050	3 026
45-99	TOTAL SERVICES	20 978	21 119	20 957	21 152	21 394	21 507	21 603	21 776
45-82	BUSINESS SECTOR SERVICES	11 794	11 877	11 639	11 763	11 996	12 082	12 073	12 144
45-82x	BUSINESS SECTOR SERVICES excluding real estate	11 414	11 496	11 288	11 414	11 639	11 726	11 716	11 790
05-82x	NON-AGRICULTURE BUSINESS SECTOR excluding real estate	..	..	..	..	..	..	..	..

.. Not available

Note: Detailed metadata at: http://metalinks.oecd.org/stan/20170410/1c43.

Information on data for Israel: http://oe.cd/israel-disclaimer.

Disclaimer: http://oe.cd/disclaimer

Table 6. Labour costs (compensation of employees), current prices

ISIC Rev. 4

Million EUR

		2007	2008	2009	2010	2011	2012	2013	2014
	TOTAL	**979 930**	**1 010 192**	**1 013 013**	**1 040 212**	**1 068 929**	**1 092 356**	**1 107 702**	**1 122 328**
01-03	**AGRICULTURE, FORESTRY AND FISHING**	**8 295**	**8 298**	**8 136**	**8 439**	**8 600**	**9 061**	**9 533**	**9 750**
05-09	**MINING AND QUARRYING**	**948**	**968**	**938**	**930**	**952**	**967**	**967**	**965**
10-33	**MANUFACTURING**	**131 889**	**133 920**	**128 695**	**129 494**	**131 740**	**133 378**	**133 907**	**134 182**
10-12	Food products, beverages and tobacco	19 637	19 991	20 159	20 595	21 347	22 073	22 508	22 822
13-14	Textiles and wearing apparel	3 348	3 213	2 756	2 612	2 611	2 580	2 534	2 508
15	Leather and related products	812	818	726	768	808	837	832	820
16	Wood, wood and cork products	2 096	2 405	2 409	2 319	2 354	2 314	2 318	2 258
17	Paper and paper products	3 449	3 293	3 047	3 044	3 105	3 168	3 098	3 061
18	Printing and reproduction of recorded media	3 797	3 652	3 385	3 279	3 146	3 018	2 983	2 871
19-23	Chemical, rubber, plastics, non-metallic products	26 530	26 805	24 905	25 112	26 026	26 126	26 249	26 293
20	Chemicals and chemical products	8 072	8 233	7 819	8 088	8 472	8 652	8 837	8 897
21	Pharmaceutical products	3 891	3 816	3 783	3 826	3 984	4 002	4 116	4 170
22-23	Rubber, plastic, non-metallic mineral products	13 728	13 838	12 537	12 397	12 775	12 652	12 484	12 390
24	Basic metals	4 516	5 032	4 322	4 315	4 483	4 425	4 407	4 361
25	Metal products, except machinery and equipment	14 011	13 834	14 009	14 156	14 180	14 157	14 336	14 330
26-28	Machinery and equipment	21 238	21 709	19 674	19 396	19 527	19 702	19 693	19 526
26	Computer, electronic and optical products	7 316	7 376	6 353	6 550	6 353	6 236	6 339	6 422
27	Electrical equipment	4 947	5 078	4 986	4 923	4 903	4 885	4 862	4 847
28	Machinery and equipment n.e.c.	8 975	9 255	8 335	7 923	8 271	8 581	8 492	8 257
29-30	Transport equipment	13 529	13 791	13 117	13 355	13 256	13 635	13 766	13 756
29	Motor vehicles, trailers and semi-trailers	8 188	8 166	7 423	7 507	7 355	7 194	7 204	7 079
30	Other transport equipment	5 341	5 625	5 694	5 848	5 901	6 441	6 562	6 677
31-33	Furniture; repair, installation of machinery and equipment	18 925	19 379	20 186	20 543	20 897	21 343	21 183	21 576
31-32	Furniture, other manufacturing	4 966	4 850	4 672	4 608	4 577	4 581	4 573	4 568
33	Repair and installation of machinery and equipment	13 959	14 529	15 514	15 935	16 320	16 762	16 610	17 008
35-39	**ELECTRICITY, GAS, WATER AND WASTE MANAGEMENT**	**15 225**	**15 831**	**16 475**	**17 134**	**17 663**	**18 546**	**19 045**	**19 259**
35	Electricity, gas, steam and air conditioning supply	9 074	9 518	10 196	10 452	10 761	11 468	11 776	11 946
36-39	Water supply; sewerage, waste, remediation activities	6 151	6 312	6 279	6 682	6 902	7 078	7 269	7 313
41-43	**CONSTRUCTION**	**63 510**	**66 902**	**67 327**	**67 353**	**68 719**	**69 022**	**69 966**	**69 069**
45-56	Distribution; transportation, accommodation, food service	198 601	204 933	204 527	210 438	214 948	219 929	221 202	223 262
45-47	**Wholesale and retail trade; motor vehicle and motorcycle repairs**	**116 834**	**120 586**	**120 875**	**123 880**	**126 089**	**128 953**	**129 493**	**131 115**
49-53	**Transportation and storage**	**55 806**	**57 475**	**56 127**	**57 211**	**58 190**	**59 451**	**59 715**	**60 058**
55-56	**Accommodation and food service activities**	**25 961**	**26 872**	**27 525**	**29 347**	**30 669**	**31 525**	**31 994**	**32 089**
58-63	**Information and communication**	**47 590**	**50 042**	**49 344**	**50 834**	**52 387**	**54 133**	**54 825**	**56 051**
58-60	Publishing, audiovisual and broadcasting activities	13 072	13 165	13 159	13 114	13 415	13 727	13 831	14 129
61	Telecommunications	8 511	8 427	8 423	8 687	8 749	8 951	8 962	9 049
62-63	IT and other information services	26 007	28 450	27 762	29 033	30 223	31 455	32 032	32 873
64-66	**Financial and insurance activities**	**43 566**	**43 182**	**45 709**	**46 839**	**47 309**	**49 140**	**48 757**	**49 399**
68	**Real estate activities**	**14 821**	**15 094**	**13 890**	**14 174**	**14 813**	**14 877**	**15 133**	**15 241**
69-82	**Professional, scientific, technical, admin., support activities**	**139 793**	**145 595**	**142 742**	**150 035**	**159 173**	**162 803**	**166 040**	**169 575**
69-75	Professional, scientific and technical activities	79 428	83 718	85 987	88 875	94 142	98 039	100 187	102 204
69-71	Legal, accounting activities; mgt consultancy; engineering	55 465	59 036	60 429	62 584	66 846	70 050	71 623	73 043
73-75	Advertising, market research; other prof., scientific, tech.	8 843	9 138	8 817	8 930	9 443	9 799	9 693	9 920
77-82	Administrative and support service activities	60 364	61 877	56 755	61 160	65 031	64 764	65 853	67 371
84-88	**Public administration, defence; social security; education; health**	**278 550**	**286 933**	**295 923**	**303 613**	**311 000**	**318 225**	**325 114**	**331 817**
84	**Public administration, defence; compulsory social security**	**100 899**	**101 965**	**105 982**	**108 027**	**110 016**	**112 530**	**114 708**	**116 059**
85	**Education**	**79 043**	**82 103**	**83 908**	**85 890**	**86 849**	**87 859**	**88 930**	**91 077**
86-88	**Human health and social work activities**	**98 608**	**102 865**	**106 033**	**109 696**	**114 135**	**117 836**	**121 476**	**124 681**
90-99	**Arts, entertainment, household goods repairs, other**	**37 141**	**38 495**	**39 307**	**40 929**	**41 625**	**42 275**	**43 213**	**43 758**
90-93	**Arts, entertainment and recreation**	**15 762**	**16 472**	**16 815**	**17 846**	**18 100**	**18 342**	**19 005**	**19 536**
94-96	**Other service activities**	**16 650**	**16 988**	**17 405**	**17 921**	**18 346**	**18 770**	**19 182**	**19 309**
97-98	**Activities of households as employers and for own use**	**4 729**	**5 036**	**5 087**	**5 162**	**5 179**	**5 163**	**5 026**	**4 913**
05-39	**INDUSTRY INCLUDING ENERGY**	**148 062**	**150 718**	**146 108**	**147 558**	**150 355**	**152 891**	**153 919**	**154 406**
45-99	**TOTAL SERVICES**	**760 063**	**784 274**	**791 442**	**816 862**	**841 255**	**861 382**	**874 284**	**889 102**
45-82	**BUSINESS SECTOR SERVICES**	**444 371**	**458 846**	**456 212**	**472 320**	**488 630**	**500 882**	**505 957**	**513 527**
45-82x	**BUSINESS SECTOR SERVICES excluding real estate**	**429 550**	**443 752**	**442 322**	**458 146**	**473 817**	**486 005**	**490 824**	**498 287**
05-82x	**NON-AGRICULTURE BUSINESS SECTOR excluding real estate**	..	..	..	..	..	..	..	..

.. Not available

Note: Detailed metadata at: http://metalinks.oecd.org/stan/20170410/1c43.

Information on data for Israel: http://oe.cd/israel-disclaimer.

Disclaimer: http://oe.cd/disclaimer

GERMANY

Table 1. Production (gross output), current prices

ISIC Rev. 4

Million EUR

		2007	2008	2009	2010	2011	2012	2013	2014
	TOTAL	**4 652 134**	**4 811 296**	**4 473 146**	**4 776 123**	**5 111 952**	**5 144 769**	**5 201 446**	**5 351 953**
01-03	**AGRICULTURE, FORESTRY AND FISHING**	**47 140**	**50 745**	**44 135**	**45 619**	**52 039**	**53 627**	**56 665**	**56 960**
05-09	**MINING AND QUARRYING**	**13 579**	**13 707**	**11 568**	**12 531**	**12 895**	**12 621**	**11 852**	**11 928**
10-33	**MANUFACTURING**	**1 663 494**	**1 692 561**	**1 377 481**	**1 566 305**	**1 758 293**	**1 756 400**	**1 750 900**	**1 790 981**
10-12	Food products, beverages and tobacco	155 691	164 769	152 541	159 167	171 171	176 784	182 043	180 977
13-14	Textiles and wearing apparel	21 982	20 912	17 299	19 110	21 265	19 806	19 601	20 742
15	Leather and related products	3 224	2 701	2 348	2 513	2 843	2 452	2 503	2 758
16	Wood, wood and cork products	24 241	21 341	19 377	21 526	22 704	22 929	23 706	24 366
17	Paper and paper products	36 448	37 447	32 871	37 153	39 512	38 167	37 730	37 509
18	Printing and reproduction of recorded media	23 423	22 873	21 685	21 867	22 292	21 463	20 185	19 245
19-23	Chemical, rubber, plastics, non-metallic products	330 845	351 753	290 015	331 025	370 150	373 458	377 594	373 565
20	Chemicals and chemical products	119 998	123 740	106 541	125 418	136 218	133 211	135 912	136 038
21	Pharmaceutical products	41 458	42 280	38 882	38 391	40 179	42 371	45 113	45 978
22-23	Rubber, plastic, non-metallic mineral products	108 709	109 173	94 790	104 799	118 286	116 397	118 615	122 072
24	Basic metals	109 871	112 001	72 212	91 190	111 995	107 347	99 072	97 439
25	Metal products, except machinery and equipment	120 007	121 799	95 356	109 478	126 078	122 688	124 116	126 329
26-28	Machinery and equipment	406 835	414 830	324 718	363 923	411 690	408 110	407 556	418 666
26	Computer, electronic and optical products	91 144	81 541	59 657	68 109	74 130	70 745	71 912	73 034
27	Electrical equipment	94 953	99 672	85 684	95 728	106 808	104 185	101 683	104 266
28	Machinery and equipment n.e.c.	220 738	233 617	179 377	200 086	230 752	233 180	233 961	241 366
29-30	Transport equipment	346 526	338 524	271 267	327 265	369 848	375 225	368 896	399 203
29	Motor vehicles, trailers and semi-trailers	315 542	305 590	239 725	293 051	334 772	337 971	329 356	357 033
30	Other transport equipment	30 984	32 934	31 542	34 214	35 076	37 254	39 540	42 170
31-33	Furniture; repair, installation of machinery and equipment	84 401	83 611	77 792	82 088	88 745	87 971	87 898	90 182
31-32	Furniture, other manufacturing	47 581	48 263	42 240	47 092	51 333	51 137	49 591	50 426
33	Repair and installation of machinery and equipment	36 820	35 348	35 552	34 996	37 412	36 834	38 307	39 756
35-39	**ELECTRICITY, GAS, WATER AND WASTE MANAGEMENT**	**159 452**	**172 863**	**175 286**	**186 979**	**191 243**	**194 966**	**188 763**	**187 514**
35	Electricity, gas, steam and air conditioning supply	112 427	124 571	129 210	137 077	135 609	138 683	132 487	125 799
36-39	Water supply; sewerage, waste, remediation activities	47 025	48 292	46 076	49 902	55 634	56 283	56 276	61 715
41-43	**CONSTRUCTION**	**207 877**	**221 117**	**221 003**	**231 376**	**251 671**	**260 057**	**264 450**	**274 340**
45-56	Distribution; transportation, accommodation, food service	711 566	749 263	713 434	751 310	790 701	782 805	793 632	831 306
45-47	**Wholesale and retail trade; motor vehicle and motorcycle repairs**	**395 016**	**414 793**	**401 014**	**413 803**	**432 673**	**414 932**	**418 463**	**447 551**
49-53	**Transportation and storage**	**250 933**	**267 684**	**245 726**	**266 034**	**283 028**	**289 890**	**295 294**	**300 269**
55-56	**Accommodation and food service activities**	**65 617**	**66 786**	**66 694**	**71 473**	**75 000**	**77 983**	**79 875**	**83 486**
58-63	**Information and communication**	**208 762**	**221 231**	**219 026**	**215 078**	**226 089**	**228 556**	**236 375**	**240 856**
58-60	Publishing, audiovisual and broadcasting activities	55 724	58 675	58 231	58 990	62 098	61 881	62 388	60 750
61	Telecommunications	78 103	80 762	80 532	71 344	68 859	63 333	61 777	62 126
62-63	IT and other information services	74 935	81 794	80 263	84 744	95 132	103 342	112 210	117 980
64-66	**Financial and insurance activities**	**226 137**	**222 255**	**235 610**	**240 275**	**239 710**	**249 167**	**245 742**	**252 050**
68	**Real estate activities**	**340 563**	**351 418**	**361 249**	**361 146**	**375 889**	**367 576**	**374 987**	**378 826**
69-82	**Professional, scientific, technical, admin., support activities**	**417 973**	**433 204**	**400 330**	**427 790**	**448 877**	**457 541**	**467 012**	**488 002**
69-75	Professional, scientific and technical activities	256 691	265 142	239 423	249 401	259 279	262 404	264 135	273 276
69-71	Legal, accounting activities; mgt consultancy; engineering	189 343	197 151	174 483	182 346	190 269	191 002	189 270	192 788
73-75	Advertising, market research; other prof., scientific, tech.	44 870	43 808	40 195	41 529	42 808	43 563	45 054	48 446
77-82	Administrative and support service activities	161 282	168 062	160 907	178 389	189 598	195 137	202 877	214 726
84-88	**Public administration, defence; social security; education; health**	**521 600**	**544 454**	**575 048**	**596 499**	**620 152**	**636 334**	**662 030**	**686 038**
84	**Public administration, defence; compulsory social security**	**190 843**	**201 343**	**213 036**	**220 903**	**228 250**	**233 297**	**240 657**	**245 339**
85	**Education**	**119 092**	**122 654**	**127 751**	**132 623**	**138 241**	**141 649**	**147 940**	**153 606**
86-88	**Human health and social work activities**	**211 665**	**220 457**	**234 261**	**242 973**	**253 661**	**261 388**	**273 433**	**287 093**
90-99	**Arts, entertainment, household goods repairs, other**	**133 991**	**138 478**	**138 976**	**141 215**	**144 393**	**145 119**	**149 038**	**153 152**
90-93	**Arts, entertainment and recreation**	**45 222**	**46 917**	**47 662**	**49 349**	**51 719**	**52 553**	**55 410**	**57 755**
94-96	**Other service activities**	**82 110**	**84 911**	**84 502**	**85 299**	**85 859**	**85 693**	**86 381**	**88 107**
97-98	**Activities of households as employers and for own use**	**6 659**	**6 650**	**6 812**	**6 567**	**6 815**	**6 873**	**7 247**	**7 290**
05-39	**INDUSTRY INCLUDING ENERGY**	**1 836 525**	**1 879 131**	**1 564 335**	**1 765 815**	**1 962 431**	**1 963 987**	**1 951 515**	**1 990 423**
45-99	**TOTAL SERVICES**	**2 560 592**	**2 660 303**	**2 643 673**	**2 733 313**	**2 845 811**	**2 867 098**	**2 928 816**	**3 030 230**
45-82	**BUSINESS SECTOR SERVICES**	**1 905 001**	**1 977 371**	**1 929 649**	**1 995 599**	**2 081 266**	**2 085 645**	**2 117 748**	**2 191 040**
45-82x	**BUSINESS SECTOR SERVICES excluding real estate**	**1 564 438**	**1 625 953**	**1 568 400**	**1 634 453**	**1 705 377**	**1 718 069**	**1 742 761**	**1 812 214**
05-82x	**NON-AGRICULTURE BUSINESS SECTOR excluding real estate**	..	..	..	..	..	..	..	..

.. Not available

Note: Detailed metadata at: http://metalinks.oecd.org/stan/20170410/1c43.

Information on data for Israel: http://oe.cd/israel-disclaimer.

Disclaimer: http://oe.cd/disclaimer

GERMANY

Table 2. Value added, current prices

ISIC Rev. 4

Million EUR

		2007	2008	2009	2010	2011	2012	2013	2014
	TOTAL	**2 261 360**	**2 304 665**	**2 207 236**	**2 321 695**	**2 428 078**	**2 478 596**	**2 542 628**	**2 631 268**
01-03	**AGRICULTURE, FORESTRY AND FISHING**	**18 667**	**20 615**	**16 248**	**16 700**	**19 967**	**19 388**	**24 005**	**20 436**
05-09	**MINING AND QUARRYING**	**5 022**	**6 429**	**5 161**	**5 301**	**5 511**	**5 902**	**5 229**	**5 047**
10-33	**MANUFACTURING**	**530 125**	**518 726**	**439 843**	**515 175**	**556 004**	**563 279**	**572 186**	**604 487**
10-12	Food products, beverages and tobacco	37 491	36 485	36 591	38 110	38 317	39 601	40 933	41 954
13-14	Textiles and wearing apparel	6 890	6 536	5 402	6 119	6 620	6 499	6 537	7 023
15	Leather and related products	885	913	786	839	918	798	771	807
16	Wood, wood and cork products	6 851	6 075	5 269	6 177	6 437	6 156	6 300	6 380
17	Paper and paper products	10 520	9 996	9 587	9 598	9 768	10 410	10 374	10 808
18	Printing and reproduction of recorded media	9 450	9 106	8 054	8 432	8 284	8 372	8 007	7 631
19-23	Chemical, rubber, plastics, non-metallic products	102 057	102 240	93 441	105 042	106 995	107 667	110 297	114 656
20	Chemicals and chemical products	38 004	38 061	34 567	40 987	41 359	40 403	40 757	42 852
21	Pharmaceutical products	19 967	21 745	20 909	20 850	21 591	22 399	22 577	23 960
22-23	Rubber, plastic, non-metallic mineral products	39 304	38 924	34 286	37 702	40 578	40 857	42 236	44 146
24	Basic metals	26 037	25 546	17 873	17 759	20 708	21 422	20 789	21 096
25	Metal products, except machinery and equipment	46 729	47 610	37 425	44 754	49 849	50 261	51 688	53 250
26-28	Machinery and equipment	154 859	155 973	125 666	147 360	161 406	161 876	164 339	172 509
26	Computer, electronic and optical products	37 052	33 225	25 545	30 508	32 818	32 155	32 906	34 606
27	Electrical equipment	35 689	37 538	34 007	39 750	41 972	41 362	41 866	44 066
28	Machinery and equipment n.e.c.	82 118	85 210	66 114	77 102	86 616	88 359	89 567	93 837
29-30	Transport equipment	95 392	85 778	68 563	96 645	109 345	112 318	114 759	129 575
29	Motor vehicles, trailers and semi-trailers	84 705	74 777	58 332	84 515	96 918	99 259	101 811	115 412
30	Other transport equipment	10 687	11 001	10 231	12 130	12 427	13 059	12 948	14 163
31-33	Furniture; repair, installation of machinery and equipment	32 964	32 468	31 186	34 340	37 357	37 899	37 392	38 798
31-32	Furniture, other manufacturing	19 821	19 653	18 047	20 827	23 109	22 998	22 357	23 287
33	Repair and installation of machinery and equipment	13 143	12 815	13 139	13 513	14 248	14 901	15 035	15 511
35-39	**ELECTRICITY, GAS, WATER AND WASTE MANAGEMENT**	**68 012**	**76 452**	**77 483**	**79 963**	**74 169**	**80 930**	**76 773**	**75 609**
35	Electricity, gas, steam and air conditioning supply	45 527	52 756	54 731	56 033	48 269	54 594	50 221	47 175
36-39	Water supply; sewerage, waste, remediation activities	22 485	23 696	22 752	23 930	25 900	26 336	26 552	28 434
41-43	**CONSTRUCTION**	**87 270**	**91 249**	**91 295**	**99 843**	**106 503**	**110 962**	**113 247**	**118 196**
45-56	Distribution; transportation, accommodation, food service	370 022	380 401	373 250	370 497	386 990	386 919	395 395	413 879
45-47	**Wholesale and retail trade; motor vehicle and motorcycle repairs**	**231 296**	**239 129**	**236 901**	**229 376**	**241 204**	**235 648**	**237 987**	**256 251**
49-53	**Transportation and storage**	**105 434**	**108 258**	**104 714**	**107 850**	**110 327**	**113 648**	**120 293**	**117 950**
55-56	**Accommodation and food service activities**	**33 292**	**33 014**	**31 635**	**33 271**	**35 459**	**37 623**	**37 115**	**39 678**
58-63	**Information and communication**	**107 420**	**108 637**	**104 580**	**103 345**	**112 130**	**116 418**	**120 539**	**125 372**
58-60	Publishing, audiovisual and broadcasting activities	26 521	27 543	27 471	28 447	30 064	31 045	29 689	29 870
61	Telecommunications	34 675	33 770	31 065	27 472	27 159	26 396	25 023	26 115
62-63	IT and other information services	46 224	47 324	46 044	47 426	54 907	58 977	65 827	69 387
64-66	**Financial and insurance activities**	**103 606**	**94 885**	**104 790**	**106 292**	**101 652**	**108 418**	**109 293**	**109 951**
68	**Real estate activities**	**259 663**	**271 034**	**266 222**	**267 279**	**281 645**	**278 631**	**286 891**	**285 979**
69-82	**Professional, scientific, technical, admin., support activities**	**248 010**	**256 348**	**233 342**	**246 332**	**255 925**	**264 606**	**276 838**	**289 623**
69-75	Professional, scientific and technical activities	145 806	151 165	135 108	140 092	143 465	148 849	154 539	156 569
69-71	Legal, accounting activities; mgt consultancy; engineering	107 207	111 803	97 620	101 747	104 617	107 912	110 752	112 268
73-75	Advertising, market research; other prof., scientific, tech.	23 896	24 208	21 625	22 153	22 123	23 055	24 716	24 361
77-82	Administrative and support service activities	102 204	105 183	98 234	106 240	112 460	115 757	122 299	133 054
84-88	**Public administration, defence; social security; education; health**	**370 132**	**383 119**	**399 793**	**414 351**	**428 936**	**442 779**	**459 011**	**476 643**
84	**Public administration, defence; compulsory social security**	**133 569**	**138 001**	**143 324**	**146 718**	**149 800**	**153 127**	**157 302**	**161 333**
85	**Education**	**93 946**	**96 454**	**100 010**	**103 667**	**107 918**	**111 069**	**114 743**	**118 966**
86-88	**Human health and social work activities**	**142 617**	**148 664**	**156 459**	**163 966**	**171 218**	**178 583**	**186 966**	**196 344**
90-99	**Arts, entertainment, household goods repairs, other**	**93 411**	**96 770**	**95 229**	**96 617**	**98 646**	**100 364**	**103 221**	**106 046**
90-93	**Arts, entertainment and recreation**	**28 995**	**29 930**	**29 655**	**30 552**	**31 932**	**32 949**	**34 916**	**36 329**
94-96	**Other service activities**	**57 757**	**60 190**	**58 762**	**59 498**	**59 899**	**60 542**	**61 058**	**62 427**
97-98	**Activities of households as employers and for own use**	**6 659**	**6 650**	**6 812**	**6 567**	**6 815**	**6 873**	**7 247**	**7 290**
05-39	**INDUSTRY INCLUDING ENERGY**	**603 159**	**601 607**	**522 487**	**600 439**	**635 684**	**650 111**	**654 188**	**685 143**
45-99	**TOTAL SERVICES**	**1 552 264**	**1 591 194**	**1 577 206**	**1 604 713**	**1 665 924**	**1 698 135**	**1 751 188**	**1 807 493**
45-82	**BUSINESS SECTOR SERVICES**	**1 088 721**	**1 111 305**	**1 082 184**	**1 093 745**	**1 138 342**	**1 154 992**	**1 188 956**	**1 224 804**
45-82x	**BUSINESS SECTOR SERVICES excluding real estate**	**829 058**	**840 271**	**815 962**	**826 466**	**856 697**	**876 361**	**902 065**	**938 825**
05-82x	**NON-AGRICULTURE BUSINESS SECTOR excluding real estate**	..	..	..	..	..	..	..	..

.. Not available

Note: Detailed metadata at: http://metalinks.oecd.org/stan/20170410/1c43.

Information on data for Israel: http://oe.cd/israel-disclaimer.

Disclaimer: http://oe.cd/disclaimer

Table 3. Value added, volumes

ISIC Rev. 4

Million 2010 EUR

		2007	2008	2009	2010	2011	2012	2013	2014
	TOTAL	**2 344 758**	**2 372 607**	**2 227 058**	**2 321 695**	**2 404 436**	**2 418 381**	**2 430 642**	**2 467 352**
01-03	**AGRICULTURE, FORESTRY AND FISHING**	**19 010**	**22 831**	**22 084**	**16 700**	**14 977**	**14 850**	**15 438**	**13 505**
05-09	**MINING AND QUARRYING**	**5 330**	**5 647**	**5 336**	**5 301**	**4 877**	**4 748**	**4 160**	**4 196**
10-33	**MANUFACTURING**	**549 746**	**538 487**	**435 053**	**515 175**	**559 054**	**546 590**	**547 307**	**577 538**
10-12	Food products, beverages and tobacco	40 633	36 373	35 054	38 110	39 192	35 725	34 661	37 532
13-14	Textiles and wearing apparel	..	..	..	..	..	..	..	..
15	Leather and related products	..	..	..	..	..	..	..	..
16	Wood, wood and cork products	6 623	6 126	5 507	6 177	6 053	5 711	5 690	5 610
17	Paper and paper products	9 721	9 533	8 854	9 598	9 462	10 408	10 459	10 769
18	Printing and reproduction of recorded media	8 509	8 463	7 828	8 432	8 566	8 595	8 085	7 802
19-23	Chemical, rubber, plastics, non-metallic products	107 904	109 395	91 010	105 042	106 849	102 880	105 905	110 813
20	Chemicals and chemical products	41 054	40 367	33 318	40 987	40 330	38 070	38 232	40 646
21	Pharmaceutical products	21 256	22 886	20 929	20 850	22 232	22 727	22 758	23 334
22-23	Rubber, plastic, non-metallic mineral products	40 366	40 562	32 873	37 702	41 859	40 804	40 991	42 354
24	Basic metals	21 542	21 562	18 231	17 759	19 935	20 636	20 866	21 499
25	Metal products, except machinery and equipment	50 241	49 774	35 631	44 754	50 486	49 075	49 589	50 966
26-28	Machinery and equipment	160 502	163 104	125 980	147 360	164 024	160 524	158 907	164 908
26	Computer, electronic and optical products	30 216	31 658	25 532	30 508	36 152	36 810	37 788	40 177
27	Electrical equipment	38 877	39 437	34 080	39 750	41 657	39 760	39 272	40 891
28	Machinery and equipment n.e.c.	92 096	92 352	66 370	77 102	86 215	84 095	82 212	84 415
29-30	Transport equipment	100 163	92 334	69 286	96 645	109 992	109 608	111 647	125 198
29	Motor vehicles, trailers and semi-trailers	89 732	81 761	59 038	84 515	97 578	96 944	99 550	112 211
30	Other transport equipment	10 781	10 850	10 228	12 130	12 414	12 662	12 100	13 016
31-33	Furniture; repair, installation of machinery and equipment	37 030	34 791	31 274	34 340	36 944	36 319	34 606	35 130
31-32	Furniture, other manufacturing	22 219	21 000	18 127	20 827	22 718	21 985	20 779	21 247
33	Repair and installation of machinery and equipment	14 802	13 782	13 144	13 513	14 226	14 340	13 834	13 892
35-39	**ELECTRICITY, GAS, WATER AND WASTE MANAGEMENT**	**68 542**	**71 269**	**79 204**	**79 963**	**69 061**	**79 223**	**76 772**	**78 035**
35	Electricity, gas, steam and air conditioning supply	46 871	48 297	54 105	56 033	45 024	54 134	50 442	48 982
36-39	Water supply; sewerage, waste, remediation activities	21 869	23 152	25 271	23 930	24 037	25 101	26 264	28 951
41-43	**CONSTRUCTION**	**95 771**	**95 528**	**92 807**	**99 843**	**103 620**	**102 450**	**100 044**	**101 458**
45-56	Distribution; transportation, accommodation, food service	397 615	400 074	376 632	370 497	385 002	396 212	393 309	394 760
45-47	**Wholesale and retail trade; motor vehicle and motorcycle repairs**	**251 635**	**250 818**	**235 843**	**229 376**	**239 288**	**249 387**	**244 576**	**252 311**
49-53	**Transportation and storage**	**107 936**	**111 889**	**106 305**	**107 850**	**110 217**	**110 305**	**113 735**	**106 812**
55-56	**Accommodation and food service activities**	**38 382**	**37 435**	**34 476**	**33 271**	**35 497**	**36 498**	**34 730**	**35 903**
58-63	**Information and communication**	**98 248**	**104 197**	**103 130**	**103 345**	**114 823**	**119 654**	**124 167**	**130 149**
58-60	Publishing, audiovisual and broadcasting activities	29 212	29 648	28 634	28 447	29 995	30 438	28 524	28 436
61	Telecommunications	25 363	27 641	28 090	27 472	29 198	29 209	28 310	30 066
62-63	IT and other information services	44 190	47 053	46 339	47 426	55 630	59 950	67 223	71 662
64-66	**Financial and insurance activities**	**112 163**	**111 149**	**103 659**	**106 292**	**106 694**	**107 679**	**118 157**	**112 462**
68	**Real estate activities**	**259 422**	**265 001**	**270 605**	**267 279**	**276 636**	**271 482**	**276 166**	**271 945**
69-82	**Professional, scientific, technical, admin., support activities**	**258 941**	**264 369**	**237 087**	**246 332**	**252 075**	**255 032**	**256 281**	**262 477**
69-75	Professional, scientific and technical activities	152 437	155 825	137 715	140 092	141 535	144 063	143 073	141 531
69-71	Legal, accounting activities; mgt consultancy; engineering	112 581	115 739	99 820	101 747	102 920	104 141	101 140	99 652
73-75	Advertising, market research; other prof., scientific, tech.	24 698	24 732	21 967	22 153	22 281	23 073	24 312	23 899
77-82	Administrative and support service activities	106 523	108 565	99 393	106 240	110 540	110 972	113 195	120 931
84-88	**Public administration, defence; social security; education; health**	**389 512**	**400 297**	**407 067**	**414 351**	**421 022**	**423 892**	**424 265**	**427 089**
84	**Public administration, defence; compulsory social security**	**140 322**	**141 974**	**144 074**	**146 718**	**147 102**	**146 597**	**147 796**	**148 685**
85	**Education**	**104 283**	**104 421**	**104 166**	**103 667**	**104 064**	**104 389**	**102 516**	**102 424**
86-88	**Human health and social work activities**	**145 329**	**154 042**	**158 885**	**163 966**	**169 856**	**172 932**	**174 028**	**176 086**
90-99	**Arts, entertainment, household goods repairs, other**	**97 571**	**99 964**	**97 290**	**96 617**	**96 595**	**96 085**	**94 457**	**94 031**
90-93	**Arts, entertainment and recreation**	**30 233**	**30 737**	**30 137**	**30 552**	**31 449**	**31 826**	**31 603**	**31 739**
94-96	**Other service activities**	**60 487**	**62 390**	**60 271**	**59 498**	**58 447**	**57 732**	**56 363**	**55 920**
97-98	**Activities of households as employers and for own use**	**6 851**	**6 842**	**6 883**	**6 567**	**6 699**	**6 531**	**6 499**	**6 377**
05-39	**INDUSTRY INCLUDING ENERGY**	**620 425**	**612 348**	**519 235**	**600 439**	**632 992**	**631 371**	**628 947**	**660 590**
45-99	**TOTAL SERVICES**	**1 611 285**	**1 643 649**	**1 595 485**	**1 604 713**	**1 652 847**	**1 669 795**	**1 686 412**	**1 693 053**
45-82	**BUSINESS SECTOR SERVICES**	**1 123 818**	**1 143 058**	**1 091 096**	**1 093 745**	**1 135 230**	**1 149 869**	**1 167 997**	**1 172 228**
45-82x	**BUSINESS SECTOR SERVICES excluding real estate**	**865 770**	**879 402**	**820 534**	**826 466**	**858 594**	**878 564**	**892 000**	**900 595**
05-82x	**NON-AGRICULTURE BUSINESS SECTOR excluding real estate**	..	..	..	..	..	..	..	..

.. Not available

Note: Detailed metadata at: http://metalinks.oecd.org/stan/20170410/1c43.
Information on data for Israel: http://oe.cd/israel-disclaimer.

Disclaimer: http://oe.cd/disclaimer

GERMANY

Table 4. Gross fixed capital formation, current prices

ISIC Rev. 4

Million EUR

		2007	2008	2009	2010	2011	2012	2013	2014
	TOTAL	**520 690**	**537 285**	**487 053**	**516 920**	**564 510**	**571 294**	**574 049**	**603 741**
01-03	**AGRICULTURE, FORESTRY AND FISHING**	**9 375**	**10 656**	**7 822**	**8 075**	**8 935**	**9 319**	**9 547**	**9 541**
05-09	**MINING AND QUARRYING**	**1 607**	**1 589**	**1 631**	**1 523**	**1 225**	**1 296**	**1 271**	**1 548**
10-33	**MANUFACTURING**	**101 378**	**107 008**	**92 344**	**93 204**	**104 399**	**109 424**	**108 144**	**113 316**
10-12	Food products, beverages and tobacco	5 842	5 555	5 514	5 447	5 722	6 038	6 032	6 583
13-14	Textiles and wearing apparel	839	698	532	538	663	679	616	611
15	Leather and related products	122	183	144	180	171	134	192	274
16	Wood, wood and cork products	1 594	952	681	787	735	748	733	792
17	Paper and paper products	1 572	2 063	1 282	1 385	1 539	1 580	1 563	1 518
18	Printing and reproduction of recorded media	1 392	1 558	1 263	1 192	1 182	1 112	1 047	1 176
19-23	Chemical, rubber, plastics, non-metallic products	21 702	22 821	21 168	20 149	20 891	21 830	21 895	23 276
20	Chemicals and chemical products	8 031	8 848	8 327	7 907	8 362	8 366	8 256	8 587
21	Pharmaceutical products	6 141	6 459	6 650	6 155	5 932	6 472	6 985	7 418
22-23	Rubber, plastic, non-metallic mineral products	5 893	6 250	5 082	5 087	5 927	6 124	5 814	6 191
24	Basic metals	3 903	4 297	3 447	2 986	3 494	3 701	3 764	3 423
25	Metal products, except machinery and equipment	5 882	6 413	4 584	4 487	5 665	5 650	5 391	5 600
26-28	Machinery and equipment	28 371	29 309	23 866	23 901	27 979	28 968	27 327	27 853
26	Computer, electronic and optical products	11 036	10 298	8 609	9 460	11 084	10 966	10 039	9 862
27	Electrical equipment	5 034	5 488	4 727	4 613	5 672	5 951	5 656	5 412
28	Machinery and equipment n.e.c.	12 301	13 523	10 530	9 828	11 223	12 051	11 632	12 579
29-30	Transport equipment	26 824	29 469	26 324	28 434	32 133	34 928	35 747	38 026
29	Motor vehicles, trailers and semi-trailers	23 952	26 663	23 596	25 645	29 073	31 559	32 669	34 923
30	Other transport equipment	2 872	2 806	2 728	2 789	3 060	3 369	3 078	3 103
31-33	Furniture; repair, installation of machinery and equipment	3 335	3 690	3 539	3 718	4 225	4 056	3 837	4 184
31-32	Furniture, other manufacturing	2 170	2 359	2 087	2 332	2 659	2 652	2 500	2 802
33	Repair and installation of machinery and equipment	1 165	1 331	1 452	1 386	1 566	1 404	1 337	1 382
35-39	**ELECTRICITY, GAS, WATER AND WASTE MANAGEMENT**	**19 674**	**21 477**	**20 766**	**21 744**	**22 331**	**21 883**	**21 210**	**24 223**
35	Electricity, gas, steam and air conditioning supply	10 179	11 781	11 895	12 967	13 005	12 425	11 843	13 957
36-39	Water supply; sewerage, waste, remediation activities	9 495	9 696	8 871	8 777	9 326	9 458	9 367	10 266
41-43	**CONSTRUCTION**	**4 492**	**4 639**	**4 097**	**5 025**	**5 470**	**6 272**	**5 944**	**6 601**
45-56	Distribution; transportation, accommodation, food service	55 316	56 246	48 118	58 483	57 840	55 542	53 823	58 320
45-47	**Wholesale and retail trade; motor vehicle and motorcycle repairs**	**18 325**	**19 539**	**17 155**	**18 553**	**22 134**	**23 192**	**21 787**	**22 772**
49-53	**Transportation and storage**	**34 120**	**33 916**	**28 209**	**36 122**	**31 661**	**28 138**	**28 058**	**31 453**
55-56	**Accommodation and food service activities**	**2 871**	**2 791**	**2 754**	**3 808**	**4 045**	**4 212**	**3 978**	**4 095**
58-63	**Information and communication**	**18 224**	**19 674**	**19 214**	**19 055**	**22 557**	**20 122**	**22 217**	**22 555**
58-60	Publishing, audiovisual and broadcasting activities	5 248	5 327	5 485	5 563	5 540	5 862	5 826	5 824
61	Telecommunications	6 982	7 291	7 358	6 328	9 143	5 787	6 613	7 429
62-63	IT and other information services	5 994	7 056	6 371	7 164	7 874	8 473	9 778	9 302
64-66	**Financial and insurance activities**	**6 516**	**8 102**	**7 238**	**9 216**	**10 112**	**10 500**	**10 908**	**11 449**
68	**Real estate activities**	**142 789**	**142 036**	**137 286**	**145 912**	**168 902**	**177 506**	**180 172**	**186 584**
69-82	**Professional, scientific, technical, admin., support activities**	**77 560**	**79 631**	**62 565**	**65 412**	**69 136**	**64 746**	**66 121**	**72 475**
69-75	Professional, scientific and technical activities	14 769	16 405	15 664	16 666	17 467	17 416	17 364	19 502
69-71	Legal, accounting activities; mgt consultancy; engineering	5 969	6 838	5 936	6 045	6 177	5 857	5 976	7 402
73-75	Advertising, market research; other prof., scientific, tech.	1 105	1 191	942	1 147	1 124	1 278	1 164	1 314
77-82	Administrative and support service activities	62 791	63 226	46 901	48 746	51 669	47 330	48 757	52 973
84-88	**Public administration, defence; social security; education; health**	**70 165**	**73 597**	**74 017**	**77 171**	**81 380**	**83 185**	**82 837**	**85 024**
84	**Public administration, defence; compulsory social security**	**27 202**	**28 844**	**31 523**	**31 509**	**32 950**	**33 766**	**32 664**	**31 874**
85	**Education**	**15 028**	**15 969**	**16 908**	**19 250**	**20 042**	**19 242**	**19 607**	**20 109**
86-88	**Human health and social work activities**	**27 935**	**28 784**	**25 586**	**26 412**	**28 388**	**30 177**	**30 566**	**33 041**
90-99	**Arts, entertainment, household goods repairs, other**	**13 594**	**12 630**	**11 955**	**12 100**	**12 223**	**11 499**	**11 855**	**12 105**
90-93	**Arts, entertainment and recreation**	**9 978**	**8 839**	**8 518**	**8 601**	**8 695**	**8 155**	**8 499**	**8 669**
94-96	**Other service activities**	**3 616**	**3 791**	**3 437**	**3 499**	**3 528**	**3 344**	**3 356**	**3 436**
97-98	**Activities of households as employers and for own use**	**0**	**0**	**0**	**0**	**0**	**0**	**0**	**0**
05-39	**INDUSTRY INCLUDING ENERGY**	**122 659**	**130 074**	**114 741**	**116 471**	**127 955**	**132 603**	**130 625**	**139 087**
45-99	**TOTAL SERVICES**	**384 164**	**391 916**	**360 393**	**387 349**	**422 150**	**423 100**	**427 933**	**448 512**
45-82	**BUSINESS SECTOR SERVICES**	**300 405**	**305 689**	**274 421**	**298 078**	**328 547**	**328 416**	**333 241**	**351 383**
45-82x	**BUSINESS SECTOR SERVICES excluding real estate**	**157 616**	**163 653**	**137 135**	**152 166**	**159 645**	**150 910**	**153 069**	**164 799**
05-82x	**NON-AGRICULTURE BUSINESS SECTOR excluding real estate**	..	..	..	..	..	..	..	..

.. Not available

Note: Detailed metadata at: http://metalinks.oecd.org/stan/20170410/1c43.
Information on data for Israel: http://oe.cd/israel-disclaimer.

Disclaimer: http://oe.cd/disclaimer

GERMANY

Table 5. Number of persons engaged, total employment

ISIC Rev. 4

Thousands

		2007	2008	2009	2010	2011	2012	2013	2014
	TOTAL	**40 325**	**40 856**	**40 892**	**41 020**	**41 577**	**42 061**	**42 328**	**42 662**
01-03	**AGRICULTURE, FORESTRY AND FISHING**	**667**	**670**	**667**	**661**	**670**	**667**	**641**	**649**
05-09	**MINING AND QUARRYING**	**80**	**77**	**74**	**71**	**68**	**67**	**63**	**62**
10-33	**MANUFACTURING**	**7 274**	**7 458**	**7 277**	**7 138**	**7 285**	**7 418**	**7 442**	**7 486**
10-12	Food products, beverages and tobacco	898	922	923	922	922	925	922	923
13-14	Textiles and wearing apparel	156	152	143	138	139	140	139	138
15	Leather and related products	23	24	23	22	23	20	19	18
16	Wood, wood and cork products	146	149	140	136	139	137	137	136
17	Paper and paper products	150	151	148	146	147	146	149	147
18	Printing and reproduction of recorded media	216	210	200	192	185	182	173	171
19-23	Chemical, rubber, plastics, non-metallic products	1 118	1 148	1 114	1 098	1 122	1 141	1 152	1 172
20	Chemicals and chemical products	336	342	335	328	335	340	344	351
21	Pharmaceutical products	116	118	119	119	119	122	125	128
22-23	Rubber, plastic, non-metallic mineral products	649	670	642	634	651	662	666	676
24	Basic metals	269	281	270	258	265	269	268	270
25	Metal products, except machinery and equipment	871	907	859	845	878	897	893	890
26-28	Machinery and equipment	1 860	1 939	1 901	1 848	1 903	1 958	1 973	1 984
26	Computer, electronic and optical products	337	348	332	317	327	335	338	341
27	Electrical equipment	497	505	495	490	505	514	512	510
28	Machinery and equipment n.e.c.	1 026	1 086	1 074	1 041	1 071	1 109	1 123	1 133
29-30	Transport equipment	955	951	922	902	919	951	968	986
29	Motor vehicles, trailers and semi-trailers	834	829	800	781	798	825	837	854
30	Other transport equipment	121	122	122	121	121	126	131	132
31-33	Furniture; repair, installation of machinery and equipment	612	624	634	631	643	652	649	651
31-32	Furniture, other manufacturing	416	412	403	398	403	407	404	407
33	Repair and installation of machinery and equipment	196	212	231	233	240	245	245	244
35-39	**ELECTRICITY, GAS, WATER AND WASTE MANAGEMENT**	**485**	**487**	**493**	**496**	**501**	**509**	**517**	**520**
35	Electricity, gas, steam and air conditioning supply	244	242	247	249	251	253	256	255
36-39	Water supply; sewerage, waste, remediation activities	241	245	246	247	250	256	261	265
41-43	**CONSTRUCTION**	**2 312**	**2 300**	**2 312**	**2 331**	**2 376**	**2 412**	**2 426**	**2 436**
45-56	Distribution; transportation, accommodation, food service	9 380	9 471	9 481	9 476	9 619	9 710	9 761	9 804
45-47	**Wholesale and retail trade; motor vehicle and motorcycle repairs**	**5 825**	**5 863**	**5 835**	**5 813**	**5 886**	**5 903**	**5 903**	**5 896**
49-53	**Transportation and storage**	**1 971**	**1 997**	**1 980**	**1 983**	**2 026**	**2 057**	**2 084**	**2 106**
55-56	**Accommodation and food service activities**	**1 584**	**1 611**	**1 666**	**1 680**	**1 707**	**1 750**	**1 774**	**1 802**
58-63	**Information and communication**	**1 189**	**1 207**	**1 189**	**1 162**	**1 176**	**1 203**	**1 218**	**1 230**
58-60	Publishing, audiovisual and broadcasting activities	366	363	367	365	367	372	367	356
61	Telecommunications	200	194	173	144	135	129	126	125
62-63	IT and other information services	623	650	649	653	674	702	725	749
64-66	**Financial and insurance activities**	**1 231**	**1 219**	**1 225**	**1 214**	**1 201**	**1 201**	**1 194**	**1 189**
68	**Real estate activities**	**474**	**477**	**464**	**463**	**463**	**467**	**460**	**463**
69-82	**Professional, scientific, technical, admin., support activities**	**4 866**	**5 001**	**4 967**	**5 172**	**5 372**	**5 471**	**5 537**	**5 618**
69-75	Professional, scientific and technical activities	2 302	2 365	2 373	2 408	2 476	2 528	2 577	2 622
69-71	Legal, accounting activities; mgt consultancy; engineering	1 693	1 751	1 766	1 794	1 853	1 892	1 936	1 967
73-75	Advertising, market research; other prof., scientific, tech.	454	453	441	447	451	453	446	454
77-82	Administrative and support service activities	2 564	2 636	2 594	2 764	2 896	2 943	2 960	2 996
84-88	**Public administration, defence; social security; education; health**	**9 433**	**9 545**	**9 761**	**9 915**	**9 910**	**10 009**	**10 107**	**10 282**
84	**Public administration, defence; compulsory social security**	**2 742**	**2 727**	**2 745**	**2 741**	**2 622**	**2 569**	**2 543**	**2 539**
85	**Education**	**2 169**	**2 210**	**2 254**	**2 292**	**2 302**	**2 334**	**2 369**	**2 390**
86-88	**Human health and social work activities**	**4 522**	**4 608**	**4 762**	**4 882**	**4 986**	**5 106**	**5 195**	**5 353**
90-99	**Arts, entertainment, household goods repairs, other**	**2 934**	**2 944**	**2 982**	**2 921**	**2 936**	**2 927**	**2 962**	**2 923**
90-93	**Arts, entertainment and recreation**	**593**	**603**	**614**	**621**	**628**	**648**	**644**	**653**
94-96	**Other service activities**	**1 472**	**1 491**	**1 503**	**1 509**	**1 498**	**1 497**	**1 488**	**1 463**
97-98	**Activities of households as employers and for own use**	**869**	**850**	**865**	**791**	**810**	**782**	**830**	**807**
05-39	**INDUSTRY INCLUDING ENERGY**	**7 839**	**8 022**	**7 844**	**7 705**	**7 854**	**7 994**	**8 022**	**8 068**
45-99	**TOTAL SERVICES**	**29 507**	**29 864**	**30 069**	**30 323**	**30 677**	**30 988**	**31 239**	**31 509**
45-82	**BUSINESS SECTOR SERVICES**	**17 140**	**17 375**	**17 326**	**17 487**	**17 831**	**18 052**	**18 170**	**18 304**
45-82x	**BUSINESS SECTOR SERVICES excluding real estate**	**16 666**	**16 898**	**16 862**	**17 024**	**17 368**	**17 585**	**17 710**	**17 841**
05-82x	**NON-AGRICULTURE BUSINESS SECTOR excluding real estate**	..	..	..	..	..	..	..	..

.. Not available

Note: Detailed metadata at: http://metalinks.oecd.org/stan/20170410/1c43.

Information on data for Israel: http://oe.cd/israel-disclaimer.

Disclaimer: http://oe.cd/disclaimer

Table 6. Labour costs (compensation of employees), current prices

ISIC Rev. 4

Million EUR

		2007	2008	2009	2010	2011	2012	2013	2014
	TOTAL	**1 197 070**	**1 241 273**	**1 245 663**	**1 281 963**	**1 337 273**	**1 388 832**	**1 427 532**	**1 482 827**
01-03	**AGRICULTURE, FORESTRY AND FISHING**	**5 821**	**5 925**	**6 048**	**6 095**	**6 613**	**6 789**	**7 102**	**7 408**
05-09	**MINING AND QUARRYING**	**4 311**	**3 726**	**4 186**	**3 960**	**4 893**	**3 948**	**4 020**	**3 879**
10-33	**MANUFACTURING**	**315 863**	**327 863**	**309 957**	**319 461**	**336 384**	**347 707**	**360 671**	**373 747**
10-12	Food products, beverages and tobacco	25 943	27 515	27 607	28 220	28 703	29 144	29 751	30 547
13-14	Textiles and wearing apparel	4 653	4 705	4 281	4 319	4 577	4 691	4 725	4 827
15	Leather and related products	599	672	623	638	690	611	572	556
16	Wood, wood and cork products	4 491	4 530	4 146	4 149	4 342	4 436	4 503	4 638
17	Paper and paper products	6 039	6 212	6 002	6 152	6 326	6 380	6 588	6 698
18	Printing and reproduction of recorded media	5 898	5 713	5 447	5 220	5 051	4 951	4 743	4 730
19-23	Chemical, rubber, plastics, non-metallic products	50 415	53 271	51 304	53 006	55 635	57 415	59 501	61 737
20	Chemicals and chemical products	18 809	20 124	19 445	20 120	21 346	21 696	22 903	23 761
21	Pharmaceutical products	6 591	6 642	7 001	7 130	7 253	7 758	8 062	8 479
22-23	Rubber, plastic, non-metallic mineral products	23 660	25 357	23 570	24 567	25 771	26 580	27 237	28 193
24	Basic metals	12 769	13 429	11 840	12 348	13 167	13 587	13 874	14 203
25	Metal products, except machinery and equipment	32 028	33 520	29 836	31 470	34 040	35 439	36 193	37 244
26-28	Machinery and equipment	91 932	98 897	91 631	94 296	99 839	103 025	107 350	111 605
26	Computer, electronic and optical products	17 426	19 358	17 374	17 810	18 125	18 107	19 183	20 059
27	Electrical equipment	23 613	26 294	24 064	25 098	25 946	25 703	27 009	28 181
28	Machinery and equipment n.e.c.	50 893	53 245	50 193	51 388	55 768	59 215	61 158	63 365
29-30	Transport equipment	57 388	54 743	51 866	53 768	57 134	60 462	64 665	68 341
29	Motor vehicles, trailers and semi-trailers	51 043	47 835	44 834	46 442	49 565	52 548	55 985	59 281
30	Other transport equipment	6 345	6 908	7 032	7 326	7 569	7 914	8 680	9 060
31-33	Furniture; repair, installation of machinery and equipment	23 708	24 656	25 374	25 875	26 880	27 566	28 206	28 621
31-32	Furniture, other manufacturing	14 130	14 262	13 841	14 159	14 684	15 294	15 614	16 087
33	Repair and installation of machinery and equipment	9 578	10 394	11 533	11 716	12 196	12 272	12 592	12 534
35-39	**ELECTRICITY, GAS, WATER AND WASTE MANAGEMENT**	**23 969**	**23 010**	**25 359**	**25 456**	**25 275**	**27 489**	**28 253**	**27 719**
35	Electricity, gas, steam and air conditioning supply	15 158	13 840	15 983	15 877	15 327	17 078	17 509	16 577
36-39	Water supply; sewerage, waste, remediation activities	8 811	9 170	9 376	9 579	9 948	10 411	10 744	11 142
41-43	**CONSTRUCTION**	**61 112**	**61 566**	**64 223**	**65 593**	**68 614**	**71 084**	**71 282**	**73 831**
45-56	Distribution; transportation, accommodation, food service	216 798	224 953	225 711	230 544	238 600	248 771	253 982	262 951
45-47	**Wholesale and retail trade; motor vehicle and motorcycle repairs**	**139 955**	**145 184**	**145 046**	**147 640**	**153 074**	**158 732**	**162 223**	**167 617**
49-53	**Transportation and storage**	**56 033**	**58 257**	**58 378**	**59 921**	**61 681**	**64 818**	**65 549**	**67 912**
55-56	**Accommodation and food service activities**	**20 810**	**21 512**	**22 287**	**22 983**	**23 845**	**25 221**	**26 210**	**27 422**
58-63	**Information and communication**	**51 125**	**53 992**	**53 565**	**53 917**	**56 633**	**60 136**	**61 443**	**65 354**
58-60	Publishing, audiovisual and broadcasting activities	12 941	13 033	13 420	13 750	14 297	14 701	15 200	15 380
61	Telecommunications	10 855	11 109	9 772	8 379	8 329	8 093	7 847	8 165
62-63	IT and other information services	27 329	29 850	30 373	31 788	34 007	37 342	38 396	41 809
64-66	**Financial and insurance activities**	**61 339**	**63 089**	**62 477**	**61 909**	**63 882**	**65 478**	**67 233**	**69 362**
68	**Real estate activities**	**10 847**	**10 894**	**10 764**	**10 907**	**11 272**	**11 708**	**11 610**	**12 218**
69-82	**Professional, scientific, technical, admin., support activities**	**108 417**	**117 215**	**115 705**	**124 654**	**135 314**	**144 597**	**147 116**	**155 975**
69-75	Professional, scientific and technical activities	63 790	70 498	70 117	75 028	80 642	86 840	87 613	93 001
69-71	Legal, accounting activities; mgt consultancy; engineering	50 260	56 345	55 451	60 074	64 866	70 071	69 815	74 281
73-75	Advertising, market research; other prof., scientific, tech.	6 414	6 599	6 962	7 080	7 577	8 082	8 358	8 664
77-82	Administrative and support service activities	44 627	46 717	45 588	49 626	54 672	57 757	59 503	62 974
84-88	**Public administration, defence; social security; education; health**	**289 079**	**299 335**	**316 343**	**327 257**	**335 865**	**345 989**	**358 597**	**372 686**
84	**Public administration, defence; compulsory social security**	**108 152**	**111 605**	**116 409**	**119 238**	**121 056**	**123 079**	**126 130**	**129 409**
85	**Education**	**77 741**	**79 264**	**83 786**	**86 827**	**89 104**	**91 472**	**94 217**	**97 387**
86-88	**Human health and social work activities**	**103 186**	**108 466**	**116 148**	**121 192**	**125 705**	**131 438**	**138 250**	**145 890**
90-99	**Arts, entertainment, household goods repairs, other**	**48 389**	**49 705**	**51 325**	**52 210**	**53 928**	**55 136**	**56 223**	**57 697**
90-93	**Arts, entertainment and recreation**	**11 643**	**12 171**	**12 472**	**12 796**	**13 679**	**14 179**	**14 711**	**15 405**
94-96	**Other service activities**	**30 087**	**30 884**	**32 041**	**32 847**	**33 434**	**34 084**	**34 265**	**35 002**
97-98	**Activities of households as employers and for own use**	**6 659**	**6 650**	**6 812**	**6 567**	**6 815**	**6 873**	**7 247**	**7 290**
05-39	**INDUSTRY INCLUDING ENERGY**	**344 143**	**354 599**	**339 502**	**348 877**	**366 552**	**379 144**	**392 944**	**405 345**
45-99	**TOTAL SERVICES**	**785 994**	**819 183**	**835 890**	**861 398**	**895 494**	**931 815**	**956 204**	**996 243**
45-82	**BUSINESS SECTOR SERVICES**	**448 526**	**470 143**	**468 222**	**481 931**	**505 701**	**530 690**	**541 384**	**565 860**
45-82x	**BUSINESS SECTOR SERVICES excluding real estate**	**437 679**	**459 249**	**457 458**	**471 024**	**494 429**	**518 982**	**529 774**	**553 642**
05-82x	**NON-AGRICULTURE BUSINESS SECTOR excluding real estate**	..	..	..	..	..	..	..	..

.. Not available

Note: Detailed metadata at: http://metalinks.oecd.org/stan/20170410/1c43.

Information on data for Israel: http://oe.cd/israel-disclaimer.

Disclaimer: http://oe.cd/disclaimer

GREECE

Table 1. Production (gross output), current prices

ISIC Rev. 4

Million EUR

		2007	2008	2009	2010	2011	2012	2013	2014
	TOTAL	**377 760**	**386 427**	**375 814**	**354 633**	**323 261**	**306 893**	**292 476**	**287 081**
01-03	**AGRICULTURE, FORESTRY AND FISHING**	**12 474**	**12 204**	**11 807**	**12 240**	**12 281**	**12 247**	**12 047**	**11 920**
05-09	**MINING AND QUARRYING**	**1 703**	**1 506**	**1 492**	**1 588**	**1 498**	**1 303**	**1 344**	**1 419**
10-33	**MANUFACTURING**	**61 330**	**65 358**	**57 541**	**59 745**	**58 694**	**59 084**	**56 759**	**56 334**
10-12	Food products, beverages and tobacco	15 413	15 431	16 936	16 320	16 408	15 996	15 982	16 209
13-14	Textiles and wearing apparel	3 163	3 088	2 747	2 393	2 082	1 791	1 561	1 422
15	Leather and related products	420	276	268	239	145	123	106	92
16	Wood, wood and cork products	1 164	1 282	1 264	778	860	587	481	427
17	Paper and paper products	1 177	1 087	1 109	1 106	1 056	1 043	1 127	1 212
18	Printing and reproduction of recorded media	2 623	1 380	1 412	1 048	837	707	596	581
19-23	Chemical, rubber, plastics, non-metallic products	19 681	23 825	18 526	21 648	22 062	24 891	24 499	24 176
20	Chemicals and chemical products	2 470	2 956	2 267	2 131	2 102	1 885	2 126	2 119
21	Pharmaceutical products	1 939	1 734	1 838	1 538	1 338	1 285	1 409	1 294
22-23	Rubber, plastic, non-metallic mineral products	5 508	5 883	5 105	4 969	3 881	3 472	3 632	3 698
24	Basic metals	6 014	6 507	4 054	4 878	5 471	4 722	4 089	4 178
25	Metal products, except machinery and equipment	4 796	4 905	4 486	4 251	3 557	3 136	3 124	3 086
26-28	Machinery and equipment	3 440	3 679	2 774	3 151	2 708	2 827	2 541	2 409
26	Computer, electronic and optical products	583	565	359	544	376	448	414	453
27	Electrical equipment	1 615	1 649	1 155	1 518	1 323	1 431	1 144	990
28	Machinery and equipment n.e.c.	1 242	1 466	1 260	1 088	1 009	948	983	965
29-30	Transport equipment	1 377	1 216	1 308	751	591	482	358	275
29	Motor vehicles, trailers and semi-trailers	306	405	296	305	200	177	175	180
30	Other transport equipment	1 070	811	1 012	445	391	305	183	94
31-33	Furniture; repair, installation of machinery and equipment	2 062	2 684	2 656	3 182	2 918	2 777	2 295	2 268
31-32	Furniture, other manufacturing	1 584	1 968	2 038	1 791	1 538	1 179	996	1 022
33	Repair and installation of machinery and equipment	478	716	618	1 391	1 380	1 598	1 299	1 246
35-39	**ELECTRICITY, GAS, WATER AND WASTE MANAGEMENT**	**10 652**	**10 671**	**11 050**	**10 104**	**9 599**	**9 966**	**10 262**	**9 756**
35	Electricity, gas, steam and air conditioning supply	6 492	6 179	6 584	6 434	6 146	6 477	6 621	6 124
36-39	Water supply; sewerage, waste, remediation activities	4 160	4 492	4 467	3 671	3 453	3 489	3 641	3 632
41-43	**CONSTRUCTION**	**41 191**	**34 799**	**31 780**	**20 959**	**16 868**	**14 960**	**12 731**	**11 395**
45-56	Distribution; transportation, accommodation, food service	100 440	105 642	98 523	96 253	85 698	78 356	76 502	77 668
45-47	**Wholesale and retail trade; motor vehicle and motorcycle repairs**	**47 605**	**49 613**	**48 472**	**45 664**	**39 931**	**34 389**	**32 087**	**32 319**
49-53	**Transportation and storage**	**32 059**	**34 998**	**30 117**	**30 631**	**27 761**	**26 198**	**24 513**	**25 451**
55-56	**Accommodation and food service activities**	**20 777**	**21 032**	**19 934**	**19 958**	**18 006**	**17 770**	**19 902**	**19 899**
58-63	**Information and communication**	**15 113**	**14 267**	**14 776**	**14 564**	**12 230**	**10 637**	**11 041**	**10 617**
58-60	Publishing, audiovisual and broadcasting activities	4 708	4 283	4 721	4 113	3 145	2 530	2 190	2 120
61	Telecommunications	9 043	8 822	8 869	8 833	7 790	6 833	7 435	7 081
62-63	IT and other information services	1 361	1 162	1 186	1 618	1 294	1 273	1 416	1 416
64-66	**Financial and insurance activities**	**13 789**	**13 955**	**14 419**	**14 363**	**13 500**	**12 431**	**12 074**	**11 176**
68	**Real estate activities**	**26 937**	**30 727**	**32 229**	**35 397**	**33 541**	**34 222**	**32 336**	**30 549**
69-82	**Professional, scientific, technical, admin., support activities**	**25 589**	**26 259**	**25 599**	**20 431**	**17 414**	**16 093**	**14 475**	**14 234**
69-75	Professional, scientific and technical activities	17 996	17 720	17 538	14 030	11 734	10 670	9 552	9 286
69-71	Legal, accounting activities; mgt consultancy; engineering	11 445	11 609	11 864	9 085	7 706	7 289	6 435	6 114
73-75	Advertising, market research; other prof., scientific, tech.	5 264	5 144	4 779	4 014	3 190	2 445	2 126	2 194
77-82	Administrative and support service activities	7 593	8 538	8 061	6 401	5 680	5 423	4 923	4 948
84-88	**Public administration, defence; social security; education; health**	**55 012**	**57 458**	**61 691**	**56 143**	**50 025**	**46 272**	**41 791**	**41 125**
84	**Public administration, defence; compulsory social security**	**26 685**	**27 152**	**30 566**	**27 276**	**24 308**	**23 057**	**20 710**	**20 708**
85	**Education**	**11 892**	**12 918**	**13 356**	**12 640**	**12 213**	**11 243**	**10 281**	**10 423**
86-88	**Human health and social work activities**	**16 434**	**17 387**	**17 769**	**16 227**	**13 504**	**11 971**	**10 801**	**9 994**
90-99	**Arts, entertainment, household goods repairs, other**	**13 531**	**13 582**	**14 907**	**12 847**	**11 913**	**11 323**	**11 114**	**10 888**
90-93	**Arts, entertainment and recreation**	**5 192**	**4 868**	**5 431**	**4 085**	**3 767**	**3 549**	**3 519**	**3 471**
94-96	**Other service activities**	**7 069**	**7 384**	**8 054**	**7 479**	**7 195**	**6 863**	**6 918**	**6 863**
97-98	**Activities of households as employers and for own use**	**1 270**	**1 330**	**1 422**	**1 283**	**951**	**911**	**677**	**554**
05-39	**INDUSTRY INCLUDING ENERGY**	**73 685**	**77 534**	**70 083**	**71 437**	**69 791**	**70 353**	**68 365**	**67 509**
45-99	**TOTAL SERVICES**	**250 410**	**261 889**	**262 143**	**249 998**	**224 321**	**209 332**	**199 332**	**196 256**
45-82	**BUSINESS SECTOR SERVICES**	**181 868**	**190 850**	**185 546**	**181 009**	**162 383**	**151 738**	**146 427**	**144 244**
45-82x	**BUSINESS SECTOR SERVICES excluding real estate**	**154 931**	**160 123**	**153 317**	**145 611**	**128 842**	**117 516**	**114 092**	**113 695**
05-82x	**NON-AGRICULTURE BUSINESS SECTOR excluding real estate**	..	..	..	..	..	..	..	..

.. Not available

Note: Detailed metadata at: http://metalinks.oecd.org/stan/20170410/1c43.

Information on data for Israel: http://oe.cd/israel-disclaimer.

Disclaimer: http://oe.cd/disclaimer

Table 2. Value added, current prices

ISIC Rev. 4

Million EUR

		2007	2008	2009	2010	2011	2012	2013	2014
	TOTAL	**205 267**	**213 819**	**212 391**	**199 644**	**181 909**	**168 979**	**160 237**	**157 187**
01-03	**AGRICULTURE, FORESTRY AND FISHING**	**7 068**	**6 793**	**6 663**	**6 519**	**6 109**	**6 191**	**5 794**	**5 843**
05-09	**MINING AND QUARRYING**	**899**	**817**	**777**	**863**	**851**	**695**	**819**	**848**
10-33	**MANUFACTURING**	**19 695**	**20 578**	**18 146**	**16 356**	**16 175**	**15 377**	**15 251**	**14 939**
10-12	Food products, beverages and tobacco	4 526	4 797	4 711	4 626	4 576	4 736	5 284	5 425
13-14	Textiles and wearing apparel	1 248	1 283	1 034	935	807	633	551	518
15	Leather and related products	176	114	109	100	71	52	47	37
16	Wood, wood and cork products	435	517	484	243	327	49	77	71
17	Paper and paper products	425	414	317	270	187	200	180	183
18	Printing and reproduction of recorded media	1 359	753	674	463	413	342	277	239
19-23	Chemical, rubber, plastics, non-metallic products	4 672	5 407	4 677	4 040	4 315	3 649	3 547	3 335
20	Chemicals and chemical products	681	723	617	637	564	735	898	859
21	Pharmaceutical products	665	580	613	623	525	454	597	561
22-23	Rubber, plastic, non-metallic mineral products	2 223	2 321	2 079	1 478	1 302	1 052	1 060	1 113
24	Basic metals	1 712	1 760	1 167	873	1 211	1 519	1 537	1 558
25	Metal products, except machinery and equipment	1 886	1 855	1 682	1 522	1 182	1 214	1 247	1 211
26-28	Machinery and equipment	1 566	1 715	1 355	1 332	1 143	1 100	1 029	996
26	Computer, electronic and optical products	303	291	229	299	209	211	171	187
27	Electrical equipment	703	715	515	517	447	392	358	315
28	Machinery and equipment n.e.c.	561	709	611	516	487	496	500	494
29-30	Transport equipment	661	582	628	352	271	267	201	144
29	Motor vehicles, trailers and semi-trailers	120	159	112	137	90	75	86	87
30	Other transport equipment	542	423	516	215	182	192	115	56
31-33	Furniture; repair, installation of machinery and equipment	1 030	1 382	1 307	1 601	1 670	1 618	1 275	1 223
31-32	Furniture, other manufacturing	746	933	928	718	706	493	363	357
33	Repair and installation of machinery and equipment	284	449	379	883	965	1 125	912	866
35-39	**ELECTRICITY, GAS, WATER AND WASTE MANAGEMENT**	**6 270**	**5 781**	**6 902**	**5 149**	**4 990**	**5 499**	**5 721**	**5 327**
35	Electricity, gas, steam and air conditioning supply	3 192	2 292	3 490	2 909	2 824	3 191	3 302	2 989
36-39	Water supply; sewerage, waste, remediation activities	3 078	3 489	3 412	2 240	2 166	2 308	2 418	2 338
41-43	**CONSTRUCTION**	**15 017**	**10 719**	**10 550**	**8 888**	**6 310**	**5 821**	**4 701**	**3 935**
45-56	Distribution; transportation, accommodation, food service	52 016	56 917	51 420	49 399	44 313	37 677	36 344	37 612
45-47	**Wholesale and retail trade; motor vehicle and motorcycle repairs**	**25 534**	**27 502**	**26 505**	**25 344**	**22 934**	**17 959**	**16 248**	**16 758**
49-53	**Transportation and storage**	**16 322**	**17 619**	**14 849**	**14 243**	**12 878**	**11 499**	**10 675**	**11 364**
55-56	**Accommodation and food service activities**	**10 160**	**11 797**	**10 066**	**9 812**	**8 502**	**8 220**	**9 421**	**9 490**
58-63	**Information and communication**	**8 279**	**8 061**	**8 568**	**7 683**	**6 355**	**5 518**	**5 749**	**5 238**
58-60	Publishing, audiovisual and broadcasting activities	2 471	2 171	2 625	1 744	1 278	1 150	985	930
61	Telecommunications	5 058	5 240	5 266	5 120	4 329	3 642	4 043	3 627
62-63	IT and other information services	750	649	677	819	748	726	721	681
64-66	**Financial and insurance activities**	**9 223**	**9 396**	**9 775**	**9 623**	**8 652**	**8 396**	**8 293**	**7 655**
68	**Real estate activities**	**24 321**	**28 303**	**29 544**	**33 515**	**31 367**	**32 324**	**30 331**	**28 787**
69-82	**Professional, scientific, technical, admin., support activities**	**13 341**	**13 649**	**13 463**	**10 593**	**9 570**	**8 683**	**7 649**	**7 558**
69-75	Professional, scientific and technical activities	8 867	8 112	8 299	7 384	6 661	6 189	5 446	5 305
69-71	Legal, accounting activities; mgt consultancy; engineering	6 535	6 272	6 527	5 851	5 240	4 679	4 078	3 886
73-75	Advertising, market research; other prof., scientific, tech.	1 731	1 471	1 384	1 057	1 004	907	792	857
77-82	Administrative and support service activities	4 474	5 537	5 164	3 209	2 909	2 494	2 203	2 253
84-88	**Public administration, defence; social security; education; health**	**40 360**	**43 968**	**46 716**	**43 238**	**40 403**	**35 920**	**32 859**	**33 045**
84	**Public administration, defence; compulsory social security**	**17 605**	**19 156**	**21 821**	**19 999**	**18 432**	**17 517**	**16 168**	**15 951**
85	**Education**	**10 813**	**11 971**	**12 362**	**11 657**	**11 440**	**10 567**	**9 673**	**9 811**
86-88	**Human health and social work activities**	**11 941**	**12 841**	**12 532**	**11 582**	**10 530**	**7 835**	**7 017**	**7 283**
90-99	**Arts, entertainment, household goods repairs, other**	**8 778**	**8 835**	**9 868**	**7 820**	**6 815**	**6 879**	**6 726**	**6 400**
90-93	**Arts, entertainment and recreation**	**3 369**	**3 072**	**3 636**	**2 559**	**2 317**	**2 157**	**2 181**	**2 178**
94-96	**Other service activities**	**4 139**	**4 434**	**4 810**	**3 978**	**3 547**	**3 811**	**3 868**	**3 668**
97-98	**Activities of households as employers and for own use**	**1 270**	**1 330**	**1 422**	**1 283**	**951**	**911**	**677**	**554**
05-39	**INDUSTRY INCLUDING ENERGY**	**26 864**	**27 176**	**25 825**	**22 368**	**22 016**	**21 571**	**21 791**	**21 113**
45-99	**TOTAL SERVICES**	**156 318**	**169 130**	**169 353**	**161 870**	**147 474**	**135 397**	**127 951**	**126 296**
45-82	**BUSINESS SECTOR SERVICES**	**107 180**	**116 327**	**112 770**	**110 812**	**100 256**	**92 598**	**88 367**	**86 851**
45-82x	**BUSINESS SECTOR SERVICES excluding real estate**	**82 860**	**88 024**	**83 225**	**77 298**	**68 890**	**60 274**	**58 035**	**58 064**
05-82x	**NON-AGRICULTURE BUSINESS SECTOR excluding real estate**	..	..	..	..	..	..	..	..

.. Not available

Note: Detailed metadata at: http://metalinks.oecd.org/stan/20170410/1c43.
Information on data for Israel: http://oe.cd/israel-disclaimer.

Disclaimer: http://oe.cd/disclaimer

GREECE

Table 3. Value added, volumes

ISIC Rev. 4

Million 2010 EUR

		2007	2008	2009	2010	2011	2012	2013	2014
	TOTAL	**219 499**	**219 092**	**211 682**	**199 644**	**181 672**	**169 968**	**165 455**	**165 491**
01-03	**AGRICULTURE, FORESTRY AND FISHING**	**5 865**	**5 933**	**6 228**	**6 519**	**6 378**	**7 063**	**6 572**	**6 841**
05-09	**MINING AND QUARRYING**	**981**	**880**	**810**	**863**	**758**	**595**	**759**	**744**
10-33	**MANUFACTURING**	**21 026**	**19 737**	**18 878**	**16 356**	**15 289**	**14 150**	**14 078**	**13 590**
10-12	Food products, beverages and tobacco	6 046	5 234	4 739	4 626	4 260	4 050	4 445	4 468
13-14	Textiles and wearing apparel	..	..	..	..	..	..	..	..
15	Leather and related products	..	..	..	..	..	..	..	..
16	Wood, wood and cork products	473	539	483	243	334	46	75	72
17	Paper and paper products	513	448	321	270	172	214	193	196
18	Printing and reproduction of recorded media	1 524	772	661	463	411	343	278	237
19-23	Chemical, rubber, plastics, non-metallic products	3 797	3 997	5 133	4 040	3 846	3 023	2 986	2 623
20	Chemicals and chemical products	661	658	479	637	493	619	706	659
21	Pharmaceutical products	672	505	519	623	616	507	673	678
22-23	Rubber, plastic, non-metallic mineral products	2 384	2 426	2 076	1 478	1 282	1 038	1 054	1 087
24	Basic metals	2 283	2 117	1 434	873	1 083	1 560	1 679	1 810
25	Metal products, except machinery and equipment	2 239	2 028	1 657	1 522	1 243	1 335	1 335	1 283
26-28	Machinery and equipment	1 788	1 782	1 408	1 332	1 110	1 021	982	975
26	Computer, electronic and optical products	313	293	229	299	211	176	140	154
27	Electrical equipment	931	764	591	517	398	326	329	307
28	Machinery and equipment n.e.c.	584	730	592	516	501	526	523	523
29-30	Transport equipment	725	614	639	352	274	265	197	140
29	Motor vehicles, trailers and semi-trailers	128	164	110	137	91	76	86	86
30	Other transport equipment	607	456	538	215	183	189	112	55
31-33	Furniture; repair, installation of machinery and equipment	1 156	1 484	1 309	1 601	1 693	1 625	1 266	1 219
31-32	Furniture, other manufacturing	842	1 022	933	718	725	479	345	334
33	Repair and installation of machinery and equipment	315	462	379	883	967	1 140	918	882
35-39	**ELECTRICITY, GAS, WATER AND WASTE MANAGEMENT**	**7 057**	**5 897**	**6 656**	**5 149**	**5 291**	**5 272**	**4 911**	**4 242**
35	Electricity, gas, steam and air conditioning supply	3 718	2 232	3 330	2 909	3 088	2 901	2 426	1 899
36-39	Water supply; sewerage, waste, remediation activities	3 472	3 749	3 337	2 240	2 203	2 359	2 508	2 444
41-43	**CONSTRUCTION**	**13 259**	**9 691**	**9 793**	**8 888**	**6 536**	**6 159**	**5 027**	**4 557**
45-56	Distribution; transportation, accommodation, food service	55 982	58 760	51 919	49 399	43 816	36 995	35 735	37 360
45-47	**Wholesale and retail trade; motor vehicle and motorcycle repairs**	**27 962**	**28 019**	**27 432**	**25 344**	**21 708**	**16 041**	**14 392**	**14 983**
49-53	**Transportation and storage**	**17 159**	**18 151**	**14 196**	**14 243**	**12 978**	**12 050**	**10 838**	**11 607**
55-56	**Accommodation and food service activities**	**11 023**	**12 744**	**10 354**	**9 812**	**9 130**	**9 140**	**11 053**	**11 319**
58-63	**Information and communication**	**8 789**	**8 721**	**8 908**	**7 683**	**6 264**	**5 532**	**5 910**	**5 227**
58-60	Publishing, audiovisual and broadcasting activities	2 755	2 194	2 653	1 744	1 303	1 240	1 028	950
61	Telecommunications	5 188	5 783	5 478	5 120	4 245	3 621	4 198	3 622
62-63	IT and other information services	926	753	748	819	716	674	667	635
64-66	**Financial and insurance activities**	**9 324**	**10 159**	**10 382**	**9 623**	**8 251**	**7 837**	**7 921**	**7 546**
68	**Real estate activities**	**26 810**	**30 046**	**30 249**	**33 515**	**31 138**	**32 823**	**33 159**	**34 196**
69-82	**Professional, scientific, technical, admin., support activities**	**14 328**	**14 331**	**13 523**	**10 593**	**9 512**	**8 737**	**7 614**	**7 350**
69-75	Professional, scientific and technical activities	9 520	8 538	8 315	7 384	6 607	6 269	5 401	4 981
69-71	Legal, accounting activities; mgt consultancy; engineering	6 597	6 459	6 442	5 851	5 237	4 785	4 130	3 730
73-75	Advertising, market research; other prof., scientific, tech.	2 519	1 782	1 564	1 057	970	903	696	665
77-82	Administrative and support service activities	4 815	5 802	5 217	3 209	2 905	2 468	2 211	2 370
84-88	**Public administration, defence; social security; education; health**	**45 714**	**45 639**	**44 254**	**43 238**	**41 717**	**37 911**	**36 642**	**37 185**
84	**Public administration, defence; compulsory social security**	**19 756**	**19 548**	**20 052**	**19 999**	**19 448**	**19 152**	**18 699**	**18 556**
85	**Education**	**11 908**	**12 346**	**11 896**	**11 657**	**11 726**	**11 057**	**10 638**	**10 985**
86-88	**Human health and social work activities**	**14 167**	**13 835**	**12 335**	**11 582**	**10 544**	**7 787**	**7 401**	**7 713**
90-99	**Arts, entertainment, household goods repairs, other**	**9 781**	**9 439**	**10 183**	**7 820**	**6 724**	**6 956**	**7 039**	**6 824**
90-93	**Arts, entertainment and recreation**	**3 628**	**3 199**	**3 643**	**2 559**	**2 299**	**2 196**	**2 336**	**2 385**
94-96	**Other service activities**	**4 739**	**4 852**	**5 066**	**3 978**	**3 489**	**3 822**	**3 954**	**3 818**
97-98	**Activities of households as employers and for own use**	**1 394**	**1 385**	**1 463**	**1 283**	**937**	**936**	**745**	**614**
05-39	**INDUSTRY INCLUDING ENERGY**	**29 130**	**26 603**	**26 390**	**22 368**	**21 338**	**19 975**	**19 732**	**18 532**
45-99	**TOTAL SERVICES**	**170 714**	**177 166**	**169 348**	**161 870**	**147 421**	**136 818**	**134 067**	**135 703**
45-82	**BUSINESS SECTOR SERVICES**	**115 415**	**122 179**	**115 009**	**110 812**	**98 980**	**91 915**	**90 325**	**91 633**
45-82x	**BUSINESS SECTOR SERVICES excluding real estate**	**88 502**	**92 076**	**84 736**	**77 298**	**67 842**	**59 124**	**57 227**	**57 554**
05-82x	**NON-AGRICULTURE BUSINESS SECTOR excluding real estate**	..	..	..	..	..	..	..	..

.. Not available

Note: Detailed metadata at: http://metalinks.oecd.org/stan/20170410/1c43.

Information on data for Israel: http://oe.cd/israel-disclaimer.

Disclaimer: http://oe.cd/disclaimer

Table 4. Gross fixed capital formation, current prices

ISIC Rev. 4

Million EUR

		2007	2008	2009	2010	2011	2012	2013	2014
	TOTAL	**60 528**	**57 627**	**49 387**	**39 698**	**31 607**	**24 140**	**21 963**	**20 625**
01-03	**AGRICULTURE, FORESTRY AND FISHING**	**2 212**	**2 583**	**2 084**	**1 635**	**1 387**	**1 122**	**1 026**	**1 120**
05-09	**MINING AND QUARRYING**	**176**	**197**	**195**	**184**	**216**	**210**	**209**	**166**
10-33	**MANUFACTURING**	**2 398**	**3 059**	**2 983**	**2 850**	**2 368**	**2 232**	**2 116**	**1 949**
10-12	Food products, beverages and tobacco	662	793	628	608	372	341	324	316
13-14	Textiles and wearing apparel	103	58	81	-6	56	51	51	47
15	Leather and related products	16	9	12	-3	1	3	1	2
16	Wood, wood and cork products	54	42	42	51	14	14	13	12
17	Paper and paper products	79	58	44	32	43	40	36	37
18	Printing and reproduction of recorded media	135	71	36	58	43	41	42	37
19-23	Chemical, rubber, plastics, non-metallic products	679	1 144	1 412	1 198	1 305	1 228	1 162	1 060
20	Chemicals and chemical products	132	152	167	48	69	60	59	57
21	Pharmaceutical products	150	191	331	71	109	100	103	95
22-23	Rubber, plastic, non-metallic mineral products	350	325	367	226	208	192	177	175
24	Basic metals	143	235	177	431	231	217	210	186
25	Metal products, except machinery and equipment	238	243	211	162	93	91	81	73
26-28	Machinery and equipment	167	217	191	157	126	121	114	110
26	Computer, electronic and optical products	47	51	42	72	39	38	37	36
27	Electrical equipment	54	80	56	41	40	38	35	35
28	Machinery and equipment n.e.c.	66	86	92	44	47	44	41	40
29-30	Transport equipment	47	53	44	56	17	17	16	16
29	Motor vehicles, trailers and semi-trailers	14	11	5	9	4	4	3	3
30	Other transport equipment	33	42	39	47	13	13	13	13
31-33	Furniture; repair, installation of machinery and equipment	74	135	105	107	66	67	64	53
31-32	Furniture, other manufacturing	59	117	75	98	67	66	65	55
33	Repair and installation of machinery and equipment	15	18	31	8	0	1	-1	-2
35-39	**ELECTRICITY, GAS, WATER AND WASTE MANAGEMENT**	**1 003**	**1 220**	**1 321**	**1 092**	**599**	**573**	**577**	**460**
35	Electricity, gas, steam and air conditioning supply	688	925	991	838	463	445	449	355
36-39	Water supply; sewerage, waste, remediation activities	315	295	330	254	135	128	129	104
41-43	**CONSTRUCTION**	**1 359**	**1 494**	**697**	**225**	**248**	**213**	**205**	**219**
45-56	Distribution; transportation, accommodation, food service	12 423	11 397	8 403	8 848	6 648	3 383	3 679	4 473
45-47	**Wholesale and retail trade; motor vehicle and motorcycle repairs**	**3 168**	**2 998**	**2 102**	**1 993**	**1 344**	**1 053**	**1 062**	**1 081**
49-53	**Transportation and storage**	**8 176**	**6 771**	**5 296**	**6 291**	**4 749**	**1 883**	**2 189**	**2 980**
55-56	**Accommodation and food service activities**	**1 078**	**1 628**	**1 005**	**565**	**555**	**448**	**428**	**412**
58-63	**Information and communication**	**1 399**	**1 532**	**1 540**	**2 170**	**1 438**	**1 226**	**1 159**	**1 194**
58-60	Publishing, audiovisual and broadcasting activities	376	542	520	390	297	253	244	250
61	Telecommunications	812	842	812	1 253	748	642	585	612
62-63	IT and other information services	211	147	207	526	394	331	330	332
64-66	**Financial and insurance activities**	**546**	**577**	**469**	**419**	**353**	**322**	**320**	**313**
68	**Real estate activities**	**26 758**	**20 941**	**16 795**	**12 295**	**10 172**	**7 484**	**5 433**	**4 238**
69-82	**Professional, scientific, technical, admin., support activities**	**2 799**	**3 513**	**3 148**	**2 168**	**1 467**	**1 166**	**1 197**	**1 225**
69-75	Professional, scientific and technical activities	1 055	1 072	1 021	916	978	814	858	849
69-71	Legal, accounting activities; mgt consultancy; engineering	428	550	462	181	311	264	249	257
73-75	Advertising, market research; other prof., scientific, tech.	82	88	159	216	140	112	107	111
77-82	Administrative and support service activities	1 744	2 441	2 127	1 252	490	351	339	376
84-88	**Public administration, defence; social security; education; health**	**8 482**	**9 945**	**9 870**	**6 315**	**4 854**	**4 507**	**4 366**	**3 784**
84	**Public administration, defence; compulsory social security**	**6 375**	**7 611**	**7 873**	**4 899**	**3 505**	**3 248**	**3 153**	**2 625**
85	**Education**	**1 535**	**1 734**	**1 396**	**1 015**	**1 032**	**987**	**956**	**894**
86-88	**Human health and social work activities**	**572**	**600**	**601**	**401**	**317**	**272**	**257**	**265**
90-99	**Arts, entertainment, household goods repairs, other**	**973**	**1 168**	**1 882**	**1 498**	**1 858**	**1 702**	**1 675**	**1 483**
90-93	**Arts, entertainment and recreation**	**410**	**522**	**326**	**277**	**231**	**187**	**192**	**187**
94-96	**Other service activities**	**562**	**647**	**1 556**	**1 221**	**1 627**	**1 515**	**1 483**	**1 295**
97-98	**Activities of households as employers and for own use**	**0**	**0**	**0**	**0**	**0**	**0**	**0**	**0**
05-39	**INDUSTRY INCLUDING ENERGY**	**3 577**	**4 476**	**4 499**	**4 126**	**3 182**	**3 015**	**2 902**	**2 574**
45-99	**TOTAL SERVICES**	**53 380**	**49 074**	**42 107**	**33 713**	**26 789**	**19 790**	**17 829**	**16 710**
45-82	**BUSINESS SECTOR SERVICES**	**43 925**	**37 961**	**30 355**	**25 900**	**20 078**	**13 581**	**11 789**	**11 444**
45-82x	**BUSINESS SECTOR SERVICES excluding real estate**	**17 167**	**17 020**	**13 560**	**13 605**	**9 906**	**6 097**	**6 356**	**7 205**
05-82x	**NON-AGRICULTURE BUSINESS SECTOR excluding real estate**	..	..	..	..	..	..	..	..

.. Not available

Note: Detailed metadata at: http://metalinks.oecd.org/stan/20170410/1c43.

Information on data for Israel: http://oe.cd/israel-disclaimer.

Disclaimer: http://oe.cd/disclaimer

GREECE

Table 5. Number of persons engaged, total employment

ISIC Rev. 4

Thousands

		2007	2008	2009	2010	2011	2012	2013	2014
	TOTAL	**4 795**	**4 856**	**4 829**	**4 705**	**4 382**	**4 105**	**3 998**	**3 999**
01-03	**AGRICULTURE, FORESTRY AND FISHING**	**532**	**529**	**543**	**535**	**499**	**491**	**489**	**488**
05-09	**MINING AND QUARRYING**	**14**	**12**	**13**	**12**	**11**	**10**	**10**	**11**
10-33	**MANUFACTURING**	**474**	**495**	**476**	**431**	**392**	**359**	**336**	**338**
10-12	Food products, beverages and tobacco	115	115	116	109	105	102	105	109
13-14	Textiles and wearing apparel	63	59	50	41	37	33	28	25
15	Leather and related products	6	6	5	4	3	2	3	3
16	Wood, wood and cork products	27	27	28	21	20	17	14	13
17	Paper and paper products	9	10	10	9	8	8	7	8
18	Printing and reproduction of recorded media	18	20	18	16	13	11	11	11
19-23	Chemical, rubber, plastics, non-metallic products	77	81	78	71	64	61	59	57
20	Chemicals and chemical products	14	14	13	13	11	11	12	13
21	Pharmaceutical products	13	13	13	12	12	13	12	12
22-23	Rubber, plastic, non-metallic mineral products	43	48	47	41	36	34	31	29
24	Basic metals	16	20	20	18	17	17	18	17
25	Metal products, except machinery and equipment	43	49	48	47	40	37	29	31
26-28	Machinery and equipment	33	36	32	33	28	24	22	24
26	Computer, electronic and optical products	6	5	4	5	3	3	3	3
27	Electrical equipment	10	10	10	10	8	8	7	8
28	Machinery and equipment n.e.c.	17	20	19	18	16	13	13	13
29-30	Transport equipment	11	13	12	11	10	9	7	6
29	Motor vehicles, trailers and semi-trailers	3	5	4	4	3	3	2	2
30	Other transport equipment	8	8	8	7	6	6	4	4
31-33	Furniture; repair, installation of machinery and equipment	56	60	59	51	47	38	34	34
31-32	Furniture, other manufacturing	48	46	47	40	36	28	23	23
33	Repair and installation of machinery and equipment	8	14	12	12	11	10	12	11
35-39	**ELECTRICITY, GAS, WATER AND WASTE MANAGEMENT**	**53**	**52**	**50**	**51**	**50**	**46**	**43**	**41**
35	Electricity, gas, steam and air conditioning supply	24	21	20	20	20	19	16	16
36-39	Water supply; sewerage, waste, remediation activities	29	30	30	31	29	27	27	25
41-43	**CONSTRUCTION**	**389**	**386**	**369**	**314**	**241**	**207**	**203**	**189**
45-56	Distribution; transportation, accommodation, food service	1 507	1 532	1 527	1 490	1 402	1 303	1 263	1 271
45-47	**Wholesale and retail trade; motor vehicle and motorcycle repairs**	**982**	**988**	**977**	**960**	**897**	**825**	**789**	**783**
49-53	**Transportation and storage**	**210**	**222**	**226**	**222**	**202**	**192**	**189**	**190**
55-56	**Accommodation and food service activities**	**314**	**322**	**324**	**307**	**302**	**286**	**285**	**299**
58-63	**Information and communication**	**89**	**90**	**87**	**90**	**85**	**84**	**86**	**87**
58-60	Publishing, audiovisual and broadcasting activities	41	39	37	37	35	33	34	33
61	Telecommunications	28	30	28	29	28	28	27	29
62-63	IT and other information services	20	21	22	23	22	23	25	25
64-66	**Financial and insurance activities**	**111**	**112**	**107**	**102**	**99**	**96**	**92**	**85**
68	**Real estate activities**	**7**	**10**	**10**	**11**	**9**	**9**	**8**	**9**
69-82	**Professional, scientific, technical, admin., support activities**	**329**	**344**	**348**	**346**	**331**	**324**	**316**	**328**
69-75	Professional, scientific and technical activities	223	236	239	236	226	223	216	213
69-71	Legal, accounting activities; mgt consultancy; engineering	174	183	183	181	176	175	172	169
73-75	Advertising, market research; other prof., scientific, tech.	39	41	44	46	43	41	38	37
77-82	Administrative and support service activities	106	108	109	111	105	101	99	115
84-88	**Public administration, defence; social security; education; health**	**990**	**982**	**978**	**984**	**945**	**890**	**871**	**867**
84	**Public administration, defence; compulsory social security**	**431**	**428**	**421**	**425**	**409**	**376**	**374**	**364**
85	**Education**	**324**	**321**	**325**	**322**	**304**	**290**	**282**	**290**
86-88	**Human health and social work activities**	**236**	**233**	**232**	**237**	**232**	**224**	**215**	**213**
90-99	**Arts, entertainment, household goods repairs, other**	**301**	**312**	**321**	**340**	**318**	**287**	**281**	**285**
90-93	**Arts, entertainment and recreation**	**52**	**55**	**52**	**47**	**46**	**43**	**43**	**45**
94-96	**Other service activities**	**181**	**186**	**190**	**206**	**198**	**188**	**188**	**191**
97-98	**Activities of households as employers and for own use**	**69**	**71**	**80**	**87**	**74**	**56**	**50**	**49**
05-39	**INDUSTRY INCLUDING ENERGY**	**541**	**558**	**539**	**494**	**452**	**415**	**390**	**390**
45-99	**TOTAL SERVICES**	**3 334**	**3 383**	**3 379**	**3 363**	**3 189**	**2 993**	**2 916**	**2 931**
45-82	**BUSINESS SECTOR SERVICES**	**2 042**	**2 088**	**2 080**	**2 039**	**1 926**	**1 815**	**1 764**	**1 780**
45-82x	**BUSINESS SECTOR SERVICES excluding real estate**	**2 036**	**2 078**	**2 070**	**2 027**	**1 917**	**1 807**	**1 756**	**1 771**
05-82x	**NON-AGRICULTURE BUSINESS SECTOR excluding real estate**	..	..	..	..	..	..	..	..

.. Not available

Note: Detailed metadata at: http://metalinks.oecd.org/stan/20170410/1c43.
Information on data for Israel: http://oe.cd/israel-disclaimer.

Disclaimer: http://oe.cd/disclaimer

Table 6. Labour costs (compensation of employees), current prices

ISIC Rev. 4

Million EUR

		2007	2008	2009	2010	2011	2012	2013	2014
	TOTAL	**78 441**	**82 947**	**84 875**	**82 130**	**73 259**	**66 080**	**59 715**	**58 363**
01-03	**AGRICULTURE, FORESTRY AND FISHING**	**1 228**	**1 124**	**970**	**967**	**924**	**862**	**816**	**780**
05-09	**MINING AND QUARRYING**	**586**	**556**	**559**	**514**	**459**	**379**	**373**	**356**
10-33	**MANUFACTURING**	**9 005**	**9 133**	**8 925**	**8 885**	**8 111**	**6 726**	**5 960**	**5 847**
10-12	Food products, beverages and tobacco	2 260	2 086	2 223	2 342	2 185	1 994	1 825	1 867
13-14	Textiles and wearing apparel	848	787	703	611	542	428	313	252
15	Leather and related products	108	72	72	61	40	33	26	22
16	Wood, wood and cork products	261	246	254	226	208	41	55	55
17	Paper and paper products	219	225	222	215	153	177	160	167
18	Printing and reproduction of recorded media	355	316	304	306	248	207	169	149
19-23	Chemical, rubber, plastics, non-metallic products	2 180	2 208	2 074	2 025	1 887	1 579	1 546	1 516
20	Chemicals and chemical products	404	415	367	352	320	309	329	361
21	Pharmaceutical products	361	330	329	328	313	293	320	323
22-23	Rubber, plastic, non-metallic mineral products	1 078	1 132	1 095	999	903	674	603	573
24	Basic metals	460	585	567	558	766	486	446	417
25	Metal products, except machinery and equipment	685	800	825	926	728	653	504	504
26-28	Machinery and equipment	653	765	669	739	589	539	470	492
26	Computer, electronic and optical products	137	115	91	145	76	70	63	70
27	Electrical equipment	248	228	215	240	204	192	156	163
28	Machinery and equipment n.e.c.	268	423	363	354	310	276	251	259
29-30	Transport equipment	324	343	340	295	230	184	102	72
29	Motor vehicles, trailers and semi-trailers	74	104	93	90	68	58	34	23
30	Other transport equipment	251	239	247	205	162	126	67	49
31-33	Furniture; repair, installation of machinery and equipment	653	700	672	579	534	404	343	332
31-32	Furniture, other manufacturing	485	475	503	415	365	235	175	177
33	Repair and installation of machinery and equipment	169	225	169	164	169	169	169	155
35-39	**ELECTRICITY, GAS, WATER AND WASTE MANAGEMENT**	**2 414**	**2 215**	**2 057**	**1 959**	**1 856**	**1 573**	**1 547**	**1 554**
35	Electricity, gas, steam and air conditioning supply	1 379	1 085	861	797	675	609	613	642
36-39	Water supply; sewerage, waste, remediation activities	1 035	1 130	1 196	1 161	1 181	964	934	912
41-43	**CONSTRUCTION**	**4 548**	**4 666**	**4 175**	**3 332**	**2 650**	**1 946**	**1 681**	**1 632**
45-56	Distribution; transportation, accommodation, food service	18 292	19 535	19 563	20 380	17 769	16 013	13 762	13 626
45-47	**Wholesale and retail trade; motor vehicle and motorcycle repairs**	**11 516**	**12 438**	**12 094**	**12 758**	**11 355**	**9 932**	**8 408**	**8 169**
49-53	**Transportation and storage**	**4 102**	**4 200**	**4 454**	**4 653**	**3 613**	**3 513**	**3 321**	**3 336**
55-56	**Accommodation and food service activities**	**2 673**	**2 896**	**3 015**	**2 969**	**2 801**	**2 568**	**2 032**	**2 121**
58-63	**Information and communication**	**2 743**	**2 816**	**2 756**	**3 173**	**2 595**	**2 345**	**2 292**	**2 141**
58-60	Publishing, audiovisual and broadcasting activities	1 063	1 031	1 011	1 192	946	874	729	604
61	Telecommunications	1 202	1 331	1 335	1 522	1 274	1 084	1 139	1 133
62-63	IT and other information services	478	454	410	459	375	388	424	404
64-66	**Financial and insurance activities**	**5 436**	**5 665**	**5 833**	**5 059**	**4 853**	**4 209**	**3 825**	**3 127**
68	**Real estate activities**	**87**	**115**	**118**	**95**	**67**	**72**	**64**	**57**
69-82	**Professional, scientific, technical, admin., support activities**	**4 094**	**4 246**	**4 197**	**5 338**	**4 432**	**3 926**	**3 498**	**3 502**
69-75	Professional, scientific and technical activities	2 375	2 521	2 454	3 441	2 743	2 343	2 173	1 988
69-71	Legal, accounting activities; mgt consultancy; engineering	1 533	1 585	1 439	2 477	1 932	1 525	1 412	1 297
73-75	Advertising, market research; other prof., scientific, tech.	502	627	661	617	626	583	576	519
77-82	Administrative and support service activities	1 719	1 725	1 743	1 897	1 689	1 583	1 325	1 514
84-88	**Public administration, defence; social security; education; health**	**25 907**	**28 437**	**30 702**	**27 992**	**25 974**	**24 182**	**21 882**	**21 923**
84	**Public administration, defence; compulsory social security**	**12 878**	**14 082**	**16 342**	**14 356**	**13 084**	**12 468**	**11 357**	**11 310**
85	**Education**	**8 517**	**9 462**	**9 355**	**8 814**	**8 534**	**7 741**	**7 130**	**7 316**
86-88	**Human health and social work activities**	**4 513**	**4 894**	**5 005**	**4 822**	**4 356**	**3 973**	**3 395**	**3 296**
90-99	**Arts, entertainment, household goods repairs, other**	**4 100**	**4 439**	**5 020**	**4 437**	**3 570**	**3 847**	**4 015**	**3 819**
90-93	**Arts, entertainment and recreation**	**613**	**588**	**562**	**560**	**650**	**633**	**643**	**667**
94-96	**Other service activities**	**2 483**	**2 752**	**3 137**	**2 604**	**1 994**	**2 390**	**2 759**	**2 653**
97-98	**Activities of households as employers and for own use**	**1 004**	**1 100**	**1 321**	**1 272**	**926**	**825**	**613**	**499**
05-39	**INDUSTRY INCLUDING ENERGY**	**12 006**	**11 905**	**11 541**	**11 358**	**10 426**	**8 678**	**7 880**	**7 757**
45-99	**TOTAL SERVICES**	**60 659**	**65 253**	**68 189**	**66 474**	**59 260**	**54 595**	**49 339**	**48 194**
45-82	**BUSINESS SECTOR SERVICES**	**30 651**	**32 377**	**32 467**	**34 045**	**29 716**	**26 566**	**23 441**	**22 452**
45-82x	**BUSINESS SECTOR SERVICES excluding real estate**	**30 564**	**32 262**	**32 349**	**33 950**	**29 650**	**26 493**	**23 378**	**22 395**
05-82x	**NON-AGRICULTURE BUSINESS SECTOR excluding real estate**	..	..	..	..	..	..	..	..

.. Not available

Note: Detailed metadata at: http://metalinks.oecd.org/stan/20170410/1c43.
Information on data for Israel: http://oe.cd/israel-disclaimer.

Disclaimer: http://oe.cd/disclaimer

Table 1. Production (gross output), current prices

ISIC Rev. 4

Million EUR

		2007	2008	2009	2010	2011	2012	2013	2014
	TOTAL	**3 209 965**	**3 267 159**	**2 981 437**	**3 117 983**	**3 214 830**	**3 132 431**	**3 084 351**	**3 101 472**
01-03	**AGRICULTURE, FORESTRY AND FISHING**	**52 144**	**54 653**	**50 731**	**51 486**	**55 953**	**57 521**	**59 739**	**56 904**
05-09	**MINING AND QUARRYING**	**9 724**	**10 063**	**8 015**	**8 488**	**9 516**	**10 893**	**10 822**	**11 321**
10-33	**MANUFACTURING**	**1 021 727**	**1 021 919**	**801 416**	**895 958**	**949 269**	**911 820**	**891 014**	**895 864**
10-12	Food products, beverages and tobacco	123 383	129 089	119 827	122 925	125 865	126 628	128 576	129 209
13-14	Textiles and wearing apparel	62 644	61 614	52 770	56 246	58 961	53 517	51 668	51 456
15	Leather and related products	28 010	26 144	20 461	23 732	27 112	27 841	29 279	30 518
16	Wood, wood and cork products	22 505	19 986	17 192	17 678	17 820	15 938	14 315	14 123
17	Paper and paper products	21 318	20 946	18 250	21 204	22 159	21 168	21 101	21 855
18	Printing and reproduction of recorded media	15 876	15 274	13 246	13 704	13 209	12 132	11 401	10 482
19-23	Chemical, rubber, plastics, non-metallic products	223 517	230 826	170 944	203 281	220 685	215 610	204 681	199 500
20	Chemicals and chemical products	56 261	55 390	41 178	49 934	53 004	51 778	51 296	50 167
21	Pharmaceutical products	23 344	24 002	21 755	23 342	24 071	25 226	25 799	24 360
22-23	Rubber, plastic, non-metallic mineral products	87 907	85 671	68 555	74 974	76 947	71 340	70 099	69 584
24	Basic metals	70 843	71 829	41 105	55 436	66 500	57 738	54 890	54 565
25	Metal products, except machinery and equipment	102 556	100 437	74 353	83 961	86 700	82 098	79 063	78 326
26-28	Machinery and equipment	192 883	191 303	149 194	168 129	177 568	173 067	171 055	173 037
26	Computer, electronic and optical products	26 706	25 194	21 290	23 235	24 175	22 615	21 581	20 851
27	Electrical equipment	45 238	43 478	35 047	42 294	42 560	39 469	38 396	38 877
28	Machinery and equipment n.e.c.	120 939	122 630	92 857	102 601	110 833	110 982	111 078	113 309
29-30	Transport equipment	89 980	87 962	68 193	71 838	73 298	68 334	69 189	75 887
29	Motor vehicles, trailers and semi-trailers	64 500	60 406	43 958	49 003	50 364	45 860	47 277	51 676
30	Other transport equipment	25 480	27 556	24 235	22 835	22 935	22 474	21 912	24 210
31-33	Furniture; repair, installation of machinery and equipment	68 211	66 509	55 881	57 825	59 390	57 752	55 796	56 906
31-32	Furniture, other manufacturing	46 328	44 418	37 804	39 478	39 726	38 078	36 902	38 393
33	Repair and installation of machinery and equipment	21 883	22 091	18 078	18 347	19 664	19 674	18 895	18 514
35-39	**ELECTRICITY, GAS, WATER AND WASTE MANAGEMENT**	**110 674**	**127 617**	**115 921**	**122 631**	**127 409**	**133 302**	**137 609**	**133 807**
35	Electricity, gas, steam and air conditioning supply	73 929	88 247	78 562	81 925	84 351	90 576	93 304	89 420
36-39	Water supply; sewerage, waste, remediation activities	36 745	39 370	37 359	40 707	43 058	42 726	44 305	44 387
41-43	**CONSTRUCTION**	**274 065**	**277 718**	**257 869**	**253 789**	**255 297**	**229 554**	**212 194**	**199 657**
45-56	Distribution; transportation, accommodation, food service	601 389	608 557	575 912	595 894	612 151	604 969	595 392	614 149
45-47	**Wholesale and retail trade; motor vehicle and motorcycle repairs**	**327 908**	**330 795**	**314 143**	**321 171**	**328 806**	**325 220**	**313 598**	**326 062**
49-53	**Transportation and storage**	**179 308**	**181 110**	**165 326**	**176 230**	**182 741**	**179 215**	**181 737**	**185 884**
55-56	**Accommodation and food service activities**	**94 173**	**96 653**	**96 443**	**98 492**	**100 604**	**100 534**	**100 057**	**102 204**
58-63	**Information and communication**	**130 547**	**129 688**	**129 468**	**129 114**	**128 802**	**121 553**	**117 348**	**114 707**
58-60	Publishing, audiovisual and broadcasting activities	31 421	30 964	29 387	29 614	29 142	26 357	24 830	24 069
61	Telecommunications	51 067	49 977	50 146	49 326	48 017	45 731	42 548	38 656
62-63	IT and other information services	48 059	48 747	49 935	50 174	51 643	49 465	49 970	51 982
64-66	**Financial and insurance activities**	**137 315**	**137 340**	**131 716**	**132 655**	**134 338**	**130 666**	**136 212**	**142 560**
68	**Real estate activities**	**200 480**	**207 938**	**214 718**	**218 428**	**225 876**	**227 616**	**227 278**	**230 004**
69-82	**Professional, scientific, technical, admin., support activities**	**256 584**	**260 360**	**252 363**	**257 921**	**263 259**	**255 919**	**247 475**	**252 098**
69-75	Professional, scientific and technical activities	163 748	167 143	163 772	165 487	164 498	159 249	154 580	156 747
69-71	Legal, accounting activities; mgt consultancy; engineering	107 592	109 628	109 585	110 332	110 508	105 616	103 394	105 495
73-75	Advertising, market research; other prof., scientific, tech.	43 148	43 961	40 963	42 250	41 201	40 130	37 846	38 104
77-82	Administrative and support service activities	92 836	93 217	88 592	92 434	98 760	96 670	92 895	95 352
84-88	**Public administration, defence; social security; education; health**	**327 717**	**341 333**	**350 079**	**353 989**	**352 629**	**348 957**	**348 733**	**349 074**
84	**Public administration, defence; compulsory social security**	**127 412**	**131 847**	**134 647**	**136 543**	**134 756**	**130 527**	**130 975**	**127 367**
85	**Education**	**74 763**	**74 380**	**75 852**	**74 505**	**72 538**	**72 829**	**72 555**	**72 654**
86-88	**Human health and social work activities**	**125 543**	**135 107**	**139 580**	**142 941**	**145 335**	**145 601**	**145 203**	**149 052**
90-99	**Arts, entertainment, household goods repairs, other**	**87 598**	**89 972**	**93 230**	**97 628**	**100 331**	**99 661**	**100 535**	**101 328**
90-93	**Arts, entertainment and recreation**	**35 917**	**36 539**	**38 272**	**41 308**	**42 369**	**41 993**	**42 002**	**42 303**
94-96	**Other service activities**	**35 893**	**36 533**	**37 211**	**38 314**	**39 897**	**39 207**	**39 433**	**40 068**
97-98	**Activities of households as employers and for own use**	**15 787**	**16 900**	**17 747**	**18 006**	**18 065**	**18 461**	**19 100**	**18 957**
05-39	**INDUSTRY INCLUDING ENERGY**	**1 142 125**	**1 159 599**	**925 352**	**1 027 078**	**1 086 194**	**1 056 015**	**1 039 444**	**1 040 991**
45-99	**TOTAL SERVICES**	**1 741 631**	**1 775 189**	**1 747 485**	**1 785 630**	**1 817 386**	**1 789 340**	**1 772 974**	**1 803 920**
45-82	**BUSINESS SECTOR SERVICES**	**1 326 316**	**1 343 884**	**1 304 176**	**1 334 012**	**1 364 427**	**1 340 722**	**1 323 706**	**1 353 518**
45-82x	**BUSINESS SECTOR SERVICES excluding real estate**	**1 125 835**	**1 135 946**	**1 089 458**	**1 115 584**	**1 138 550**	**1 113 107**	**1 096 428**	**1 123 514**
05-82x	**NON-AGRICULTURE BUSINESS SECTOR excluding real estate**	..	..	..	..	..	..	..	..

.. Not available

Note: Detailed metadata at: http://metalinks.oecd.org/stan/20170410/1c43.

Information on data for Israel: http://oe.cd/israel-disclaimer.

Disclaimer: http://oe.cd/disclaimer

Table 2. Value added, current prices

ISIC Rev. 4

Million EUR

		2007	2008	2009	2010	2011	2012	2013	2014
	TOTAL	**1 445 765**	**1 473 045**	**1 421 651**	**1 443 247**	**1 470 334**	**1 448 021**	**1 444 106**	**1 456 419**
01-03	**AGRICULTURE, FORESTRY AND FISHING**	**30 432**	**30 471**	**28 150**	**28 417**	**30 880**	**31 698**	**33 614**	**31 431**
05-09	**MINING AND QUARRYING**	**5 536**	**6 046**	**4 390**	**4 597**	**5 467**	**6 802**	**6 580**	**5 692**
10-33	**MANUFACTURING**	**256 643**	**251 913**	**215 612**	**228 279**	**232 204**	**222 812**	**222 141**	**225 725**
10-12	Food products, beverages and tobacco	24 326	24 500	24 339	24 801	24 426	23 831	24 185	24 771
13-14	Textiles and wearing apparel	18 402	18 025	15 538	15 239	16 384	14 635	14 629	15 028
15	Leather and related products	7 171	6 962	5 563	6 836	6 934	7 520	7 945	8 135
16	Wood, wood and cork products	6 656	6 422	5 686	5 622	5 608	4 954	4 710	4 623
17	Paper and paper products	4 759	4 582	4 593	4 711	4 912	4 827	4 775	5 183
18	Printing and reproduction of recorded media	6 296	6 047	5 073	5 082	4 912	4 631	4 359	4 261
19-23	Chemical, rubber, plastics, non-metallic products	48 351	46 157	39 952	42 246	41 857	40 271	39 804	37 741
20	Chemicals and chemical products	10 186	9 415	8 586	9 894	9 682	9 581	9 829	9 884
21	Pharmaceutical products	7 906	8 293	8 046	8 361	8 546	8 479	8 621	8 112
22-23	Rubber, plastic, non-metallic mineral products	25 441	23 785	21 467	21 828	21 283	20 442	20 305	20 503
24	Basic metals	11 173	10 294	5 938	7 882	8 530	7 444	7 018	7 682
25	Metal products, except machinery and equipment	32 316	32 416	27 133	28 414	28 886	27 587	27 253	27 957
26-28	Machinery and equipment	54 079	53 941	45 524	49 796	52 076	51 515	51 765	52 684
26	Computer, electronic and optical products	8 691	8 248	7 415	8 164	8 565	8 341	7 931	7 997
27	Electrical equipment	11 870	11 839	10 300	11 297	11 354	11 021	10 892	10 277
28	Machinery and equipment n.e.c.	33 518	33 854	27 809	30 336	32 157	32 154	32 942	34 410
29-30	Transport equipment	20 473	20 138	16 290	17 528	17 190	15 691	15 814	17 449
29	Motor vehicles, trailers and semi-trailers	13 083	11 879	9 454	11 102	10 923	9 511	10 228	10 658
30	Other transport equipment	7 391	8 259	6 836	6 426	6 267	6 181	5 586	6 790
31-33	Furniture; repair, installation of machinery and equipment	22 641	22 431	19 984	20 122	20 489	19 905	19 883	20 213
31-32	Furniture, other manufacturing	13 948	13 603	12 099	12 157	12 209	11 461	11 550	12 046
33	Repair and installation of machinery and equipment	8 693	8 828	7 886	7 965	8 280	8 444	8 334	8 167
35-39	**ELECTRICITY, GAS, WATER AND WASTE MANAGEMENT**	**34 345**	**38 274**	**39 927**	**37 703**	**36 220**	**38 168**	**39 251**	**39 022**
35	Electricity, gas, steam and air conditioning supply	24 066	27 568	28 413	25 238	23 935	25 891	26 571	25 772
36-39	Water supply; sewerage, waste, remediation activities	10 279	10 706	11 514	12 465	12 285	12 277	12 680	13 250
41-43	**CONSTRUCTION**	**86 411**	**88 710**	**85 055**	**81 207**	**82 072**	**77 886**	**74 255**	**70 045**
45-56	Distribution; transportation, accommodation, food service	293 742	296 295	286 337	290 228	297 838	291 286	288 774	295 874
45-47	**Wholesale and retail trade; motor vehicle and motorcycle repairs**	**166 005**	**167 084**	**157 817**	**160 670**	**165 772**	**162 011**	**159 788**	**164 751**
49-53	**Transportation and storage**	**76 580**	**77 630**	**76 157**	**77 902**	**78 910**	**76 602**	**77 531**	**78 466**
55-56	**Accommodation and food service activities**	**51 156**	**51 582**	**52 363**	**51 656**	**53 156**	**52 673**	**51 455**	**52 658**
58-63	**Information and communication**	**62 644**	**62 989**	**62 556**	**62 264**	**61 592**	**58 108**	**54 568**	**53 684**
58-60	Publishing, audiovisual and broadcasting activities	11 749	11 750	11 465	11 700	11 077	9 502	8 944	8 427
61	Telecommunications	27 562	27 119	26 343	25 488	24 643	22 758	19 477	18 145
62-63	IT and other information services	23 333	24 120	24 748	25 076	25 871	25 847	26 146	27 111
64-66	**Financial and insurance activities**	**80 768**	**79 946**	**73 067**	**75 910**	**78 824**	**77 968**	**80 669**	**84 338**
68	**Real estate activities**	**174 806**	**182 570**	**187 240**	**188 746**	**195 793**	**199 878**	**201 031**	**203 463**
69-82	**Professional, scientific, technical, admin., support activities**	**132 050**	**136 675**	**132 672**	**135 963**	**138 145**	**136 324**	**135 565**	**137 845**
69-75	Professional, scientific and technical activities	92 825	96 073	93 575	95 174	94 243	93 199	92 652	93 703
69-71	Legal, accounting activities; mgt consultancy; engineering	65 066	67 509	67 628	68 720	68 344	66 611	66 687	67 192
73-75	Advertising, market research; other prof., scientific, tech.	19 590	20 265	17 775	17 971	17 544	18 017	17 263	17 865
77-82	Administrative and support service activities	39 225	40 603	39 097	40 788	43 902	43 125	42 913	44 142
84-88	**Public administration, defence; social security; education; health**	**237 250**	**245 499**	**251 219**	**252 869**	**252 171**	**249 204**	**249 398**	**250 440**
84	**Public administration, defence; compulsory social security**	**96 706**	**99 460**	**101 604**	**103 094**	**103 240**	**100 263**	**100 494**	**99 026**
85	**Education**	**63 572**	**63 766**	**65 471**	**63 723**	**61 818**	**61 851**	**61 728**	**62 124**
86-88	**Human health and social work activities**	**76 972**	**82 273**	**84 144**	**86 052**	**87 113**	**87 090**	**87 176**	**89 289**
90-99	**Arts, entertainment, household goods repairs, other**	**51 136**	**53 656**	**55 427**	**57 065**	**59 129**	**57 889**	**58 259**	**58 859**
90-93	**Arts, entertainment and recreation**	**14 933**	**15 636**	**15 610**	**16 621**	**17 135**	**16 137**	**15 803**	**16 414**
94-96	**Other service activities**	**20 417**	**21 120**	**22 070**	**22 438**	**23 929**	**23 291**	**23 356**	**23 489**
97-98	**Activities of households as employers and for own use**	**15 787**	**16 900**	**17 747**	**18 006**	**18 065**	**18 461**	**19 100**	**18 957**
05-39	INDUSTRY INCLUDING ENERGY	296 524	296 234	259 929	270 579	273 891	267 781	267 973	270 440
45-99	TOTAL SERVICES	1 032 397	1 057 629	1 048 517	1 063 043	1 083 491	1 070 656	1 068 264	1 084 503
45-82	BUSINESS SECTOR SERVICES	744 011	758 475	741 872	753 110	772 192	763 563	760 607	775 204
45-82x	BUSINESS SECTOR SERVICES excluding real estate	569 204	575 906	554 632	564 364	576 398	563 685	559 576	571 740
05-82x	NON-AGRICULTURE BUSINESS SECTOR excluding real estate	..	..	..	..	..	..	..	..

.. Not available

Note: Detailed metadata at: http://metalinks.oecd.org/stan/20170410/1c43.
Information on data for Israel: http://oe.cd/israel-disclaimer.

Disclaimer: http://oe.cd/disclaimer

Table 3. Value added, volumes

ISIC Rev. 4

Million 2010 EUR

		2007	2008	2009	2010	2011	2012	2013	2014
	TOTAL	**1 514 368**	**1 501 603**	**1 418 573**	**1 443 247**	**1 451 697**	**1 416 148**	**1 395 029**	**1 396 994**
01-03	**AGRICULTURE, FORESTRY AND FISHING**	**28 452**	**28 782**	**28 314**	**28 417**	**28 960**	**28 210**	**28 603**	**27 955**
05-09	**MINING AND QUARRYING**	**5 890**	**5 628**	**5 253**	**4 597**	**5 590**	**6 378**	**6 235**	**6 946**
10-33	**MANUFACTURING**	**263 268**	**254 721**	**209 759**	**228 279**	**232 880**	**224 835**	**221 287**	**221 657**
10-12	Food products, beverages and tobacco	26 312	25 596	24 073	24 801	25 797	25 784	25 651	25 817
13-14	Textiles and wearing apparel	..	..	..	..	..	..	..	..
15	Leather and related products	..	..	..	..	..	..	..	..
16	Wood, wood and cork products	7 007	6 172	5 537	5 622	5 721	4 939	4 596	4 385
17	Paper and paper products	4 608	4 528	4 552	4 711	4 611	4 846	4 873	5 039
18	Printing and reproduction of recorded media	6 034	5 796	4 776	5 082	5 300	4 992	4 855	4 828
19-23	Chemical, rubber, plastics, non-metallic products	47 349	45 701	38 587	42 246	42 331	40 967	40 415	38 526
20	Chemicals and chemical products	10 540	10 589	8 094	9 894	9 255	9 573	9 936	9 967
21	Pharmaceutical products	8 039	8 409	7 696	8 361	8 898	8 711	8 899	8 819
22-23	Rubber, plastic, non-metallic mineral products	24 896	23 663	20 447	21 828	21 790	20 633	20 164	20 342
24	Basic metals	9 192	8 733	6 374	7 882	8 750	9 928	10 155	11 218
25	Metal products, except machinery and equipment	34 834	34 103	26 187	28 414	28 267	26 763	26 233	26 396
26-28	Machinery and equipment	54 846	54 515	44 058	49 796	51 286	49 590	49 010	48 568
26	Computer, electronic and optical products	9 864	9 144	7 769	8 164	7 952	7 844	7 471	7 274
27	Electrical equipment	12 215	12 142	9 804	11 297	10 792	10 189	10 203	9 778
28	Machinery and equipment n.e.c.	32 865	33 237	26 533	30 336	32 542	31 559	31 342	31 529
29-30	Transport equipment	22 952	22 242	16 600	17 528	17 995	16 653	15 931	17 046
29	Motor vehicles, trailers and semi-trailers	14 269	13 242	9 344	11 102	11 783	10 413	10 231	10 612
30	Other transport equipment	8 778	9 145	7 361	6 426	6 212	6 200	5 684	6 423
31-33	Furniture; repair, installation of machinery and equipment	24 454	22 856	19 751	20 122	19 479	17 871	17 513	17 794
31-32	Furniture, other manufacturing	14 915	13 791	11 821	12 157	11 739	10 260	10 088	10 292
33	Repair and installation of machinery and equipment	9 537	9 068	7 933	7 965	7 740	7 596	7 411	7 487
35-39	**ELECTRICITY, GAS, WATER AND WASTE MANAGEMENT**	**39 625**	**41 119**	**38 990**	**37 703**	**35 206**	**35 376**	**33 210**	**30 945**
35	Electricity, gas, steam and air conditioning supply	27 589	28 745	26 980	25 238	23 846	24 573	22 989	21 353
36-39	Water supply; sewerage, waste, remediation activities	11 928	12 260	11 929	12 465	11 360	10 847	10 257	9 621
41-43	**CONSTRUCTION**	**94 343**	**91 609**	**84 350**	**81 207**	**76 979**	**71 649**	**68 017**	**64 220**
45-56	Distribution; transportation, accommodation, food service	310 304	305 928	284 097	290 228	294 939	284 642	280 032	285 340
45-47	**Wholesale and retail trade; motor vehicle and motorcycle repairs**	**175 574**	**172 909**	**155 320**	**160 670**	**166 011**	**159 122**	**158 064**	**162 939**
49-53	**Transportation and storage**	**83 096**	**81 073**	**77 253**	**77 902**	**76 834**	**73 886**	**72 223**	**71 479**
55-56	**Accommodation and food service activities**	**51 803**	**52 048**	**51 554**	**51 656**	**52 095**	**51 612**	**49 735**	**51 034**
58-63	**Information and communication**	**59 165**	**60 451**	**61 389**	**62 264**	**62 263**	**60 479**	**59 250**	**59 300**
58-60	Publishing, audiovisual and broadcasting activities	11 843	11 586	11 209	11 700	10 763	9 394	8 489	7 855
61	Telecommunications	22 542	23 703	24 533	25 488	25 925	25 700	24 828	24 509
62-63	IT and other information services	25 095	25 307	25 737	25 076	25 576	25 435	25 934	26 889
64-66	**Financial and insurance activities**	**73 096**	**72 738**	**72 028**	**75 910**	**77 534**	**78 948**	**76 592**	**75 655**
68	**Real estate activities**	**188 769**	**191 436**	**191 598**	**188 746**	**192 186**	**191 186**	**189 889**	**192 540**
69-82	**Professional, scientific, technical, admin., support activities**	**144 078**	**141 941**	**133 802**	**135 963**	**134 503**	**129 092**	**128 597**	**127 379**
69-75	Professional, scientific and technical activities	101 021	99 430	94 389	95 174	91 939	88 587	87 812	86 333
69-71	Legal, accounting activities; mgt consultancy; engineering	71 923	70 538	68 116	68 720	66 208	62 298	62 260	60 342
73-75	Advertising, market research; other prof., scientific, tech.	20 789	20 726	17 882	17 971	17 175	17 282	16 649	17 124
77-82	Administrative and support service activities	43 065	42 519	39 413	40 788	42 565	40 508	40 782	41 045
84-88	**Public administration, defence; social security; education; health**	**252 325**	**252 159**	**253 401**	**252 869**	**252 297**	**248 955**	**247 905**	**249 158**
84	**Public administration, defence; compulsory social security**	**103 436**	**102 639**	**103 163**	**103 094**	**102 200**	**100 923**	**100 161**	**99 204**
85	**Education**	**63 399**	**64 029**	**63 956**	**63 723**	**63 960**	**63 453**	**62 887**	**63 169**
86-88	**Human health and social work activities**	**85 522**	**85 474**	**86 278**	**86 052**	**86 138**	**84 595**	**84 845**	**86 736**
90-99	**Arts, entertainment, household goods repairs, other**	**55 832**	**55 908**	**56 267**	**57 065**	**58 361**	**56 577**	**55 671**	**56 801**
90-93	**Arts, entertainment and recreation**	**16 406**	**16 419**	**16 125**	**16 621**	**16 743**	**15 746**	**15 203**	**15 938**
94-96	**Other service activities**	**21 641**	**21 691**	**22 214**	**22 438**	**23 572**	**22 475**	**22 055**	**21 951**
97-98	**Activities of households as employers and for own use**	**17 789**	**17 800**	**17 922**	**18 006**	**18 045**	**18 372**	**18 437**	**18 946**
05-39	**INDUSTRY INCLUDING ENERGY**	**309 087**	**301 495**	**253 812**	**270 579**	**273 676**	**266 606**	**260 626**	**259 114**
45-99	**TOTAL SERVICES**	**1 082 917**	**1 080 031**	**1 052 382**	**1 063 043**	**1 072 083**	**1 049 871**	**1 038 024**	**1 046 279**
45-82	**BUSINESS SECTOR SERVICES**	**774 643**	**771 869**	**742 734**	**753 110**	**761 425**	**744 365**	**734 516**	**740 362**
45-82x	**BUSINESS SECTOR SERVICES excluding real estate**	**585 577**	**580 295**	**551 292**	**564 364**	**569 239**	**553 159**	**544 575**	**547 736**
05-82x	**NON-AGRICULTURE BUSINESS SECTOR excluding real estate**	..	..	..	..	..	..	..	..

.. Not available

Note: Detailed metadata at: http://metalinks.oecd.org/stan/20170410/1c43.

Information on data for Israel: http://oe.cd/israel-disclaimer.

Disclaimer: http://oe.cd/disclaimer

ITALY

Table 4. Gross fixed capital formation, current prices

ISIC Rev. 4

Million EUR

		2007	2008	2009	2010	2011	2012	2013	2014
	TOTAL	**347 176**	**346 691**	**314 360**	**320 002**	**321 837**	**296 166**	**276 668**	**269 330**
01-03	**AGRICULTURE, FORESTRY AND FISHING**	**12 547**	**11 893**	**10 174**	**10 806**	**12 037**	**11 194**	**9 225**	**8 830**
05-09	**MINING AND QUARRYING**	**1 889**	**1 749**	**1 533**	**1 842**	**1 821**	**1 643**	**1 568**	**1 967**
10-33	**MANUFACTURING**	**60 002**	**60 971**	**51 385**	**57 111**	**58 025**	**55 705**	**51 449**	**52 347**
10-12	Food products, beverages and tobacco	6 619	6 732	5 056	6 321	6 350	6 666	5 865	6 121
13-14	Textiles and wearing apparel	2 657	2 614	2 084	2 425	2 276	2 226	1 999	2 010
15	Leather and related products	614	910	915	881	1 135	1 142	1 075	1 230
16	Wood, wood and cork products	1 148	1 147	977	1 322	1 080	833	1 273	..
17	Paper and paper products	1 589	1 436	1 023	968	1 324	1 367	1 045	..
18	Printing and reproduction of recorded media	866	880	719	1 001	909	876	496	..
19-23	Chemical, rubber, plastics, non-metallic products	15 285	15 349	12 891	14 621	14 581	13 572	12 503	12 571
20	Chemicals and chemical products	4 021	3 761	3 606	3 721	3 732	3 237	3 259	3 362
21	Pharmaceutical products	2 065	1 921	2 143	2 322	2 244	2 231	2 239	2 361
22-23	Rubber, plastic, non-metallic mineral products	6 193	6 975	4 598	5 845	5 840	5 489	5 184	4 991
24	Basic metals	3 655	4 019	3 323	2 736	3 348	3 428	2 839	3 184
25	Metal products, except machinery and equipment	5 942	5 542	4 669	5 996	5 442	5 120	4 315	4 431
26-28	Machinery and equipment	11 783	11 994	10 209	11 421	11 706	10 876	9 990	10 304
26	Computer, electronic and optical products	3 087	2 681	2 916	2 983	2 989	3 007	2 342	2 640
27	Electrical equipment	2 925	2 881	2 416	2 768	2 868	2 287	2 024	1 956
28	Machinery and equipment n.e.c.	5 771	6 432	4 876	5 670	5 848	5 582	5 623	5 708
29-30	Transport equipment	5 973	6 850	6 001	6 027	6 474	7 014	7 583	7 422
29	Motor vehicles, trailers and semi-trailers	4 149	5 174	4 195	4 402	4 372	4 596	6 436	5 915
30	Other transport equipment	1 824	1 676	1 806	1 625	2 102	2 418	1 147	1 506
31-33	Furniture; repair, installation of machinery and equipment	3 872	3 497	3 520	3 391	3 400	2 583	2 466	2 482
31-32	Furniture, other manufacturing	2 250	2 151	1 721	2 395	2 295	1 766	1 630	..
33	Repair and installation of machinery and equipment	1 622	1 346	1 799	997	1 105	817	835	..
35-39	**ELECTRICITY, GAS, WATER AND WASTE MANAGEMENT**	**21 691**	**23 209**	**18 985**	**14 479**	**18 163**	**14 832**	**15 098**	**12 545**
35	Electricity, gas, steam and air conditioning supply	17 685	19 563	15 531	10 727	14 503	10 682	11 936	9 553
36-39	Water supply; sewerage, waste, remediation activities	4 006	3 647	3 455	3 752	3 660	4 150	3 161	2 992
41-43	**CONSTRUCTION**	**10 346**	**9 938**	**7 612**	**8 726**	**8 673**	**6 514**	**5 549**	**5 399**
45-56	Distribution; transportation, accommodation, food service	53 220	50 781	45 876	48 830	51 341	41 562	38 532	36 138
45-47	**Wholesale and retail trade; motor vehicle and motorcycle repairs**	**20 924**	**18 502**	**16 667**	**18 078**	**18 987**	**15 236**	**15 137**	**12 595**
49-53	**Transportation and storage**	**24 984**	**24 427**	**23 263**	**24 280**	**25 786**	**21 728**	**19 942**	**20 002**
55-56	**Accommodation and food service activities**	**7 311**	**7 852**	**5 947**	**6 471**	**6 567**	**4 598**	**3 453**	**3 540**
58-63	**Information and communication**	**15 174**	**14 294**	**12 790**	**14 791**	**14 774**	**15 930**	**15 940**	**15 416**
58-60	Publishing, audiovisual and broadcasting activities	3 107	3 237	2 491	3 172	3 113	3 383	2 521	2 242
61	Telecommunications	5 220	5 520	4 608	5 613	5 612	6 723	6 578	6 897
62-63	IT and other information services	6 847	5 536	5 691	6 005	6 050	5 824	6 842	6 277
64-66	**Financial and insurance activities**	**5 489**	**5 731**	**4 698**	**5 530**	**4 610**	**3 880**	**4 002**	**4 418**
68	**Real estate activities**	**104 778**	**106 140**	**98 175**	**99 700**	**95 810**	**91 556**	**87 313**	**85 183**
69-82	**Professional, scientific, technical, admin., support activities**	**15 922**	**15 937**	**12 116**	**13 096**	**13 547**	**13 383**	**10 996**	**11 404**
69-75	Professional, scientific and technical activities	6 850	6 792	5 642	6 221	6 187	6 177	6 065	5 799
69-71	Legal, accounting activities; mgt consultancy; engineering	3 805	3 642	2 969	3 350	3 416	3 363	3 303	3 308
73-75	Advertising, market research; other prof., scientific, tech.	1 434	1 398	1 140	1 304	1 302	1 364	1 249	1 033
77-82	Administrative and support service activities	9 072	9 144	6 473	6 875	7 360	7 207	4 930	5 605
84-88	**Public administration, defence; social security; education; health**	**39 632**	**39 979**	**45 148**	**39 476**	**37 230**	**35 407**	**32 571**	**31 147**
84	**Public administration, defence; compulsory social security**	**28 038**	**29 555**	**33 533**	**27 820**	**26 790**	**24 703**	**22 646**	**21 761**
85	**Education**	**2 482**	**2 422**	**2 378**	**2 038**	**2 019**	**3 002**	**2 899**	**2 870**
86-88	**Human health and social work activities**	**9 113**	**8 002**	**9 237**	**9 618**	**8 421**	**7 702**	**7 026**	**6 516**
90-99	**Arts, entertainment, household goods repairs, other**	**6 486**	**6 072**	**5 868**	**5 615**	**5 806**	**4 560**	**4 424**	**4 536**
90-93	**Arts, entertainment and recreation**	**4 142**	**3 588**	**4 081**	**3 453**	**3 597**	**2 764**	**2 993**	**2 712**
94-96	**Other service activities**	**2 344**	**2 484**	**1 786**	**2 162**	**2 209**	**1 796**	**1 431**	**1 824**
97-98	**Activities of households as employers and for own use**	**0**	**0**	**0**	**0**	**0**	**0**	**0**	**0**
05-39	**INDUSTRY INCLUDING ENERGY**	**83 581**	**85 929**	**71 903**	**73 431**	**78 009**	**72 180**	**68 114**	**66 859**
45-99	**TOTAL SERVICES**	**240 702**	**238 932**	**224 671**	**227 038**	**223 118**	**206 278**	**193 779**	**188 242**
45-82	**BUSINESS SECTOR SERVICES**	**194 583**	**192 882**	**173 655**	**181 947**	**180 082**	**166 311**	**156 784**	**152 560**
45-82x	**BUSINESS SECTOR SERVICES excluding real estate**	**89 805**	**86 742**	**75 480**	**82 246**	**84 272**	**74 755**	**69 471**	**67 376**
05-82x	**NON-AGRICULTURE BUSINESS SECTOR excluding real estate**	..	..	..	..	..	..	..	..

.. Not available

Note: Detailed metadata at: http://metalinks.oecd.org/stan/20170410/1c43.

Information on data for Israel: http://oe.cd/israel-disclaimer.

Disclaimer: http://oe.cd/disclaimer

Table 5. Number of persons engaged, total employment

ISIC Rev. 4

Thousands

		2007	2008	2009	2010	2011	2012	2013	2014
	TOTAL	**25 295**	**25 349**	**24 926**	**24 766**	**24 843**	**24 765**	**24 323**	**24 339**
01-03	**AGRICULTURE, FORESTRY AND FISHING**	**985**	**963**	**942**	**960**	**942**	**919**	**892**	**891**
05-09	**MINING AND QUARRYING**	**29**	**28**	**27**	**26**	**26**	**26**	**24**	**24**
10-33	**MANUFACTURING**	**4 599**	**4 551**	**4 328**	**4 166**	**4 135**	**4 057**	**3 941**	**3 868**
10-12	Food products, beverages and tobacco	456	462	449	443	452	449	450	449
13-14	Textiles and wearing apparel	493	485	445	415	411	382	359	351
15	Leather and related products	156	157	143	138	140	151	152	153
16	Wood, wood and cork products	169	166	157	155	149	139	129	124
17	Paper and paper products	82	80	79	78	77	76	73	73
18	Printing and reproduction of recorded media	117	116	111	105	102	98	94	90
19-23	Chemical, rubber, plastics, non-metallic products	686	668	637	615	603	594	570	548
20	Chemicals and chemical products	122	119	115	113	113	115	114	112
21	Pharmaceutical products	73	70	67	65	64	64	62	59
22-23	Rubber, plastic, non-metallic mineral products	469	457	435	415	404	395	376	361
24	Basic metals	155	154	148	142	140	137	132	131
25	Metal products, except machinery and equipment	649	643	608	578	574	559	535	526
26-28	Machinery and equipment	815	809	782	761	760	751	740	732
26	Computer, electronic and optical products	130	126	119	114	116	114	109	103
27	Electrical equipment	197	193	183	180	178	177	171	168
28	Machinery and equipment n.e.c.	488	490	480	467	466	460	460	461
29-30	Transport equipment	296	296	284	272	268	263	258	254
29	Motor vehicles, trailers and semi-trailers	193	192	184	177	176	173	171	167
30	Other transport equipment	104	104	101	95	92	90	88	87
31-33	Furniture; repair, installation of machinery and equipment	525	514	485	464	460	458	449	438
31-32	Furniture, other manufacturing	346	334	315	296	292	284	276	271
33	Repair and installation of machinery and equipment	179	180	171	168	168	174	173	167
35-39	**ELECTRICITY, GAS, WATER AND WASTE MANAGEMENT**	**279**	**277**	**278**	**278**	**279**	**287**	**286**	**287**
35	Electricity, gas, steam and air conditioning supply	90	87	85	85	85	87	87	88
36-39	Water supply; sewerage, waste, remediation activities	189	190	193	193	194	200	199	199
41-43	**CONSTRUCTION**	**1 961**	**1 966**	**1 945**	**1 912**	**1 868**	**1 779**	**1 643**	**1 578**
45-56	Distribution; transportation, accommodation, food service	6 223	6 254	6 150	6 133	6 188	6 210	6 114	6 125
45-47	**Wholesale and retail trade; motor vehicle and motorcycle repairs**	**3 771**	**3 770**	**3 720**	**3 699**	**3 715**	**3 706**	**3 636**	**3 613**
49-53	**Transportation and storage**	**1 159**	**1 169**	**1 142**	**1 134**	**1 143**	**1 122**	**1 104**	**1 106**
55-56	**Accommodation and food service activities**	**1 293**	**1 315**	**1 289**	**1 300**	**1 330**	**1 382**	**1 374**	**1 406**
58-63	**Information and communication**	**603**	**604**	**609**	**597**	**595**	**591**	**585**	**577**
58-60	Publishing, audiovisual and broadcasting activities	111	111	109	108	107	103	96	92
61	Telecommunications	118	116	113	108	104	99	95	89
62-63	IT and other information services	374	376	387	381	384	389	394	397
64-66	**Financial and insurance activities**	**708**	**710**	**700**	**690**	**685**	**682**	**670**	**669**
68	**Real estate activities**	**176**	**174**	**172**	**177**	**181**	**186**	**180**	**175**
69-82	**Professional, scientific, technical, admin., support activities**	**2 670**	**2 725**	**2 654**	**2 701**	**2 782**	**2 825**	**2 814**	**2 868**
69-75	Professional, scientific and technical activities	1 520	1 543	1 531	1 551	1 576	1 605	1 601	1 623
69-71	Legal, accounting activities; mgt consultancy; engineering	1 067	1 081	1 071	1 086	1 113	1 120	1 122	1 138
73-75	Advertising, market research; other prof., scientific, tech.	335	343	339	342	343	363	358	360
77-82	Administrative and support service activities	1 150	1 182	1 123	1 150	1 207	1 221	1 214	1 244
84-88	**Public administration, defence; social security; education; health**	**4 687**	**4 700**	**4 667**	**4 636**	**4 632**	**4 596**	**4 578**	**4 614**
84	**Public administration, defence; compulsory social security**	**1 390**	**1 374**	**1 367**	**1 363**	**1 345**	**1 316**	**1 291**	**1 277**
85	**Education**	**1 647**	**1 630**	**1 588**	**1 546**	**1 525**	**1 500**	**1 488**	**1 503**
86-88	**Human health and social work activities**	**1 651**	**1 697**	**1 712**	**1 727**	**1 763**	**1 780**	**1 799**	**1 835**
90-99	**Arts, entertainment, household goods repairs, other**	**2 376**	**2 396**	**2 453**	**2 489**	**2 530**	**2 608**	**2 596**	**2 663**
90-93	**Arts, entertainment and recreation**	**304**	**312**	**307**	**318**	**318**	**319**	**315**	**315**
94-96	**Other service activities**	**687**	**680**	**697**	**702**	**704**	**723**	**714**	**727**
97-98	**Activities of households as employers and for own use**	**1 386**	**1 405**	**1 449**	**1 470**	**1 508**	**1 566**	**1 566**	**1 621**
05-39	**INDUSTRY INCLUDING ENERGY**	**4 906**	**4 856**	**4 633**	**4 470**	**4 440**	**4 370**	**4 251**	**4 179**
45-99	**TOTAL SERVICES**	**17 443**	**17 564**	**17 405**	**17 424**	**17 593**	**17 698**	**17 536**	**17 692**
45-82	**BUSINESS SECTOR SERVICES**	**10 380**	**10 467**	**10 285**	**10 299**	**10 431**	**10 494**	**10 363**	**10 414**
45-82x	**BUSINESS SECTOR SERVICES excluding real estate**	**10 204**	**10 293**	**10 113**	**10 121**	**10 250**	**10 308**	**10 183**	**10 239**
05-82x	**NON-AGRICULTURE BUSINESS SECTOR excluding real estate**	..	..	..	..	..	..	..	..

.. Not available

Note: Detailed metadata at: http://metalinks.oecd.org/stan/20170410/1c43.

Information on data for Israel: http://oe.cd/israel-disclaimer.

Disclaimer: http://oe.cd/disclaimer

Table 6. Labour costs (compensation of employees), current prices

ISIC Rev. 4

Million EUR

		2007	2008	2009	2010	2011	2012	2013	2014
	TOTAL	**617 212**	**639 168**	**634 815**	**642 342**	**651 470**	**643 066**	**637 180**	**638 719**
01-03	**AGRICULTURE, FORESTRY AND FISHING**	**7 860**	**7 661**	**7 703**	**8 041**	**8 260**	**8 283**	**8 103**	**8 411**
05-09	**MINING AND QUARRYING**	**1 136**	**1 146**	**1 131**	**1 103**	**1 135**	**1 111**	**1 147**	**1 148**
10-33	**MANUFACTURING**	**138 033**	**141 331**	**130 290**	**131 023**	**134 790**	**132 537**	**131 848**	**132 086**
10-12	Food products, beverages and tobacco	11 621	11 996	12 149	12 414	12 800	12 663	13 090	13 256
13-14	Textiles and wearing apparel	10 726	10 733	9 603	9 199	9 307	8 863	8 518	8 569
15	Leather and related products	3 401	3 487	3 197	3 311	3 624	3 807	3 927	3 996
16	Wood, wood and cork products	3 149	3 267	3 014	2 911	2 877	2 636	2 419	2 309
17	Paper and paper products	2 822	2 801	2 783	2 800	2 887	2 864	2 839	2 902
18	Printing and reproduction of recorded media	2 940	2 995	2 846	2 698	2 617	2 501	2 384	2 295
19-23	Chemical, rubber, plastics, non-metallic products	25 548	25 766	24 178	24 152	24 476	24 232	23 683	23 083
20	Chemicals and chemical products	5 408	5 447	5 173	5 289	5 423	5 592	5 670	5 584
21	Pharmaceutical products	4 261	4 260	4 067	4 030	4 133	4 191	4 094	3 966
22-23	Rubber, plastic, non-metallic mineral products	14 539	14 688	13 583	13 488	13 519	13 161	12 654	12 464
24	Basic metals	5 933	6 101	5 261	5 475	5 650	5 532	5 372	5 428
25	Metal products, except machinery and equipment	17 357	18 053	16 240	16 277	16 857	16 563	16 280	16 298
26-28	Machinery and equipment	30 636	31 717	29 070	29 967	31 485	31 309	31 729	31 986
26	Computer, electronic and optical products	5 022	5 048	4 659	4 728	4 977	4 904	4 967	4 638
27	Electrical equipment	6 570	6 705	6 244	6 496	6 605	6 469	6 386	6 508
28	Machinery and equipment n.e.c.	19 044	19 964	18 167	18 743	19 903	19 936	20 376	20 840
29-30	Transport equipment	12 093	12 212	10 628	10 648	10 959	10 475	10 594	11 052
29	Motor vehicles, trailers and semi-trailers	7 742	7 653	6 368	6 558	6 916	6 549	6 638	7 021
30	Other transport equipment	4 352	4 559	4 260	4 090	4 043	3 926	3 956	4 031
31-33	Furniture; repair, installation of machinery and equipment	11 808	12 203	11 322	11 171	11 250	11 092	11 014	10 912
31-32	Furniture, other manufacturing	7 439	7 612	7 040	6 817	6 844	6 525	6 505	6 564
33	Repair and installation of machinery and equipment	4 369	4 591	4 282	4 355	4 406	4 566	4 509	4 348
35-39	**ELECTRICITY, GAS, WATER AND WASTE MANAGEMENT**	**11 331**	**11 591**	**12 216**	**12 399**	**12 730**	**13 168**	**13 189**	**13 330**
35	Electricity, gas, steam and air conditioning supply	4 877	4 843	4 978	5 024	5 115	5 403	5 295	5 364
36-39	Water supply; sewerage, waste, remediation activities	6 454	6 748	7 238	7 375	7 615	7 765	7 895	7 967
41-43	**CONSTRUCTION**	**36 294**	**37 958**	**38 290**	**37 736**	**37 581**	**34 856**	**31 648**	**30 024**
45-56	Distribution; transportation, accommodation, food service	116 401	121 084	122 514	124 364	127 333	127 204	126 558	127 432
45-47	**Wholesale and retail trade; motor vehicle and motorcycle repairs**	**60 444**	**63 326**	**64 704**	**65 808**	**67 451**	**67 283**	**66 699**	**66 959**
49-53	**Transportation and storage**	**34 667**	**35 488**	**35 149**	**35 392**	**35 888**	**35 383**	**35 671**	**35 838**
55-56	**Accommodation and food service activities**	**21 289**	**22 270**	**22 661**	**23 163**	**23 995**	**24 538**	**24 188**	**24 635**
58-63	**Information and communication**	**21 665**	**22 229**	**23 287**	**23 287**	**23 340**	**23 276**	**23 359**	**23 230**
58-60	Publishing, audiovisual and broadcasting activities	4 905	4 955	5 047	5 020	4 928	4 842	4 698	4 483
61	Telecommunications	5 446	5 548	5 537	5 409	5 245	5 083	4 723	4 378
62-63	IT and other information services	11 313	11 726	12 704	12 858	13 167	13 351	13 938	14 370
64-66	**Financial and insurance activities**	**37 041**	**37 590**	**36 102**	**36 467**	**36 899**	**35 943**	**34 000**	**34 565**
68	**Real estate activities**	**2 151**	**2 187**	**2 301**	**2 357**	**2 461**	**2 367**	**2 226**	**2 178**
69-82	**Professional, scientific, technical, admin., support activities**	**42 497**	**45 119**	**45 951**	**48 367**	**50 516**	**49 903**	**51 042**	**52 221**
69-75	Professional, scientific and technical activities	21 631	23 082	24 457	25 097	25 470	24 689	25 149	25 646
69-71	Legal, accounting activities; mgt consultancy; engineering	12 098	12 952	14 177	14 493	15 021	14 424	14 475	15 024
73-75	Advertising, market research; other prof., scientific, tech.	3 637	3 927	4 027	4 182	4 240	4 176	4 392	4 452
77-82	Administrative and support service activities	20 866	22 037	21 494	23 270	25 046	25 214	25 894	26 575
84-88	**Public administration, defence; social security; education; health**	**173 018**	**179 755**	**181 903**	**183 565**	**182 359**	**179 268**	**178 271**	**178 012**
84	**Public administration, defence; compulsory social security**	**67 011**	**68 725**	**69 473**	**70 406**	**70 657**	**69 013**	**68 209**	**66 835**
85	**Education**	**55 695**	**56 102**	**58 028**	**56 581**	**54 864**	**53 959**	**53 792**	**54 467**
86-88	**Human health and social work activities**	**50 312**	**54 928**	**54 402**	**56 578**	**56 838**	**56 296**	**56 270**	**56 710**
90-99	**Arts, entertainment, household goods repairs, other**	**29 787**	**31 517**	**33 125**	**33 633**	**34 068**	**35 150**	**35 788**	**36 081**
90-93	**Arts, entertainment and recreation**	**6 762**	**7 138**	**7 285**	**7 446**	**7 653**	**7 579**	**7 650**	**7 552**
94-96	**Other service activities**	**7 238**	**7 479**	**8 094**	**8 181**	**8 350**	**9 111**	**9 038**	**9 572**
97-98	**Activities of households as employers and for own use**	**15 787**	**16 900**	**17 747**	**18 006**	**18 065**	**18 461**	**19 100**	**18 957**
05-39	**INDUSTRY INCLUDING ENERGY**	**150 500**	**154 067**	**143 637**	**144 524**	**148 655**	**146 815**	**146 184**	**146 564**
45-99	**TOTAL SERVICES**	**422 559**	**439 481**	**445 185**	**452 040**	**456 975**	**453 111**	**451 244**	**453 720**
45-82	**BUSINESS SECTOR SERVICES**	**219 753**	**228 209**	**230 156**	**234 841**	**240 548**	**238 693**	**237 185**	**239 627**
45-82x	**BUSINESS SECTOR SERVICES excluding real estate**	**217 602**	**226 021**	**227 855**	**232 484**	**238 088**	**236 327**	**234 959**	**237 449**
05-82x	**NON-AGRICULTURE BUSINESS SECTOR excluding real estate**	..	..	..	..	..	..	..	..

.. Not available

Note: Detailed metadata at: http://metalinks.oecd.org/stan/20170410/1c43.

Information on data for Israel: http://oe.cd/israel-disclaimer

Disclaimer: http://oe.cd/disclaimer

LUXEMBOURG

Table 1. Production (gross output), current prices

ISIC Rev. 4

Million EUR

		2007	2008	2009	2010	2011	2012	2013	2014
	TOTAL	**107 832**	**110 498**	**98 959**	**115 290**	**124 010**	**131 166**	**143 593**	**164 791**
01-03	**AGRICULTURE, FORESTRY AND FISHING**	**373**	**383**	**341**	**345**	**371**	**453**	**465**	**469**
05-09	**MINING AND QUARRYING**	**78**	**77**	**73**	**67**	**74**	**72**	**71**	**70**
10-33	**MANUFACTURING**	**10 040**	**10 349**	**7 411**	**9 287**	**9 588**	**8 780**	**8 876**	**9 254**
10-12	Food products, beverages and tobacco	715	748	759	791	916	883	907	1 000
13-14	Textiles and wearing apparel	..	..	..	..	..	..	..	..
15	Leather and related products	..	..	..	..	..	..	..	..
16	Wood, wood and cork products	198	174	161	190	174	..	..	..
17	Paper and paper products	339	362	366	370	190	..	..	..
18	Printing and reproduction of recorded media	129	130	112	110	76	..	..	..
19-23	Chemical, rubber, plastics, non-metallic products	2 344	2 236	1 785	2 439	2 590	2 129	2 361	2 658
20	Chemicals and chemical products	384	344	242	355	325	..	..	..
21	Pharmaceutical products	2	1	1	0	0	..	..	..
22-23	Rubber, plastic, non-metallic mineral products	1 959	1 891	1 542	2 084	2 265	1 833	2 015	2 263
24	Basic metals	2 879	3 439	1 760	2 327	2 539	..	..	..
25	Metal products, except machinery and equipment	1 060	997	683	760	786	..	..	..
26-28	Machinery and equipment	1 281	1 169	972	1 248	1 397	1 397	1 424	1 586
26	Computer, electronic and optical products	260	155	167	220	257	..	..	..
27	Electrical equipment	167	185	164	189	213	..	..	..
28	Machinery and equipment n.e.c.	854	828	640	839	927	..	..	..
29-30	Transport equipment	124	141	91	96	118	120	121	141
29	Motor vehicles, trailers and semi-trailers	122	139	89	94	117	..	..	..
30	Other transport equipment	2	3	2	3	2	..	..	..
31-33	Furniture; repair, installation of machinery and equipment	283	304	208	358	179	194	182	191
31-32	Furniture, other manufacturing	55	61	63	63	25	70	74	82
33	Repair and installation of machinery and equipment	228	244	144	295	155	123	108	110
35-39	**ELECTRICITY, GAS, WATER AND WASTE MANAGEMENT**	**1 604**	**1 793**	**1 409**	**1 499**	**1 775**	**1 741**	**1 869**	**1 797**
35	Electricity, gas, steam and air conditioning supply	1 232	1 401	1 015	1 088	1 280	1 293	1 411	1 309
36-39	Water supply; sewerage, waste, remediation activities	372	392	394	411	495	448	458	488
41-43	**CONSTRUCTION**	**4 868**	**5 135**	**4 998**	**4 859**	**5 379**	**5 210**	**5 416**	**6 173**
45-56	Distribution; transportation, accommodation, food service	11 269	13 702	12 697	14 485	17 398	18 803	21 048	21 987
45-47	**Wholesale and retail trade; motor vehicle and motorcycle repairs**	**6 208**	**8 223**	**7 753**	**8 976**	**11 528**	**12 919**	**14 939**	**15 563**
49-53	**Transportation and storage**	**3 916**	**4 260**	**3 712**	**4 220**	**4 495**	**4 449**	**4 621**	**4 857**
55-56	**Accommodation and food service activities**	**1 146**	**1 219**	**1 231**	**1 289**	**1 374**	**1 435**	**1 488**	**1 566**
58-63	**Information and communication**	**5 602**	**5 374**	**5 821**	**7 192**	**6 926**	**7 930**	**9 265**	**11 882**
58-60	Publishing, audiovisual and broadcasting activities	669	567	459	484	480	521	718	720
61	Telecommunications	2 177	2 589	3 163	4 013	3 931	3 964	3 882	3 983
62-63	IT and other information services	2 756	2 217	2 199	2 694	2 515	3 445	4 665	7 179
64-66	**Financial and insurance activities**	**58 076**	**54 249**	**46 945**	**56 333**	**60 065**	**63 109**	**69 777**	**80 542**
68	**Real estate activities**	**3 400**	**3 643**	**3 765**	**3 936**	**4 151**	**4 330**	**4 530**	**4 802**
69-82	**Professional, scientific, technical, admin., support activities**	**5 677**	**8 382**	**7 494**	**8 895**	**9 227**	**10 973**	**11 963**	**17 311**
69-75	Professional, scientific and technical activities	3 493	4 243	4 376	4 294	4 914	5 037	5 957	7 101
69-71	Legal, accounting activities; mgt consultancy; engineering	..	..	..	..	..	..	..	..
73-75	Advertising, market research; other prof., scientific, tech.	..	..	..	..	..	..	..	..
77-82	Administrative and support service activities	2 184	4 139	3 119	4 601	4 312	5 936	6 006	10 210
84-88	**Public administration, defence; social security; education; health**	**5 931**	**6 409**	**6 916**	**7 300**	**7 860**	**8 524**	**8 995**	**9 165**
84	**Public administration, defence; compulsory social security**	**2 444**	**2 630**	**2 814**	**2 835**	**3 139**	**3 448**	**3 560**	**3 492**
85	**Education**	**1 330**	**1 441**	**1 580**	**1 784**	**1 892**	**2 031**	**2 037**	**2 122**
86-88	**Human health and social work activities**	**2 157**	**2 338**	**2 523**	**2 681**	**2 828**	**3 046**	**3 399**	**3 551**
90-99	**Arts, entertainment, household goods repairs, other**	**915**	**1 002**	**1 089**	**1 092**	**1 197**	**1 243**	**1 318**	**1 339**
90-93	**Arts, entertainment and recreation**	**406**	**463**	**510**	**477**	**519**	**543**	**569**	**603**
94-96	**Other service activities**	**399**	**428**	**465**	**498**	**559**	**583**	**624**	**611**
97-98	**Activities of households as employers and for own use**	**109**	**111**	**114**	**117**	**119**	**117**	**125**	**125**
05-39	**INDUSTRY INCLUDING ENERGY**	**11 721**	**12 220**	**8 892**	**10 852**	**11 436**	**10 593**	**10 816**	**11 121**
45-99	**TOTAL SERVICES**	**90 870**	**92 761**	**84 728**	**99 233**	**106 824**	**114 911**	**126 896**	**147 028**
45-82	**BUSINESS SECTOR SERVICES**	**84 024**	**85 349**	**76 723**	**90 842**	**97 767**	**105 144**	**116 583**	**136 524**
45-82x	**BUSINESS SECTOR SERVICES excluding real estate**	**80 624**	**81 706**	**72 958**	**86 905**	**93 616**	**100 814**	**112 053**	**131 722**
05-82x	**NON-AGRICULTURE BUSINESS SECTOR excluding real estate**	..	..	..	..	..	..	..	..

.. Not available

Note: Detailed metadata at: http://metalinks.oecd.org/stan/20170410/1c43.

Information on data for Israel: http://oe.cd/israel-disclaimer.

Disclaimer: http://oe.cd/disclaimer

LUXEMBOURG

Table 2. Value added, current prices

ISIC Rev. 4

Million EUR

		2007	2008	2009	2010	2011	2012	2013	2014
	TOTAL	**33 035**	**33 889**	**32 602**	**35 916**	**38 433**	**39 181**	**41 384**	**43 844**
01-03	**AGRICULTURE, FORESTRY AND FISHING**	**152**	**119**	**93**	**99**	**109**	**159**	**123**	**128**
05-09	**MINING AND QUARRYING**	**36**	**32**	**31**	**30**	**33**	**30**	**29**	**29**
10-33	**MANUFACTURING**	**3 011**	**2 697**	**1 713**	**2 080**	**2 124**	**2 093**	**2 298**	**2 500**
10-12	Food products, beverages and tobacco	255	232	216	260	249	258	264	274
13-14	Textiles and wearing apparel	..	..	..	..	..	..	..	..
15	Leather and related products	..	..	..	..	..	..	..	..
16	Wood, wood and cork products	42	38	34	47	43	..	..	..
17	Paper and paper products	37	35	40	34	40	..	..	..
18	Printing and reproduction of recorded media	61	58	48	48	37	..	..	..
19-23	Chemical, rubber, plastics, non-metallic products	684	628	509	567	540	479	655	852
20	Chemicals and chemical products	80	99	74	..	..	..	..	..
21	Pharmaceutical products	1	1	0	..	..	..	..	..
22-23	Rubber, plastic, non-metallic mineral products	603	529	434	489	455	407	570	747
24	Basic metals	876	787	104	206	279	..	..	..
25	Metal products, except machinery and equipment	290	274	209	224	227	..	..	..
26-28	Machinery and equipment	429	387	354	417	435	454	490	462
26	Computer, electronic and optical products	99	62	57	72	77	..	..	..
27	Electrical equipment	57	76	65	77	78	..	..	..
28	Machinery and equipment n.e.c.	272	249	231	268	280	..	..	..
29-30	Transport equipment	51	49	25	32	36	38	40	46
29	Motor vehicles, trailers and semi-trailers	50	48	24	31	36	..	..	..
30	Other transport equipment	1	1	1	1	1	..	..	..
31-33	Furniture; repair, installation of machinery and equipment	91	78	67	73	68	68	69	78
31-32	Furniture, other manufacturing	28	32	36	32	31	31	32	38
33	Repair and installation of machinery and equipment	63	46	32	41	37	37	37	40
35-39	**ELECTRICITY, GAS, WATER AND WASTE MANAGEMENT**	**536**	**516**	**555**	**524**	**538**	**540**	**583**	**667**
35	Electricity, gas, steam and air conditioning supply	347	314	346	300	303	296	313	381
36-39	Water supply; sewerage, waste, remediation activities	189	202	210	224	235	244	270	286
41-43	**CONSTRUCTION**	**1 926**	**1 937**	**1 912**	**1 927**	**2 121**	**2 034**	**2 129**	**2 447**
45-56	Distribution; transportation, accommodation, food service	4 831	5 794	5 214	6 045	7 286	7 030	7 689	7 914
45-47	**Wholesale and retail trade; motor vehicle and motorcycle repairs**	**2 661**	**3 559**	**3 118**	**3 697**	**4 873**	**4 593**	**5 172**	**5 192**
49-53	**Transportation and storage**	**1 577**	**1 613**	**1 460**	**1 693**	**1 716**	**1 709**	**1 774**	**1 920**
55-56	**Accommodation and food service activities**	**592**	**622**	**635**	**655**	**697**	**728**	**742**	**802**
58-63	**Information and communication**	**1 931**	**2 002**	**2 002**	**2 261**	**2 071**	**2 199**	**2 059**	**2 217**
58-60	Publishing, audiovisual and broadcasting activities	286	200	194	220	228	270	281	324
61	Telecommunications	1 123	1 199	1 243	1 429	1 494	1 599	1 342	1 395
62-63	IT and other information services	522	603	565	612	349	330	436	497
64-66	**Financial and insurance activities**	**9 772**	**8 910**	**8 822**	**10 196**	**10 211**	**10 353**	**10 833**	**11 712**
68	**Real estate activities**	**2 883**	**2 932**	**2 919**	**2 974**	**3 195**	**3 345**	**3 511**	**3 658**
69-82	**Professional, scientific, technical, admin., support activities**	**2 904**	**3 569**	**3 588**	**3 569**	**4 009**	**4 119**	**4 363**	**4 712**
69-75	Professional, scientific and technical activities	1 972	2 423	2 583	2 512	2 872	2 910	3 149	3 289
69-71	Legal, accounting activities; mgt consultancy; engineering	..	..	..	..	..	..	..	..
73-75	Advertising, market research; other prof., scientific, tech.	..	..	..	..	..	..	..	..
77-82	Administrative and support service activities	932	1 146	1 004	1 057	1 138	1 210	1 214	1 423
84-88	**Public administration, defence; social security; education; health**	**4 445**	**4 736**	**5 081**	**5 519**	**5 991**	**6 505**	**6 921**	**7 007**
84	**Public administration, defence; compulsory social security**	**1 724**	**1 812**	**1 941**	**2 071**	**2 355**	**2 562**	**2 651**	**2 583**
85	**Education**	**1 167**	**1 252**	**1 343**	**1 517**	**1 608**	**1 719**	**1 767**	**1 838**
86-88	**Human health and social work activities**	**1 554**	**1 672**	**1 798**	**1 931**	**2 028**	**2 224**	**2 502**	**2 587**
90-99	**Arts, entertainment, household goods repairs, other**	**609**	**646**	**673**	**691**	**744**	**773**	**846**	**853**
90-93	**Arts, entertainment and recreation**	**230**	**242**	**245**	**247**	**257**	**271**	**303**	**321**
94-96	**Other service activities**	**270**	**293**	**314**	**327**	**368**	**386**	**419**	**406**
97-98	**Activities of households as employers and for own use**	**109**	**111**	**114**	**117**	**119**	**117**	**125**	**125**
05-39	**INDUSTRY INCLUDING ENERGY**	**3 583**	**3 245**	**2 299**	**2 635**	**2 695**	**2 663**	**2 910**	**3 196**
45-99	**TOTAL SERVICES**	**27 374**	**28 588**	**28 297**	**31 255**	**33 508**	**34 325**	**36 222**	**38 073**
45-82	**BUSINESS SECTOR SERVICES**	**22 320**	**23 206**	**22 543**	**25 045**	**26 773**	**27 047**	**28 455**	**30 213**
45-82x	**BUSINESS SECTOR SERVICES excluding real estate**	**19 437**	**20 274**	**19 625**	**22 071**	**23 578**	**23 702**	**24 944**	**26 555**
05-82x	**NON-AGRICULTURE BUSINESS SECTOR excluding real estate**	..	..	..	..	..	..	..	..

.. Not available

Note: Detailed metadata at: http://metalinks.oecd.org/stan/20170410/1c43.

Information on data for Israel: http://oe.cd/israel-disclaimer.

Disclaimer: http://oe.cd/disclaimer

Table 3. Value added, volumes

ISIC Rev. 4

Million 2010 EUR

		2007	2008	2009	2010	2011	2012	2013	2014
	TOTAL	**36 483**	**36 070**	**34 015**	**35 916**	**36 406**	**36 249**	**37 803**	**39 413**
01-03	**AGRICULTURE, FORESTRY AND FISHING**	**111**	**81**	**95**	**99**	**78**	**101**	**72**	**77**
05-09	**MINING AND QUARRYING**	**42**	**36**	**32**	**30**	**27**	**26**	**26**	**24**
10-33	**MANUFACTURING**	**2 929**	**2 328**	**1 802**	**2 080**	**1 781**	**1 854**	**2 200**	**2 467**
10-12	Food products, beverages and tobacco	345	259	216	260	215	221	220	212
13-14	Textiles and wearing apparel	..	..	..	..	..	..	..	..
15	Leather and related products	..	..	..	..	..	..	..	..
16	Wood, wood and cork products	27	28	32	47	39	..	..	..
17	Paper and paper products	29	26	58	34	21	..	..	..
18	Printing and reproduction of recorded media	66	63	45	48	42	..	..	..
19-23	Chemical, rubber, plastics, non-metallic products	745	648	535	567	464	454	712	966
20	Chemicals and chemical products	..	..	..	..	..	..	..	..
21	Pharmaceutical products	..	..	..	..	..	..	..	..
22-23	Rubber, plastic, non-metallic mineral products	631	523	445	489	378	380	613	819
24	Basic metals	311	219	121	206	162	..	..	..
25	Metal products, except machinery and equipment	302	263	248	224	167	..	..	..
26-28	Machinery and equipment	520	432	361	417	403	468	521	502
26	Computer, electronic and optical products	133	86	64	72	81	..	..	..
27	Electrical equipment	69	84	66	77	72	..	..	..
28	Machinery and equipment n.e.c.	323	265	231	268	250	..	..	..
29-30	Transport equipment	63	54	24	32	25	20	21	24
29	Motor vehicles, trailers and semi-trailers	..	..	..	..	..	..	..	..
30	Other transport equipment	..	..	..	..	..	..	..	..
31-33	Furniture; repair, installation of machinery and equipment	105	87	73	73	62	64	65	75
31-32	Furniture, other manufacturing	35	32	35	32	23	..	..	..
33	Repair and installation of machinery and equipment	71	56	38	41	40	..	..	..
35-39	**ELECTRICITY, GAS, WATER AND WASTE MANAGEMENT**	**731**	**621**	**629**	**524**	**566**	**554**	**606**	**616**
35	Electricity, gas, steam and air conditioning supply	470	378	371	300	377	353	387	395
36-39	Water supply; sewerage, waste, remediation activities	258	242	256	224	189	195	213	216
41-43	**CONSTRUCTION**	**2 061**	**1 973**	**1 904**	**1 927**	**2 050**	**1 874**	**1 901**	**2 109**
45-56	Distribution; transportation, accommodation, food service	5 440	5 951	5 404	6 045	6 585	6 152	6 675	6 889
45-47	**Wholesale and retail trade; motor vehicle and motorcycle repairs**	**3 032**	**3 689**	**3 217**	**3 697**	**4 290**	**3 918**	**4 299**	**4 367**
49-53	**Transportation and storage**	**1 752**	**1 609**	**1 545**	**1 693**	**1 615**	**1 551**	**1 692**	**1 832**
55-56	**Accommodation and food service activities**	**648**	**656**	**642**	**655**	**680**	**691**	**686**	**703**
58-63	**Information and communication**	**1 790**	**1 869**	**1 910**	**2 261**	**2 124**	**2 271**	**2 080**	**2 215**
58-60	Publishing, audiovisual and broadcasting activities	324	222	197	220	218	248	244	277
61	Telecommunications	894	1 002	1 151	1 429	1 579	1 804	1 561	1 610
62-63	IT and other information services	648	696	566	612	328	233	257	288
64-66	**Financial and insurance activities**	**11 057**	**10 278**	**9 532**	**10 196**	**9 713**	**9 493**	**9 799**	**10 222**
68	**Real estate activities**	**2 982**	**3 021**	**2 978**	**2 974**	**3 092**	**3 181**	**3 342**	**3 471**
69-82	**Professional, scientific, technical, admin., support activities**	**3 490**	**3 982**	**3 700**	**3 569**	**3 927**	**3 975**	**4 023**	**4 294**
69-75	Professional, scientific and technical activities	2 473	2 763	2 695	2 512	2 810	2 813	2 880	2 977
69-71	Legal, accounting activities; mgt consultancy; engineering	..	..	..	..	..	..	..	..
73-75	Advertising, market research; other prof., scientific, tech.	..	..	..	..	..	..	..	..
77-82	Administrative and support service activities	1 017	1 212	1 009	1 057	1 117	1 161	1 143	1 320
84-88	**Public administration, defence; social security; education; health**	**5 015**	**5 175**	**5 342**	**5 519**	**5 740**	**6 064**	**6 293**	**6 267**
84	**Public administration, defence; compulsory social security**	**1 955**	**2 004**	**2 071**	**2 071**	**2 301**	**2 473**	**2 509**	**2 399**
85	**Education**	**1 470**	**1 491**	**1 496**	**1 517**	**1 522**	**1 538**	**1 566**	**1 573**
86-88	**Human health and social work activities**	**1 608**	**1 693**	**1 783**	**1 931**	**1 918**	**2 054**	**2 218**	**2 289**
90-99	**Arts, entertainment, household goods repairs, other**	**692**	**707**	**705**	**691**	**723**	**722**	**761**	**750**
90-93	**Arts, entertainment and recreation**	**255**	**261**	**250**	**247**	**254**	**257**	**280**	**291**
94-96	**Other service activities**	**303**	**319**	**332**	**327**	**358**	**364**	**381**	**365**
97-98	**Activities of households as employers and for own use**	**134**	**127**	**122**	**117**	**111**	**102**	**102**	**95**
05-39	**INDUSTRY INCLUDING ENERGY**	**3 754**	**3 017**	**2 453**	**2 635**	**2 373**	**2 439**	**2 843**	**3 123**
45-99	**TOTAL SERVICES**	**30 438**	**30 942**	**29 558**	**31 255**	**31 905**	**31 818**	**32 981**	**34 106**
45-82	**BUSINESS SECTOR SERVICES**	**24 726**	**25 056**	**23 512**	**25 045**	**25 442**	**25 035**	**25 930**	**27 093**
45-82x	**BUSINESS SECTOR SERVICES excluding real estate**	**21 747**	**22 038**	**20 529**	**22 071**	**22 350**	**21 857**	**22 593**	**23 625**
05-82x	**NON-AGRICULTURE BUSINESS SECTOR excluding real estate**	..	..	..	..	..	..	..	..

.. Not available

Note: Detailed metadata at: http://metalinks.oecd.org/stan/20170410/1c43.

Information on data for Israel: http://oe.cd/israel-disclaimer.

Disclaimer: http://oe.cd/disclaimer

Table 4. Gross fixed capital formation, current prices

ISIC Rev. 4

Million EUR

		2007	2008	2009	2010	2011	2012	2013	2014
	TOTAL	**7 396**	**8 084**	**7 127**	**7 026**	**8 370**	**9 026**	**9 017**	**9 587**
01-03	**AGRICULTURE, FORESTRY AND FISHING**	**152**	**197**	**148**	**128**	**177**	**202**	**211**	**245**
05-09	**MINING AND QUARRYING**	**9**	**8**	**11**	**3**	**6**	**6**	**6**	**11**
10-33	**MANUFACTURING**	**676**	**796**	**507**	**554**	**578**	**581**	**607**	**619**
10-12	Food products, beverages and tobacco	80	92	84	163	83	66	53	50
13-14	Textiles and wearing apparel	..	..	..	..	..	..	..	..
15	Leather and related products	..	..	..	..	..	..	..	..
16	Wood, wood and cork products	..	..	..	..	..	..	..	..
17	Paper and paper products	..	..	..	..	..	..	..	..
18	Printing and reproduction of recorded media	..	..	..	..	..	..	..	..
19-23	Chemical, rubber, plastics, non-metallic products	233	196	148	135	141	160	201	181
20	Chemicals and chemical products	..	..	..	..	..	..	..	..
21	Pharmaceutical products	..	..	..	..	..	..	..	..
22-23	Rubber, plastic, non-metallic mineral products	233	196	148	135	141	160	201	181
24	Basic metals	..	..	..	..	..	..	..	..
25	Metal products, except machinery and equipment	..	..	..	..	..	..	..	..
26-28	Machinery and equipment	98	118	64	73	112	141	136	133
26	Computer, electronic and optical products	..	..	..	..	..	..	..	..
27	Electrical equipment	..	..	..	..	..	..	..	..
28	Machinery and equipment n.e.c.	..	..	..	..	..	..	..	..
29-30	Transport equipment	10	4	-2	9	8	10	10	11
29	Motor vehicles, trailers and semi-trailers	..	..	..	..	..	..	..	..
30	Other transport equipment	..	..	..	..	..	..	..	..
31-33	Furniture; repair, installation of machinery and equipment	11	11	8	5	11	7	9	7
31-32	Furniture, other manufacturing	3	3	5	2	3	3	3	5
33	Repair and installation of machinery and equipment	8	8	3	3	8	5	6	2
35-39	**ELECTRICITY, GAS, WATER AND WASTE MANAGEMENT**	**424**	**510**	**459**	**383**	**434**	**466**	**481**	**489**
35	Electricity, gas, steam and air conditioning supply	289	336	299	266	293	325	317	314
36-39	Water supply; sewerage, waste, remediation activities	135	174	160	118	140	142	164	175
41-43	**CONSTRUCTION**	**139**	**138**	**153**	**130**	**223**	**196**	**240**	**230**
45-56	Distribution; transportation, accommodation, food service	918	1 456	943	799	1 256	1 690	1 493	1 510
45-47	**Wholesale and retail trade; motor vehicle and motorcycle repairs**	**371**	**374**	**382**	**345**	**446**	**468**	**497**	**563**
49-53	**Transportation and storage**	**485**	**1 018**	**456**	**409**	**717**	**1 144**	**917**	**874**
55-56	**Accommodation and food service activities**	**63**	**64**	**105**	**44**	**93**	**78**	**78**	**72**
58-63	**Information and communication**	**594**	**478**	**513**	**640**	**813**	**1 071**	**1 110**	**1 284**
58-60	Publishing, audiovisual and broadcasting activities	..	..	..	..	60	54	..	..
61	Telecommunications	..	..	..	..	737	979	..	..
62-63	IT and other information services	..	..	..	..	16	38	..	..
64-66	**Financial and insurance activities**	**282**	**189**	**272**	**398**	**434**	**421**	**337**	**398**
68	**Real estate activities**	**2 360**	**2 622**	**2 212**	**1 647**	**2 155**	**2 057**	**2 365**	**2 584**
69-82	**Professional, scientific, technical, admin., support activities**	**508**	**342**	**384**	**506**	**570**	**662**	**682**	**674**
69-75	Professional, scientific and technical activities	112	117	140	104	176	205	242	222
69-71	Legal, accounting activities; mgt consultancy; engineering	..	..	..	..	..	..	..	..
73-75	Advertising, market research; other prof., scientific, tech.	..	..	..	..	..	..	..	..
77-82	Administrative and support service activities	396	225	244	401	393	457	440	453
84-88	**Public administration, defence; social security; education; health**	**1 192**	**1 202**	**1 371**	**1 720**	**1 589**	**1 526**	**1 362**	**1 425**
84	**Public administration, defence; compulsory social security**	**802**	**828**	**960**	**1 204**	**1 091**	**1 036**	**868**	**959**
85	**Education**	**203**	**239**	**259**	**300**	**297**	**245**	**239**	**263**
86-88	**Human health and social work activities**	**187**	**136**	**152**	**215**	**200**	**246**	**255**	**203**
90-99	**Arts, entertainment, household goods repairs, other**	**140**	**145**	**154**	**119**	**136**	**148**	**121**	**119**
90-93	**Arts, entertainment and recreation**	**122**	**129**	**137**	**111**	**113**	**127**	**102**	**101**
94-96	**Other service activities**	**18**	**16**	**17**	**8**	**23**	**21**	**20**	**18**
97-98	**Activities of households as employers and for own use**	**0**	**0**	**0**	**0**	**0**	**0**	**0**	**0**
05-39	**INDUSTRY INCLUDING ENERGY**	**1 109**	**1 315**	**977**	**940**	**1 018**	**1 053**	**1 094**	**1 119**
45-99	**TOTAL SERVICES**	**5 995**	**6 434**	**5 849**	**5 828**	**6 953**	**7 575**	**7 472**	**7 993**
45-82	**BUSINESS SECTOR SERVICES**	**4 663**	**5 087**	**4 324**	**3 989**	**5 228**	**5 901**	**5 988**	**6 449**
45-82x	**BUSINESS SECTOR SERVICES excluding real estate**	**2 302**	**2 465**	**2 112**	**2 343**	**3 073**	**3 844**	**3 623**	**3 866**
05-82x	**NON-AGRICULTURE BUSINESS SECTOR excluding real estate**	..	..	..	..	..	..	..	..

.. Not available

Note: Detailed metadata at: http://metalinks.oecd.org/stan/20170410/1c43.

Information on data for Israel: http://oe.cd/israel-disclaimer.

Disclaimer: http://oe.cd/disclaimer

Table 5. Number of persons engaged, total employment

ISIC Rev. 4

Thousands

		2007	2008	2009	2010	2011	2012	2013	2014
	TOTAL	**333**	**349**	**353**	**359**	**370**	**379**	**386**	**396**
01-03	**AGRICULTURE, FORESTRY AND FISHING**	**5**	**5**	**5**	**4**	**4**	**4**	**4**	**4**
05-09	**MINING AND QUARRYING**	**0**	**0**	**0**	**0**	**0**	**0**	**0**	**0**
10-33	**MANUFACTURING**	**34**	**34**	**33**	**33**	**33**	**33**	**32**	**32**
10-12	Food products, beverages and tobacco	5	5	5	5	5	5	5	6
13-14	Textiles and wearing apparel	..	..	..	..	..	..	..	..
15	Leather and related products	..	..	..	..	..	..	..	..
16	Wood, wood and cork products	1	1	1	1	1	..	..	..
17	Paper and paper products	0	0	0	0	0	..	..	..
18	Printing and reproduction of recorded media	1	1	1	1	1	..	..	..
19-23	Chemical, rubber, plastics, non-metallic products	8	8	8	7	7	7	7	8
20	Chemicals and chemical products	..	..	..	..	..	..	..	..
21	Pharmaceutical products	..	..	..	..	..	..	..	..
22-23	Rubber, plastic, non-metallic mineral products	7	7	7	6	7	6	7	7
24	Basic metals	6	6	5	5	5	..	..	..
25	Metal products, except machinery and equipment	5	5	4	4	4	..	..	..
26-28	Machinery and equipment	6	6	6	6	6	6	6	6
26	Computer, electronic and optical products	2	2	2	1	1	..	..	..
27	Electrical equipment	1	1	1	1	1	..	..	..
28	Machinery and equipment n.e.c.	3	3	3	3	3	..	..	..
29-30	Transport equipment	1	1	1	0	0	0	0	0
29	Motor vehicles, trailers and semi-trailers	..	..	..	..	..	..	..	..
30	Other transport equipment	..	..	..	..	..	..	..	..
31-33	Furniture; repair, installation of machinery and equipment	1	1	1	1	1	1	1	1
31-32	Furniture, other manufacturing	1	1	1	1	1	1	1	1
33	Repair and installation of machinery and equipment	0	0	0	0	1	1	0	0
35-39	**ELECTRICITY, GAS, WATER AND WASTE MANAGEMENT**	**4**	**4**	**4**	**4**	**4**	**4**	**4**	**4**
35	Electricity, gas, steam and air conditioning supply	1	1	1	1	1	1	1	1
36-39	Water supply; sewerage, waste, remediation activities	2	2	3	3	3	3	3	3
41-43	**CONSTRUCTION**	**38**	**39**	**39**	**39**	**40**	**40**	**40**	**41**
45-56	Distribution; transportation, accommodation, food service	80	83	84	86	88	90	92	94
45-47	**Wholesale and retail trade; motor vehicle and motorcycle repairs**	**42**	**43**	**44**	**45**	**47**	**48**	**49**	**50**
49-53	**Transportation and storage**	**23**	**25**	**24**	**24**	**25**	**25**	**25**	**25**
55-56	**Accommodation and food service activities**	**15**	**15**	**16**	**16**	**17**	**18**	**18**	**19**
58-63	**Information and communication**	**13**	**13**	**14**	**14**	**15**	**15**	**16**	**16**
58-60	Publishing, audiovisual and broadcasting activities	3	3	3	3	3	3	3	3
61	Telecommunications	3	3	3	3	3	3	3	4
62-63	IT and other information services	7	8	8	8	9	9	10	10
64-66	**Financial and insurance activities**	**39**	**41**	**41**	**41**	**41**	**42**	**43**	**43**
68	**Real estate activities**	**3**	**3**	**3**	**3**	**3**	**3**	**3**	**4**
69-82	**Professional, scientific, technical, admin., support activities**	**45**	**49**	**49**	**52**	**54**	**56**	**58**	**60**
69-75	Professional, scientific and technical activities	24	27	29	29	31	33	34	35
69-71	Legal, accounting activities; mgt consultancy; engineering	..	..	..	..	..	..	..	..
73-75	Advertising, market research; other prof., scientific, tech.	..	..	..	..	..	..	..	..
77-82	Administrative and support service activities	21	22	20	22	23	23	24	25
84-88	**Public administration, defence; social security; education; health**	**60**	**63**	**66**	**68**	**71**	**75**	**78**	**81**
84	**Public administration, defence; compulsory social security**	**19**	**19**	**20**	**20**	**21**	**21**	**22**	**23**
85	**Education**	**15**	**15**	**16**	**16**	**17**	**18**	**18**	**18**
86-88	**Human health and social work activities**	**27**	**29**	**30**	**32**	**34**	**36**	**38**	**40**
90-99	**Arts, entertainment, household goods repairs, other**	**14**	**15**	**15**	**15**	**16**	**16**	**17**	**17**
90-93	**Arts, entertainment and recreation**	**3**	**3**	**3**	**3**	**4**	**4**	**4**	**4**
94-96	**Other service activities**	**7**	**7**	**7**	**7**	**7**	**8**	**8**	**8**
97-98	**Activities of households as employers and for own use**	**4**	**5**	**5**	**5**	**5**	**5**	**5**	**5**
05-39	**INDUSTRY INCLUDING ENERGY**	**38**	**38**	**37**	**37**	**37**	**37**	**36**	**36**
45-99	**TOTAL SERVICES**	**253**	**267**	**272**	**279**	**289**	**298**	**305**	**315**
45-82	**BUSINESS SECTOR SERVICES**	**179**	**190**	**191**	**195**	**201**	**206**	**211**	**217**
45-82x	**BUSINESS SECTOR SERVICES excluding real estate**	**176**	**187**	**188**	**192**	**198**	**203**	**207**	**213**
05-82x	**NON-AGRICULTURE BUSINESS SECTOR excluding real estate**	..	..	..	..	..	..	..	..

.. Not available

Note: Detailed metadata at: http://metalinks.oecd.org/stan/20170410/1c43.

Information on data for Israel: http://oe.cd/israel-disclaimer.

Disclaimer: http://oe.cd/disclaimer

Table 6. Labour costs (compensation of employees), current prices

ISIC Rev. 4

Million EUR

		2007	2008	2009	2010	2011	2012	2013	2014
	TOTAL	**17 193**	**18 514**	**19 010**	**19 899**	**20 858**	**21 756**	**22 655**	**23 820**
01-03	**AGRICULTURE, FORESTRY AND FISHING**	**43**	**45**	**49**	**34**	**36**	**38**	**38**	**41**
05-09	**MINING AND QUARRYING**	**15**	**16**	**17**	**17**	**15**	**15**	**14**	**14**
10-33	**MANUFACTURING**	**1 672**	**1 741**	**1 683**	**1 682**	**1 722**	**1 708**	**1 726**	**1 766**
10-12	Food products, beverages and tobacco	157	163	176	182	184	194	197	200
13-14	Textiles and wearing apparel	..	..	..	..	..	..	..	..
15	Leather and related products	..	..	..	..	..	..	..	..
16	Wood, wood and cork products	26	27	28	27	29	..	..	..
17	Paper and paper products	22	20	22	22	23	..	..	..
18	Printing and reproduction of recorded media	46	46	45	38	36	..	..	..
19-23	Chemical, rubber, plastics, non-metallic products	394	400	397	395	405	406	431	442
20	Chemicals and chemical products	35	38	41	42	..	..	..	..
21	Pharmaceutical products	0	0	0	0	..	..	..	..
22-23	Rubber, plastic, non-metallic mineral products	359	362	356	352	360	363	383	391
24	Basic metals	390	419	401	368	364	..	..	..
25	Metal products, except machinery and equipment	193	207	178	180	188	..	..	..
26-28	Machinery and equipment	293	306	285	306	324	322	323	345
26	Computer, electronic and optical products	69	51	62	64	63	..	..	..
27	Electrical equipment	52	61	60	63	63	..	..	..
28	Machinery and equipment n.e.c.	172	194	163	179	198	..	..	..
29-30	Transport equipment	19	20	17	17	18	18	19	18
29	Motor vehicles, trailers and semi-trailers	18	19	16	16	17	..	..	..
30	Other transport equipment	1	1	1	1	1	..	..	..
31-33	Furniture; repair, installation of machinery and equipment	47	49	52	63	61	55	57	64
31-32	Furniture, other manufacturing	19	24	26	26	25	23	31	33
33	Repair and installation of machinery and equipment	29	25	26	36	36	32	27	31
35-39	**ELECTRICITY, GAS, WATER AND WASTE MANAGEMENT**	**232**	**247**	**259**	**266**	**270**	**289**	**283**	**299**
35	Electricity, gas, steam and air conditioning supply	104	110	117	121	122	130	137	146
36-39	Water supply; sewerage, waste, remediation activities	128	137	142	145	149	159	147	153
41-43	**CONSTRUCTION**	**1 414**	**1 529**	**1 573**	**1 562**	**1 624**	**1 661**	**1 675**	**1 777**
45-56	Distribution; transportation, accommodation, food service	3 113	3 390	3 519	3 647	3 865	4 007	4 120	4 373
45-47	**Wholesale and retail trade; motor vehicle and motorcycle repairs**	**1 528**	**1 663**	**1 737**	**1 811**	**1 941**	**2 035**	**2 106**	**2 268**
49-53	**Transportation and storage**	**1 189**	**1 306**	**1 333**	**1 363**	**1 425**	**1 439**	**1 457**	**1 507**
55-56	**Accommodation and food service activities**	**396**	**421**	**449**	**473**	**499**	**533**	**558**	**597**
58-63	**Information and communication**	**824**	**897**	**929**	**974**	**1 037**	**1 076**	**1 119**	**1 207**
58-60	Publishing, audiovisual and broadcasting activities	169	173	171	173	177	176	174	183
61	Telecommunications	201	208	233	262	270	282	295	313
62-63	IT and other information services	454	516	526	538	590	618	650	711
64-66	**Financial and insurance activities**	**3 654**	**3 841**	**3 828**	**3 989**	**4 058**	**4 229**	**4 443**	**4 580**
68	**Real estate activities**	**68**	**77**	**85**	**85**	**96**	**107**	**115**	**125**
69-82	**Professional, scientific, technical, admin., support activities**	**2 131**	**2 423**	**2 452**	**2 616**	**2 804**	**2 964**	**3 144**	**3 347**
69-75	Professional, scientific and technical activities	1 487	1 722	1 794	1 887	2 046	2 179	2 318	2 451
69-71	Legal, accounting activities; mgt consultancy; engineering	..	..	..	..	..	..	..	..
73-75	Advertising, market research; other prof., scientific, tech.	..	..	..	..	..	..	..	..
77-82	Administrative and support service activities	644	701	658	728	758	785	826	896
84-88	**Public administration, defence; social security; education; health**	**3 575**	**3 830**	**4 100**	**4 492**	**4 768**	**5 077**	**5 366**	**5 664**
84	**Public administration, defence; compulsory social security**	**1 307**	**1 362**	**1 457**	**1 566**	**1 667**	**1 735**	**1 811**	**1 913**
85	**Education**	**1 081**	**1 152**	**1 243**	**1 412**	**1 492**	**1 599**	**1 631**	**1 722**
86-88	**Human health and social work activities**	**1 187**	**1 315**	**1 400**	**1 513**	**1 609**	**1 743**	**1 924**	**2 028**
90-99	**Arts, entertainment, household goods repairs, other**	**452**	**478**	**515**	**536**	**564**	**584**	**611**	**628**
90-93	**Arts, entertainment and recreation**	**134**	**144**	**160**	**164**	**173**	**185**	**192**	**199**
94-96	**Other service activities**	**209**	**223**	**241**	**256**	**272**	**282**	**295**	**303**
97-98	**Activities of households as employers and for own use**	**109**	**111**	**114**	**117**	**119**	**117**	**124**	**125**
05-39	**INDUSTRY INCLUDING ENERGY**	**1 919**	**2 004**	**1 959**	**1 965**	**2 007**	**2 013**	**2 023**	**2 079**
45-99	**TOTAL SERVICES**	**13 818**	**14 936**	**15 429**	**16 339**	**17 191**	**18 044**	**18 919**	**19 923**
45-82	**BUSINESS SECTOR SERVICES**	**9 791**	**10 629**	**10 814**	**11 311**	**11 860**	**12 384**	**12 941**	**13 631**
45-82x	**BUSINESS SECTOR SERVICES excluding real estate**	**9 723**	**10 552**	**10 729**	**11 225**	**11 764**	**12 277**	**12 826**	**13 507**
05-82x	**NON-AGRICULTURE BUSINESS SECTOR excluding real estate**	..	..	..	..	..	..	..	..

.. Not available

Note: Detailed metadata at: http://metalinks.oecd.org/stan/20170410/1c43.
Information on data for Israel: http://oe.cd/israel-disclaimer.

Disclaimer: http://oe.cd/disclaimer

Table 1. Production (gross output), current prices

ISIC Rev. 4

Million MXN

		2007	2008	2009	2010	2011	2012	2013	2014
	TOTAL	**18 952 139**	**20 682 566**	**19 874 836**	**21 994 278**	**24 272 414**	**26 326 044**	**26 880 075**	**28 296 470**
01-03	**AGRICULTURE, FORESTRY AND FISHING**	**557 299**	**610 193**	**622 654**	**672 905**	**709 628**	**794 034**	**804 716**	**862 791**
05-09	**MINING AND QUARRYING**	**1 052 922**	**1 231 118**	**960 432**	**1 170 877**	**1 531 936**	**1 573 301**	**1 485 337**	**1 464 765**
10-33	**MANUFACTURING**	**6 528 373**	**7 035 435**	**6 518 962**	**7 469 394**	**8 248 559**	**9 113 755**	**9 218 539**	**9 731 923**
10-12	Food products, beverages and tobacco	1 312 378	1 438 868	1 555 399	1 642 535	1 804 191	1 977 556	2 061 617	2 130 484
13-14	Textiles and wearing apparel	212 565	207 435	210 594	226 161	230 600	243 030	247 113	248 277
15	Leather and related products	46 466	46 357	47 699	53 131	55 512	61 496	63 566	64 628
16	Wood, wood and cork products	49 642	47 170	46 486	49 776	55 232	64 900	64 270	65 978
17	Paper and paper products	130 037	138 965	144 522	157 965	160 787	172 104	178 171	184 645
18	Printing and reproduction of recorded media	41 790	44 424	45 247	46 351	50 839	52 333	52 658	54 687
19-23	Chemical, rubber, plastics, non-metallic products	1 760 248	2 058 641	1 721 915	1 943 527	2 236 944	2 424 506	2 385 037	2 430 787
20	Chemicals and chemical products	583 868	680 387	547 018	601 973	656 074	649 879	702 796	744 702
21	Pharmaceutical products	168 510	177 626	179 771	165 914	157 279	174 104	174 226	152 048
22-23	Rubber, plastic, non-metallic mineral products	423 948	434 102	412 454	452 841	499 295	547 761	547 401	592 474
24	Basic metals	395 912	451 994	348 550	424 669	499 821	537 816	481 930	508 574
25	Metal products, except machinery and equipment	203 659	224 152	198 506	232 806	256 862	285 094	284 159	307 021
26-28	Machinery and equipment	1 215 780	1 193 143	1 172 778	1 335 002	1 329 596	1 450 867	1 435 050	1 509 591
26	Computer, electronic and optical products	788 541	752 062	741 058	761 223	731 906	791 362	788 219	821 720
27	Electrical equipment	251 586	254 339	245 390	301 055	297 762	322 462	320 165	352 020
28	Machinery and equipment n.e.c.	175 653	186 742	186 330	272 724	299 928	337 043	326 666	335 851
29-30	Transport equipment	934 853	951 999	789 870	1 079 967	1 266 068	1 518 456	1 640 066	1 874 271
29	Motor vehicles, trailers and semi-trailers	897 715	910 076	756 173	1 044 642	1 210 299	1 443 978	1 556 583	1 776 144
30	Other transport equipment	37 138	41 923	33 697	35 325	55 769	74 478	83 483	98 127
31-33	Furniture; repair, installation of machinery and equipment	225 042	232 289	237 396	277 503	302 107	325 596	324 902	352 979
31-32	Furniture, other manufacturing	202 338	208 323	213 678	253 114	276 012	297 872	295 043	320 256
33	Repair and installation of machinery and equipment	22 704	23 966	23 718	24 389	26 095	27 724	29 859	32 723
35-39	**ELECTRICITY, GAS, WATER AND WASTE MANAGEMENT**	**391 710**	**468 287**	**442 583**	**453 341**	**468 513**	**482 035**	**494 629**	**541 234**
35	Electricity, gas, steam and air conditioning supply	335 382	412 302	373 970	380 656	383 654	393 088	398 764	438 246
36-39	Water supply; sewerage, waste, remediation activities	56 328	55 985	68 613	72 685	84 859	88 947	95 865	102 988
41-43	**CONSTRUCTION**	**1 655 790**	**1 859 700**	**1 789 709**	**1 861 633**	**2 061 329**	**2 201 727**	**2 070 370**	**2 173 933**
45-56	Distribution; transportation, accommodation, food service	3 664 869	3 926 385	3 747 921	4 255 438	4 751 467	5 175 544	5 452 246	5 833 497
45-47	**Wholesale and retail trade; motor vehicle and motorcycle repairs**	**2 166 692**	**2 357 250**	**2 206 465**	**2 523 672**	**2 882 530**	**3 128 580**	**3 293 089**	**3 535 351**
49-53	**Transportation and storage**	**1 100 441**	**1 160 324**	**1 156 175**	**1 322 162**	**1 431 336**	**1 571 578**	**1 657 089**	**1 761 432**
55-56	**Accommodation and food service activities**	**397 736**	**408 811**	**385 281**	**409 604**	**437 601**	**475 386**	**502 068**	**536 714**
58-63	**Information and communication**	**496 749**	**523 680**	**557 232**	**568 741**	**572 234**	**595 310**	**610 739**	**622 273**
58-60	Publishing, audiovisual and broadcasting activities	77 435	84 158	85 501	92 223	98 518	105 100	109 688	112 223
61	Telecommunications	397 378	415 060	446 465	450 729	447 571	462 337	473 790	479 490
62-63	IT and other information services	21 936	24 462	25 266	25 789	26 145	27 873	27 261	30 560
64-66	**Financial and insurance activities**	**571 577**	**640 709**	**666 229**	**716 230**	**766 832**	**834 256**	**909 934**	**935 141**
68	**Real estate activities**	**1 404 543**	**1 519 853**	**1 572 826**	**1 664 516**	**1 763 146**	**1 845 931**	**1 912 114**	**1 982 207**
69-82	**Professional, scientific, technical, admin., support activities**	**896 293**	**977 671**	**967 241**	**997 108**	**1 081 745**	**1 177 076**	**1 243 287**	**1 300 146**
69-75	Professional, scientific and technical activities	403 553	444 743	440 215	449 695	484 788	520 096	539 452	571 388
69-71	Legal, accounting activities; mgt consultancy; engineering	325 683	361 064	357 621	361 674	391 601	422 858	436 801	459 200
73-75	Advertising, market research; other prof., scientific, tech.	62 282	66 109	63 687	66 117	70 338	74 333	76 854	83 244
77-82	Administrative and support service activities	492 740	532 928	527 026	547 413	596 957	656 980	703 835	728 758
84-88	**Public administration, defence; social security; education; health**	**1 419 439**	**1 560 185**	**1 685 071**	**1 800 113**	**1 936 616**	**2 124 078**	**2 250 936**	**2 405 124**
84	**Public administration, defence; compulsory social security**	**604 509**	**657 615**	**725 705**	**780 690**	**833 256**	**927 505**	**961 550**	**1 040 425**
85	**Education**	**491 314**	**537 213**	**569 539**	**600 288**	**646 050**	**707 022**	**750 058**	**796 572**
86-88	**Human health and social work activities**	**323 616**	**365 357**	**389 827**	**419 135**	**457 310**	**489 551**	**539 328**	**568 127**
90-99	**Arts, entertainment, household goods repairs, other**	**312 574**	**329 351**	**343 976**	**363 982**	**380 408**	**408 997**	**427 229**	**443 435**
90-93	**Arts, entertainment and recreation**	**73 894**	**78 134**	**79 639**	**86 504**	**89 723**	**94 496**	**98 895**	**100 248**
94-96	**Other service activities**	**183 058**	**192 981**	**204 174**	**213 790**	**224 487**	**240 398**	**249 803**	**261 904**
97-98	**Activities of households as employers and for own use**	**55 050**	**57 703**	**59 613**	**63 131**	**65 617**	**73 504**	**77 908**	**80 636**
05-39	**INDUSTRY INCLUDING ENERGY**	**7 973 005**	**8 734 840**	**7 921 977**	**9 093 612**	**10 249 008**	**11 169 091**	**11 198 505**	**11 737 922**
45-99	**TOTAL SERVICES**	**8 766 044**	**9 477 833**	**9 540 496**	**10 366 128**	**11 252 449**	**12 161 192**	**12 806 485**	**13 521 823**
45-82	**BUSINESS SECTOR SERVICES**	**7 034 031**	**7 588 297**	**7 511 449**	**8 202 033**	**8 935 425**	**9 628 117**	**10 128 320**	**10 673 264**
45-82x	**BUSINESS SECTOR SERVICES excluding real estate**	**5 629 488**	**6 068 444**	**5 938 623**	**6 537 517**	**7 172 279**	**7 782 186**	**8 216 206**	**8 691 057**
05-82x	**NON-AGRICULTURE BUSINESS SECTOR excluding real estate**	..	..	..	..	..	..	..	..

.. Not available

Note: Detailed metadata at: http://metalinks.oecd.org/stan/20170410/1c43.

Information on data for Israel: http://oe.cd/israel-disclaimer.

Disclaimer: http://oe.cd/disclaimer

Table 2. Value added, current prices

ISIC Rev. 4

Million MXN

		2007	2008	2009	2010	2011	2012	2013	2014
	TOTAL	10 962 144	11 941 199	11 568 456	12 723 475	14 021 257	15 116 998	15 444 778	16 306 606
01-03	AGRICULTURE, FORESTRY AND FISHING	360 285	392 984	387 015	425 590	448 103	505 675	506 394	538 018
05-09	MINING AND QUARRYING	901 739	1 054 691	786 997	966 823	1 298 146	1 315 847	1 176 101	1 168 070
10-33	MANUFACTURING	1 916 994	2 038 933	1 939 580	2 211 130	2 406 288	2 717 000	2 729 593	2 896 938
10-12	Food products, beverages and tobacco	511 885	553 318	595 716	631 611	690 438	753 672	786 766	819 330
13-14	Textiles and wearing apparel	83 523	85 494	82 201	90 212	95 562	101 864	105 449	107 942
15	Leather and related products	17 217	17 297	17 502	19 518	20 687	22 801	23 307	23 738
16	Wood, wood and cork products	20 328	19 213	19 171	20 809	23 210	27 462	27 379	28 467
17	Paper and paper products	37 558	40 732	43 561	47 408	48 614	52 708	54 900	57 737
18	Printing and reproduction of recorded media	15 179	16 438	16 514	16 921	19 011	19 751	19 925	20 803
19-23	Chemical, rubber, plastics, non-metallic products	485 907	525 090	479 823	536 039	550 395	651 381	611 624	622 885
20	Chemicals and chemical products	153 711	173 585	169 108	185 555	190 392	228 251	231 919	201 101
21	Pharmaceutical products	91 720	95 161	95 740	88 848	83 002	92 074	92 612	82 640
22-23	Rubber, plastic, non-metallic mineral products	168 461	172 274	165 097	178 956	193 789	210 689	207 808	224 460
24	Basic metals	126 201	146 715	111 325	135 212	157 147	168 558	155 637	165 330
25	Metal products, except machinery and equipment	61 794	68 356	60 041	68 007	75 061	84 145	84 291	89 684
26-28	Machinery and equipment	228 559	228 279	217 907	261 716	276 650	306 014	301 034	327 307
26	Computer, electronic and optical products	96 510	89 888	89 987	95 576	97 521	106 843	103 422	119 159
27	Electrical equipment	65 326	67 151	62 106	71 675	73 408	80 890	79 462	87 432
28	Machinery and equipment n.e.c.	66 723	71 240	65 814	94 465	105 721	118 281	118 150	120 716
29-30	Transport equipment	248 100	253 223	210 133	290 368	346 282	417 936	448 490	514 304
29	Motor vehicles, trailers and semi-trailers	233 688	237 938	197 109	277 001	325 415	389 406	416 563	477 462
30	Other transport equipment	14 412	15 285	13 024	13 367	20 867	28 530	31 927	36 842
31-33	Furniture; repair, installation of machinery and equipment	80 744	84 778	85 686	93 309	103 231	110 709	110 792	119 412
31-32	Furniture, other manufacturing	68 047	71 414	72 597	79 700	88 613	95 243	94 309	101 474
33	Repair and installation of machinery and equipment	12 697	13 364	13 089	13 609	14 618	15 466	16 483	17 938
35-39	ELECTRICITY, GAS, WATER AND WASTE MANAGEMENT	232 692	257 997	273 106	268 296	262 850	255 299	275 669	335 007
35	Electricity, gas, steam and air conditioning supply	193 405	219 215	225 147	217 444	203 479	192 991	208 437	262 778
36-39	Water supply; sewerage, waste, remediation activities	39 287	38 782	47 959	50 852	59 371	62 308	67 232	72 229
41-43	CONSTRUCTION	910 388	1 014 746	971 978	1 021 503	1 131 690	1 214 269	1 143 634	1 205 761
45-56	Distribution; transportation, accommodation, food service	2 603 801	2 806 002	2 657 683	3 016 500	3 379 841	3 675 698	3 879 676	4 158 106
45-47	Wholesale and retail trade; motor vehicle and motorcycle repairs	1 666 330	1 827 623	1 704 508	1 939 934	2 221 066	2 406 453	2 537 051	2 730 170
49-53	Transportation and storage	666 691	700 557	691 371	796 765	860 889	945 708	1 001 762	1 062 472
55-56	Accommodation and food service activities	270 780	277 822	261 804	279 801	297 886	323 537	340 863	365 464
58-63	Information and communication	317 798	334 738	350 751	365 071	359 108	361 568	369 249	377 238
58-60	Publishing, audiovisual and broadcasting activities	37 330	40 139	40 620	44 642	47 692	50 843	52 997	53 807
61	Telecommunications	268 505	281 495	296 803	306 300	297 006	295 283	301 072	306 392
62-63	IT and other information services	11 963	13 104	13 328	14 129	14 410	15 442	15 180	17 039
64-66	Financial and insurance activities	386 157	424 568	442 216	473 702	489 112	512 512	574 797	610 591
68	Real estate activities	1 295 475	1 400 723	1 455 896	1 540 637	1 630 464	1 706 583	1 767 169	1 834 238
69-82	Professional, scientific, technical, admin., support activities	715 915	778 270	768 142	795 259	865 317	940 873	994 281	1 038 711
69-75	Professional, scientific and technical activities	307 214	335 664	330 586	341 730	369 566	394 814	410 084	434 614
69-71	Legal, accounting activities; mgt consultancy; engineering	251 853	276 685	272 495	278 344	302 717	324 902	336 266	354 514
73-75	Advertising, market research; other prof., scientific, tech.	43 846	46 361	44 378	47 046	50 359	53 498	55 048	59 368
77-82	Administrative and support service activities	408 701	442 606	437 556	453 529	495 751	546 059	584 197	604 097
84-88	Public administration, defence; social security; education; health	1 075 547	1 180 247	1 269 088	1 356 712	1 456 897	1 598 569	1 696 692	1 800 241
84	Public administration, defence; compulsory social security	418 876	457 979	503 819	540 869	578 181	640 417	669 303	713 824
85	Education	432 887	472 159	499 021	529 239	567 719	623 822	662 898	704 399
86-88	Human health and social work activities	223 784	250 109	266 248	286 604	310 997	334 330	364 491	382 018
90-99	Arts, entertainment, household goods repairs, other	245 354	257 300	266 004	282 253	293 440	313 105	331 523	343 688
90-93	Arts, entertainment and recreation	55 171	57 684	58 405	63 731	65 619	69 337	73 787	74 483
94-96	Other service activities	134 992	141 828	147 898	155 302	162 111	170 168	179 728	188 466
97-98	Activities of households as employers and for own use	55 050	57 703	59 613	63 131	65 617	73 504	77 908	80 636
05-39	INDUSTRY INCLUDING ENERGY	3 051 425	3 351 621	2 999 683	3 446 249	3 967 284	4 288 146	4 181 363	4 400 015
45-99	TOTAL SERVICES	6 640 046	7 181 848	7 209 780	7 830 133	8 474 180	9 108 908	9 613 387	10 162 812
45-82	BUSINESS SECTOR SERVICES	5 319 146	5 744 301	5 674 688	6 191 169	6 723 842	7 197 234	7 585 172	8 018 884
45-82x	BUSINESS SECTOR SERVICES excluding real estate	4 023 671	4 343 578	4 218 792	4 650 532	5 093 378	5 490 651	5 818 003	6 184 646
05-82x	NON-AGRICULTURE BUSINESS SECTOR excluding real estate	..	..	..	..	..	..	..	..

.. Not available

Note: Detailed metadata at: http://metalinks.oecd.org/stan/20170410/1c43.

Information on data for Israel: http://oe.cd/israel-disclaimer.

Disclaimer: http://oe.cd/disclaimer

MEXICO

Table 3. Value added, volumes

ISIC Rev. 4

Million 2010 MXN

		2007	2008	2009	2010	2011	2012	2013	2014
	TOTAL	**12 524 530**	**12 697 126**	**12 094 691**	**12 723 475**	**13 222 249**	**13 756 066**	**13 950 010**	**14 252 332**
01-03	**AGRICULTURE, FORESTRY AND FISHING**	**426 177**	**428 378**	**411 879**	**425 590**	**399 432**	**432 869**	**444 789**	**460 423**
05-09	**MINING AND QUARRYING**	**1 040 254**	**999 833**	**959 431**	**966 823**	**963 241**	**972 646**	**972 670**	**959 464**
10-33	**MANUFACTURING**	**2 252 299**	**2 226 162**	**2 040 342**	**2 211 130**	**2 312 326**	**2 409 747**	**2 443 173**	**2 543 957**
10-12	Food products, beverages and tobacco	620 194	627 501	626 360	631 611	647 801	665 335	670 406	678 531
13-14	Textiles and wearing apparel	94 898	93 102	86 035	90 212	89 098	89 452	91 454	90 457
15	Leather and related products	20 126	19 148	18 230	19 518	19 381	20 080	19 990	19 665
16	Wood, wood and cork products	22 594	20 824	19 850	20 809	21 880	24 720	24 190	24 472
17	Paper and paper products	45 238	46 263	45 985	47 408	47 040	49 289	50 397	52 019
18	Printing and reproduction of recorded media	15 808	16 554	15 472	16 921	17 639	16 918	15 770	15 361
19-23	Chemical, rubber, plastics, non-metallic products	572 823	557 742	531 863	536 039	540 500	549 951	551 958	553 183
20	Chemicals and chemical products	187 601	181 512	178 711	185 555	188 590	188 079	191 370	191 006
21	Pharmaceutical products	106 579	105 339	99 024	88 848	85 385	85 423	84 718	81 705
22-23	Rubber, plastic, non-metallic mineral products	193 341	185 966	167 884	178 956	187 045	195 659	190 733	198 865
24	Basic metals	146 646	144 784	120 999	135 212	140 904	146 353	149 924	162 773
25	Metal products, except machinery and equipment	73 167	72 256	61 360	68 007	71 694	74 616	73 325	79 222
26-28	Machinery and equipment	270 322	258 153	224 343	261 716	280 527	289 148	292 183	312 337
26	Computer, electronic and optical products	113 230	103 198	92 707	95 576	102 010	102 644	106 456	118 333
27	Electrical equipment	75 420	73 245	65 939	71 675	71 416	72 822	71 171	77 554
28	Machinery and equipment n.e.c.	82 288	82 468	66 190	94 465	107 101	113 635	114 670	116 709
29-30	Transport equipment	279 037	278 955	205 585	290 368	339 276	386 636	409 684	461 144
29	Motor vehicles, trailers and semi-trailers	263 260	262 535	192 364	277 001	319 827	361 489	381 446	429 232
30	Other transport equipment	16 087	16 724	13 436	13 367	19 449	24 992	27 986	31 621
31-33	Furniture; repair, installation of machinery and equipment	96 507	96 138	91 176	93 309	96 586	97 902	95 557	99 397
31-32	Furniture, other manufacturing	82 034	81 469	77 356	79 700	82 655	83 693	80 772	83 765
33	Repair and installation of machinery and equipment	14 477	14 660	13 815	13 609	13 931	14 210	14 829	15 690
35-39	**ELECTRICITY, GAS, WATER AND WASTE MANAGEMENT**	**251 470**	**254 092**	**257 402**	**268 296**	**285 827**	**291 963**	**293 872**	**315 402**
35	Electricity, gas, steam and air conditioning supply	200 706	206 265	207 239	217 444	234 997	240 473	242 143	264 170
36-39	Water supply; sewerage, waste, remediation activities	51 337	47 507	50 357	50 852	50 830	51 602	51 874	52 827
41-43	**CONSTRUCTION**	**1 047 187**	**1 083 668**	**1 014 079**	**1 021 503**	**1 063 159**	**1 090 124**	**1 038 486**	**1 059 969**
45-56	Distribution; transportation, accommodation, food service	3 085 712	3 084 947	2 754 487	3 016 500	3 238 332	3 391 615	3 473 095	3 580 262
45-47	**Wholesale and retail trade; motor vehicle and motorcycle repairs**	**1 980 940**	**1 982 450**	**1 740 260**	**1 939 934**	**2 125 268**	**2 228 172**	**2 281 415**	**2 351 361**
49-53	**Transportation and storage**	**800 085**	**798 140**	**740 550**	**796 765**	**828 980**	**863 556**	**885 827**	**914 260**
55-56	**Accommodation and food service activities**	**304 431**	**304 099**	**274 814**	**279 801**	**284 083**	**299 849**	**305 793**	**314 561**
58-63	**Information and communication**	**315 866**	**334 338**	**361 838**	**365 071**	**380 558**	**441 541**	**463 611**	**465 631**
58-60	Publishing, audiovisual and broadcasting activities	43 194	44 504	42 774	44 642	46 171	47 424	48 037	47 586
61	Telecommunications	260 470	276 586	305 369	306 300	320 398	380 822	403 523	404 266
62-63	IT and other information services	12 966	13 876	13 662	14 129	13 989	14 221	14 049	15 486
64-66	**Financial and insurance activities**	**322 074**	**386 607**	**396 757**	**473 702**	**506 835**	**545 671**	**599 113**	**594 598**
68	**Real estate activities**	**1 438 844**	**1 482 158**	**1 501 668**	**1 540 637**	**1 585 078**	**1 625 086**	**1 641 668**	**1 675 374**
69-82	**Professional, scientific, technical, admin., support activities**	**813 133**	**838 907**	**788 870**	**795 259**	**838 256**	**869 107**	**896 117**	**904 981**
69-75	Professional, scientific and technical activities	342 339	356 667	340 034	341 730	358 307	367 199	371 201	380 506
69-71	Legal, accounting activities; mgt consultancy; engineering	278 558	292 399	279 360	278 344	294 063	302 777	304 136	310 382
73-75	Advertising, market research; other prof., scientific, tech.	49 268	50 003	46 444	47 046	48 973	49 859	50 566	52 960
77-82	Administrative and support service activities	471 035	482 370	448 839	453 529	479 949	501 903	524 823	524 423
84-88	**Public administration, defence; social security; education; health**	**1 309 901**	**1 327 385**	**1 344 568**	**1 356 712**	**1 363 560**	**1 403 110**	**1 408 541**	**1 417 350**
84	**Public administration, defence; compulsory social security**	**508 768**	**518 046**	**528 549**	**540 869**	**533 337**	**553 614**	**551 886**	**562 087**
85	**Education**	**522 825**	**527 929**	**528 900**	**529 239**	**537 540**	**550 130**	**555 244**	**555 566**
86-88	**Human health and social work activities**	**278 386**	**281 485**	**287 253**	**286 604**	**292 683**	**299 251**	**301 388**	**299 614**
90-99	**Arts, entertainment, household goods repairs, other**	**279 064**	**280 189**	**277 776**	**282 253**	**285 645**	**295 281**	**302 754**	**305 231**
90-93	**Arts, entertainment and recreation**	**63 817**	**63 914**	**61 293**	**63 731**	**63 250**	**65 153**	**67 473**	**66 508**
94-96	**Other service activities**	**154 866**	**155 750**	**155 068**	**155 302**	**158 113**	**160 768**	**164 687**	**167 242**
97-98	**Activities of households as employers and for own use**	**60 363**	**60 534**	**61 340**	**63 131**	**64 191**	**69 279**	**70 509**	**71 395**
05-39	**INDUSTRY INCLUDING ENERGY**	**3 531 387**	**3 467 900**	**3 251 184**	**3 446 249**	**3 561 394**	**3 668 846**	**3 702 546**	**3 805 995**
45-99	**TOTAL SERVICES**	**7 519 317**	**7 714 486**	**7 417 136**	**7 830 133**	**8 198 263**	**8 566 048**	**8 770 433**	**8 931 393**
45-82	**BUSINESS SECTOR SERVICES**	**5 930 202**	**6 105 240**	**5 797 144**	**6 191 169**	**6 549 058**	**6 868 538**	**7 062 483**	**7 214 349**
45-82x	**BUSINESS SECTOR SERVICES excluding real estate**	**4 492 725**	**4 624 485**	**4 296 225**	**4 650 532**	**4 963 981**	**5 243 546**	**5 420 996**	**5 539 165**
05-82x	**NON-AGRICULTURE BUSINESS SECTOR excluding real estate**	..	..	..	..	..	..	..	..

.. Not available

Note: Detailed metadata at: http://metalinks.oecd.org/stan/20170410/1c43.

Information on data for Israel: http://oe.cd/israel-disclaimer.

Disclaimer: http://oe.cd/disclaimer

Table 5. Number of persons engaged, total employment

ISIC Rev. 4

Thousands

		2007	2008	2009	2010	2011	2012	2013	2014
	TOTAL	**37 917**	**38 486**	**37 097**	**37 636**	**38 172**	**39 261**	**39 021**	**39 436**
01-03	**AGRICULTURE, FORESTRY AND FISHING**	**6 697**	**6 669**	**6 523**	**6 805**	**6 524**	**6 888**	**6 935**	**7 106**
05-09	**MINING AND QUARRYING**	**249**	**257**	**256**	**258**	**261**	**267**	**271**	**273**
10-33	**MANUFACTURING**	**4 569**	**4 374**	**3 982**	**4 042**	**4 060**	**4 095**	**4 087**	**4 192**
10-12	Food products, beverages and tobacco	1 173	1 165	1 161	1 151	1 166	1 179	1 181	1 197
13-14	Textiles and wearing apparel	435	390	350	350	328	318	322	321
15	Leather and related products	133	123	118	122	121	125	125	125
16	Wood, wood and cork products	141	127	123	125	122	120	118	112
17	Paper and paper products	88	87	84	85	84	83	84	85
18	Printing and reproduction of recorded media	89	85	83	82	85	75	74	73
19-23	Chemical, rubber, plastics, non-metallic products	710	679	609	633	630	629	614	610
20	Chemicals and chemical products	125	120	115	116	116	116	114	112
21	Pharmaceutical products	64	61	61	60	61	60	53	53
22-23	Rubber, plastic, non-metallic mineral products	492	468	404	428	424	423	417	413
24	Basic metals	63	63	57	57	59	60	58	57
25	Metal products, except machinery and equipment	259	254	215	214	219	217	209	214
26-28	Machinery and equipment	622	593	514	535	525	526	519	568
26	Computer, electronic and optical products	317	297	251	256	244	238	239	268
27	Electrical equipment	183	170	149	156	152	155	152	166
28	Machinery and equipment n.e.c.	121	125	115	123	129	132	128	134
29-30	Transport equipment	417	383	278	291	324	354	391	421
29	Motor vehicles, trailers and semi-trailers	386	354	259	274	302	332	367	394
30	Other transport equipment	30	28	19	17	22	22	24	27
31-33	Furniture; repair, installation of machinery and equipment	439	426	390	395	396	407	392	409
31-32	Furniture, other manufacturing	371	357	321	324	324	334	317	331
33	Repair and installation of machinery and equipment	68	69	69	71	72	73	75	78
35-39	**ELECTRICITY, GAS, WATER AND WASTE MANAGEMENT**	**251**	**251**	**238**	**218**	**228**	**235**	**232**	**228**
35	Electricity, gas, steam and air conditioning supply	129	132	119	96	103	105	104	103
36-39	Water supply; sewerage, waste, remediation activities	121	119	119	122	125	130	128	125
41-43	**CONSTRUCTION**	**5 653**	**6 064**	**5 489**	**5 446**	**5 796**	**5 885**	**5 348**	**5 375**
45-56	Distribution; transportation, accommodation, food service	8 547	8 712	8 517	8 660	8 851	9 028	9 153	9 158
45-47	**Wholesale and retail trade; motor vehicle and motorcycle repairs**	**5 326**	**5 472**	**5 324**	**5 428**	**5 600**	**5 772**	**5 857**	**5 808**
49-53	**Transportation and storage**	**1 942**	**1 953**	**1 933**	**1 972**	**2 004**	**1 995**	**2 021**	**2 072**
55-56	**Accommodation and food service activities**	**1 279**	**1 288**	**1 259**	**1 260**	**1 248**	**1 261**	**1 275**	**1 278**
58-63	**Information and communication**	**221**	**226**	**226**	**215**	**215**	**214**	**213**	**215**
58-60	Publishing, audiovisual and broadcasting activities	56	56	56	56	57	57	57	56
61	Telecommunications	128	131	133	123	121	121	120	121
62-63	IT and other information services	37	39	37	37	36	37	36	38
64-66	**Financial and insurance activities**	**253**	**242**	**245**	**267**	**290**	**294**	**309**	**323**
68	**Real estate activities**	**317**	**327**	**302**	**293**	**292**	**295**	**293**	**296**
69-82	**Professional, scientific, technical, admin., support activities**	**3 392**	**3 506**	**3 389**	**3 395**	**3 539**	**3 683**	**3 756**	**3 758**
69-75	Professional, scientific and technical activities	593	607	607	613	620	612	627	629
69-71	Legal, accounting activities; mgt consultancy; engineering	416	430	432	430	440	433	439	440
73-75	Advertising, market research; other prof., scientific, tech.	134	135	134	134	135	137	139	139
77-82	Administrative and support service activities	2 800	2 899	2 782	2 782	2 919	3 070	3 129	3 128
84-88	**Public administration, defence; social security; education; health**	**5 343**	**5 420**	**5 466**	**5 504**	**5 543**	**5 633**	**5 641**	**5 696**
84	**Public administration, defence; compulsory social security**	**2 195**	**2 243**	**2 271**	**2 285**	**2 292**	**2 347**	**2 336**	**2 381**
85	**Education**	**2 179**	**2 198**	**2 204**	**2 210**	**2 230**	**2 256**	**2 267**	**2 265**
86-88	**Human health and social work activities**	**969**	**979**	**991**	**1 009**	**1 020**	**1 029**	**1 038**	**1 050**
90-99	**Arts, entertainment, household goods repairs, other**	**2 424**	**2 438**	**2 464**	**2 535**	**2 570**	**2 744**	**2 784**	**2 816**
90-93	**Arts, entertainment and recreation**	**106**	**108**	**107**	**111**	**110**	**111**	**113**	**111**
94-96	**Other service activities**	**321**	**324**	**325**	**329**	**331**	**337**	**338**	**342**
97-98	**Activities of households as employers and for own use**	**1 996**	**2 005**	**2 032**	**2 094**	**2 129**	**2 295**	**2 332**	**2 362**
05-39	**INDUSTRY INCLUDING ENERGY**	**5 069**	**4 882**	**4 476**	**4 518**	**4 550**	**4 597**	**4 590**	**4 693**
45-99	**TOTAL SERVICES**	**20 498**	**20 871**	**20 609**	**20 868**	**21 302**	**21 891**	**22 148**	**22 261**
45-82	**BUSINESS SECTOR SERVICES**	**12 731**	**13 014**	**12 678**	**12 830**	**13 188**	**13 514**	**13 723**	**13 749**
45-82x	**BUSINESS SECTOR SERVICES excluding real estate**	**12 414**	**12 687**	**12 377**	**12 537**	**12 896**	**13 219**	**13 430**	**13 453**
05-82x	**NON-AGRICULTURE BUSINESS SECTOR excluding real estate**	..	..	..	..	..	..	..	..

.. Not available

Note: Detailed metadata at: http://metalinks.oecd.org/stan/20170410/1c43.
Information on data for Israel: http://oe.cd/israel-disclaimer.

Disclaimer: http://oe.cd/disclaimer

MEXICO

Table 6. Labour costs (compensation of employees), current prices

ISIC Rev. 4

Million MXN

		2007	2008	2009	2010	2011	2012	2013	2014
	TOTAL	**3 155 458**	**3 411 296**	**3 469 534**	**3 659 099**	**3 923 845**	**4 228 946**	**4 419 472**	**4 671 756**
01-03	**AGRICULTURE, FORESTRY AND FISHING**	**60 395**	**62 690**	**64 729**	**70 941**	**72 368**	**78 557**	**83 126**	**89 136**
05-09	**MINING AND QUARRYING**	**50 970**	**59 213**	**64 093**	**63 451**	**70 466**	**77 739**	**84 626**	**85 998**
10-33	**MANUFACTURING**	**433 982**	**438 238**	**414 400**	**429 862**	**450 286**	**484 282**	**499 026**	**522 549**
10-12	Food products, beverages and tobacco	80 598	81 651	83 081	85 699	89 599	95 535	99 000	102 967
13-14	Textiles and wearing apparel	25 591	24 379	22 651	23 383	22 950	23 125	24 097	24 731
15	Leather and related products	7 310	6 871	6 686	7 084	7 407	7 980	8 347	8 728
16	Wood, wood and cork products	7 428	7 195	7 173	7 606	7 647	7 848	8 013	7 942
17	Paper and paper products	9 237	9 592	9 552	10 023	10 413	10 756	11 282	11 806
18	Printing and reproduction of recorded media	6 426	6 430	6 676	6 836	7 295	7 046	7 157	7 411
19-23	Chemical, rubber, plastics, non-metallic products	100 632	102 586	101 555	104 073	108 484	115 523	116 598	116 607
20	Chemicals and chemical products	28 362	29 128	30 637	30 701	33 090	35 100	36 449	36 659
21	Pharmaceutical products	16 696	16 917	17 220	16 899	17 400	17 335	16 992	15 202
22-23	Rubber, plastic, non-metallic mineral products	39 547	39 693	35 696	38 045	38 624	40 456	39 781	40 667
24	Basic metals	11 463	11 700	11 289	11 478	12 297	14 080	14 007	14 731
25	Metal products, except machinery and equipment	21 862	22 382	20 615	21 586	22 745	24 744	25 190	27 482
26-28	Machinery and equipment	75 830	77 083	70 571	73 919	74 447	82 217	82 736	91 267
26	Computer, electronic and optical products	39 610	38 794	35 145	35 352	33 965	37 536	37 356	42 579
27	Electrical equipment	20 378	20 733	18 589	19 662	19 455	21 309	21 741	23 735
28	Machinery and equipment n.e.c.	15 842	17 556	16 837	18 905	21 027	23 372	23 639	24 953
29-30	Transport equipment	55 991	55 638	43 670	45 527	52 691	59 435	67 193	70 826
29	Motor vehicles, trailers and semi-trailers	51 831	51 861	40 498	42 648	48 762	55 441	62 642	65 630
30	Other transport equipment	4 160	3 777	3 172	2 879	3 929	3 994	4 551	5 196
31-33	Furniture; repair, installation of machinery and equipment	31 615	32 730	30 881	32 648	34 311	35 993	35 405	38 051
31-32	Furniture, other manufacturing	27 028	27 796	25 715	27 054	28 364	29 744	28 636	30 743
33	Repair and installation of machinery and equipment	4 587	4 934	5 166	5 594	5 947	6 249	6 769	7 308
35-39	**ELECTRICITY, GAS, WATER AND WASTE MANAGEMENT**	**47 351**	**50 798**	**52 252**	**48 573**	**55 346**	**60 603**	**63 376**	**67 205**
35	Electricity, gas, steam and air conditioning supply	34 675	37 573	38 351	34 035	40 127	44 569	46 592	49 855
36-39	Water supply; sewerage, waste, remediation activities	12 676	13 225	13 901	14 538	15 219	16 034	16 784	17 350
41-43	**CONSTRUCTION**	**409 585**	**457 570**	**427 995**	**439 679**	**487 192**	**519 494**	**491 758**	**512 503**
45-56	Distribution; transportation, accommodation, food service	587 675	627 146	633 749	671 985	710 712	750 358	802 123	854 793
45-47	**Wholesale and retail trade; motor vehicle and motorcycle repairs**	**314 471**	**338 201**	**336 196**	**352 928**	**370 856**	**392 982**	**424 019**	**453 982**
49-53	**Transportation and storage**	**211 742**	**224 079**	**231 336**	**248 952**	**267 509**	**281 299**	**297 256**	**316 909**
55-56	**Accommodation and food service activities**	**61 462**	**64 866**	**66 217**	**70 105**	**72 347**	**76 077**	**80 848**	**83 902**
58-63	**Information and communication**	**76 410**	**80 851**	**85 548**	**86 429**	**89 706**	**87 215**	**89 432**	**91 761**
58-60	Publishing, audiovisual and broadcasting activities	7 731	8 352	8 641	9 041	9 668	10 206	10 694	10 799
61	Telecommunications	63 577	66 927	71 218	71 490	73 880	70 410	71 816	73 521
62-63	IT and other information services	5 102	5 572	5 689	5 898	6 158	6 599	6 922	7 441
64-66	**Financial and insurance activities**	**93 960**	**108 632**	**110 890**	**121 467**	**130 940**	**138 022**	**143 958**	**160 863**
68	**Real estate activities**	**20 649**	**22 274**	**21 390**	**21 891**	**22 984**	**24 002**	**24 696**	**25 624**
69-82	**Professional, scientific, technical, admin., support activities**	**322 405**	**349 571**	**352 234**	**371 660**	**405 466**	**439 036**	**472 685**	**495 194**
69-75	Professional, scientific and technical activities	83 071	90 471	91 494	98 155	104 808	108 473	117 355	124 486
69-71	Legal, accounting activities; mgt consultancy; engineering	60 721	66 495	66 156	69 589	75 283	78 164	83 990	88 515
73-75	Advertising, market research; other prof., scientific, tech.	11 554	12 201	12 571	13 207	13 930	14 889	15 725	16 440
77-82	Administrative and support service activities	239 334	259 100	260 740	273 505	300 658	330 563	355 330	370 708
84-88	**Public administration, defence; social security; education; health**	**964 004**	**1 062 148**	**1 146 336**	**1 230 705**	**1 321 817**	**1 452 928**	**1 541 008**	**1 637 653**
84	**Public administration, defence; compulsory social security**	**412 277**	**451 393**	**495 974**	**532 480**	**566 499**	**627 104**	**654 165**	**699 912**
85	**Education**	**388 010**	**423 997**	**448 472**	**476 494**	**511 642**	**563 456**	**597 977**	**633 976**
86-88	**Human health and social work activities**	**163 717**	**186 758**	**201 890**	**221 731**	**243 676**	**262 368**	**288 866**	**303 765**
90-99	**Arts, entertainment, household goods repairs, other**	**88 073**	**92 166**	**95 919**	**102 457**	**106 561**	**116 710**	**123 659**	**128 476**
90-93	**Arts, entertainment and recreation**	**12 400**	**12 858**	**13 561**	**15 463**	**15 887**	**16 703**	**18 014**	**18 646**
94-96	**Other service activities**	**20 483**	**21 520**	**22 657**	**23 774**	**24 964**	**26 407**	**27 638**	**29 091**
97-98	**Activities of households as employers and for own use**	**55 050**	**57 703**	**59 613**	**63 131**	**65 617**	**73 504**	**77 908**	**80 636**
05-39	**INDUSTRY INCLUDING ENERGY**	532 303	548 249	530 745	541 886	576 098	622 624	647 028	675 752
45-99	**TOTAL SERVICES**	2 153 175	2 342 787	2 446 065	2 606 593	2 788 187	3 008 271	3 197 560	3 394 365
45-82	**BUSINESS SECTOR SERVICES**	1 101 099	1 188 474	1 203 811	1 273 432	1 359 808	1 438 633	1 532 894	1 628 235
45-82x	**BUSINESS SECTOR SERVICES excluding real estate**	1 080 450	1 166 200	1 182 421	1 251 541	1 336 824	1 414 631	1 508 198	1 602 611
05-82x	**NON-AGRICULTURE BUSINESS SECTOR excluding real estate**	..	..	..	..	..	..	..	..

.. Not available

Note: Detailed metadata at: http://metalinks.oecd.org/stan/20170410/1c43.

Information on data for Israel: http://oe.cd/israel-disclaimer.

Disclaimer: http://oe.cd/disclaimer

NETHERLANDS

Table 1. Production (gross output), current prices

ISIC Rev. 4

Million EUR

		2007	2008	2009	2010	2011	2012	2013	2014
	TOTAL	**1 130 668**	**1 190 059**	**1 140 435**	**1 177 286**	**1 236 753**	**1 254 164**	**1 252 249**	**1 265 728**
01-03	**AGRICULTURE, FORESTRY AND FISHING**	**26 489**	**27 445**	**25 716**	**27 953**	**28 449**	**29 406**	**30 835**	**29 648**
05-09	**MINING AND QUARRYING**	**19 715**	**25 363**	**19 874**	**20 846**	**22 399**	**25 434**	**26 497**	**21 828**
10-33	**MANUFACTURING**	**263 869**	**275 138**	**234 739**	**258 384**	**291 758**	**297 727**	**293 296**	**293 446**
10-12	Food products, beverages and tobacco	51 067	54 592	50 625	52 890	57 961	61 023	64 086	64 922
13-14	Textiles and wearing apparel	3 208	3 072	2 748	2 840	3 147	2 961	2 983	2 989
15	Leather and related products	323	309	276	318	352	383	387	376
16	Wood, wood and cork products	3 079	3 119	2 698	2 581	2 703	2 407	2 212	2 355
17	Paper and paper products	6 358	6 107	5 288	5 771	5 992	5 917	5 821	5 870
18	Printing and reproduction of recorded media	5 716	5 493	5 154	4 734	4 688	4 337	4 189	4 020
19-23	Chemical, rubber, plastics, non-metallic products	85 626	90 606	71 335	83 847	99 830	106 694	99 682	94 947
20	Chemicals and chemical products	41 452	41 398	33 119	39 467	47 941	50 355	46 834	45 376
21	Pharmaceutical products	6 127	5 834	5 647	5 741	5 497	5 776	4 324	4 334
22-23	Rubber, plastic, non-metallic mineral products	13 714	13 979	12 274	12 287	13 523	13 098	13 166	13 278
24	Basic metals	8 972	8 786	6 042	8 005	8 799	7 807	7 414	7 488
25	Metal products, except machinery and equipment	16 966	18 231	15 659	16 881	18 641	18 012	17 803	18 235
26-28	Machinery and equipment	50 368	50 964	46 812	50 830	58 621	56 822	57 741	59 876
26	Computer, electronic and optical products	23 811	24 439	24 177	24 871	27 719	27 909	28 247	29 154
27	Electrical equipment	5 923	6 003	5 072	4 932	5 671	5 528	5 415	5 232
28	Machinery and equipment n.e.c.	20 634	20 522	17 563	21 027	25 231	23 385	24 079	25 490
29-30	Transport equipment	14 639	15 550	11 187	12 454	13 327	13 173	13 300	14 257
29	Motor vehicles, trailers and semi-trailers	8 261	8 440	4 350	5 924	7 289	6 585	6 303	6 829
30	Other transport equipment	6 378	7 110	6 837	6 530	6 038	6 588	6 997	7 428
31-33	Furniture; repair, installation of machinery and equipment	17 547	18 309	16 915	17 233	17 697	18 191	17 678	18 111
31-32	Furniture, other manufacturing	10 076	10 395	9 309	9 367	9 442	9 390	8 956	9 074
33	Repair and installation of machinery and equipment	7 471	7 914	7 606	7 866	8 255	8 801	8 722	9 037
35-39	**ELECTRICITY, GAS, WATER AND WASTE MANAGEMENT**	**24 242**	**25 885**	**26 587**	**26 586**	**28 019**	**27 533**	**26 848**	**25 879**
35	Electricity, gas, steam and air conditioning supply	16 193	17 095	18 071	17 772	18 540	18 392	17 664	16 584
36-39	Water supply; sewerage, waste, remediation activities	8 049	8 790	8 516	8 814	9 479	9 141	9 184	9 295
41-43	**CONSTRUCTION**	**91 580**	**98 935**	**96 326**	**87 521**	**91 131**	**83 931**	**79 002**	**80 232**
45-56	Distribution; transportation, accommodation, food service	213 143	220 840	208 218	215 946	224 959	227 404	230 458	235 401
45-47	**Wholesale and retail trade; motor vehicle and motorcycle repairs**	**129 414**	**133 108**	**126 407**	**131 814**	**136 624**	**137 260**	**139 264**	**140 842**
49-53	**Transportation and storage**	**63 645**	**67 578**	**62 248**	**64 921**	**68 285**	**69 836**	**70 566**	**72 873**
55-56	**Accommodation and food service activities**	**20 084**	**20 154**	**19 563**	**19 211**	**20 050**	**20 308**	**20 628**	**21 686**
58-63	**Information and communication**	**52 999**	**53 781**	**51 307**	**51 302**	**52 056**	**51 881**	**52 258**	**54 628**
58-60	Publishing, audiovisual and broadcasting activities	11 501	11 481	10 986	10 589	10 496	10 243	10 041	10 175
61	Telecommunications	19 256	18 318	17 265	17 244	17 057	16 745	16 531	16 449
62-63	IT and other information services	22 242	23 982	23 056	23 469	24 503	24 893	25 686	28 004
64-66	**Financial and insurance activities**	**61 579**	**62 364**	**70 039**	**76 281**	**76 004**	**78 286**	**77 189**	**77 841**
68	**Real estate activities**	**63 998**	**66 256**	**67 061**	**68 660**	**69 809**	**70 670**	**72 068**	**74 725**
69-82	**Professional, scientific, technical, admin., support activities**	**129 194**	**137 559**	**132 691**	**131 253**	**137 447**	**142 834**	**143 021**	**148 842**
69-75	Professional, scientific and technical activities	81 613	86 586	84 238	82 941	86 511	90 527	90 256	92 933
69-71	Legal, accounting activities; mgt consultancy; engineering	63 535	67 697	66 069	64 489	67 942	71 823	71 608	74 295
73-75	Advertising, market research; other prof., scientific, tech.	13 797	14 449	13 668	13 858	14 175	14 298	14 065	14 066
77-82	Administrative and support service activities	47 581	50 973	48 453	48 312	50 936	52 307	52 765	55 909
84-88	**Public administration, defence; social security; education; health**	**159 629**	**171 277**	**182 343**	**186 579**	**188 101**	**192 373**	**193 888**	**195 770**
84	**Public administration, defence; compulsory social security**	**65 869**	**70 264**	**74 738**	**75 319**	**74 463**	**75 153**	**74 967**	**75 837**
85	**Education**	**33 190**	**35 391**	**36 915**	**37 741**	**37 910**	**37 970**	**38 111**	**38 671**
86-88	**Human health and social work activities**	**60 570**	**65 622**	**70 690**	**73 519**	**75 728**	**79 250**	**80 810**	**81 262**
90-99	**Arts, entertainment, household goods repairs, other**	**24 231**	**25 216**	**25 534**	**25 975**	**26 621**	**26 685**	**26 889**	**27 488**
90-93	**Arts, entertainment and recreation**	**13 025**	**13 454**	**13 527**	**13 774**	**14 168**	**14 201**	**14 313**	**14 749**
94-96	**Other service activities**	**10 923**	**11 440**	**11 631**	**11 776**	**12 008**	**11 998**	**12 094**	**12 255**
97-98	**Activities of households as employers and for own use**	**283**	**322**	**376**	**425**	**445**	**486**	**482**	**484**
05-39	**INDUSTRY INCLUDING ENERGY**	**307 826**	**326 386**	**281 200**	**305 816**	**342 176**	**350 694**	**346 641**	**341 153**
45-99	**TOTAL SERVICES**	**704 773**	**737 293**	**737 193**	**755 996**	**774 997**	**790 133**	**795 771**	**814 695**
45-82	**BUSINESS SECTOR SERVICES**	**520 913**	**540 800**	**529 316**	**543 442**	**560 275**	**571 075**	**574 994**	**591 437**
45-82x	**BUSINESS SECTOR SERVICES excluding real estate**	**456 915**	**474 544**	**462 255**	**474 782**	**490 466**	**500 405**	**502 926**	**516 712**
05-82x	**NON-AGRICULTURE BUSINESS SECTOR excluding real estate**	..	..	..	..	..	..	..	..

.. Not available

Note: Detailed metadata at: http://metalinks.oecd.org/stan/20170410/1c43.

Information on data for Israel: http://oe.cd/israel-disclaimer.

Disclaimer: http://oe.cd/disclaimer

NETHERLANDS

Table 2. Value added, current prices

ISIC Rev. 4

Million EUR

		2007	2008	2009	2010	2011	2012	2013	2014
	TOTAL	**547 518**	**570 887**	**553 689**	**567 757**	**579 590**	**583 832**	**588 535**	**597 414**
01-03	**AGRICULTURE, FORESTRY AND FISHING**	**10 760**	**10 099**	**9 192**	**10 828**	**9 697**	**10 225**	**11 198**	**10 996**
05-09	**MINING AND QUARRYING**	**16 071**	**21 507**	**16 239**	**17 283**	**18 559**	**21 327**	**22 161**	**17 072**
10-33	**MANUFACTURING**	**74 866**	**73 899**	**65 005**	**67 024**	**69 979**	**69 074**	**66 676**	**68 004**
10-12	Food products, beverages and tobacco	11 629	11 136	11 664	11 507	11 843	12 819	13 188	13 842
13-14	Textiles and wearing apparel	1 002	985	894	916	1 002	939	953	974
15	Leather and related products	141	131	110	117	123	138	139	130
16	Wood, wood and cork products	1 060	1 126	1 001	878	942	863	766	821
17	Paper and paper products	1 818	1 710	1 562	1 580	1 586	1 477	1 421	1 524
18	Printing and reproduction of recorded media	2 393	2 343	2 227	1 958	1 850	1 697	1 559	1 396
19-23	Chemical, rubber, plastics, non-metallic products	20 006	19 757	16 313	15 950	17 047	16 947	14 641	13 745
20	Chemicals and chemical products	10 527	9 918	7 438	8 293	8 963	8 734	8 120	8 082
21	Pharmaceutical products	2 710	2 758	2 855	2 758	2 670	2 939	1 627	1 526
22-23	Rubber, plastic, non-metallic mineral products	4 768	4 733	4 662	4 229	4 432	4 230	4 222	4 436
24	Basic metals	3 016	2 582	1 633	1 888	1 774	1 734	1 707	2 000
25	Metal products, except machinery and equipment	5 929	6 257	5 768	5 966	6 372	6 302	6 122	6 467
26-28	Machinery and equipment	15 295	14 701	12 539	14 291	15 170	13 995	14 156	14 770
26	Computer, electronic and optical products	5 391	4 675	4 401	4 453	4 087	3 899	3 846	3 846
27	Electrical equipment	2 619	2 762	2 081	2 001	2 279	2 202	2 155	2 069
28	Machinery and equipment n.e.c.	7 285	7 264	6 057	7 837	8 804	7 894	8 155	8 855
29-30	Transport equipment	4 352	4 604	3 145	3 720	3 765	3 410	3 597	3 742
29	Motor vehicles, trailers and semi-trailers	2 427	2 507	1 185	1 784	2 148	1 814	1 816	1 901
30	Other transport equipment	1 925	2 097	1 960	1 936	1 617	1 596	1 781	1 841
31-33	Furniture; repair, installation of machinery and equipment	8 225	8 567	8 149	8 253	8 505	8 753	8 427	8 593
31-32	Furniture, other manufacturing	5 632	5 838	5 558	5 513	5 457	5 476	5 278	5 325
33	Repair and installation of machinery and equipment	2 593	2 729	2 591	2 740	3 048	3 277	3 149	3 268
35-39	**ELECTRICITY, GAS, WATER AND WASTE MANAGEMENT**	**9 626**	**9 317**	**11 357**	**10 842**	**10 943**	**11 055**	**10 821**	**10 201**
35	Electricity, gas, steam and air conditioning supply	6 202	5 633	7 829	7 301	7 277	7 458	7 206	6 479
36-39	Water supply; sewerage, waste, remediation activities	3 424	3 684	3 528	3 541	3 666	3 597	3 615	3 722
41-43	**CONSTRUCTION**	**31 033**	**33 369**	**33 636**	**30 531**	**30 295**	**27 826**	**26 456**	**27 223**
45-56	Distribution; transportation, accommodation, food service	110 693	112 358	105 546	110 472	113 924	115 141	118 253	121 772
45-47	**Wholesale and retail trade; motor vehicle and motorcycle repairs**	**73 527**	**74 773**	**70 503**	**74 663**	**77 429**	**77 951**	**80 231**	**81 544**
49-53	**Transportation and storage**	**27 901**	**28 478**	**26 114**	**26 991**	**27 181**	**27 784**	**28 408**	**29 886**
55-56	**Accommodation and food service activities**	**9 265**	**9 107**	**8 929**	**8 818**	**9 314**	**9 406**	**9 614**	**10 342**
58-63	**Information and communication**	**28 158**	**28 778**	**27 493**	**27 843**	**27 889**	**27 751**	**27 920**	**28 473**
58-60	Publishing, audiovisual and broadcasting activities	5 203	5 207	5 129	5 082	4 908	4 844	4 740	4 891
61	Telecommunications	10 008	9 641	9 076	9 161	9 128	8 710	8 207	7 953
62-63	IT and other information services	12 947	13 930	13 288	13 600	13 853	14 197	14 973	15 629
64-66	**Financial and insurance activities**	**30 365**	**31 628**	**41 448**	**47 722**	**45 918**	**49 908**	**49 142**	**48 526**
68	**Real estate activities**	**43 228**	**44 669**	**33 169**	**31 599**	**33 405**	**29 050**	**31 173**	**34 716**
69-82	**Professional, scientific, technical, admin., support activities**	**74 090**	**79 179**	**76 776**	**75 234**	**78 267**	**78 699**	**79 131**	**83 331**
69-75	Professional, scientific and technical activities	43 380	46 297	45 277	44 623	46 094	45 598	44 982	46 919
69-71	Legal, accounting activities; mgt consultancy; engineering	35 617	38 008	37 164	36 144	37 548	37 047	36 270	38 192
73-75	Advertising, market research; other prof., scientific, tech.	5 526	5 967	5 649	5 953	6 147	6 172	6 084	6 046
77-82	Administrative and support service activities	30 710	32 882	31 499	30 611	32 173	33 101	34 149	36 412
84-88	**Public administration, defence; social security; education; health**	**105 572**	**112 464**	**119 717**	**123 746**	**125 690**	**128 584**	**130 442**	**131 453**
84	**Public administration, defence; compulsory social security**	**38 365**	**40 292**	**42 203**	**43 404**	**43 433**	**44 155**	**44 848**	**44 905**
85	**Education**	**25 992**	**27 692**	**28 994**	**29 571**	**29 849**	**29 971**	**30 076**	**30 550**
86-88	**Human health and social work activities**	**41 215**	**44 480**	**48 520**	**50 771**	**52 408**	**54 458**	**55 518**	**55 998**
90-99	**Arts, entertainment, household goods repairs, other**	**13 056**	**13 620**	**14 111**	**14 633**	**15 024**	**15 192**	**15 162**	**15 647**
90-93	**Arts, entertainment and recreation**	**6 582**	**6 845**	**7 051**	**7 343**	**7 546**	**7 633**	**7 644**	**8 010**
94-96	**Other service activities**	**6 191**	**6 453**	**6 684**	**6 865**	**7 033**	**7 073**	**7 036**	**7 153**
97-98	**Activities of households as employers and for own use**	**283**	**322**	**376**	**425**	**445**	**486**	**482**	**484**
05-39	**INDUSTRY INCLUDING ENERGY**	**100 563**	**104 723**	**92 601**	**95 149**	**99 481**	**101 456**	**99 658**	**95 277**
45-99	**TOTAL SERVICES**	**405 162**	**422 696**	**418 260**	**431 249**	**440 117**	**444 325**	**451 223**	**463 918**
45-82	**BUSINESS SECTOR SERVICES**	**286 534**	**296 612**	**284 432**	**292 870**	**299 403**	**300 549**	**305 619**	**316 818**
45-82x	**BUSINESS SECTOR SERVICES excluding real estate**	**243 306**	**251 943**	**251 263**	**261 271**	**265 998**	**271 499**	**274 446**	**282 102**
05-82x	**NON-AGRICULTURE BUSINESS SECTOR excluding real estate**	..	..	..	..	..	..	..	..

.. Not available

Note: Detailed metadata at: http://metalinks.oecd.org/stan/20170410/1c43.

Information on data for Israel: http://oe.cd/israel-disclaimer.

Disclaimer: http://oe.cd/disclaimer

NETHERLANDS

Table 3. Value added, volumes

ISIC Rev. 4

Million 2010 EUR

		2007	2008	2009	2010	2011	2012	2013	2014
	TOTAL	**566 969**	**577 990**	**558 157**	**567 757**	**579 152**	**574 694**	**575 515**	**584 159**
01-03	**AGRICULTURE, FORESTRY AND FISHING**	**10 194**	**10 474**	**10 819**	**10 828**	**10 674**	**10 541**	**10 595**	**11 052**
05-09	**MINING AND QUARRYING**	**15 159**	**16 144**	**15 279**	**17 283**	**15 852**	**15 833**	**17 018**	**14 849**
10-33	**MANUFACTURING**	**72 788**	**71 398**	**63 666**	**67 024**	**69 443**	**68 443**	**67 605**	**68 802**
10-12	Food products, beverages and tobacco	12 145	11 764	11 585	11 507	11 534	12 056	12 429	12 831
13-14	Textiles and wearing apparel	..	..	..	..	..	..	..	..
15	Leather and related products	..	..	..	..	..	..	..	..
16	Wood, wood and cork products	1 051	1 054	930	878	932	850	768	811
17	Paper and paper products	1 610	1 581	1 465	1 580	1 522	1 496	1 430	1 489
18	Printing and reproduction of recorded media	2 183	2 159	2 078	1 958	1 942	1 781	1 752	1 604
19-23	Chemical, rubber, plastics, non-metallic products	17 701	16 613	15 545	15 950	16 228	16 549	15 828	15 373
20	Chemicals and chemical products	9 017	8 374	7 792	8 293	8 195	8 480	7 720	7 268
21	Pharmaceutical products	3 102	2 710	2 762	2 758	2 645	3 029	3 027	2 865
22-23	Rubber, plastic, non-metallic mineral products	5 100	5 019	4 327	4 229	4 458	4 128	4 127	4 278
24	Basic metals	1 821	1 850	1 474	1 888	1 692	1 661	1 705	1 845
25	Metal products, except machinery and equipment	6 198	6 240	5 437	5 966	6 485	6 149	5 792	5 963
26-28	Machinery and equipment	15 604	15 626	12 771	14 291	15 804	14 900	15 279	16 128
26	Computer, electronic and optical products	5 077	5 220	4 579	4 453	4 803	5 046	5 532	5 977
27	Electrical equipment	2 742	2 791	2 160	2 001	2 215	2 097	2 010	1 960
28	Machinery and equipment n.e.c.	7 821	7 630	6 067	7 837	8 786	7 835	7 906	8 420
29-30	Transport equipment	4 246	4 305	3 084	3 720	3 826	3 473	3 561	3 681
29	Motor vehicles, trailers and semi-trailers	2 475	2 440	1 184	1 784	2 109	1 770	1 742	1 819
30	Other transport equipment	1 815	1 903	1 890	1 936	1 717	1 715	1 838	1 881
31-33	Furniture; repair, installation of machinery and equipment	9 008	9 091	8 319	8 253	8 325	8 380	7 945	7 942
31-32	Furniture, other manufacturing	6 159	6 219	5 624	5 513	5 437	5 370	5 084	5 138
33	Repair and installation of machinery and equipment	2 848	2 871	2 693	2 740	2 888	3 005	2 856	2 802
35-39	**ELECTRICITY, GAS, WATER AND WASTE MANAGEMENT**	**10 777**	**10 935**	**10 695**	**10 842**	**10 844**	**10 675**	**10 958**	**11 162**
35	Electricity, gas, steam and air conditioning supply	7 222	7 280	7 121	7 301	7 275	7 150	7 293	7 311
36-39	Water supply; sewerage, waste, remediation activities	3 569	3 665	3 584	3 541	3 569	3 525	3 666	3 852
41-43	**CONSTRUCTION**	**34 465**	**35 849**	**34 259**	**30 531**	**30 818**	**28 308**	**26 836**	**28 014**
45-56	Distribution; transportation, accommodation, food service	113 930	114 149	106 221	110 472	115 245	114 878	115 335	118 647
45-47	**Wholesale and retail trade; motor vehicle and motorcycle repairs**	**75 760**	**76 081**	**71 164**	**74 663**	**78 195**	**77 717**	**78 372**	**80 702**
49-53	**Transportation and storage**	**27 474**	**27 855**	**25 757**	**26 991**	**27 936**	**28 199**	**27 981**	**28 687**
55-56	**Accommodation and food service activities**	**10 833**	**10 266**	**9 334**	**8 818**	**9 114**	**8 971**	**8 987**	**9 261**
58-63	**Information and communication**	**27 920**	**28 805**	**27 931**	**27 843**	**28 284**	**28 473**	**29 037**	**30 067**
58-60	Publishing, audiovisual and broadcasting activities	5 675	5 567	5 281	5 082	4 878	4 703	4 485	4 545
61	Telecommunications	9 395	9 579	9 247	9 161	8 820	8 461	8 224	8 398
62-63	IT and other information services	12 882	13 673	13 408	13 600	14 586	15 359	16 461	17 288
64-66	**Financial and insurance activities**	**44 589**	**46 464**	**46 397**	**47 722**	**47 165**	**45 717**	**44 650**	**43 436**
68	**Real estate activities**	**30 518**	**30 861**	**30 784**	**31 599**	**32 055**	**32 814**	**34 445**	**36 118**
69-82	**Professional, scientific, technical, admin., support activities**	**77 583**	**80 892**	**76 862**	**75 234**	**77 677**	**78 242**	**77 984**	**81 762**
69-75	Professional, scientific and technical activities	44 712	46 482	45 113	44 623	45 948	45 973	45 357	47 288
69-71	Legal, accounting activities; mgt consultancy; engineering	36 448	37 895	36 946	36 144	37 309	37 209	36 370	38 470
73-75	Advertising, market research; other prof., scientific, tech.	5 824	6 131	5 693	5 953	6 242	6 383	6 380	6 189
77-82	Administrative and support service activities	32 914	34 460	31 754	30 611	31 729	32 265	32 609	34 440
84-88	**Public administration, defence; social security; education; health**	**113 324**	**116 753**	**120 812**	**123 746**	**126 304**	**125 973**	**126 403**	**126 655**
84	**Public administration, defence; compulsory social security**	**40 549**	**41 157**	**42 163**	**43 404**	**43 073**	**43 037**	**43 473**	**43 321**
85	**Education**	**29 104**	**29 518**	**29 481**	**29 571**	**30 129**	**30 105**	**30 134**	**30 310**
86-88	**Human health and social work activities**	**43 719**	**46 106**	**49 173**	**50 771**	**53 102**	**52 829**	**52 794**	**53 023**
90-99	**Arts, entertainment, household goods repairs, other**	**14 748**	**14 885**	**14 654**	**14 633**	**14 791**	**14 676**	**14 402**	**14 386**
90-93	**Arts, entertainment and recreation**	**7 377**	**7 440**	**7 363**	**7 343**	**7 472**	**7 364**	**7 220**	**7 284**
94-96	**Other service activities**	**7 072**	**7 115**	**6 913**	**6 865**	**6 878**	**6 837**	**6 713**	**6 635**
97-98	**Activities of households as employers and for own use**	**305**	**335**	**380**	**425**	**441**	**475**	**469**	**467**
05-39	**INDUSTRY INCLUDING ENERGY**	**98 654**	**98 415**	**89 619**	**95 149**	**96 139**	**94 979**	**95 956**	**94 567**
45-99	**TOTAL SERVICES**	**423 233**	**432 994**	**423 691**	**431 249**	**441 521**	**440 846**	**442 021**	**450 484**
45-82	**BUSINESS SECTOR SERVICES**	**295 006**	**301 213**	**288 235**	**292 870**	**300 426**	**300 199**	**301 226**	**309 502**
45-82x	**BUSINESS SECTOR SERVICES excluding real estate**	**265 078**	**271 116**	**257 484**	**261 271**	**268 371**	**267 345**	**266 936**	**273 630**
05-82x	**NON-AGRICULTURE BUSINESS SECTOR excluding real estate**	**..**	**..**	**..**	**..**	**..**	**..**	**..**	**..**

.. Not available

Note: Detailed metadata at: http://metalinks.oecd.org/stan/20170410/1c43.

Information on data for Israel: http://oe.cd/israel-disclaimer.

Disclaimer: http://oe.cd/disclaimer

NETHERLANDS

Table 4. Gross fixed capital formation, current prices

ISIC Rev. 4

Million EUR

		2007	2008	2009	2010	2011	2012	2013	2014
	TOTAL	137 113	145 658	134 753	128 114	133 730	124 775	120 088	122 735
01-03	AGRICULTURE, FORESTRY AND FISHING	4 333	4 627	4 341	4 527	5 663	5 208	4 764	5 106
05-09	MINING AND QUARRYING	1 847	2 522	2 366	2 347	3 880	3 462	3 246	3 729
10-33	MANUFACTURING	12 553	13 076	11 902	10 879	12 241	12 780	12 617	13 355
10-12	Food products, beverages and tobacco	1 950	2 018	1 814	1 800	1 706	1 960	2 230	2 510
13-14	Textiles and wearing apparel	112	130	53	65	74	74	72	96
15	Leather and related products	11	23	20	13	6	7	22	12
16	Wood, wood and cork products	161	121	85	73	87	74	78	74
17	Paper and paper products	247	212	185	157	176	186	203	175
18	Printing and reproduction of recorded media	338	394	269	207	256	234	228	250
19-23	Chemical, rubber, plastics, non-metallic products	4 018	4 573	4 152	3 685	4 591	4 764	4 188	4 358
20	Chemicals and chemical products	2 152	2 504	2 203	1 832	2 493	2 628	2 280	2 136
21	Pharmaceutical products	658	720	807	789	746	688	657	731
22-23	Rubber, plastic, non-metallic mineral products	779	746	623	555	683	582	637	619
24	Basic metals	464	289	527	188	202	246	235	260
25	Metal products, except machinery and equipment	805	882	644	611	625	627	644	707
26-28	Machinery and equipment	3 049	3 001	2 890	2 799	3 183	3 211	3 150	3 389
26	Computer, electronic and optical products	938	917	798	713	755	807	843	1 022
27	Electrical equipment	703	768	728	660	699	750	697	739
28	Machinery and equipment n.e.c.	1 408	1 316	1 364	1 426	1 729	1 654	1 610	1 628
29-30	Transport equipment	658	556	393	428	499	542	673	615
29	Motor vehicles, trailers and semi-trailers	426	361	231	240	287	320	432	383
30	Other transport equipment	232	195	162	188	212	222	241	232
31-33	Furniture; repair, installation of machinery and equipment	740	877	870	853	836	855	894	909
31-32	Furniture, other manufacturing	471	622	508	433	508	471	470	468
33	Repair and installation of machinery and equipment	269	255	362	420	328	384	424	441
35-39	ELECTRICITY, GAS, WATER AND WASTE MANAGEMENT	3 656	4 081	4 428	5 161	6 659	6 626	6 510	7 644
35	Electricity, gas, steam and air conditioning supply	2 923	2 781	3 135	3 606	4 843	5 500	5 501	6 469
36-39	Water supply; sewerage, waste, remediation activities	733	1 300	1 293	1 555	1 816	1 126	1 009	1 175
41-43	CONSTRUCTION	2 455	2 732	2 225	2 209	2 655	2 180	2 296	2 291
45-56	Distribution; transportation, accommodation, food service	15 098	16 774	14 387	14 245	16 620	15 418	15 476	14 982
45-47	Wholesale and retail trade; motor vehicle and motorcycle repairs	8 053	8 562	6 587	5 949	7 090	6 618	6 991	7 061
49-53	Transportation and storage	6 124	7 242	6 994	7 542	8 629	7 997	7 696	7 137
55-56	Accommodation and food service activities	921	970	806	754	901	803	789	784
58-63	Information and communication	4 221	4 460	3 883	3 871	4 127	4 159	4 125	4 689
58-60	Publishing, audiovisual and broadcasting activities	443	527	520	599	539	506	533	531
61	Telecommunications	2 319	2 422	2 079	1 859	2 162	2 048	2 090	2 603
62-63	IT and other information services	1 459	1 511	1 284	1 413	1 426	1 605	1 502	1 555
64-66	Financial and insurance activities	4 300	4 254	4 527	5 287	5 062	4 195	4 230	4 196
68	Real estate activities	45 474	47 667	42 994	35 743	32 429	27 710	24 899	26 219
69-82	Professional, scientific, technical, admin., support activities	12 269	12 576	9 880	10 004	11 440	11 517	10 741	10 911
69-75	Professional, scientific and technical activities	5 078	5 393	5 159	5 029	5 314	5 137	5 606	5 358
69-71	Legal, accounting activities; mgt consultancy; engineering	2 822	2 944	2 807	2 594	2 859	2 865	3 266	3 061
73-75	Advertising, market research; other prof., scientific, tech.	685	734	570	534	662	564	610	578
77-82	Administrative and support service activities	7 191	7 183	4 721	4 975	6 126	6 380	5 135	5 553
84-88	Public administration, defence; social security; education; health	29 021	30 900	32 081	32 045	31 142	29 716	29 283	27 607
84	Public administration, defence; compulsory social security	17 829	19 287	19 943	19 640	18 858	17 518	17 190	16 041
85	Education	5 506	5 775	5 700	5 424	5 547	5 415	5 431	5 803
86-88	Human health and social work activities	5 686	5 838	6 438	6 981	6 737	6 783	6 662	5 763
90-99	Arts, entertainment, household goods repairs, other	1 886	1 989	1 739	1 796	1 812	1 804	1 901	2 006
90-93	Arts, entertainment and recreation	1 029	1 037	983	1 042	1 047	1 073	1 120	1 211
94-96	Other service activities	857	952	756	754	765	731	781	795
97-98	Activities of households as employers and for own use	0	0	0	0	0	0	0	0
05-39	INDUSTRY INCLUDING ENERGY	18 056	19 679	18 696	18 387	22 780	22 868	22 373	24 728
45-99	TOTAL SERVICES	112 269	118 620	109 491	102 991	102 632	94 519	90 655	90 610
45-82	BUSINESS SECTOR SERVICES	81 362	85 731	75 671	69 150	69 678	62 999	59 471	60 997
45-82x	BUSINESS SECTOR SERVICES excluding real estate	35 888	38 064	32 677	33 407	37 249	35 289	34 572	34 778
05-82x	NON-AGRICULTURE BUSINESS SECTOR excluding real estate	..	..	..	..	..	..	..	..

.. Not available

Note: Detailed metadata at: http://metalinks.oecd.org/stan/20170410/1c43.

Information on data for Israel: http://oe.cd/israel-disclaimer.

Disclaimer: http://oe.cd/disclaimer

Table 5. Number of persons engaged, total employment

ISIC Rev. 4

Thousands

		2007	2008	2009	2010	2011	2012	2013	2014
	TOTAL	**8 771**	**8 914**	**8 838**	**8 778**	**8 854**	**8 836**	**8 732**	**8 711**
01-03	**AGRICULTURE, FORESTRY AND FISHING**	**213**	**209**	**204**	**203**	**201**	**199**	**196**	**193**
05-09	**MINING AND QUARRYING**	**8**	**8**	**8**	**8**	**8**	**9**	**9**	**10**
10-33	**MANUFACTURING**	**844**	**847**	**822**	**799**	**792**	**783**	**769**	**765**
10-12	Food products, beverages and tobacco	128	129	130	129	126	127	127	127
13-14	Textiles and wearing apparel	18	18	16	16	16	15	16	15
15	Leather and related products	2	2	2	2	2	2	2	2
16	Wood, wood and cork products	20	20	18	16	16	15	13	13
17	Paper and paper products	20	19	18	18	18	18	18	17
18	Printing and reproduction of recorded media	40	39	35	31	29	27	25	23
19-23	Chemical, rubber, plastics, non-metallic products	132	131	126	123	121	118	116	113
20	Chemicals and chemical products	47	47	44	45	44	44	45	44
21	Pharmaceutical products	17	16	17	16	15	13	12	12
22-23	Rubber, plastic, non-metallic mineral products	62	62	59	56	56	55	53	51
24	Basic metals	22	22	21	21	21	20	20	19
25	Metal products, except machinery and equipment	97	99	92	89	90	89	87	88
26-28	Machinery and equipment	130	133	128	121	124	125	126	125
26	Computer, electronic and optical products	28	29	28	28	27	27	27	26
27	Electrical equipment	25	25	22	20	22	22	21	20
28	Machinery and equipment n.e.c.	77	79	78	73	75	76	78	79
29-30	Transport equipment	39	41	40	38	38	37	37	37
29	Motor vehicles, trailers and semi-trailers	23	24	22	19	19	19	18	18
30	Other transport equipment	16	17	18	19	18	18	18	18
31-33	Furniture; repair, installation of machinery and equipment	196	196	196	194	192	190	184	186
31-32	Furniture, other manufacturing	155	153	153	152	150	147	140	142
33	Repair and installation of machinery and equipment	41	43	43	42	42	43	44	44
35-39	**ELECTRICITY, GAS, WATER AND WASTE MANAGEMENT**	**53**	**54**	**54**	**56**	**57**	**55**	**56**	**57**
35	Electricity, gas, steam and air conditioning supply	22	23	22	24	24	23	24	24
36-39	Water supply; sewerage, waste, remediation activities	31	31	32	32	33	32	32	33
41-43	**CONSTRUCTION**	**546**	**555**	**549**	**523**	**522**	**509**	**478**	**462**
45-56	Distribution; transportation, accommodation, food service	2 152	2 165	2 129	2 124	2 159	2 164	2 141	2 147
45-47	**Wholesale and retail trade; motor vehicle and motorcycle repairs**	**1 408**	**1 421**	**1 400**	**1 396**	**1 414**	**1 415**	**1 394**	**1 394**
49-53	**Transportation and storage**	**401**	**400**	**392**	**385**	**390**	**388**	**383**	**379**
55-56	**Accommodation and food service activities**	**343**	**344**	**337**	**343**	**355**	**361**	**364**	**374**
58-63	**Information and communication**	**257**	**265**	**260**	**252**	**256**	**259**	**256**	**261**
58-60	Publishing, audiovisual and broadcasting activities	64	64	62	59	59	59	57	55
61	Telecommunications	41	39	36	33	32	32	31	31
62-63	IT and other information services	152	162	162	160	165	168	168	175
64-66	**Financial and insurance activities**	**284**	**279**	**275**	**266**	**261**	**257**	**252**	**242**
68	**Real estate activities**	**80**	**83**	**83**	**79**	**79**	**76**	**75**	**74**
69-82	**Professional, scientific, technical, admin., support activities**	**1 726**	**1 764**	**1 702**	**1 653**	**1 683**	**1 685**	**1 680**	**1 711**
69-75	Professional, scientific and technical activities	670	691	691	668	674	680	672	682
69-71	Legal, accounting activities; mgt consultancy; engineering	460	479	481	455	460	464	460	465
73-75	Advertising, market research; other prof., scientific, tech.	178	179	177	180	181	183	179	183
77-82	Administrative and support service activities	1 055	1 073	1 011	985	1 009	1 005	1 008	1 029
84-88	**Public administration, defence; social security; education; health**	**2 262**	**2 324**	**2 381**	**2 445**	**2 457**	**2 464**	**2 448**	**2 417**
84	**Public administration, defence; compulsory social security**	**495**	**498**	**509**	**523**	**507**	**501**	**499**	**495**
85	**Education**	**500**	**514**	**523**	**522**	**524**	**520**	**515**	**516**
86-88	**Human health and social work activities**	**1 266**	**1 312**	**1 349**	**1 400**	**1 426**	**1 443**	**1 434**	**1 406**
90-99	**Arts, entertainment, household goods repairs, other**	**347**	**362**	**370**	**370**	**379**	**376**	**372**	**373**
90-93	**Arts, entertainment and recreation**	**146**	**152**	**155**	**155**	**158**	**158**	**158**	**159**
94-96	**Other service activities**	**183**	**191**	**195**	**195**	**198**	**195**	**193**	**192**
97-98	**Activities of households as employers and for own use**	**18**	**19**	**20**	**20**	**23**	**23**	**21**	**21**
05-39	**INDUSTRY INCLUDING ENERGY**	**905**	**909**	**884**	**863**	**857**	**847**	**834**	**832**
45-99	**TOTAL SERVICES**	**7 107**	**7 241**	**7 201**	**7 189**	**7 274**	**7 281**	**7 224**	**7 224**
45-82	**BUSINESS SECTOR SERVICES**	**4 498**	**4 555**	**4 450**	**4 374**	**4 438**	**4 441**	**4 404**	**4 434**
45-82x	**BUSINESS SECTOR SERVICES excluding real estate**	**4 418**	**4 472**	**4 366**	**4 295**	**4 359**	**4 365**	**4 329**	**4 360**
05-82x	**NON-AGRICULTURE BUSINESS SECTOR excluding real estate**	..	..	..	..	..	..	..	..

.. Not available

Note: Detailed metadata at: http://metalinks.oecd.org/stan/20170410/1c43.

Information on data for Israel: http://oe.cd/israel-disclaimer.

Disclaimer: http://oe.cd/disclaimer

Table 6. Labour costs (compensation of employees), current prices

ISIC Rev. 4

Million EUR

		2007	2008	2009	2010	2011	2012	2013	2014
	TOTAL	**290 933**	**307 355**	**311 679**	**310 471**	**318 040**	**322 825**	**324 595**	**327 963**
01-03	**AGRICULTURE, FORESTRY AND FISHING**	**2 480**	**2 543**	**2 563**	**2 603**	**2 677**	**2 739**	**2 792**	**2 799**
05-09	**MINING AND QUARRYING**	**729**	**768**	**776**	**809**	**912**	**964**	**1 052**	**1 162**
10-33	**MANUFACTURING**	**36 505**	**38 518**	**39 125**	**36 912**	**37 771**	**38 285**	**38 555**	**39 645**
10-12	Food products, beverages and tobacco	5 417	5 432	5 472	5 526	5 536	5 738	5 899	6 037
13-14	Textiles and wearing apparel	589	592	554	553	558	557	577	577
15	Leather and related products	63	66	62	58	68	77	69	65
16	Wood, wood and cork products	697	727	672	630	602	569	512	491
17	Paper and paper products	1 005	1 003	937	976	1 001	1 006	1 022	1 033
18	Printing and reproduction of recorded media	1 446	1 469	1 367	1 255	1 147	1 121	1 050	953
19-23	Chemical, rubber, plastics, non-metallic products	7 484	8 260	9 423	7 481	7 742	7 679	7 683	7 834
20	Chemicals and chemical products	3 171	3 246	3 142	3 165	3 298	3 370	3 469	3 531
21	Pharmaceutical products	1 084	1 083	1 076	1 062	1 018	884	892	868
22-23	Rubber, plastic, non-metallic mineral products	2 704	2 825	2 731	2 674	2 708	2 809	2 815	2 751
24	Basic metals	1 291	1 351	1 218	1 183	1 234	1 216	1 213	1 238
25	Metal products, except machinery and equipment	3 823	4 086	3 903	3 842	3 936	4 009	3 973	4 070
26-28	Machinery and equipment	6 622	7 079	6 962	6 873	7 332	7 604	7 989	8 693
26	Computer, electronic and optical products	1 575	1 689	1 676	1 760	1 804	1 819	1 911	2 198
27	Electrical equipment	1 234	1 293	1 146	1 067	1 150	1 188	1 169	1 458
28	Machinery and equipment n.e.c.	3 813	4 097	4 140	4 046	4 378	4 597	4 909	5 037
29-30	Transport equipment	1 748	1 889	1 913	1 889	1 973	1 994	2 002	2 091
29	Motor vehicles, trailers and semi-trailers	1 039	1 107	1 039	965	1 004	1 032	1 004	1 047
30	Other transport equipment	709	782	874	924	969	962	998	1 044
31-33	Furniture; repair, installation of machinery and equipment	6 320	6 564	6 642	6 646	6 642	6 715	6 566	6 563
31-32	Furniture, other manufacturing	4 276	4 418	4 462	4 516	4 412	4 399	4 248	4 196
33	Repair and installation of machinery and equipment	2 044	2 146	2 180	2 130	2 230	2 316	2 318	2 367
35-39	**ELECTRICITY, GAS, WATER AND WASTE MANAGEMENT**	**2 926**	**3 086**	**3 202**	**3 321**	**3 458**	**3 492**	**3 604**	**3 605**
35	Electricity, gas, steam and air conditioning supply	1 409	1 506	1 544	1 609	1 679	1 716	1 808	1 800
36-39	Water supply; sewerage, waste, remediation activities	1 517	1 580	1 658	1 712	1 779	1 776	1 796	1 805
41-43	**CONSTRUCTION**	**18 372**	**19 250**	**19 115**	**18 765**	**18 786**	**18 660**	**17 277**	**16 652**
45-56	Distribution; transportation, accommodation, food service	57 329	60 214	60 461	60 724	62 806	64 182	64 446	64 763
45-47	**Wholesale and retail trade; motor vehicle and motorcycle repairs**	**37 144**	**39 210**	**39 431**	**39 679**	**41 033**	**42 146**	**42 111**	**42 358**
49-53	**Transportation and storage**	**15 649**	**16 291**	**16 282**	**16 148**	**16 670**	**16 792**	**16 974**	**16 787**
55-56	**Accommodation and food service activities**	**4 536**	**4 713**	**4 748**	**4 897**	**5 103**	**5 244**	**5 361**	**5 618**
58-63	**Information and communication**	**13 140**	**14 092**	**14 442**	**13 768**	**14 128**	**14 513**	**14 458**	**14 588**
58-60	Publishing, audiovisual and broadcasting activities	2 782	2 886	2 792	2 680	2 690	2 694	2 592	2 527
61	Telecommunications	2 329	2 291	2 319	2 129	2 086	2 136	2 084	2 154
62-63	IT and other information services	8 029	8 915	9 331	8 959	9 352	9 683	9 782	9 907
64-66	**Financial and insurance activities**	**19 439**	**19 781**	**19 126**	**18 987**	**19 306**	**19 383**	**20 503**	**20 512**
68	**Real estate activities**	**3 631**	**3 851**	**3 861**	**3 735**	**3 751**	**3 731**	**3 685**	**3 632**
69-82	**Professional, scientific, technical, admin., support activities**	**48 548**	**52 125**	**50 852**	**49 479**	**51 360**	**51 995**	**52 274**	**54 010**
69-75	Professional, scientific and technical activities	28 961	31 168	31 492	30 154	30 855	31 357	31 360	32 083
69-71	Legal, accounting activities; mgt consultancy; engineering	24 258	26 161	26 372	25 098	25 718	26 185	26 167	26 639
73-75	Advertising, market research; other prof., scientific, tech.	2 953	3 149	3 109	3 111	3 078	3 131	3 072	3 045
77-82	Administrative and support service activities	19 587	20 957	19 360	19 325	20 505	20 638	20 914	21 927
84-88	**Public administration, defence; social security; education; health**	**80 384**	**85 287**	**89 982**	**92 952**	**94 469**	**96 321**	**97 512**	**98 044**
84	**Public administration, defence; compulsory social security**	**26 688**	**27 955**	**29 597**	**30 264**	**29 944**	**30 349**	**30 581**	**30 461**
85	**Education**	**19 842**	**21 301**	**22 407**	**22 882**	**23 020**	**23 138**	**23 130**	**23 466**
86-88	**Human health and social work activities**	**33 854**	**36 031**	**37 978**	**39 806**	**41 505**	**42 834**	**43 801**	**44 117**
90-99	**Arts, entertainment, household goods repairs, other**	**7 450**	**7 840**	**8 174**	**8 416**	**8 616**	**8 560**	**8 437**	**8 551**
90-93	**Arts, entertainment and recreation**	**3 309**	**3 482**	**3 570**	**3 621**	**3 647**	**3 652**	**3 592**	**3 661**
94-96	**Other service activities**	**3 858**	**4 036**	**4 228**	**4 370**	**4 524**	**4 422**	**4 363**	**4 406**
97-98	**Activities of households as employers and for own use**	**283**	**322**	**376**	**425**	**445**	**486**	**482**	**484**
05-39	**INDUSTRY INCLUDING ENERGY**	**40 160**	**42 372**	**43 103**	**41 042**	**42 141**	**42 741**	**43 211**	**44 412**
45-99	**TOTAL SERVICES**	**229 921**	**243 190**	**246 898**	**248 061**	**254 436**	**258 685**	**261 315**	**264 100**
45-82	**BUSINESS SECTOR SERVICES**	**142 087**	**150 063**	**148 742**	**146 693**	**151 351**	**153 804**	**155 366**	**157 505**
45-82x	**BUSINESS SECTOR SERVICES excluding real estate**	**138 456**	**146 212**	**144 881**	**142 958**	**147 600**	**150 073**	**151 681**	**153 873**
05-82x	**NON-AGRICULTURE BUSINESS SECTOR excluding real estate**	..	..	..	..	..	..	..	..

.. Not available

Note: Detailed metadata at: http://metalinks.oecd.org/stan/20170410/1c43.

Information on data for Israel: http://oe.cd/israel-disclaimer.

Disclaimer: http://oe.cd/disclaimer

NORWAY

Table 1. Production (gross output), current prices

ISIC Rev. 4

Million NOK

		2007	2008	2009	2010	2011	2012	2013	2014
	TOTAL	**3 905 762**	**4 336 111**	**4 043 585**	**4 231 238**	**4 568 500**	**4 841 466**	**5 038 585**	**5 223 615**
01-03	**AGRICULTURE, FORESTRY AND FISHING**	**67 743**	**70 529**	**75 314**	**87 164**	**89 200**	**90 035**	**98 671**	**107 916**
05-09	**MINING AND QUARRYING**	**596 468**	**759 960**	**591 971**	**644 573**	**765 824**	**818 770**	**821 159**	**786 384**
10-33	**MANUFACTURING**	**736 785**	**766 833**	**677 396**	**689 780**	**737 473**	**755 001**	**780 972**	**817 043**
10-12	Food products, beverages and tobacco	145 673	148 283	147 169	148 973	157 216	163 697	170 008	189 076
13-14	Textiles and wearing apparel	6 937	7 112	5 893	6 217	6 850	6 458	6 150	6 641
15	Leather and related products	368	379	290	256	255	212	212	113
16	Wood, wood and cork products	28 962	26 094	21 635	23 608	25 587	25 329	24 177	25 094
17	Paper and paper products	20 278	20 238	14 540	16 755	16 579	11 422	10 072	9 584
18	Printing and reproduction of recorded media	11 769	12 173	10 897	10 881	10 670	10 432	9 783	9 333
19-23	Chemical, rubber, plastics, non-metallic products	155 567	170 763	140 380	162 755	189 180	185 711	186 193	180 325
20	Chemicals and chemical products	30 402	38 819	30 461	36 418	39 154	31 271	29 380	32 842
21	Pharmaceutical products	89 442	93 040	75 998	92 897	112 652	116 211	117 181	106 821
22-23	Rubber, plastic, non-metallic mineral products	35 723	38 904	33 921	33 440	37 374	38 229	39 632	40 662
24	Basic metals	82 239	73 127	51 082	63 563	67 186	59 096	53 495	60 324
25	Metal products, except machinery and equipment	39 314	46 035	44 774	42 998	44 956	47 793	47 260	47 681
26-28	Machinery and equipment	104 462	121 066	119 759	107 455	103 801	118 462	132 935	146 626
26	Computer, electronic and optical products	24 474	25 532	22 313	22 398	22 156	21 972	22 679	24 668
27	Electrical equipment	20 395	21 806	18 315	17 653	18 685	20 670	22 266	22 978
28	Machinery and equipment n.e.c.	59 593	73 728	79 131	67 404	62 960	75 820	87 990	98 980
29-30	Transport equipment	87 735	90 115	73 199	60 435	65 734	74 727	82 394	84 051
29	Motor vehicles, trailers and semi-trailers	9 045	8 746	5 356	6 498	7 356	7 156	7 502	6 738
30	Other transport equipment	78 690	81 369	67 843	53 937	58 378	67 571	74 892	77 313
31-33	Furniture; repair, installation of machinery and equipment	53 481	51 448	47 778	45 884	49 459	51 662	58 293	58 195
31-32	Furniture, other manufacturing	19 545	16 431	13 769	13 092	13 740	13 607	13 595	13 842
33	Repair and installation of machinery and equipment	33 936	35 017	34 009	32 792	35 719	38 055	44 698	44 353
35-39	**ELECTRICITY, GAS, WATER AND WASTE MANAGEMENT**	**85 674**	**107 803**	**101 701**	**114 178**	**111 985**	**110 520**	**113 929**	**115 362**
35	Electricity, gas, steam and air conditioning supply	56 159	73 032	67 608	77 041	72 334	69 893	72 089	71 465
36-39	Water supply; sewerage, waste, remediation activities	29 515	34 771	34 093	37 137	39 651	40 627	41 840	43 897
41-43	**CONSTRUCTION**	**331 235**	**359 750**	**323 880**	**327 969**	**373 876**	**426 140**	**445 764**	**471 986**
45-56	Distribution; transportation, accommodation, food service	705 228	771 904	702 550	727 574	765 596	802 551	831 415	881 489
45-47	**Wholesale and retail trade; motor vehicle and motorcycle repairs**	**335 270**	**375 647**	**334 084**	**342 407**	**362 310**	**376 111**	**378 897**	**395 979**
49-53	**Transportation and storage**	**313 951**	**336 192**	**307 933**	**322 173**	**335 893**	**355 083**	**377 405**	**407 014**
55-56	**Accommodation and food service activities**	**56 007**	**60 065**	**60 533**	**62 994**	**67 393**	**71 357**	**75 113**	**78 496**
58-63	**Information and communication**	**171 320**	**182 870**	**182 226**	**192 235**	**198 133**	**203 289**	**211 268**	**222 781**
58-60	Publishing, audiovisual and broadcasting activities	58 307	60 782	58 821	60 841	61 698	62 598	64 105	65 829
61	Telecommunications	63 137	65 590	66 172	68 340	65 142	65 173	66 913	70 581
62-63	IT and other information services	49 876	56 498	57 233	63 054	71 293	75 518	80 250	86 371
64-66	**Financial and insurance activities**	**140 306**	**137 784**	**153 549**	**156 285**	**153 503**	**176 683**	**199 156**	**209 476**
68	**Real estate activities**	**215 032**	**229 826**	**240 427**	**248 948**	**262 289**	**277 405**	**292 176**	**303 081**
69-82	**Professional, scientific, technical, admin., support activities**	**260 577**	**300 857**	**295 388**	**307 839**	**333 249**	**361 936**	**381 047**	**393 744**
69-75	Professional, scientific and technical activities	162 448	190 901	186 206	190 976	200 415	218 316	232 610	239 807
69-71	Legal, accounting activities; mgt consultancy; engineering	124 584	141 137	144 049	147 259	152 934	167 766	179 743	185 198
73-75	Advertising, market research; other prof., scientific, tech.	26 441	36 808	29 217	30 323	34 086	35 423	36 709	36 675
77-82	Administrative and support service activities	98 129	109 956	109 182	116 863	132 834	143 620	148 437	153 937
84-88	**Public administration, defence; social security; education; health**	**520 449**	**568 314**	**614 995**	**648 667**	**686 681**	**724 894**	**764 789**	**810 645**
84	**Public administration, defence; compulsory social security**	**172 133**	**187 172**	**205 837**	**217 941**	**228 375**	**243 317**	**255 462**	**271 994**
85	**Education**	**116 993**	**125 913**	**136 151**	**143 034**	**149 420**	**155 863**	**163 886**	**170 924**
86-88	**Human health and social work activities**	**231 323**	**255 229**	**273 007**	**287 692**	**308 886**	**325 714**	**345 441**	**367 727**
90-99	**Arts, entertainment, household goods repairs, other**	**74 945**	**79 681**	**84 188**	**86 026**	**90 691**	**94 242**	**98 239**	**103 708**
90-93	**Arts, entertainment and recreation**	**42 079**	**43 910**	**46 169**	**46 469**	**48 379**	**49 712**	**50 300**	**53 087**
94-96	**Other service activities**	**32 578**	**35 413**	**37 645**	**39 187**	**41 935**	**44 069**	**47 467**	**50 110**
97-98	**Activities of households as employers and for own use**	**288**	**358**	**374**	**370**	**377**	**461**	**472**	**511**
05-39	**INDUSTRY INCLUDING ENERGY**	1 418 927	1 634 596	1 371 068	1 448 531	1 615 282	1 684 291	1 716 060	1 718 789
45-99	**TOTAL SERVICES**	2 087 857	2 271 236	2 273 323	2 367 574	2 490 142	2 641 000	2 778 090	2 924 924
45-82	**BUSINESS SECTOR SERVICES**	1 492 463	1 623 241	1 574 140	1 632 881	1 712 770	1 821 864	1 915 062	2 010 571
45-82x	**BUSINESS SECTOR SERVICES excluding real estate**	1 277 431	1 393 415	1 333 713	1 383 933	1 450 481	1 544 459	1 622 886	1 707 490
05-82x	**NON-AGRICULTURE BUSINESS SECTOR excluding real estate**	..	..	..	..	..	..	..	..

.. Not available

Note: Detailed metadata at: http://metalinks.oecd.org/stan/20170410/1c43.

Information on data for Israel: http://oe.cd/israel-disclaimer.

Disclaimer: http://oe.cd/disclaimer

NORWAY

Table 2. Value added, current prices

ISIC Rev. 4

Million NOK

		2007	2008	2009	2010	2011	2012	2013	2014
	TOTAL	**2 085 049**	**2 344 746**	**2 168 415**	**2 306 443**	**2 496 919**	**2 656 794**	**2 749 018**	**2 807 857**
01-03	**AGRICULTURE, FORESTRY AND FISHING**	**29 139**	**29 408**	**31 578**	**40 650**	**37 552**	**33 433**	**40 396**	**45 317**
05-09	**MINING AND QUARRYING**	**510 065**	**656 072**	**470 265**	**519 009**	**640 008**	**673 692**	**660 481**	**615 015**
10-33	**MANUFACTURING**	**194 744**	**201 794**	**178 412**	**186 383**	**188 581**	**196 056**	**203 246**	**213 801**
10-12	Food products, beverages and tobacco	33 056	31 585	30 364	33 703	34 217	35 017	36 611	39 347
13-14	Textiles and wearing apparel	2 584	2 648	2 178	2 484	2 676	2 508	2 677	2 653
15	Leather and related products	109	208	113	66	62	58	66	42
16	Wood, wood and cork products	8 849	7 640	6 540	7 017	7 658	7 699	7 284	7 422
17	Paper and paper products	4 360	3 647	2 516	2 679	1 511	2 686	2 358	2 357
18	Printing and reproduction of recorded media	4 847	4 905	4 133	4 415	4 366	4 307	4 169	3 903
19-23	Chemical, rubber, plastics, non-metallic products	36 649	38 496	32 207	33 638	32 311	30 817	32 841	34 309
20	Chemicals and chemical products	9 519	12 490	7 986	9 242	7 851	5 642	6 820	8 509
21	Pharmaceutical products	15 089	13 422	13 408	13 617	12 621	12 817	13 431	12 008
22-23	Rubber, plastic, non-metallic mineral products	12 041	12 584	10 813	10 779	11 839	12 358	12 590	13 792
24	Basic metals	15 297	16 464	6 618	10 127	10 164	9 430	8 041	10 877
25	Metal products, except machinery and equipment	15 696	16 710	16 048	15 709	17 080	19 412	19 288	19 268
26-28	Machinery and equipment	33 814	39 663	40 115	38 138	39 757	42 067	43 583	47 291
26	Computer, electronic and optical products	10 069	9 934	9 176	9 208	9 145	9 487	9 880	10 569
27	Electrical equipment	6 465	6 915	6 575	6 975	7 057	7 413	8 232	8 508
28	Machinery and equipment n.e.c.	17 280	22 814	24 364	21 955	23 555	25 167	25 471	28 214
29-30	Transport equipment	20 446	21 703	19 895	19 743	20 068	21 067	23 014	22 941
29	Motor vehicles, trailers and semi-trailers	2 700	2 551	1 817	2 003	2 227	2 271	2 444	2 396
30	Other transport equipment	17 746	19 152	18 078	17 740	17 841	18 796	20 570	20 545
31-33	Furniture; repair, installation of machinery and equipment	19 037	18 125	17 685	18 664	18 711	20 988	23 314	23 391
31-32	Furniture, other manufacturing	7 203	6 196	5 687	5 744	5 698	5 732	5 903	5 532
33	Repair and installation of machinery and equipment	11 834	11 929	11 998	12 920	13 013	15 256	17 411	17 859
35-39	**ELECTRICITY, GAS, WATER AND WASTE MANAGEMENT**	**52 644**	**68 652**	**62 874**	**72 429**	**70 306**	**69 422**	**72 227**	**72 582**
35	Electricity, gas, steam and air conditioning supply	41 882	56 199	50 456	58 670	55 652	53 846	56 451	55 823
36-39	Water supply; sewerage, waste, remediation activities	10 762	12 453	12 418	13 759	14 654	15 576	15 776	16 759
41-43	**CONSTRUCTION**	**116 291**	**124 004**	**121 460**	**123 191**	**135 139**	**152 827**	**158 615**	**167 475**
45-56	Distribution; transportation, accommodation, food service	323 919	341 731	324 520	340 584	346 771	365 363	380 801	400 449
45-47	**Wholesale and retail trade; motor vehicle and motorcycle repairs**	**175 242**	**183 863**	**169 075**	**180 905**	**183 129**	**193 995**	**193 697**	**209 308**
49-53	**Transportation and storage**	**121 679**	**129 279**	**126 646**	**130 400**	**132 290**	**138 075**	**151 819**	**153 986**
55-56	**Accommodation and food service activities**	**26 998**	**28 589**	**28 799**	**29 279**	**31 352**	**33 293**	**35 285**	**37 155**
58-63	**Information and communication**	**79 346**	**81 320**	**85 047**	**90 767**	**93 928**	**99 419**	**103 827**	**105 920**
58-60	Publishing, audiovisual and broadcasting activities	27 356	27 997	28 235	29 699	29 754	30 224	31 245	31 526
61	Telecommunications	22 564	19 556	22 684	23 821	23 719	26 336	25 660	26 694
62-63	IT and other information services	29 426	33 767	34 128	37 247	40 455	42 859	46 922	47 700
64-66	**Financial and insurance activities**	**79 212**	**81 893**	**97 528**	**97 082**	**94 771**	**117 341**	**131 581**	**137 135**
68	**Real estate activities**	**143 195**	**149 437**	**153 722**	**160 999**	**171 497**	**177 281**	**184 820**	**193 447**
69-82	**Professional, scientific, technical, admin., support activities**	**137 099**	**153 160**	**153 722**	**158 603**	**168 750**	**187 238**	**198 157**	**206 088**
69-75	Professional, scientific and technical activities	83 542	96 288	96 855	100 668	102 970	116 011	124 469	129 664
69-71	Legal, accounting activities; mgt consultancy; engineering	64 570	75 455	76 915	79 806	81 588	93 188	101 079	105 514
73-75	Advertising, market research; other prof., scientific, tech.	11 260	12 496	10 825	11 195	11 971	12 439	12 591	13 028
77-82	Administrative and support service activities	53 557	56 872	56 867	57 935	65 780	71 227	73 688	76 424
84-88	**Public administration, defence; social security; education; health**	**378 984**	**415 346**	**445 762**	**471 426**	**502 923**	**536 205**	**564 642**	**597 572**
84	**Public administration, defence; compulsory social security**	**107 841**	**117 424**	**127 225**	**135 219**	**143 218**	**153 058**	**158 817**	**169 876**
85	**Education**	**90 914**	**98 466**	**106 145**	**112 638**	**118 459**	**125 309**	**132 417**	**137 363**
86-88	**Human health and social work activities**	**180 229**	**199 456**	**212 392**	**223 569**	**241 246**	**257 838**	**273 408**	**290 333**
90-99	**Arts, entertainment, household goods repairs, other**	**40 411**	**41 929**	**43 525**	**45 320**	**46 693**	**48 517**	**50 225**	**53 056**
90-93	**Arts, entertainment and recreation**	**22 141**	**22 464**	**22 713**	**23 818**	**23 594**	**23 846**	**23 894**	**25 485**
94-96	**Other service activities**	**17 982**	**19 107**	**20 438**	**21 132**	**22 722**	**24 210**	**25 859**	**27 060**
97-98	**Activities of households as employers and for own use**	**288**	**358**	**374**	**370**	**377**	**461**	**472**	**511**
05-39	**INDUSTRY INCLUDING ENERGY**	**757 453**	**926 518**	**711 551**	**777 821**	**898 895**	**939 170**	**935 954**	**901 398**
45-99	**TOTAL SERVICES**	**1 182 166**	**1 264 816**	**1 303 826**	**1 364 781**	**1 425 333**	**1 531 364**	**1 614 053**	**1 693 667**
45-82	**BUSINESS SECTOR SERVICES**	**762 771**	**807 541**	**814 539**	**848 035**	**875 717**	**946 642**	**999 186**	**1 043 039**
45-82x	**BUSINESS SECTOR SERVICES excluding real estate**	**619 576**	**658 104**	**660 817**	**687 036**	**704 220**	**769 361**	**814 366**	**849 592**
05-82x	**NON-AGRICULTURE BUSINESS SECTOR excluding real estate**	..	..	..	..	..	..	..	..

.. Not available

Note: Detailed metadata at: http://metalinks.oecd.org/stan/20170410/1c43.

Information on data for Israel: http://oe.cd/israel-disclaimer.

Disclaimer: http://oe.cd/disclaimer

NORWAY

Table 3. Value added, volumes

ISIC Rev. 4

Million 2010 NOK

		2007	2008	2009	2010	2011	2012	2013	2014
	TOTAL	**2 326 912**	**2 340 683**	**2 299 581**	**2 306 443**	**2 322 167**	**2 384 532**	**2 406 170**	**2 452 085**
01-03	**AGRICULTURE, FORESTRY AND FISHING**	**35 596**	**37 118**	**37 649**	**40 650**	**42 191**	**44 304**	**42 503**	**45 428**
05-09	**MINING AND QUARRYING**	**565 563**	**551 373**	**543 761**	**519 009**	**499 492**	**494 124**	**481 151**	**482 426**
10-33	**MANUFACTURING**	**192 458**	**197 670**	**183 145**	**186 383**	**189 646**	**193 632**	**200 159**	**206 165**
10-12	Food products, beverages and tobacco	31 090	30 815	32 149	33 703	33 458	35 061	35 031	36 096
13-14	Textiles and wearing apparel	..	..	..	..	..	..	..	..
15	Leather and related products	..	..	..	..	..	..	..	..
16	Wood, wood and cork products	9 944	8 349	6 524	7 017	7 823	7 673	7 036	6 958
17	Paper and paper products	3 091	2 867	2 407	2 679	1 373	2 138	2 050	1 755
18	Printing and reproduction of recorded media	4 586	4 567	4 227	4 415	4 194	3 996	3 729	3 445
19-23	Chemical, rubber, plastics, non-metallic products	32 020	33 409	31 095	33 638	35 903	33 988	35 084	34 962
20	Chemicals and chemical products	..	..	..	..	..	..	..	..
21	Pharmaceutical products	..	..	..	..	..	..	..	..
22-23	Rubber, plastic, non-metallic mineral products	..	..	..	..	..	..	..	..
24	Basic metals	11 407	13 715	9 038	10 127	9 624	9 020	8 643	9 499
25	Metal products, except machinery and equipment	17 802	16 766	16 415	15 709	16 177	17 034	16 747	17 715
26-28	Machinery and equipment	34 741	39 910	40 382	38 138	40 088	41 416	43 869	47 397
26	Computer, electronic and optical products	9 071	8 693	10 049	9 208	9 351	9 474	9 891	10 165
27	Electrical equipment	5 809	6 172	6 535	6 975	7 320	7 189	7 716	8 138
28	Machinery and equipment n.e.c.	19 718	25 477	23 816	21 955	23 417	24 733	26 237	29 101
29-30	Transport equipment	24 760	24 858	20 285	19 743	19 921	20 711	23 293	24 107
29	Motor vehicles, trailers and semi-trailers	2 153	1 775	1 609	2 003	2 394	2 224	2 404	2 540
30	Other transport equipment	22 618	23 326	18 753	17 740	17 527	18 464	20 864	21 539
31-33	Furniture; repair, installation of machinery and equipment	20 794	18 870	18 152	18 664	18 106	19 452	21 267	21 000
31-32	Furniture, other manufacturing	8 658	7 260	5 814	5 744	5 513	5 413	5 432	5 062
33	Repair and installation of machinery and equipment	12 426	11 798	12 337	12 920	12 593	14 039	15 823	15 923
35-39	**ELECTRICITY, GAS, WATER AND WASTE MANAGEMENT**	**80 604**	**79 203**	**74 250**	**72 429**	**72 591**	**83 339**	**81 930**	**87 220**
35	Electricity, gas, steam and air conditioning supply	67 124	64 695	60 435	58 670	59 177	69 578	68 209	73 090
36-39	Water supply; sewerage, waste, remediation activities	13 759	14 526	13 836	13 759	13 414	13 989	13 886	14 436
41-43	**CONSTRUCTION**	**134 456**	**136 310**	**126 488**	**123 191**	**126 569**	**135 700**	**137 996**	**140 668**
45-56	Distribution; transportation, accommodation, food service	344 989	341 351	329 820	340 584	349 988	362 479	372 436	382 631
45-47	**Wholesale and retail trade; motor vehicle and motorcycle repairs**	**172 196**	**177 154**	**171 859**	**180 905**	**184 327**	**193 734**	**196 479**	**207 120**
49-53	**Transportation and storage**	**142 997**	**132 488**	**127 838**	**130 400**	**135 650**	**138 371**	**143 986**	**142 332**
55-56	**Accommodation and food service activities**	**31 292**	**31 849**	**30 166**	**29 279**	**30 011**	**30 372**	**31 908**	**33 426**
58-63	**Information and communication**	**78 724**	**80 476**	**84 374**	**90 767**	**93 392**	**97 012**	**100 043**	**101 273**
58-60	Publishing, audiovisual and broadcasting activities	30 455	29 654	28 568	29 699	28 831	28 565	28 157	27 784
61	Telecommunications	18 507	18 028	21 613	23 821	24 732	27 159	27 505	29 558
62-63	IT and other information services	30 040	33 173	34 229	37 247	39 830	41 392	44 485	44 271
64-66	**Financial and insurance activities**	**99 363**	**99 124**	**100 856**	**97 082**	**94 170**	**97 744**	**101 754**	**106 236**
68	**Real estate activities**	**155 354**	**157 500**	**158 898**	**160 999**	**166 507**	**171 087**	**175 659**	**177 374**
69-82	**Professional, scientific, technical, admin., support activities**	**157 014**	**164 383**	**158 537**	**158 603**	**163 170**	**175 087**	**180 236**	**182 435**
69-75	Professional, scientific and technical activities	97 135	104 232	100 578	100 668	100 075	107 735	111 755	113 070
69-71	Legal, accounting activities; mgt consultancy; engineering	75 218	81 242	79 815	79 806	79 939	86 913	90 905	92 098
73-75	Advertising, market research; other prof., scientific, tech.	13 113	13 870	11 317	11 195	11 214	11 447	11 465	11 538
77-82	Administrative and support service activities	59 781	60 149	57 958	57 935	63 095	67 356	68 470	69 356
84-88	**Public administration, defence; social security; education; health**	**439 786**	**452 376**	**459 550**	**471 426**	**478 687**	**488 890**	**494 285**	**503 714**
84	**Public administration, defence; compulsory social security**	**121 285**	**125 288**	**130 352**	**135 219**	**139 607**	**142 428**	**142 390**	**150 017**
85	**Education**	**107 953**	**108 290**	**109 170**	**112 638**	**113 773**	**114 971**	**118 391**	**118 624**
86-88	**Human health and social work activities**	**210 716**	**218 907**	**220 048**	**223 569**	**225 307**	**231 451**	**233 453**	**235 164**
90-99	**Arts, entertainment, household goods repairs, other**	**45 688**	**46 264**	**45 413**	**45 320**	**45 765**	**46 309**	**47 282**	**48 792**
90-93	**Arts, entertainment and recreation**	**24 767**	**24 945**	**23 820**	**23 818**	**23 701**	**23 400**	**23 707**	**25 013**
94-96	**Other service activities**	**20 636**	**20 962**	**21 215**	**21 132**	**21 688**	**22 429**	**23 078**	**23 314**
97-98	**Activities of households as employers and for own use**	**297**	**365**	**376**	**370**	**375**	**454**	**460**	**483**
05-39	INDUSTRY INCLUDING ENERGY	834 472	825 174	800 078	777 821	761 728	768 080	758 060	768 195
45-99	TOTAL SERVICES	1 321 884	1 341 932	1 337 180	1 364 781	1 391 679	1 438 478	1 471 482	1 502 564
45-82	BUSINESS SECTOR SERVICES	835 764	842 963	832 217	848 035	867 227	903 527	930 443	950 667
45-82x	BUSINESS SECTOR SERVICES excluding real estate	680 392	685 436	673 331	687 036	700 720	732 500	754 838	773 296
05-82x	NON-AGRICULTURE BUSINESS SECTOR excluding real estate	..	..	..	..	..	..	..	..

.. Not available

Note: Detailed metadata at: http://metalinks.oecd.org/stan/20170410/1c43.
Information on data for Israel: http://oe.cd/israel-disclaimer.

Disclaimer: http://oe.cd/disclaimer

NORWAY

Table 4. Gross fixed capital formation, current prices

ISIC Rev. 4

Million NOK

		2007	2008	2009	2010	2011	2012	2013	2014
	TOTAL	**550 940**	**584 604**	**561 397**	**533 044**	**595 150**	**659 479**	**717 132**	**739 271**
01-03	**AGRICULTURE, FORESTRY AND FISHING**	**9 234**	**11 508**	**9 871**	**10 933**	**11 685**	**9 861**	**11 819**	**11 261**
05-09	**MINING AND QUARRYING**	**116 730**	**134 463**	**149 339**	**129 863**	**148 835**	**186 420**	**216 938**	**216 947**
10-33	**MANUFACTURING**	**36 517**	**45 306**	**30 409**	**26 269**	**28 882**	**31 200**	**30 292**	**32 864**
10-12	Food products, beverages and tobacco	4 627	7 517	5 897	7 449	8 137	7 567	6 388	7 934
13-14	Textiles and wearing apparel	335	366	120	273	278	276	392	238
15	Leather and related products	7	13	16	8	5	3	7	4
16	Wood, wood and cork products	1 084	1 403	931	924	973	866	926	758
17	Paper and paper products	1 206	853	521	409	559	662	582	510
18	Printing and reproduction of recorded media	577	325	349	198	323	319	435	469
19-23	Chemical, rubber, plastics, non-metallic products	10 891	17 441	10 851	6 742	6 293	7 496	6 409	7 140
20	Chemicals and chemical products	3 238	8 601	5 310	2 457	2 266	2 915	2 674	2 844
21	Pharmaceutical products	3 103	6 451	3 632	2 757	2 431	2 910	2 082	2 668
22-23	Rubber, plastic, non-metallic mineral products	4 550	2 389	1 909	1 528	1 596	1 671	1 653	1 628
24	Basic metals	2 645	3 331	2 155	1 947	1 996	2 155	2 127	2 206
25	Metal products, except machinery and equipment	1 564	2 101	1 639	1 531	2 204	2 298	2 127	2 776
26-28	Machinery and equipment	5 529	6 253	4 918	4 105	4 764	5 040	6 127	6 064
26	Computer, electronic and optical products	2 668	2 485	2 209	1 787	1 837	1 787	1 916	2 096
27	Electrical equipment	750	869	856	748	1 017	989	902	991
28	Machinery and equipment n.e.c.	2 111	2 899	1 853	1 570	1 910	2 264	3 309	2 977
29-30	Transport equipment	5 866	3 094	1 362	1 082	1 314	2 311	2 247	2 131
29	Motor vehicles, trailers and semi-trailers	422	479	404	232	303	455	547	484
30	Other transport equipment	5 444	2 615	958	850	1 011	1 856	1 700	1 647
31-33	Furniture; repair, installation of machinery and equipment	2 186	2 609	1 650	1 601	2 036	2 207	2 525	2 634
31-32	Furniture, other manufacturing	807	787	425	523	570	582	724	641
33	Repair and installation of machinery and equipment	1 379	1 822	1 225	1 078	1 466	1 625	1 801	1 993
35-39	**ELECTRICITY, GAS, WATER AND WASTE MANAGEMENT**	**18 034**	**24 615**	**22 287**	**24 098**	**25 291**	**28 094**	**28 625**	**33 361**
35	Electricity, gas, steam and air conditioning supply	12 211	14 702	12 468	14 842	16 638	18 461	19 779	21 691
36-39	Water supply; sewerage, waste, remediation activities	5 823	9 913	9 819	9 256	8 653	9 633	8 846	11 670
41-43	**CONSTRUCTION**	**16 398**	**13 921**	**12 815**	**11 861**	**13 477**	**17 130**	**14 594**	**14 111**
45-56	Distribution; transportation, accommodation, food service	49 757	44 755	52 260	46 865	52 267	45 992	42 131	38 989
45-47	**Wholesale and retail trade; motor vehicle and motorcycle repairs**	**15 115**	**14 020**	**10 211**	**10 973**	**12 947**	**12 680**	**14 854**	**15 433**
49-53	**Transportation and storage**	**31 835**	**28 628**	**40 000**	**34 036**	**37 589**	**31 101**	**25 057**	**20 973**
55-56	**Accommodation and food service activities**	**2 807**	**2 107**	**2 049**	**1 856**	**1 731**	**2 211**	**2 220**	**2 583**
58-63	**Information and communication**	**14 933**	**19 079**	**16 661**	**17 511**	**17 093**	**18 952**	**20 709**	**19 551**
58-60	Publishing, audiovisual and broadcasting activities	4 393	5 134	4 437	4 811	4 825	4 578	4 586	5 293
61	Telecommunications	7 274	9 087	8 382	7 684	7 297	9 135	10 230	8 938
62-63	IT and other information services	3 266	4 858	3 842	5 016	4 971	5 239	5 893	5 320
64-66	**Financial and insurance activities**	**9 449**	**11 190**	**7 086**	**5 637**	**9 609**	**6 204**	**7 595**	**7 116**
68	**Real estate activities**	**164 738**	**156 225**	**131 414**	**132 202**	**153 937**	**176 532**	**187 334**	**195 787**
69-82	**Professional, scientific, technical, admin., support activities**	**22 094**	**19 686**	**15 162**	**16 366**	**16 758**	**20 276**	**21 447**	**21 749**
69-75	Professional, scientific and technical activities	13 016	11 964	10 913	10 496	9 845	13 071	14 779	15 050
69-71	Legal, accounting activities; mgt consultancy; engineering	8 279	6 680	5 997	4 555	4 373	6 596	8 208	8 774
73-75	Advertising, market research; other prof., scientific, tech.	1 065	1 117	640	994	994	1 009	1 085	1 111
77-82	Administrative and support service activities	9 078	7 722	4 249	5 870	6 913	7 205	6 668	6 699
84-88	**Public administration, defence; social security; education; health**	**87 023**	**97 355**	**107 040**	**104 802**	**110 239**	**111 898**	**128 433**	**139 458**
84	**Public administration, defence; compulsory social security**	**44 267**	**53 660**	**60 940**	**60 098**	**65 647**	**65 242**	**74 119**	**80 747**
85	**Education**	**22 713**	**24 319**	**27 803**	**27 885**	**27 026**	**27 199**	**30 538**	**32 518**
86-88	**Human health and social work activities**	**20 043**	**19 376**	**18 297**	**16 819**	**17 566**	**19 457**	**23 776**	**26 193**
90-99	**Arts, entertainment, household goods repairs, other**	**6 033**	**6 501**	**7 053**	**6 637**	**7 077**	**6 920**	**7 215**	**8 077**
90-93	**Arts, entertainment and recreation**	**4 281**	**4 486**	**5 168**	**4 496**	**4 127**	**4 606**	**4 491**	**5 076**
94-96	**Other service activities**	**1 752**	**2 015**	**1 885**	**2 141**	**2 950**	**2 314**	**2 724**	**3 001**
97-98	**Activities of households as employers and for own use**	**0**	**0**	**0**	**0**	**0**	**0**	**0**	**0**
05-39	**INDUSTRY INCLUDING ENERGY**	**171 281**	**204 384**	**202 035**	**180 230**	**203 008**	**245 714**	**275 855**	**283 172**
45-99	**TOTAL SERVICES**	**354 027**	**354 791**	**336 676**	**330 020**	**366 980**	**386 774**	**414 864**	**430 727**
45-82	**BUSINESS SECTOR SERVICES**	**260 971**	**250 935**	**222 583**	**218 581**	**249 664**	**267 956**	**279 216**	**283 192**
45-82x	**BUSINESS SECTOR SERVICES excluding real estate**	**96 233**	**94 710**	**91 169**	**86 379**	**95 727**	**91 424**	**91 882**	**87 405**
05-82x	**NON-AGRICULTURE BUSINESS SECTOR excluding real estate**	..	..	..	..	..	..	..	..

.. Not available

Note: Detailed metadata at: http://metalinks.oecd.org/stan/20170410/1c43.

Information on data for Israel: http://oe.cd/israel-disclaimer.

Disclaimer: http://oe.cd/disclaimer

NORWAY

Table 5. Number of persons engaged, total employment

ISIC Rev. 4

Thousands

		2007	2008	2009	2010	2011	2012	2013	2014
	TOTAL	**2 535**	**2 617**	**2 605**	**2 592**	**2 630**	**2 685**	**2 713**	**2 746**
01-03	**AGRICULTURE, FORESTRY AND FISHING**	**74**	**72**	**70**	**71**	**71**	**70**	**69**	**69**
05-09	**MINING AND QUARRYING**	**49**	**53**	**55**	**58**	**61**	**66**	**69**	**70**
10-33	**MANUFACTURING**	**265**	**270**	**258**	**247**	**246**	**248**	**251**	**251**
10-12	Food products, beverages and tobacco	51	51	53	52	52	53	53	53
13-14	Textiles and wearing apparel	5	6	5	5	5	5	4	4
15	Leather and related products	0	0	0	0	0	0	0	0
16	Wood, wood and cork products	17	16	14	14	15	15	14	14
17	Paper and paper products	7	7	6	6	5	4	4	3
18	Printing and reproduction of recorded media	8	8	8	7	7	7	6	6
19-23	Chemical, rubber, plastics, non-metallic products	34	35	31	30	30	29	29	29
20	Chemicals and chemical products	7	6	6	6	6	6	6	6
21	Pharmaceutical products	10	10	8	8	8	8	8	8
22-23	Rubber, plastic, non-metallic mineral products	18	18	16	16	16	16	16	15
24	Basic metals	13	14	12	11	11	10	10	10
25	Metal products, except machinery and equipment	25	26	26	25	26	27	27	27
26-28	Machinery and equipment	40	40	40	38	38	41	43	44
26	Computer, electronic and optical products	10	10	10	10	10	9	9	9
27	Electrical equipment	8	8	8	8	8	8	9	9
28	Machinery and equipment n.e.c.	21	21	22	21	21	23	25	26
29-30	Transport equipment	34	35	32	29	28	30	31	31
29	Motor vehicles, trailers and semi-trailers	5	5	3	3	3	3	3	3
30	Other transport equipment	29	30	28	26	25	26	27	28
31-33	Furniture; repair, installation of machinery and equipment	31	33	31	29	29	30	30	31
31-32	Furniture, other manufacturing	14	13	12	10	10	10	9	9
33	Repair and installation of machinery and equipment	18	20	19	19	19	20	21	22
35-39	**ELECTRICITY, GAS, WATER AND WASTE MANAGEMENT**	**27**	**28**	**27**	**27**	**27**	**27**	**27**	**28**
35	Electricity, gas, steam and air conditioning supply	13	13	13	12	13	13	13	13
36-39	Water supply; sewerage, waste, remediation activities	14	15	14	14	14	14	14	15
41-43	**CONSTRUCTION**	**193**	**199**	**190**	**188**	**194**	**205**	**211**	**216**
45-56	Distribution; transportation, accommodation, food service	619	639	630	620	619	628	630	638
45-47	**Wholesale and retail trade; motor vehicle and motorcycle repairs**	**368**	**382**	**376**	**369**	**366**	**371**	**370**	**374**
49-53	**Transportation and storage**	**172**	**174**	**174**	**172**	**171**	**173**	**174**	**175**
55-56	**Accommodation and food service activities**	**80**	**83**	**80**	**80**	**82**	**84**	**86**	**89**
58-63	**Information and communication**	**84**	**85**	**86**	**86**	**87**	**88**	**89**	**91**
58-60	Publishing, audiovisual and broadcasting activities	36	34	36	34	35	35	34	34
61	Telecommunications	13	13	13	13	13	13	13	13
62-63	IT and other information services	35	37	37	38	39	41	42	44
64-66	**Financial and insurance activities**	**49**	**50**	**53**	**52**	**50**	**50**	**50**	**49**
68	**Real estate activities**	**22**	**24**	**23**	**23**	**24**	**25**	**24**	**25**
69-82	**Professional, scientific, technical, admin., support activities**	**224**	**240**	**233**	**229**	**238**	**247**	**251**	**255**
69-75	Professional, scientific and technical activities	109	116	117	116	117	121	124	126
69-71	Legal, accounting activities; mgt consultancy; engineering	82	85	89	89	90	93	95	97
73-75	Advertising, market research; other prof., scientific, tech.	19	21	19	18	19	20	20	20
77-82	Administrative and support service activities	114	124	116	113	120	126	127	128
84-88	**Public administration, defence; social security; education; health**	**846**	**867**	**888**	**899**	**921**	**935**	**947**	**959**
84	**Public administration, defence; compulsory social security**	**173**	**177**	**184**	**186**	**190**	**192**	**193**	**195**
85	**Education**	**186**	**188**	**192**	**193**	**196**	**198**	**200**	**203**
86-88	**Human health and social work activities**	**487**	**501**	**512**	**520**	**535**	**545**	**554**	**561**
90-99	**Arts, entertainment, household goods repairs, other**	**84**	**91**	**94**	**94**	**94**	**94**	**94**	**95**
90-93	**Arts, entertainment and recreation**	**40**	**45**	**47**	**47**	**47**	**47**	**46**	**47**
94-96	**Other service activities**	**41**	**42**	**43**	**43**	**43**	**43**	**44**	**45**
97-98	**Activities of households as employers and for own use**	**2**	**4**	**4**	**4**	**4**	**4**	**4**	**4**
05-39	**INDUSTRY INCLUDING ENERGY**	**341**	**350**	**340**	**331**	**333**	**341**	**347**	**350**
45-99	**TOTAL SERVICES**	**1 927**	**1 996**	**2 005**	**2 003**	**2 032**	**2 068**	**2 085**	**2 111**
45-82	**BUSINESS SECTOR SERVICES**	**998**	**1 038**	**1 024**	**1 010**	**1 017**	**1 039**	**1 044**	**1 057**
45-82x	**BUSINESS SECTOR SERVICES excluding real estate**	**976**	**1 014**	**1 001**	**987**	**994**	**1 014**	**1 020**	**1 033**
05-82x	**NON-AGRICULTURE BUSINESS SECTOR excluding real estate**	..	..	..	..	..	..	..	..

.. Not available

Note: Detailed metadata at: http://metalinks.oecd.org/stan/20170410/1c43.

Information on data for Israel: http://oe.cd/israel-disclaimer.

Disclaimer: http://oe.cd/disclaimer

Table 6. Labour costs (compensation of employees), current prices

ISIC Rev. 4

Million NOK

		2007	2008	2009	2010	2011	2012	2013	2014
	TOTAL	988 513	1 086 996	1 119 397	1 151 134	1 225 068	1 308 760	1 384 564	1 448 528
01-03	AGRICULTURE, FORESTRY AND FISHING	7 435	8 009	8 248	9 216	9 919	10 325	10 774	11 548
05-09	MINING AND QUARRYING	39 214	47 257	54 460	56 913	64 473	73 059	81 712	84 956
10-33	MANUFACTURING	123 636	131 243	125 827	123 504	128 582	136 534	143 521	149 136
10-12	Food products, beverages and tobacco	20 603	21 617	22 106	22 201	23 156	24 583	25 429	26 146
13-14	Textiles and wearing apparel	1 688	1 715	1 537	1 551	1 648	1 641	1 648	1 674
15	Leather and related products	80	81	72	45	38	40	43	32
16	Wood, wood and cork products	6 078	6 087	5 447	5 660	5 955	6 096	6 065	6 137
17	Paper and paper products	3 150	3 181	3 000	2 750	2 703	2 158	2 030	1 844
18	Printing and reproduction of recorded media	3 527	3 629	3 353	3 265	3 230	3 253	3 174	3 018
19-23	Chemical, rubber, plastics, non-metallic products	17 850	18 322	16 789	17 224	17 967	18 063	18 919	19 172
20	Chemicals and chemical products	4 211	4 017	3 791	4 388	4 441	4 076	4 174	4 404
21	Pharmaceutical products	5 744	5 828	5 194	5 194	5 444	5 488	6 065	5 830
22-23	Rubber, plastic, non-metallic mineral products	7 895	8 477	7 804	7 642	8 082	8 499	8 680	8 938
24	Basic metals	6 381	7 001	6 498	5 928	6 152	6 108	6 001	6 269
25	Metal products, except machinery and equipment	11 324	12 356	12 199	11 713	12 484	13 730	14 532	14 999
26-28	Machinery and equipment	20 744	22 733	24 025	23 055	24 055	26 671	28 791	31 269
26	Computer, electronic and optical products	5 437	5 893	6 039	5 895	6 142	6 079	6 317	6 602
27	Electrical equipment	4 421	4 698	4 748	4 640	4 935	5 439	5 650	6 109
28	Machinery and equipment n.e.c.	10 886	12 142	13 238	12 520	12 978	15 153	16 824	18 558
29-30	Transport equipment	17 476	18 760	16 754	15 739	16 312	18 051	19 355	20 354
29	Motor vehicles, trailers and semi-trailers	2 073	2 181	1 588	1 522	1 668	1 714	1 876	1 896
30	Other transport equipment	15 403	16 579	15 166	14 217	14 644	16 337	17 479	18 458
31-33	Furniture; repair, installation of machinery and equipment	14 735	15 761	14 047	14 373	14 882	16 140	17 534	18 222
31-32	Furniture, other manufacturing	5 027	4 784	4 388	4 192	4 071	4 216	4 131	4 095
33	Repair and installation of machinery and equipment	9 708	10 977	9 659	10 181	10 811	11 924	13 403	14 127
35-39	ELECTRICITY, GAS, WATER AND WASTE MANAGEMENT	13 448	15 094	14 528	14 778	15 820	16 881	17 921	19 139
35	Electricity, gas, steam and air conditioning supply	7 464	8 183	7 957	7 765	8 350	9 028	9 479	10 114
36-39	Water supply; sewerage, waste, remediation activities	5 984	6 911	6 571	7 013	7 470	7 853	8 442	9 025
41-43	CONSTRUCTION	72 593	81 153	80 135	81 008	87 915	97 091	104 223	109 935
45-56	Distribution; transportation, accommodation, food service	208 232	225 737	226 851	231 123	239 904	251 886	263 703	271 879
45-47	Wholesale and retail trade; motor vehicle and motorcycle repairs	120 138	131 277	132 289	135 033	138 842	146 040	152 209	155 817
49-53	Transportation and storage	68 352	73 277	73 229	73 741	77 297	81 031	84 983	87 835
55-56	Accommodation and food service activities	19 742	21 183	21 333	22 349	23 765	24 815	26 511	28 227
58-63	Information and communication	49 478	54 393	55 571	56 635	60 505	64 352	67 182	70 743
58-60	Publishing, audiovisual and broadcasting activities	19 267	20 657	20 622	20 013	20 928	21 572	22 550	23 193
61	Telecommunications	8 556	9 484	9 776	9 846	10 222	10 741	10 866	11 182
62-63	IT and other information services	21 655	24 252	25 173	26 776	29 355	32 039	33 766	36 368
64-66	Financial and insurance activities	33 733	37 392	39 146	39 555	40 355	42 285	43 501	45 482
68	Real estate activities	9 371	10 629	10 582	10 932	11 938	13 397	13 808	14 450
69-82	Professional, scientific, technical, admin., support activities	94 849	107 206	107 934	110 893	121 543	132 040	140 950	146 991
69-75	Professional, scientific and technical activities	56 240	63 551	66 285	68 493	72 382	79 241	85 579	89 721
69-71	Legal, accounting activities; mgt consultancy; engineering	43 328	48 882	52 367	54 404	57 247	63 550	68 972	72 427
73-75	Advertising, market research; other prof., scientific, tech.	7 627	8 717	7 615	7 690	8 531	8 576	9 208	9 484
77-82	Administrative and support service activities	38 609	43 655	41 649	42 400	49 161	52 799	55 371	57 270
84-88	Public administration, defence; social security; education; health	311 878	341 538	366 849	386 277	412 104	437 458	462 473	488 017
84	Public administration, defence; compulsory social security	77 806	84 728	91 278	96 790	102 254	108 325	113 141	120 541
85	Education	75 693	81 633	88 010	92 355	96 660	101 334	107 198	110 980
86-88	Human health and social work activities	158 379	175 177	187 561	197 132	213 190	227 799	242 134	256 496
90-99	Arts, entertainment, household goods repairs, other	24 646	27 345	29 266	30 300	32 010	33 452	34 796	36 252
90-93	Arts, entertainment and recreation	12 088	13 532	14 447	14 816	15 299	15 921	15 974	16 736
94-96	Other service activities	12 270	13 455	14 445	15 105	16 306	17 070	18 350	19 005
97-98	Activities of households as employers and for own use	288	358	374	379	405	461	472	511
05-39	INDUSTRY INCLUDING ENERGY	176 298	193 594	194 815	195 195	208 875	226 474	243 154	253 231
45-99	TOTAL SERVICES	732 187	804 240	836 199	865 715	918 359	974 870	1 026 413	1 073 814
45-82	BUSINESS SECTOR SERVICES	395 663	435 357	440 084	449 138	474 245	503 960	529 144	549 545
45-82x	BUSINESS SECTOR SERVICES excluding real estate	386 292	424 728	429 502	438 206	462 307	490 563	515 336	535 095
05-82x	NON-AGRICULTURE BUSINESS SECTOR excluding real estate	..	..	..	..	..	..	..	..

.. Not available

Note: Detailed metadata at: http://metalinks.oecd.org/stan/20170410/1c43.

Information on data for Israel: http://oe.cd/israel-disclaimer.

Disclaimer: http://oe.cd/disclaimer

PORTUGAL

Table 1. Production (gross output), current prices

ISIC Rev. 4

Million EUR

		2007	2008	2009	2010	2011	2012	2013	2014
	TOTAL	**324 607**	**337 839**	**318 332**	**328 475**	**326 819**	**309 437**	**307 861**	**310 198**
01-03	**AGRICULTURE, FORESTRY AND FISHING**	**7 507**	**7 789**	**7 316**	**7 567**	**7 722**	**7 866**	**8 052**	**8 070**
05-09	**MINING AND QUARRYING**	**1 559**	**1 387**	**1 239**	**1 360**	**1 335**	**1 277**	**1 162**	**1 113**
10-33	**MANUFACTURING**	**80 412**	**82 430**	**68 919**	**76 143**	**80 457**	**78 933**	**79 655**	**80 534**
10-12	Food products, beverages and tobacco	14 394	15 579	14 741	14 811	15 364	15 549	15 907	15 960
13-14	Textiles and wearing apparel	7 660	6 980	6 047	6 460	6 540	6 412	6 781	7 140
15	Leather and related products	2 220	2 175	2 054	2 222	2 474	2 511	2 717	2 916
16	Wood, wood and cork products	2 990	2 880	2 435	2 762	2 801	2 791	2 778	2 948
17	Paper and paper products	3 644	3 510	2 967	3 366	3 675	3 676	3 697	3 710
18	Printing and reproduction of recorded media	1 309	1 261	1 066	1 210	1 110	990	944	969
19-23	Chemical, rubber, plastics, non-metallic products	19 917	21 464	16 175	19 690	21 637	21 928	22 058	21 035
20	Chemicals and chemical products	4 122	4 053	3 121	4 211	4 658	4 678	4 604	4 413
21	Pharmaceutical products	1 130	1 092	1 125	1 115	1 150	1 120	1 121	1 042
22-23	Rubber, plastic, non-metallic mineral products	8 042	8 116	7 088	7 502	7 624	7 079	6 935	7 194
24	Basic metals	2 558	2 673	2 098	2 264	2 767	2 673	2 524	2 509
25	Metal products, except machinery and equipment	6 355	6 642	5 214	5 625	5 527	5 189	5 212	5 509
26-28	Machinery and equipment	8 238	8 228	6 641	6 872	6 780	6 256	6 310	6 567
26	Computer, electronic and optical products	3 206	2 837	1 819	1 915	1 940	1 750	1 583	1 528
27	Electrical equipment	2 035	2 271	2 377	2 552	2 539	2 329	2 441	2 446
28	Machinery and equipment n.e.c.	2 996	3 120	2 445	2 405	2 301	2 177	2 286	2 594
29-30	Transport equipment	7 064	6 693	5 252	6 510	7 610	7 037	6 826	7 214
29	Motor vehicles, trailers and semi-trailers	6 698	6 346	4 980	6 173	7 219	6 645	6 372	6 723
30	Other transport equipment	366	347	272	337	391	392	453	491
31-33	Furniture; repair, installation of machinery and equipment	4 062	4 347	4 227	4 351	4 174	3 921	3 902	4 057
31-32	Furniture, other manufacturing	2 291	2 451	2 384	2 454	2 390	2 256	2 297	2 432
33	Repair and installation of machinery and equipment	1 771	1 895	1 843	1 897	1 784	1 665	1 604	1 625
35-39	**ELECTRICITY, GAS, WATER AND WASTE MANAGEMENT**	**15 277**	**17 568**	**16 045**	**16 691**	**17 806**	**18 561**	**18 296**	**17 865**
35	Electricity, gas, steam and air conditioning supply	11 664	13 708	12 374	12 625	13 514	14 410	14 294	13 989
36-39	Water supply; sewerage, waste, remediation activities	3 613	3 861	3 671	4 065	4 292	4 150	4 002	3 876
41-43	**CONSTRUCTION**	**33 510**	**33 674**	**30 991**	**30 333**	**27 104**	**20 763**	**18 284**	**16 878**
45-56	Distribution; transportation, accommodation, food service	67 400	69 481	67 413	69 343	68 572	65 814	65 929	68 170
45-47	**Wholesale and retail trade; motor vehicle and motorcycle repairs**	**36 882**	**38 012**	**36 971**	**37 212**	**36 342**	**35 085**	**34 982**	**36 048**
49-53	**Transportation and storage**	**17 035**	**17 967**	**16 782**	**18 152**	**18 437**	**17 464**	**17 672**	**17 875**
55-56	**Accommodation and food service activities**	**13 482**	**13 501**	**13 661**	**13 980**	**13 793**	**13 264**	**13 275**	**14 247**
58-63	**Information and communication**	**13 100**	**13 878**	**13 719**	**13 602**	**12 690**	**12 154**	**11 684**	**11 387**
58-60	Publishing, audiovisual and broadcasting activities	2 972	3 192	2 993	2 965	2 737	2 410	2 274	2 327
61	Telecommunications	7 453	7 740	7 603	7 433	6 671	6 445	6 037	5 498
62-63	IT and other information services	2 676	2 946	3 124	3 203	3 281	3 300	3 374	3 562
64-66	**Financial and insurance activities**	**18 132**	**19 161**	**17 590**	**17 195**	**17 570**	**16 209**	**15 340**	**14 760**
68	**Real estate activities**	**17 279**	**18 123**	**18 554**	**19 392**	**19 253**	**19 093**	**19 774**	**20 621**
69-82	**Professional, scientific, technical, admin., support activities**	**19 941**	**21 321**	**21 159**	**21 359**	**20 621**	**19 081**	**18 845**	**20 002**
69-75	Professional, scientific and technical activities	11 864	12 651	12 566	12 503	12 091	11 169	10 976	11 796
69-71	Legal, accounting activities; mgt consultancy; engineering	8 293	8 940	9 102	8 975	8 753	8 188	7 991	8 566
73-75	Advertising, market research; other prof., scientific, tech.	3 003	3 056	2 778	2 830	2 664	2 305	2 265	2 407
77-82	Administrative and support service activities	8 077	8 670	8 594	8 856	8 530	7 913	7 869	8 206
84-88	**Public administration, defence; social security; education; health**	**43 606**	**45 544**	**47 830**	**47 824**	**46 299**	**42 580**	**43 897**	**43 623**
84	**Public administration, defence; compulsory social security**	**17 391**	**17 911**	**19 045**	**18 222**	**17 515**	**16 244**	**16 988**	**16 625**
85	**Education**	**11 533**	**12 113**	**12 623**	**12 892**	**12 074**	**10 647**	**11 088**	**10 901**
86-88	**Human health and social work activities**	**14 682**	**15 519**	**16 162**	**16 710**	**16 710**	**15 689**	**15 821**	**16 097**
90-99	**Arts, entertainment, household goods repairs, other**	**6 884**	**7 483**	**7 555**	**7 666**	**7 391**	**7 105**	**6 943**	**7 177**
90-93	**Arts, entertainment and recreation**	**2 499**	**2 678**	**2 684**	**2 727**	**2 603**	**2 376**	**2 271**	**2 474**
94-96	**Other service activities**	**3 308**	**3 649**	**3 662**	**3 706**	**3 587**	**3 578**	**3 543**	**3 567**
97-98	**Activities of households as employers and for own use**	**1 077**	**1 156**	**1 210**	**1 232**	**1 201**	**1 151**	**1 129**	**1 137**
05-39	**INDUSTRY INCLUDING ENERGY**	**97 247**	**101 386**	**86 202**	**94 194**	**99 598**	**98 770**	**99 113**	**99 512**
45-99	**TOTAL SERVICES**	**186 343**	**194 990**	**193 822**	**196 380**	**192 395**	**182 037**	**182 412**	**185 739**
45-82	**BUSINESS SECTOR SERVICES**	**135 853**	**141 964**	**138 436**	**140 890**	**138 706**	**132 352**	**131 573**	**134 938**
45-82x	**BUSINESS SECTOR SERVICES excluding real estate**	**118 574**	**123 841**	**119 882**	**121 499**	**119 453**	**113 259**	**111 799**	**114 318**
05-82x	**NON-AGRICULTURE BUSINESS SECTOR excluding real estate**	..	..	..	..	..	..	..	..

.. Not available

Note: Detailed metadata at: http://metalinks.oecd.org/stan/20170410/1c43.

Information on data for Israel: http://oe.cd/israel-disclaimer.

Disclaimer: http://oe.cd/disclaimer

PORTUGAL

Table 2. Value added, current prices

ISIC Rev. 4

Million EUR

		2007	2008	2009	2010	2011	2012	2013	2014
	TOTAL	**152 183**	**156 016**	**155 506**	**158 326**	**154 243**	**147 362**	**149 768**	**151 365**
01-03	**AGRICULTURE, FORESTRY AND FISHING**	**3 502**	**3 507**	**3 409**	**3 463**	**3 209**	**3 212**	**3 542**	**3 511**
05-09	**MINING AND QUARRYING**	**804**	**608**	**646**	**714**	**650**	**636**	**570**	**530**
10-33	**MANUFACTURING**	**21 486**	**21 365**	**19 529**	**20 822**	**19 959**	**19 166**	**19 680**	**20 421**
10-12	Food products, beverages and tobacco	3 221	3 359	3 543	3 568	3 418	3 354	3 509	3 743
13-14	Textiles and wearing apparel	2 839	2 742	2 535	2 545	2 499	2 455	2 567	2 728
15	Leather and related products	747	747	783	819	885	920	996	1 057
16	Wood, wood and cork products	1 019	922	808	941	912	871	882	907
17	Paper and paper products	1 053	936	828	973	880	806	821	752
18	Printing and reproduction of recorded media	577	533	461	533	471	419	405	416
19-23	Chemical, rubber, plastics, non-metallic products	4 458	4 448	3 785	4 182	3 964	3 673	3 702	3 677
20	Chemicals and chemical products	852	740	682	806	814	672	709	704
21	Pharmaceutical products	437	440	468	428	429	449	487	454
22-23	Rubber, plastic, non-metallic mineral products	2 624	2 567	2 477	2 518	2 412	2 296	2 295	2 331
24	Basic metals	330	363	337	349	366	322	338	363
25	Metal products, except machinery and equipment	2 122	2 250	1 866	1 985	1 870	1 836	1 861	1 981
26-28	Machinery and equipment	2 174	2 146	1 804	1 956	1 711	1 657	1 724	1 811
26	Computer, electronic and optical products	786	696	449	576	452	399	407	404
27	Electrical equipment	634	663	630	668	606	557	579	581
28	Machinery and equipment n.e.c.	754	787	725	712	654	701	738	826
29-30	Transport equipment	1 425	1 302	1 101	1 284	1 324	1 258	1 293	1 343
29	Motor vehicles, trailers and semi-trailers	1 313	1 198	1 016	1 182	1 222	1 165	1 160	1 247
30	Other transport equipment	112	104	85	102	102	93	133	96
31-33	Furniture; repair, installation of machinery and equipment	1 520	1 619	1 678	1 688	1 659	1 596	1 583	1 642
31-32	Furniture, other manufacturing	892	950	981	988	953	902	922	966
33	Repair and installation of machinery and equipment	628	668	697	699	706	694	660	676
35-39	**ELECTRICITY, GAS, WATER AND WASTE MANAGEMENT**	**4 540**	**4 059**	**4 889**	**5 058**	**4 978**	**5 189**	**5 150**	**5 537**
35	Electricity, gas, steam and air conditioning supply	3 158	2 646	3 396	3 343	3 193	3 394	3 387	3 790
36-39	Water supply; sewerage, waste, remediation activities	1 381	1 414	1 493	1 715	1 785	1 796	1 763	1 747
41-43	**CONSTRUCTION**	**10 286**	**10 523**	**9 763**	**9 226**	**8 465**	**7 171**	**6 751**	**6 278**
45-56	Distribution; transportation, accommodation, food service	34 074	34 499	35 494	36 095	36 245	36 017	36 713	37 274
45-47	**Wholesale and retail trade; motor vehicle and motorcycle repairs**	**19 949**	**20 357**	**20 950**	**20 971**	**21 480**	**21 535**	**21 931**	**22 093**
49-53	**Transportation and storage**	**6 834**	**6 828**	**7 022**	**7 437**	**7 165**	**6 945**	**7 221**	**7 119**
55-56	**Accommodation and food service activities**	**7 291**	**7 314**	**7 522**	**7 687**	**7 600**	**7 537**	**7 561**	**8 062**
58-63	**Information and communication**	**5 799**	**5 977**	**5 985**	**5 739**	**5 723**	**5 416**	**5 217**	**5 192**
58-60	Publishing, audiovisual and broadcasting activities	1 087	1 097	1 122	1 092	1 016	878	888	889
61	Telecommunications	3 394	3 435	3 322	3 042	3 048	2 870	2 579	2 442
62-63	IT and other information services	1 318	1 445	1 541	1 605	1 660	1 667	1 750	1 861
64-66	**Financial and insurance activities**	**11 712**	**12 640**	**10 992**	**10 424**	**10 808**	**9 268**	**8 255**	**8 089**
68	**Real estate activities**	**13 958**	**14 672**	**15 244**	**16 795**	**16 597**	**17 424**	**18 573**	**18 891**
69-82	**Professional, scientific, technical, admin., support activities**	**10 338**	**11 125**	**11 086**	**11 244**	**10 744**	**9 997**	**10 119**	**10 856**
69-75	Professional, scientific and technical activities	5 480	5 979	5 898	5 827	5 542	5 165	5 270	5 717
69-71	Legal, accounting activities; mgt consultancy; engineering	4 145	4 549	4 511	4 423	4 215	3 894	3 936	4 261
73-75	Advertising, market research; other prof., scientific, tech.	981	1 013	945	951	900	809	821	844
77-82	Administrative and support service activities	4 858	5 146	5 188	5 417	5 201	4 832	4 849	5 139
84-88	**Public administration, defence; social security; education; health**	**31 826**	**32 822**	**34 131**	**34 254**	**32 411**	**29 528**	**30 910**	**30 391**
84	**Public administration, defence; compulsory social security**	**12 696**	**13 092**	**13 737**	**13 388**	**12 724**	**11 330**	**12 185**	**11 629**
85	**Education**	**10 046**	**10 476**	**10 828**	**11 083**	**10 184**	**9 030**	**9 453**	**9 432**
86-88	**Human health and social work activities**	**9 085**	**9 254**	**9 567**	**9 782**	**9 503**	**9 168**	**9 271**	**9 330**
90-99	**Arts, entertainment, household goods repairs, other**	**3 859**	**4 219**	**4 338**	**4 491**	**4 455**	**4 338**	**4 288**	**4 395**
90-93	**Arts, entertainment and recreation**	**1 113**	**1 193**	**1 225**	**1 256**	**1 239**	**1 084**	**1 056**	**1 128**
94-96	**Other service activities**	**1 669**	**1 870**	**1 903**	**2 003**	**2 015**	**2 104**	**2 104**	**2 130**
97-98	**Activities of households as employers and for own use**	**1 077**	**1 156**	**1 210**	**1 232**	**1 201**	**1 151**	**1 129**	**1 137**
05-39	**INDUSTRY INCLUDING ENERGY**	**26 829**	**26 033**	**25 065**	**26 594**	**25 588**	**24 991**	**25 399**	**26 488**
45-99	**TOTAL SERVICES**	**111 566**	**115 953**	**117 269**	**119 043**	**116 982**	**111 987**	**114 076**	**115 088**
45-82	**BUSINESS SECTOR SERVICES**	**75 881**	**78 912**	**78 800**	**80 298**	**80 116**	**78 121**	**78 878**	**80 302**
45-82x	**BUSINESS SECTOR SERVICES excluding real estate**	**61 923**	**64 240**	**63 556**	**63 503**	**63 520**	**60 697**	**60 304**	**61 411**
05-82x	**NON-AGRICULTURE BUSINESS SECTOR excluding real estate**	..	..	..	..	..	..	..	..

.. Not available

Note: Detailed metadata at: http://metalinks.oecd.org/stan/20170410/1c43.

Information on data for Israel: http://oe.cd/israel-disclaimer.

Disclaimer: http://oe.cd/disclaimer

Table 3. Value added, volumes

ISIC Rev. 4

Million 2010 EUR

		2007	2008	2009	2010	2011	2012	2013	2014
	TOTAL	**158 635**	**159 508**	**155 473**	**158 326**	**156 513**	**151 465**	**150 304**	**150 957**
01-03	**AGRICULTURE, FORESTRY AND FISHING**	**3 443**	**3 562**	**3 443**	**3 463**	**3 492**	**3 471**	**3 569**	**3 510**
05-09	**MINING AND QUARRYING**	**910**	**852**	**745**	**714**	**715**	**670**	**652**	**641**
10-33	**MANUFACTURING**	**22 328**	**21 814**	**19 438**	**20 822**	**20 950**	**20 230**	**20 364**	**20 909**
10-12	Food products, beverages and tobacco	3 564	3 600	3 374	3 568	3 700	3 706	3 716	3 782
13-14	Textiles and wearing apparel	..	..	..	..	..	..	..	..
15	Leather and related products	..	..	..	..	..	..	..	..
16	Wood, wood and cork products	1 105	979	878	941	928	873	868	893
17	Paper and paper products	1 163	1 008	906	973	986	939	958	958
18	Printing and reproduction of recorded media	612	557	498	533	489	447	430	437
19-23	Chemical, rubber, plastics, non-metallic products	4 423	4 391	3 785	4 182	4 018	3 675	3 644	3 652
20	Chemicals and chemical products	989	841	726	806	788	770	759	771
21	Pharmaceutical products	389	429	452	428	458	482	489	482
22-23	Rubber, plastic, non-metallic mineral products	2 753	2 662	2 404	2 518	2 550	2 383	2 324	2 407
24	Basic metals	370	381	312	349	374	368	383	399
25	Metal products, except machinery and equipment	2 217	2 235	1 864	1 985	1 929	1 897	1 904	2 024
26-28	Machinery and equipment	1 896	1 957	1 689	1 956	1 887	1 806	1 893	1 958
26	Computer, electronic and optical products	495	528	415	576	494	448	452	459
27	Electrical equipment	586	622	550	668	692	646	709	734
28	Machinery and equipment n.e.c.	829	806	737	712	700	710	733	765
29-30	Transport equipment	1 437	1 352	1 180	1 284	1 436	1 417	1 412	1 470
29	Motor vehicles, trailers and semi-trailers	1 324	1 245	1 091	1 182	1 337	1 325	1 313	1 389
30	Other transport equipment	113	107	89	102	100	93	99	89
31-33	Furniture; repair, installation of machinery and equipment	1 662	1 693	1 676	1 688	1 708	1 673	1 639	1 683
31-32	Furniture, other manufacturing	972	992	981	988	977	947	930	967
33	Repair and installation of machinery and equipment	690	702	695	699	731	726	709	715
35-39	**ELECTRICITY, GAS, WATER AND WASTE MANAGEMENT**	**4 900**	**4 905**	**5 143**	**5 058**	**4 942**	**4 905**	**4 583**	**4 631**
35	Electricity, gas, steam and air conditioning supply	3 286	3 299	3 479	3 343	3 245	3 250	2 996	3 087
36-39	Water supply; sewerage, waste, remediation activities	1 607	1 598	1 658	1 715	1 696	1 657	1 587	1 543
41-43	**CONSTRUCTION**	**11 594**	**11 073**	**9 857**	**9 226**	**8 627**	**7 317**	**6 809**	**6 232**
45-56	Distribution; transportation, accommodation, food service	35 346	35 138	34 815	36 095	35 856	35 529	35 994	36 951
45-47	**Wholesale and retail trade; motor vehicle and motorcycle repairs**	**20 303**	**20 236**	**20 273**	**20 971**	**20 992**	**20 817**	**21 390**	**22 295**
49-53	**Transportation and storage**	**7 377**	**7 456**	**7 035**	**7 437**	**7 345**	**7 248**	**7 126**	**6 851**
55-56	**Accommodation and food service activities**	**7 693**	**7 472**	**7 505**	**7 687**	**7 520**	**7 462**	**7 457**	**7 781**
58-63	**Information and communication**	**5 667**	**5 908**	**5 955**	**5 739**	**6 059**	**5 817**	**5 691**	**5 629**
58-60	Publishing, audiovisual and broadcasting activities	1 169	1 151	1 141	1 092	1 026	947	940	926
61	Telecommunications	3 115	3 286	3 269	3 042	3 344	3 138	2 860	2 673
62-63	IT and other information services	1 386	1 467	1 543	1 605	1 689	1 727	1 875	2 009
64-66	**Financial and insurance activities**	**10 036**	**10 618**	**10 610**	**10 424**	**10 448**	**9 454**	**8 878**	**8 057**
68	**Real estate activities**	**15 619**	**15 818**	**15 983**	**16 795**	**16 938**	**16 661**	**16 781**	**16 776**
69-82	**Professional, scientific, technical, admin., support activities**	**10 630**	**11 039**	**10 881**	**11 244**	**10 916**	**10 403**	**10 573**	**11 473**
69-75	Professional, scientific and technical activities	5 805	6 104	5 859	5 827	5 726	5 488	5 641	6 138
69-71	Legal, accounting activities; mgt consultancy; engineering	4 433	4 711	4 480	4 423	4 328	4 048	4 128	4 509
73-75	Advertising, market research; other prof., scientific, tech.	978	970	938	951	953	962	985	993
77-82	Administrative and support service activities	4 835	4 950	5 028	5 417	5 190	4 917	4 935	5 340
84-88	**Public administration, defence; social security; education; health**	**34 197**	**34 381**	**34 200**	**34 254**	**33 143**	**32 616**	**32 018**	**31 592**
84	**Public administration, defence; compulsory social security**	**14 014**	**14 057**	**13 767**	**13 388**	**12 961**	**12 800**	**12 429**	**12 306**
85	**Education**	**10 762**	**10 936**	**10 993**	**11 083**	**10 738**	**10 461**	**10 250**	**10 111**
86-88	**Human health and social work activities**	**9 432**	**9 400**	**9 445**	**9 782**	**9 445**	**9 351**	**9 318**	**9 155**
90-99	**Arts, entertainment, household goods repairs, other**	**4 149**	**4 417**	**4 406**	**4 491**	**4 428**	**4 399**	**4 373**	**4 482**
90-93	**Arts, entertainment and recreation**	**1 120**	**1 197**	**1 195**	**1 256**	**1 231**	**1 165**	**1 141**	**1 225**
94-96	**Other service activities**	**1 774**	**1 936**	**1 937**	**2 003**	**2 021**	**2 109**	**2 128**	**2 162**
97-98	**Activities of households as employers and for own use**	**1 265**	**1 289**	**1 277**	**1 232**	**1 176**	**1 127**	**1 105**	**1 100**
05-39	INDUSTRY INCLUDING ENERGY	28 212	27 642	25 300	26 594	26 606	25 813	25 574	26 149
45-99	TOTAL SERVICES	115 565	117 347	116 873	119 043	117 788	114 861	114 357	115 068
45-82	BUSINESS SECTOR SERVICES	77 232	78 555	78 272	80 298	80 217	77 851	77 927	78 928
45-82x	BUSINESS SECTOR SERVICES excluding real estate	61 575	62 690	62 264	63 503	63 279	61 196	61 146	62 179
05-82x	NON-AGRICULTURE BUSINESS SECTOR excluding real estate	..	..	..	..	..	..	..	..

.. Not available

Note: Detailed metadata at: http://metalinks.oecd.org/stan/20170410/1c43.
Information on data for Israel: http://oe.cd/israel-disclaimer.

Disclaimer: http://oe.cd/disclaimer

PORTUGAL

Table 4. Gross fixed capital formation, current prices

ISIC Rev. 4

Million EUR

		2007	2008	2009	2010	2011	2012	2013	2014
	TOTAL	**39 447**	**40 850**	**37 107**	**36 938**	**32 452**	**26 672**	**25 122**	**25 993**
01-03	**AGRICULTURE, FORESTRY AND FISHING**	**997**	**1 052**	**870**	**929**	**921**	**857**	**883**	**942**
05-09	**MINING AND QUARRYING**	**175**	**141**	**124**	**174**	**161**	**135**	**149**	**168**
10-33	**MANUFACTURING**	**4 258**	**5 281**	**4 362**	**4 486**	**4 353**	**3 801**	**3 613**	**4 135**
10-12	Food products, beverages and tobacco	753	896	727	703	726	699	667	736
13-14	Textiles and wearing apparel	144	167	127	154	161	177	239	302
15	Leather and related products	38	52	35	57	67	79	92	102
16	Wood, wood and cork products	146	200	122	98	115	115	134	168
17	Paper and paper products	152	427	584	210	108	101	102	163
18	Printing and reproduction of recorded media	161	152	93	80	70	70	82	67
19-23	Chemical, rubber, plastics, non-metallic products	1 274	1 695	1 309	1 639	1 648	1 157	992	1 046
20	Chemicals and chemical products	260	322	310	230	374	325	272	193
21	Pharmaceutical products	146	142	148	142	153	153	143	150
22-23	Rubber, plastic, non-metallic mineral products	744	904	499	479	473	489	514	599
24	Basic metals	92	114	56	69	65	63	71	64
25	Metal products, except machinery and equipment	380	407	288	293	283	268	316	394
26-28	Machinery and equipment	675	596	479	431	460	437	388	446
26	Computer, electronic and optical products	318	169	125	134	152	146	115	153
27	Electrical equipment	151	244	198	163	180	145	132	141
28	Machinery and equipment n.e.c.	206	182	155	134	129	146	142	153
29-30	Transport equipment	153	324	262	488	406	399	335	355
29	Motor vehicles, trailers and semi-trailers	135	288	244	454	315	290	237	277
30	Other transport equipment	18	36	18	34	91	109	98	78
31-33	Furniture; repair, installation of machinery and equipment	289	250	281	265	245	236	194	292
31-32	Furniture, other manufacturing	209	194	205	210	172	169	142	215
33	Repair and installation of machinery and equipment	79	56	76	56	73	67	52	76
35-39	**ELECTRICITY, GAS, WATER AND WASTE MANAGEMENT**	**3 105**	**3 251**	**3 435**	**3 275**	**2 936**	**2 559**	**2 503**	**2 227**
35	Electricity, gas, steam and air conditioning supply	1 908	2 316	2 471	1 897	1 850	1 687	1 800	1 498
36-39	Water supply; sewerage, waste, remediation activities	1 196	935	964	1 379	1 086	872	703	729
41-43	**CONSTRUCTION**	**1 686**	**1 493**	**1 292**	**1 120**	**1 079**	**751**	**666**	**690**
45-56	Distribution; transportation, accommodation, food service	6 704	7 384	6 491	4 642	4 916	3 743	3 626	3 973
45-47	**Wholesale and retail trade; motor vehicle and motorcycle repairs**	**2 741**	**2 810**	**2 251**	**2 163**	**1 761**	**1 519**	**1 566**	**1 930**
49-53	**Transportation and storage**	**2 925**	**3 233**	**3 168**	**1 341**	**2 243**	**1 447**	**1 431**	**1 343**
55-56	**Accommodation and food service activities**	**1 038**	**1 341**	**1 072**	**1 138**	**911**	**778**	**629**	**700**
58-63	**Information and communication**	**2 517**	**2 147**	**2 052**	**2 602**	**2 175**	**2 054**	**2 077**	**2 162**
58-60	Publishing, audiovisual and broadcasting activities	602	629	539	513	474	413	393	426
61	Telecommunications	1 407	1 003	938	1 545	1 174	1 096	1 097	1 164
62-63	IT and other information services	508	515	575	544	527	545	587	572
64-66	**Financial and insurance activities**	**1 278**	**1 548**	**1 235**	**827**	**904**	**539**	**815**	**119**
68	**Real estate activities**	**10 010**	**9 140**	**7 726**	**7 226**	**6 206**	**5 469**	**4 541**	**5 286**
69-82	**Professional, scientific, technical, admin., support activities**	**2 221**	**2 252**	**1 845**	**1 921**	**1 821**	**1 410**	**1 503**	**1 877**
69-75	Professional, scientific and technical activities	1 223	1 320	1 327	1 219	1 149	949	1 054	1 191
69-71	Legal, accounting activities; mgt consultancy; engineering	653	684	768	598	595	435	468	531
73-75	Advertising, market research; other prof., scientific, tech.	154	158	124	126	124	100	88	99
77-82	Administrative and support service activities	998	932	518	702	673	461	449	686
84-88	**Public administration, defence; social security; education; health**	**5 768**	**6 379**	**7 088**	**9 138**	**6 430**	**4 782**	**4 242**	**3 769**
84	**Public administration, defence; compulsory social security**	**3 280**	**3 828**	**4 166**	**6 133**	**3 526**	**2 212**	**1 900**	**1 619**
85	**Education**	**1 161**	**1 188**	**1 382**	**1 321**	**1 292**	**1 194**	**1 059**	**1 080**
86-88	**Human health and social work activities**	**1 327**	**1 363**	**1 540**	**1 685**	**1 612**	**1 375**	**1 283**	**1 070**
90-99	**Arts, entertainment, household goods repairs, other**	**730**	**782**	**586**	**597**	**551**	**571**	**504**	**646**
90-93	**Arts, entertainment and recreation**	**527**	**612**	**407**	**424**	**368**	**314**	**282**	**359**
94-96	**Other service activities**	**203**	**170**	**179**	**173**	**183**	**257**	**222**	**287**
97-98	**Activities of households as employers and for own use**	**0**	**0**	**0**	**0**	**0**	**0**	**0**	**0**
05-39	**INDUSTRY INCLUDING ENERGY**	**7 538**	**8 674**	**7 921**	**7 935**	**7 450**	**6 495**	**6 265**	**6 530**
45-99	**TOTAL SERVICES**	**29 227**	**29 632**	**27 024**	**26 953**	**23 003**	**18 569**	**17 307**	**17 831**
45-82	**BUSINESS SECTOR SERVICES**	**22 729**	**22 471**	**19 350**	**17 218**	**16 022**	**13 216**	**12 561**	**13 416**
45-82x	**BUSINESS SECTOR SERVICES excluding real estate**	**12 720**	**13 331**	**11 624**	**9 992**	**9 816**	**7 747**	**8 021**	**8 130**
05-82x	**NON-AGRICULTURE BUSINESS SECTOR excluding real estate**	..	..	..	..	..	..	..	..

.. Not available

Note: Detailed metadata at: http://metalinks.oecd.org/stan/20170410/1c43.

Information on data for Israel: http://oe.cd/israel-disclaimer.

Disclaimer: http://oe.cd/disclaimer

PORTUGAL

Table 5. Number of persons engaged, total employment

ISIC Rev. 4

Thousands

		2007	2008	2009	2010	2011	2012	2013	2014
	TOTAL	5 062	5 080	4 942	4 871	4 777	4 581	4 450	4 513
01-03	AGRICULTURE, FORESTRY AND FISHING	586	580	571	543	528	538	509	486
05-09	MINING AND QUARRYING	16	16	15	15	14	13	12	12
10-33	MANUFACTURING	841	817	747	727	713	686	674	689
10-12	Food products, beverages and tobacco	116	115	111	112	109	105	103	105
13-14	Textiles and wearing apparel	202	190	166	156	151	143	142	147
15	Leather and related products	53	51	49	48	51	53	54	57
16	Wood, wood and cork products	46	44	39	38	36	34	32	32
17	Paper and paper products	14	13	12	12	12	11	11	11
18	Printing and reproduction of recorded media	23	22	20	19	17	16	15	15
19-23	Chemical, rubber, plastics, non-metallic products	107	103	94	92	89	85	82	82
20	Chemicals and chemical products	15	15	14	13	13	12	12	12
21	Pharmaceutical products	6	6	6	6	6	6	6	6
22-23	Rubber, plastic, non-metallic mineral products	84	81	73	71	68	65	62	63
24	Basic metals	9	9	9	8	9	8	8	8
25	Metal products, except machinery and equipment	90	90	84	82	81	77	75	77
26-28	Machinery and equipment	56	55	50	48	48	46	47	48
26	Computer, electronic and optical products	12	12	10	10	10	10	10	10
27	Electrical equipment	18	18	17	17	17	16	17	17
28	Machinery and equipment n.e.c.	25	25	23	21	21	20	20	21
29-30	Transport equipment	44	44	37	37	36	36	35	36
29	Motor vehicles, trailers and semi-trailers	38	38	32	32	32	32	31	32
30	Other transport equipment	6	6	5	5	4	4	4	4
31-33	Furniture; repair, installation of machinery and equipment	82	81	78	76	76	72	69	70
31-32	Furniture, other manufacturing	58	58	56	54	53	50	47	48
33	Repair and installation of machinery and equipment	23	23	22	22	23	22	22	22
35-39	ELECTRICITY, GAS, WATER AND WASTE MANAGEMENT	46	47	49	48	50	49	48	48
35	Electricity, gas, steam and air conditioning supply	10	9	9	9	9	8	8	8
36-39	Water supply; sewerage, waste, remediation activities	36	38	40	40	41	41	40	40
41-43	CONSTRUCTION	516	501	455	436	396	315	283	270
45-56	Distribution; transportation, accommodation, food service	1 192	1 207	1 170	1 162	1 155	1 100	1 068	1 111
45-47	Wholesale and retail trade; motor vehicle and motorcycle repairs	751	754	726	713	709	674	648	679
49-53	Transportation and storage	166	168	166	170	167	160	157	160
55-56	Accommodation and food service activities	275	285	277	278	279	266	263	272
58-63	Information and communication	64	68	70	71	72	74	75	78
58-60	Publishing, audiovisual and broadcasting activities	23	24	24	22	21	19	18	19
61	Telecommunications	13	14	14	14	14	15	15	15
62-63	IT and other information services	28	30	33	35	38	40	42	45
64-66	Financial and insurance activities	89	90	93	94	95	92	89	86
68	Real estate activities	28	29	28	28	27	25	25	27
69-82	Professional, scientific, technical, admin., support activities	443	467	473	476	470	449	445	482
69-75	Professional, scientific and technical activities	169	178	178	179	177	169	169	180
69-71	Legal, accounting activities; mgt consultancy; engineering	132	139	140	140	138	131	132	141
73-75	Advertising, market research; other prof., scientific, tech.	29	31	30	30	31	29	29	31
77-82	Administrative and support service activities	274	289	295	297	293	280	276	302
84-88	Public administration, defence; social security; education; health	958	969	984	986	976	967	953	952
84	Public administration, defence; compulsory social security	328	325	325	320	306	302	292	291
85	Education	311	313	318	323	320	315	310	302
86-88	Human health and social work activities	320	331	341	344	350	350	351	359
90-99	Arts, entertainment, household goods repairs, other	280	290	287	284	280	273	269	273
90-93	Arts, entertainment and recreation	40	42	42	43	40	40	39	42
94-96	Other service activities	100	104	102	103	108	104	103	107
97-98	Activities of households as employers and for own use	140	144	143	138	132	130	126	124
05-39	INDUSTRY INCLUDING ENERGY	904	880	811	791	777	748	734	748
45-99	TOTAL SERVICES	3 056	3 119	3 104	3 101	3 076	2 980	2 924	3 009
45-82	BUSINESS SECTOR SERVICES	1 817	1 860	1 834	1 831	1 820	1 740	1 702	1 784
45-82x	BUSINESS SECTOR SERVICES excluding real estate	1 789	1 831	1 806	1 803	1 792	1 714	1 677	1 757
05-82x	NON-AGRICULTURE BUSINESS SECTOR excluding real estate	..	..	..	..	..	..	..	..

.. Not available

Note: Detailed metadata at: http://metalinks.oecd.org/stan/20170410/1c43.
Information on data for Israel: http://oe.cd/israel-disclaimer.

Disclaimer: http://oe.cd/disclaimer

Table 6. Labour costs (compensation of employees), current prices

ISIC Rev. 4

Million EUR

		2007	2008	2009	2010	2011	2012	2013	2014
	TOTAL	**81 028**	**83 639**	**83 625**	**84 842**	**81 617**	**75 305**	**76 280**	**76 472**
01-03	**AGRICULTURE, FORESTRY AND FISHING**	**908**	**928**	**923**	**936**	**903**	**899**	**924**	**964**
05-09	**MINING AND QUARRYING**	**262**	**271**	**245**	**244**	**240**	**230**	**215**	**219**
10-33	**MANUFACTURING**	**12 145**	**12 245**	**11 293**	**11 500**	**11 380**	**10 914**	**10 834**	**11 180**
10-12	Food products, beverages and tobacco	1 628	1 699	1 646	1 708	1 667	1 620	1 613	1 643
13-14	Textiles and wearing apparel	..	1 820	1 619	1 579	1 550	1 481	1 496	1 586
15	Leather and related products	..	503	482	508	541	563	599	651
16	Wood, wood and cork products	534	533	471	471	462	449	434	454
17	Paper and paper products	355	312	305	327	312	278	277	246
18	Printing and reproduction of recorded media	367	376	354	346	321	295	279	283
19-23	Chemical, rubber, plastics, non-metallic products	2 182	2 154	1 992	2 061	2 003	1 923	1 838	1 850
20	Chemicals and chemical products	414	402	381	390	384	372	357	356
21	Pharmaceutical products	197	200	191	210	206	191	192	194
22-23	Rubber, plastic, non-metallic mineral products	1 439	1 429	1 300	1 319	1 294	1 226	1 165	1 177
24	Basic metals	197	212	175	184	199	187	183	189
25	Metal products, except machinery and equipment	1 391	1 458	1 362	1 374	1 369	1 300	1 290	1 338
26-28	Machinery and equipment	1 144	1 154	1 038	1 031	1 058	1 002	1 027	1 077
26	Computer, electronic and optical products	330	313	263	257	283	278	261	273
27	Electrical equipment	347	359	345	364	364	346	373	387
28	Machinery and equipment n.e.c.	467	481	430	410	411	378	394	417
29-30	Transport equipment	912	913	777	808	803	787	808	823
29	Motor vehicles, trailers and semi-trailers	806	734	680	724	715	706	739	746
30	Other transport equipment	106	179	97	84	88	80	69	77
31-33	Furniture; repair, installation of machinery and equipment	1 049	1 112	1 072	1 101	1 095	1 029	992	1 042
31-32	Furniture, other manufacturing	570	703	621	639	641	592	532	555
33	Repair and installation of machinery and equipment	479	409	451	462	454	437	459	487
35-39	**ELECTRICITY, GAS, WATER AND WASTE MANAGEMENT**	**1 151**	**1 172**	**1 251**	**1 250**	**1 249**	**1 179**	**1 203**	**1 148**
35	Electricity, gas, steam and air conditioning supply	442	421	458	486	472	465	445	422
36-39	Water supply; sewerage, waste, remediation activities	709	751	793	764	777	715	758	726
41-43	**CONSTRUCTION**	**6 648**	**6 690**	**6 179**	**6 078**	**5 599**	**4 559**	**4 161**	**3 917**
45-56	Distribution; transportation, accommodation, food service	18 403	19 106	18 820	19 390	18 979	17 742	17 398	17 983
45-47	**Wholesale and retail trade; motor vehicle and motorcycle repairs**	**10 765**	**11 181**	**10 983**	**11 205**	**11 090**	**10 350**	**10 016**	**10 420**
49-53	**Transportation and storage**	**3 880**	**4 001**	**3 961**	**4 202**	**3 966**	**3 701**	**3 831**	**3 907**
55-56	**Accommodation and food service activities**	**3 757**	**3 925**	**3 875**	**3 983**	**3 922**	**3 691**	**3 551**	**3 656**
58-63	**Information and communication**	**2 265**	**2 375**	**2 460**	**2 553**	**2 586**	**2 488**	**2 603**	**2 558**
58-60	Publishing, audiovisual and broadcasting activities	736	738	716	709	679	603	563	566
61	Telecommunications	583	592	609	619	597	589	661	553
62-63	IT and other information services	947	1 045	1 135	1 225	1 310	1 296	1 380	1 439
64-66	**Financial and insurance activities**	**4 055**	**4 175**	**4 174**	**4 216**	**4 024**	**4 000**	**4 102**	**3 787**
68	**Real estate activities**	**529**	**536**	**497**	**512**	**484**	**425**	**418**	**435**
69-82	**Professional, scientific, technical, admin., support activities**	**6 236**	**6 829**	**7 007**	**7 194**	**7 106**	**6 724**	**6 727**	**7 120**
69-75	Professional, scientific and technical activities	3 227	3 548	3 628	3 686	3 704	3 527	3 525	3 730
69-71	Legal, accounting activities; mgt consultancy; engineering	2 532	2 814	2 884	2 939	2 960	2 817	2 805	2 953
73-75	Advertising, market research; other prof., scientific, tech.	507	518	522	524	531	496	498	526
77-82	Administrative and support service activities	3 009	3 281	3 378	3 507	3 401	3 197	3 202	3 390
84-88	**Public administration, defence; social security; education; health**	**25 712**	**26 389**	**27 751**	**27 822**	**25 968**	**23 122**	**24 702**	**24 103**
84	**Public administration, defence; compulsory social security**	**9 889**	**10 080**	**10 784**	**10 610**	**9 843**	**8 436**	**9 333**	**8 797**
85	**Education**	**8 803**	**9 115**	**9 381**	**9 531**	**8 787**	**7 598**	**8 112**	**8 007**
86-88	**Human health and social work activities**	**7 020**	**7 194**	**7 586**	**7 680**	**7 338**	**7 088**	**7 257**	**7 300**
90-99	**Arts, entertainment, household goods repairs, other**	**2 714**	**2 924**	**3 024**	**3 148**	**3 100**	**3 022**	**2 993**	**3 058**
90-93	**Arts, entertainment and recreation**	**711**	**770**	**783**	**826**	**826**	**820**	**792**	**827**
94-96	**Other service activities**	**926**	**998**	**1 032**	**1 090**	**1 074**	**1 052**	**1 072**	**1 095**
97-98	**Activities of households as employers and for own use**	**1 077**	**1 156**	**1 210**	**1 232**	**1 201**	**1 151**	**1 129**	**1 137**
05-39	**INDUSTRY INCLUDING ENERGY**	**13 558**	**13 688**	**12 790**	**12 994**	**12 870**	**12 323**	**12 252**	**12 547**
45-99	**TOTAL SERVICES**	**59 913**	**62 333**	**63 733**	**64 834**	**62 246**	**57 524**	**58 943**	**59 045**
45-82	**BUSINESS SECTOR SERVICES**	**31 488**	**33 020**	**32 957**	**33 864**	**33 178**	**31 379**	**31 248**	**31 884**
45-82x	**BUSINESS SECTOR SERVICES excluding real estate**	**30 959**	**32 485**	**32 461**	**33 352**	**32 694**	**30 954**	**30 830**	**31 449**
05-82x	**NON-AGRICULTURE BUSINESS SECTOR excluding real estate**	..	..	..	..	..	..	..	..

.. Not available

Note: Detailed metadata at: http://metalinks.oecd.org/stan/20170410/1c43.

Information on data for Israel: http://oe.cd/israel-disclaimer.

Disclaimer: http://oe.cd/disclaimer

SLOVAK REPUBLIC

Table 1. Production (gross output), current prices

ISIC Rev. 4

Million EUR

		2007	2008	2009	2010	2011	2012	2013	2014
	TOTAL	**142 514**	**157 092**	**138 989**	**150 839**	**164 166**	**169 940**	**171 090**	**174 025**
01-03	**AGRICULTURE, FORESTRY AND FISHING**	**4 563**	**4 957**	**4 033**	**3 872**	**4 425**	**4 783**	**5 221**	**5 524**
05-09	**MINING AND QUARRYING**	**496**	**591**	**559**	**509**	**534**	**523**	**546**	**559**
10-33	**MANUFACTURING**	**56 793**	**59 094**	**45 484**	**54 008**	**61 971**	**65 647**	**66 010**	**68 962**
10-12	Food products, beverages and tobacco	3 760	4 121	3 464	3 407	3 781	3 798	3 724	3 999
13-14	Textiles and wearing apparel	1 232	1 132	741	719	856	856	865	915
15	Leather and related products	524	465	443	507	564	607	583	623
16	Wood, wood and cork products	1 610	1 616	1 306	1 464	1 567	1 495	1 537	1 945
17	Paper and paper products	1 305	1 325	1 162	1 209	1 229	1 346	1 308	1 237
18	Printing and reproduction of recorded media	490	507	425	468	424	440	454	469
19-23	Chemical, rubber, plastics, non-metallic products	10 828	11 446	8 745	10 075	12 923	12 633	12 060	11 597
20	Chemicals and chemical products	2 263	2 214	1 802	2 152	2 719	2 472	1 936	1 950
21	Pharmaceutical products	299	305	292	336	357	356	203	210
22-23	Rubber, plastic, non-metallic mineral products	4 466	4 903	3 781	4 192	5 195	5 270	5 413	5 548
24	Basic metals	4 853	4 844	2 945	4 265	4 316	4 265	3 982	4 104
25	Metal products, except machinery and equipment	4 139	4 792	3 739	4 139	4 921	5 226	5 286	6 226
26-28	Machinery and equipment	11 323	11 658	9 937	11 495	11 518	11 910	12 136	13 253
26	Computer, electronic and optical products	5 835	6 113	6 026	6 547	5 807	5 879	5 493	5 896
27	Electrical equipment	2 419	2 439	1 992	2 274	2 564	2 582	2 932	3 262
28	Machinery and equipment n.e.c.	3 068	3 106	1 920	2 674	3 147	3 448	3 711	4 094
29-30	Transport equipment	13 658	14 005	10 103	13 652	17 107	20 306	21 347	21 590
29	Motor vehicles, trailers and semi-trailers	13 343	13 627	9 768	13 283	16 725	19 925	21 031	21 192
30	Other transport equipment	314	378	335	368	383	380	316	398
31-33	Furniture; repair, installation of machinery and equipment	3 071	3 185	2 473	2 608	2 764	2 765	2 729	3 006
31-32	Furniture, other manufacturing	1 599	1 508	1 237	1 242	1 260	1 270	1 333	1 516
33	Repair and installation of machinery and equipment	1 472	1 676	1 236	1 366	1 504	1 495	1 395	1 490
35-39	**ELECTRICITY, GAS, WATER AND WASTE MANAGEMENT**	**10 089**	**11 940**	**11 635**	**11 823**	**12 893**	**13 495**	**13 053**	**11 212**
35	Electricity, gas, steam and air conditioning supply	9 122	10 929	10 616	10 766	11 805	12 346	11 743	9 865
36-39	Water supply; sewerage, waste, remediation activities	966	1 012	1 019	1 058	1 089	1 149	1 310	1 347
41-43	**CONSTRUCTION**	**11 860**	**14 749**	**13 918**	**13 351**	**13 755**	**12 775**	**11 959**	**12 444**
45-56	Distribution; transportation, accommodation, food service	25 250	28 526	24 816	26 651	29 382	29 472	28 770	29 352
45-47	**Wholesale and retail trade; motor vehicle and motorcycle repairs**	**16 032**	**17 799**	**15 170**	**16 432**	**18 193**	**17 853**	**17 152**	**16 724**
49-53	**Transportation and storage**	**7 916**	**9 223**	**8 160**	**8 831**	**9 740**	**9 923**	**9 772**	**10 761**
55-56	**Accommodation and food service activities**	**1 302**	**1 504**	**1 486**	**1 388**	**1 448**	**1 696**	**1 845**	**1 867**
58-63	**Information and communication**	**4 172**	**4 647**	**4 990**	**4 983**	**5 159**	**5 499**	**5 379**	**5 501**
58-60	Publishing, audiovisual and broadcasting activities	849	988	1 027	1 035	968	984	856	806
61	Telecommunications	2 012	2 131	2 145	2 059	2 010	1 992	1 923	2 007
62-63	IT and other information services	1 311	1 529	1 817	1 889	2 181	2 522	2 600	2 687
64-66	**Financial and insurance activities**	**3 607**	**4 030**	**4 013**	**4 286**	**4 666**	**4 804**	**4 857**	**5 165**
68	**Real estate activities**	**5 399**	**5 790**	**5 825**	**6 654**	**6 754**	**7 226**	**8 210**	**7 118**
69-82	**Professional, scientific, technical, admin., support activities**	**7 065**	**8 270**	**8 078**	**8 735**	**8 459**	**9 005**	**9 827**	**10 983**
69-75	Professional, scientific and technical activities	4 868	5 643	5 386	5 683	5 667	6 069	6 405	7 617
69-71	Legal, accounting activities; mgt consultancy; engineering	3 224	3 691	3 726	3 968	3 947	4 117	4 489	4 873
73-75	Advertising, market research; other prof., scientific, tech.	1 369	1 695	1 451	1 493	1 487	1 715	1 640	2 464
77-82	Administrative and support service activities	2 197	2 627	2 691	3 052	2 792	2 937	3 422	3 366
84-88	**Public administration, defence; social security; education; health**	**10 447**	**11 523**	**12 854**	**13 067**	**13 087**	**13 404**	**13 886**	**13 565**
84	**Public administration, defence; compulsory social security**	**5 472**	**5 825**	**6 750**	**6 796**	**6 641**	**6 516**	**6 763**	**6 165**
85	**Education**	**2 199**	**2 556**	**2 722**	**2 821**	**2 917**	**3 169**	**3 262**	**3 451**
86-88	**Human health and social work activities**	**2 777**	**3 141**	**3 382**	**3 450**	**3 529**	**3 719**	**3 861**	**3 948**
90-99	**Arts, entertainment, household goods repairs, other**	**2 774**	**2 974**	**2 787**	**2 899**	**3 081**	**3 307**	**3 372**	**3 640**
90-93	**Arts, entertainment and recreation**	**1 613**	**1 891**	**1 692**	**1 764**	**1 950**	**2 100**	**2 107**	**2 418**
94-96	**Other service activities**	**1 161**	**1 084**	**1 095**	**1 135**	**1 131**	**1 207**	**1 265**	**1 222**
97-98	**Activities of households as employers and for own use**	**0**	**0**	**0**	**0**	**0**	**0**	**0**	**0**
05-39	**INDUSTRY INCLUDING ENERGY**	**67 377**	**71 626**	**57 678**	**66 340**	**75 398**	**79 665**	**79 610**	**80 734**
45-99	**TOTAL SERVICES**	**58 713**	**65 760**	**63 361**	**67 276**	**70 587**	**72 717**	**74 300**	**75 323**
45-82	**BUSINESS SECTOR SERVICES**	**45 492**	**51 263**	**47 720**	**51 309**	**54 419**	**56 006**	**57 042**	**58 118**
45-82x	**BUSINESS SECTOR SERVICES excluding real estate**	**40 093**	**45 473**	**41 895**	**44 655**	**47 665**	**48 780**	**48 832**	**51 000**
05-82x	**NON-AGRICULTURE BUSINESS SECTOR excluding real estate**	..	..	..	..	..	..	..	..

.. Not available

Note: Detailed metadata at: http://metalinks.oecd.org/stan/20170410/1c43.

Information on data for Israel: http://oe.cd/israel-disclaimer.

Disclaimer: http://oe.cd/disclaimer

Table 2. Value added, current prices

ISIC Rev. 4

Million EUR

		2007	2008	2009	2010	2011	2012	2013	2014
	TOTAL	**56 812**	**62 122**	**58 033**	**61 368**	**63 982**	**66 410**	**67 522**	**68 766**
01-03	**AGRICULTURE, FORESTRY AND FISHING**	**2 272**	**2 535**	**1 936**	**1 727**	**2 160**	**2 351**	**2 685**	**3 005**
05-09	**MINING AND QUARRYING**	**329**	**380**	**366**	**321**	**344**	**335**	**340**	**331**
10-33	**MANUFACTURING**	**13 232**	**13 828**	**10 290**	**12 770**	**13 474**	**13 849**	**13 654**	**15 046**
10-12	Food products, beverages and tobacco	1 075	1 134	976	985	992	1 032	955	1 052
13-14	Textiles and wearing apparel	531	433	318	389	420	413	415	450
15	Leather and related products	152	82	104	266	119	140	143	175
16	Wood, wood and cork products	608	677	563	640	652	639	664	816
17	Paper and paper products	316	297	299	302	302	325	307	316
18	Printing and reproduction of recorded media	179	199	156	180	159	172	171	183
19-23	Chemical, rubber, plastics, non-metallic products	2 418	2 384	1 922	2 031	2 272	2 425	2 269	2 449
20	Chemicals and chemical products	442	469	375	414	487	429	390	401
21	Pharmaceutical products	100	117	151	171	170	175	29	81
22-23	Rubber, plastic, non-metallic mineral products	1 391	1 411	1 222	1 255	1 431	1 584	1 658	1 744
24	Basic metals	1 493	1 209	596	974	778	852	818	796
25	Metal products, except machinery and equipment	1 675	1 891	1 503	1 676	1 981	2 098	1 943	2 263
26-28	Machinery and equipment	1 965	2 387	1 499	2 139	2 237	2 229	2 330	2 546
26	Computer, electronic and optical products	583	775	495	685	707	642	580	670
27	Electrical equipment	540	673	416	593	613	647	735	661
28	Machinery and equipment n.e.c.	843	939	588	861	916	940	1 015	1 215
29-30	Transport equipment	1 792	2 076	1 401	2 084	2 437	2 458	2 526	2 909
29	Motor vehicles, trailers and semi-trailers	1 724	1 983	1 323	1 928	2 320	2 325	2 415	2 792
30	Other transport equipment	68	93	78	156	117	133	111	117
31-33	Furniture; repair, installation of machinery and equipment	1 026	1 060	953	1 103	1 125	1 067	1 114	1 092
31-32	Furniture, other manufacturing	448	440	432	539	474	478	509	499
33	Repair and installation of machinery and equipment	579	620	521	565	651	589	606	593
35-39	**ELECTRICITY, GAS, WATER AND WASTE MANAGEMENT**	**3 466**	**3 490**	**3 409**	**3 077**	**3 190**	**3 320**	**3 057**	**3 046**
35	Electricity, gas, steam and air conditioning supply	2 939	2 953	2 863	2 487	2 613	2 639	2 258	2 331
36-39	Water supply; sewerage, waste, remediation activities	527	536	546	590	578	681	800	715
41-43	**CONSTRUCTION**	**4 490**	**5 886**	**5 634**	**5 450**	**5 713**	**5 986**	**5 277**	**5 302**
45-56	Distribution; transportation, accommodation, food service	12 258	13 674	12 576	13 146	13 681	14 004	13 927	14 740
45-47	**Wholesale and retail trade; motor vehicle and motorcycle repairs**	**8 390**	**9 506**	**8 727**	**9 177**	**9 082**	**9 129**	**8 917**	**8 892**
49-53	**Transportation and storage**	**3 142**	**3 329**	**3 067**	**3 218**	**3 830**	**3 918**	**4 068**	**4 933**
55-56	**Accommodation and food service activities**	**726**	**838**	**781**	**751**	**769**	**957**	**943**	**916**
58-63	**Information and communication**	**2 327**	**2 495**	**2 748**	**2 752**	**2 833**	**3 120**	**2 879**	**2 769**
58-60	Publishing, audiovisual and broadcasting activities	457	477	516	481	418	507	350	346
61	Telecommunications	1 074	1 131	1 152	1 147	1 100	1 089	1 068	1 091
62-63	IT and other information services	796	887	1 080	1 124	1 314	1 524	1 461	1 331
64-66	**Financial and insurance activities**	**1 957**	**2 004**	**2 249**	**2 469**	**2 687**	**2 710**	**2 706**	**2 859**
68	**Real estate activities**	**3 856**	**4 230**	**4 058**	**4 221**	**4 316**	**4 501**	**5 933**	**4 513**
69-82	**Professional, scientific, technical, admin., support activities**	**3 714**	**4 348**	**4 356**	**4 553**	**4 575**	**4 784**	**5 119**	**5 383**
69-75	Professional, scientific and technical activities	2 525	2 903	2 860	2 991	3 106	3 215	3 293	3 745
69-71	Legal, accounting activities; mgt consultancy; engineering	1 787	2 028	2 103	2 248	2 400	2 337	2 393	2 748
73-75	Advertising, market research; other prof., scientific, tech.	571	711	614	593	546	723	697	823
77-82	Administrative and support service activities	1 189	1 444	1 496	1 562	1 468	1 570	1 826	1 637
84-88	**Public administration, defence; social security; education; health**	**7 328**	**7 917**	**8 599**	**9 009**	**8 942**	**9 181**	**9 634**	**9 300**
84	**Public administration, defence; compulsory social security**	**3 772**	**3 917**	**4 469**	**4 722**	**4 537**	**4 539**	**4 718**	**4 315**
85	**Education**	**1 690**	**1 981**	**2 075**	**2 130**	**2 227**	**2 365**	**2 508**	**2 567**
86-88	**Human health and social work activities**	**1 866**	**2 020**	**2 056**	**2 158**	**2 178**	**2 277**	**2 407**	**2 418**
90-99	**Arts, entertainment, household goods repairs, other**	**1 585**	**1 334**	**1 812**	**1 873**	**2 067**	**2 269**	**2 310**	**2 473**
90-93	**Arts, entertainment and recreation**	**989**	**718**	**1 199**	**1 243**	**1 419**	**1 585**	**1 591**	**1 758**
94-96	**Other service activities**	**596**	**616**	**612**	**630**	**647**	**684**	**720**	**715**
97-98	**Activities of households as employers and for own use**	**0**	**0**	**0**	**0**	**0**	**0**	**0**	**0**
05-39	INDUSTRY INCLUDING ENERGY	17 027	17 698	14 065	16 167	17 009	17 504	17 051	18 422
45-99	TOTAL SERVICES	33 024	36 002	36 398	38 024	39 099	40 569	42 509	42 037
45-82	BUSINESS SECTOR SERVICES	24 112	26 751	25 987	27 142	28 091	29 119	30 564	30 263
45-82x	BUSINESS SECTOR SERVICES excluding real estate	20 256	22 521	21 929	22 920	23 775	24 618	24 632	25 750
05-82x	NON-AGRICULTURE BUSINESS SECTOR excluding real estate	..	..	..	..	..	..	..	..

.. Not available

Note: Detailed metadata at: http://metalinks.oecd.org/stan/20170410/1c43.

Information on data for Israel: http://oe.cd/israel-disclaimer.

Disclaimer: http://oe.cd/disclaimer

SLOVAK REPUBLIC

Table 3. Value added, volumes

ISIC Rev. 4

Million 2010 EUR

		2007	2008	2009	2010	2011	2012	2013	2014
	TOTAL	**58 022**	**61 692**	**58 314**	**61 368**	**62 899**	**64 434**	**65 168**	**66 580**
01-03	**AGRICULTURE, FORESTRY AND FISHING**	**1 887**	**2 096**	**2 026**	**1 727**	**2 046**	**2 105**	**2 497**	**2 923**
05-09	**MINING AND QUARRYING**	**322**	**366**	**372**	**321**	**344**	**338**	**338**	**325**
10-33	**MANUFACTURING**	**11 203**	**11 912**	**10 073**	**12 770**	**13 280**	**13 357**	**13 343**	**15 517**
10-12	Food products, beverages and tobacco	928	989	988	985	1 030	1 037	942	936
13-14	Textiles and wearing apparel	641	526	408	389	420	394	385	405
15	Leather and related products	182	93	110	266	108	109	106	107
16	Wood, wood and cork products	452	505	507	640	643	664	710	851
17	Paper and paper products	360	351	389	302	274	356	309	323
18	Printing and reproduction of recorded media	160	173	157	180	152	140	135	112
19-23	Chemical, rubber, plastics, non-metallic products	2 042	2 095	1 881	2 031	2 154	2 322	2 228	2 627
20	Chemicals and chemical products	396	437	484	414	439	410	313	290
21	Pharmaceutical products	95	113	153	171	166	159	30	79
22-23	Rubber, plastic, non-metallic mineral products	1 253	1 256	1 048	1 255	1 435	1 552	1 673	1 985
24	Basic metals	1 534	1 269	879	974	813	934	941	1 024
25	Metal products, except machinery and equipment	1 663	1 908	1 487	1 676	1 871	1 990	1 847	2 397
26-28	Machinery and equipment	1 022	1 287	1 125	2 139	2 648	2 415	2 495	2 908
26	Computer, electronic and optical products	177	264	312	685	1 063	752	686	942
27	Electrical equipment	284	333	286	593	605	687	820	838
28	Machinery and equipment n.e.c.	772	888	562	861	980	902	907	1 044
29-30	Transport equipment	1 760	2 042	1 428	2 084	2 044	1 980	2 218	2 841
29	Motor vehicles, trailers and semi-trailers	1 699	1 961	1 350	1 928	1 926	1 852	2 109	2 734
30	Other transport equipment	64	84	78	156	118	130	105	99
31-33	Furniture; repair, installation of machinery and equipment	1 085	1 098	982	1 103	1 123	976	950	896
31-32	Furniture, other manufacturing	459	442	446	539	477	423	399	374
33	Repair and installation of machinery and equipment	629	660	536	565	646	553	552	524
35-39	**ELECTRICITY, GAS, WATER AND WASTE MANAGEMENT**	**4 425**	**4 047**	**3 052**	**3 077**	**3 215**	**3 169**	**2 958**	**3 064**
35	Electricity, gas, steam and air conditioning supply	3 787	3 453	2 470	2 487	2 662	2 546	2 251	2 475
36-39	Water supply; sewerage, waste, remediation activities	645	601	582	590	553	618	695	595
41-43	**CONSTRUCTION**	**5 009**	**6 094**	**5 787**	**5 450**	**5 741**	**6 091**	**5 350**	**5 328**
45-56	Distribution; transportation, accommodation, food service	12 563	13 987	12 884	13 146	13 171	13 340	12 899	13 427
45-47	**Wholesale and retail trade; motor vehicle and motorcycle repairs**	**8 816**	**9 703**	**9 082**	**9 177**	**8 722**	**8 634**	**8 287**	**7 933**
49-53	**Transportation and storage**	**2 920**	**3 377**	**3 016**	**3 218**	**3 699**	**3 796**	**3 726**	**4 648**
55-56	**Accommodation and food service activities**	**854**	**917**	**792**	**751**	**750**	**913**	**890**	**837**
58-63	**Information and communication**	**2 527**	**2 520**	**2 738**	**2 752**	**2 846**	**3 217**	**3 024**	**2 784**
58-60	Publishing, audiovisual and broadcasting activities	488	491	489	481	408	469	322	305
61	Telecommunications	1 255	1 182	1 162	1 147	1 101	1 166	1 178	1 179
62-63	IT and other information services	804	858	1 087	1 124	1 337	1 582	1 542	1 319
64-66	**Financial and insurance activities**	**2 261**	**2 167**	**2 332**	**2 469**	**2 584**	**2 607**	**2 721**	**2 997**
68	**Real estate activities**	**4 291**	**4 498**	**4 212**	**4 221**	**4 453**	**4 640**	**5 939**	**4 330**
69-82	**Professional, scientific, technical, admin., support activities**	**3 874**	**4 290**	**4 361**	**4 553**	**4 525**	**4 764**	**5 012**	**5 188**
69-75	Professional, scientific and technical activities	2 615	2 829	2 827	2 991	3 003	3 129	3 172	3 612
69-71	Legal, accounting activities; mgt consultancy; engineering	1 895	2 029	2 129	2 248	2 284	2 259	2 287	2 677
73-75	Advertising, market research; other prof., scientific, tech.	554	646	554	593	563	729	702	792
77-82	Administrative and support service activities	1 257	1 461	1 535	1 562	1 522	1 638	1 850	1 571
84-88	**Public administration, defence; social security; education; health**	**7 999**	**8 250**	**8 724**	**9 009**	**8 677**	**8 649**	**8 930**	**8 415**
84	**Public administration, defence; compulsory social security**	**3 824**	**3 836**	**4 410**	**4 722**	**4 457**	**4 384**	**4 524**	**4 082**
85	**Education**	**1 993**	**2 179**	**2 181**	**2 130**	**2 134**	**2 125**	**2 218**	**2 152**
86-88	**Human health and social work activities**	**2 222**	**2 294**	**2 143**	**2 158**	**2 087**	**2 138**	**2 186**	**2 167**
90-99	**Arts, entertainment, household goods repairs, other**	**1 769**	**1 398**	**1 836**	**1 873**	**2 018**	**2 175**	**2 181**	**2 251**
90-93	**Arts, entertainment and recreation**	**1 104**	**751**	**1 214**	**1 243**	**1 392**	**1 520**	**1 508**	**1 607**
94-96	**Other service activities**	**666**	**647**	**623**	**630**	**626**	**655**	**674**	**645**
97-98	**Activities of households as employers and for own use**	..	..	..	..	..	..	..	..
05-39	**INDUSTRY INCLUDING ENERGY**	**15 743**	**16 286**	**13 538**	**16 167**	**16 839**	**16 864**	**16 638**	**18 903**
45-99	**TOTAL SERVICES**	**35 218**	**37 121**	**37 085**	**38 024**	**38 273**	**39 374**	**40 618**	**39 381**
45-82	**BUSINESS SECTOR SERVICES**	**25 465**	**27 457**	**26 525**	**27 142**	**27 578**	**28 553**	**29 511**	**28 726**
45-82x	**BUSINESS SECTOR SERVICES excluding real estate**	**21 187**	**22 967**	**22 315**	**22 920**	**23 125**	**23 914**	**23 640**	**24 403**
05-82x	**NON-AGRICULTURE BUSINESS SECTOR excluding real estate**	..	..	..	..	..	..	..	..

.. Not available

Note: Detailed metadata at: http://metalinks.oecd.org/stan/20170410/1c43.

Information on data for Israel: http://oe.cd/israel-disclaimer.

Disclaimer: http://oe.cd/disclaimer

Table 4. Gross fixed capital formation, current prices

ISIC Rev. 4

Million EUR

		2007	2008	2009	2010	2011	2012	2013	2014
	TOTAL	**16 897**	**17 499**	**13 923**	**14 910**	**16 946**	**15 446**	**15 374**	**15 495**
01-03	**AGRICULTURE, FORESTRY AND FISHING**	**372**	**689**	**353**	**346**	**458**	**379**	**404**	**364**
05-09	**MINING AND QUARRYING**	**94**	**78**	**113**	**127**	**60**	**149**	**45**	**34**
10-33	**MANUFACTURING**	**4 042**	**4 523**	**2 776**	**2 851**	**4 673**	**3 862**	**3 459**	**3 771**
10-12	Food products, beverages and tobacco	460	374	325	282	235	42	234	209
13-14	Textiles and wearing apparel	27	16	14	13	37	19	24	91
15	Leather and related products	11	12	7	14	23	11	1	33
16	Wood, wood and cork products	220	128	61	25	62	69	45	48
17	Paper and paper products	92	153	76	62	62	94	82	214
18	Printing and reproduction of recorded media	40	38	20	30	49	35	25	15
19-23	Chemical, rubber, plastics, non-metallic products	803	1 122	661	614	710	889	946	948
20	Chemicals and chemical products	67	155	167	205	164	257	67	131
21	Pharmaceutical products	10	21	28	18	21	12	33	20
22-23	Rubber, plastic, non-metallic mineral products	637	752	393	317	461	495	381	464
24	Basic metals	322	276	186	178	420	155	125	164
25	Metal products, except machinery and equipment	240	364	208	193	327	278	229	298
26-28	Machinery and equipment	827	969	505	593	1 435	806	535	692
26	Computer, electronic and optical products	241	317	174	278	853	123	93	98
27	Electrical equipment	236	194	127	123	232	311	187	271
28	Machinery and equipment n.e.c.	350	458	203	193	350	372	255	323
29-30	Transport equipment	795	846	699	730	1 197	1 331	931	851
29	Motor vehicles, trailers and semi-trailers	776	795	640	692	1 182	1 315	916	843
30	Other transport equipment	19	51	59	37	15	16	15	8
31-33	Furniture; repair, installation of machinery and equipment	205	223	14	115	116	135	283	207
31-32	Furniture, other manufacturing	130	107	-42	30	50	83	208	111
33	Repair and installation of machinery and equipment	75	116	56	86	66	52	75	96
35-39	**ELECTRICITY, GAS, WATER AND WASTE MANAGEMENT**	**3 463**	**1 845**	**1 742**	**1 733**	**2 184**	**2 118**	**1 540**	**2 237**
35	Electricity, gas, steam and air conditioning supply	3 028	1 220	1 332	1 470	1 911	1 743	1 039	1 690
36-39	Water supply; sewerage, waste, remediation activities	435	625	409	262	274	375	500	547
41-43	**CONSTRUCTION**	**337**	**522**	**247**	**332**	**291**	**273**	**330**	**271**
45-56	Distribution; transportation, accommodation, food service	2 275	2 872	1 914	2 121	1 819	2 055	2 643	2 610
45-47	**Wholesale and retail trade; motor vehicle and motorcycle repairs**	**931**	**1 231**	**780**	**898**	**932**	**877**	**834**	**729**
49-53	**Transportation and storage**	**1 222**	**1 543**	**1 054**	**1 172**	**781**	**1 105**	**1 393**	**1 810**
55-56	**Accommodation and food service activities**	**122**	**98**	**80**	**51**	**106**	**73**	**416**	**72**
58-63	**Information and communication**	**940**	**1 119**	**802**	**1 500**	**666**	**656**	**595**	**509**
58-60	Publishing, audiovisual and broadcasting activities	111	132	135	52	71	56	27	68
61	Telecommunications	768	894	548	1 331	471	412	303	288
62-63	IT and other information services	61	93	118	117	124	188	265	154
64-66	**Financial and insurance activities**	**261**	**283**	**159**	**161**	**283**	**237**	**237**	**234**
68	**Real estate activities**	**2 289**	**2 646**	**2 717**	**2 488**	**2 964**	**2 668**	**2 713**	**2 632**
69-82	**Professional, scientific, technical, admin., support activities**	**724**	**753**	**641**	**752**	**682**	**670**	**902**	**912**
69-75	Professional, scientific and technical activities	230	134	181	216	200	135	435	282
69-71	Legal, accounting activities; mgt consultancy; engineering	146	98	140	155	137	71	276	134
73-75	Advertising, market research; other prof., scientific, tech.	33	25	19	23	23	23	84	25
77-82	Administrative and support service activities	494	619	460	536	481	536	467	630
84-88	**Public administration, defence; social security; education; health**	**1 983**	**1 930**	**2 362**	**2 345**	**2 583**	**2 203**	**2 314**	**1 791**
84	**Public administration, defence; compulsory social security**	**1 391**	**1 376**	**1 728**	**1 664**	**1 973**	**1 600**	**1 704**	**1 419**
85	**Education**	**162**	**160**	**220**	**257**	**292**	**270**	**267**	**182**
86-88	**Human health and social work activities**	**430**	**394**	**414**	**423**	**318**	**333**	**343**	**189**
90-99	**Arts, entertainment, household goods repairs, other**	**117**	**240**	**97**	**154**	**283**	**177**	**192**	**131**
90-93	**Arts, entertainment and recreation**	**67**	**195**	**57**	**116**	**255**	**153**	**163**	**107**
94-96	**Other service activities**	**51**	**44**	**40**	**38**	**28**	**24**	**29**	**24**
97-98	**Activities of households as employers and for own use**	**0**	**0**	**0**	**0**	**0**	**0**	**0**	**0**
05-39	**INDUSTRY INCLUDING ENERGY**	**7 599**	**6 446**	**4 631**	**4 711**	**6 918**	**6 129**	**5 044**	**6 042**
45-99	**TOTAL SERVICES**	**8 588**	**9 842**	**8 693**	**9 521**	**9 279**	**8 665**	**9 596**	**8 818**
45-82	**BUSINESS SECTOR SERVICES**	**6 488**	**7 672**	**6 233**	**7 022**	**6 413**	**6 286**	**7 090**	**6 897**
45-82x	**BUSINESS SECTOR SERVICES excluding real estate**	**4 199**	**5 026**	**3 517**	**4 534**	**3 449**	**3 618**	**4 377**	**4 265**
05-82x	**NON-AGRICULTURE BUSINESS SECTOR excluding real estate**	..	..	..	..	..	..	..	..

.. Not available

Note: Detailed metadata at: http://metalinks.oecd.org/stan/20170410/1c43.

Information on data for Israel: http://oe.cd/israel-disclaimer.

Disclaimer: http://oe.cd/disclaimer

SLOVAK REPUBLIC

Table 5. Number of persons engaged, total employment

ISIC Rev. 4

Thousands

		2007	2008	2009	2010	2011	2012	2013	2014
	TOTAL	**2 177**	**2 247**	**2 203**	**2 170**	**2 208**	**2 209**	**2 192**	**2 223**
01-03	**AGRICULTURE, FORESTRY AND FISHING**	**83**	**82**	**78**	**73**	**73**	**71**	**74**	**72**
05-09	**MINING AND QUARRYING**	**9**	**8**	**8**	**7**	**8**	**7**	**7**	**7**
10-33	**MANUFACTURING**	**516**	**538**	**480**	**461**	**480**	**476**	**469**	**479**
10-12	Food products, beverages and tobacco	49	50	49	46	45	45	43	42
13-14	Textiles and wearing apparel	43	39	33	28	29	28	27	27
15	Leather and related products	15	13	12	11	11	12	11	11
16	Wood, wood and cork products	31	33	30	29	30	25	26	28
17	Paper and paper products	8	8	8	8	7	7	7	7
18	Printing and reproduction of recorded media	8	8	9	8	8	8	7	7
19-23	Chemical, rubber, plastics, non-metallic products	68	71	66	62	67	65	62	63
20	Chemicals and chemical products	10	10	10	9	10	10	9	9
21	Pharmaceutical products	3	3	2	2	2	2	2	2
22-23	Rubber, plastic, non-metallic mineral products	52	56	51	48	52	51	48	49
24	Basic metals	28	27	24	23	24	24	24	24
25	Metal products, except machinery and equipment	64	74	66	64	67	69	68	72
26-28	Machinery and equipment	100	102	84	83	85	84	86	88
26	Computer, electronic and optical products	20	23	22	20	18	16	16	15
27	Electrical equipment	37	34	28	28	30	28	29	31
28	Machinery and equipment n.e.c.	44	45	34	35	38	40	41	42
29-30	Transport equipment	53	62	53	55	62	66	65	67
29	Motor vehicles, trailers and semi-trailers	49	58	49	51	58	62	61	63
30	Other transport equipment	4	4	4	4	5	5	4	4
31-33	Furniture; repair, installation of machinery and equipment	50	50	47	45	44	43	44	43
31-32	Furniture, other manufacturing	28	28	26	25	24	24	23	25
33	Repair and installation of machinery and equipment	22	22	20	20	20	19	20	19
35-39	**ELECTRICITY, GAS, WATER AND WASTE MANAGEMENT**	**48**	**45**	**43**	**43**	**42**	**41**	**41**	**41**
35	Electricity, gas, steam and air conditioning supply	24	22	20	20	19	18	18	18
36-39	Water supply; sewerage, waste, remediation activities	25	24	23	23	23	23	23	23
41-43	**CONSTRUCTION**	**166**	**181**	**187**	**184**	**177**	**172**	**167**	**164**
45-56	Distribution; transportation, accommodation, food service	574	595	595	586	597	599	594	604
45-47	**Wholesale and retail trade; motor vehicle and motorcycle repairs**	**382**	**394**	**388**	**379**	**384**	**383**	**370**	**375**
49-53	**Transportation and storage**	**125**	**132**	**133**	**134**	**133**	**131**	**135**	**134**
55-56	**Accommodation and food service activities**	**67**	**70**	**74**	**74**	**80**	**85**	**88**	**95**
58-63	**Information and communication**	**48**	**51**	**52**	**50**	**55**	**55**	**57**	**59**
58-60	Publishing, audiovisual and broadcasting activities	16	15	15	14	14	12	12	12
61	Telecommunications	9	10	10	10	10	10	11	11
62-63	IT and other information services	23	26	28	27	32	33	35	35
64-66	**Financial and insurance activities**	**38**	**41**	**41**	**40**	**41**	**42**	**42**	**44**
68	**Real estate activities**	**22**	**20**	**20**	**22**	**24**	**24**	**23**	**22**
69-82	**Professional, scientific, technical, admin., support activities**	**176**	**182**	**190**	**190**	**199**	**214**	**210**	**210**
69-75	Professional, scientific and technical activities	104	104	113	109	111	123	123	121
69-71	Legal, accounting activities; mgt consultancy; engineering	67	68	78	74	76	83	87	83
73-75	Advertising, market research; other prof., scientific, tech.	25	26	26	26	26	32	27	29
77-82	Administrative and support service activities	72	78	76	81	88	91	87	90
84-88	**Public administration, defence; social security; education; health**	**445**	**449**	**450**	**454**	**454**	**449**	**448**	**457**
84	**Public administration, defence; compulsory social security**	**152**	**152**	**157**	**159**	**156**	**155**	**155**	**158**
85	**Education**	**167**	**168**	**171**	**172**	**173**	**170**	**170**	**171**
86-88	**Human health and social work activities**	**127**	**128**	**122**	**123**	**125**	**125**	**124**	**129**
90-99	**Arts, entertainment, household goods repairs, other**	**52**	**55**	**59**	**59**	**59**	**59**	**60**	**62**
90-93	**Arts, entertainment and recreation**	**23**	**24**	**25**	**25**	**26**	**26**	**26**	**30**
94-96	**Other service activities**	**29**	**30**	**34**	**34**	**34**	**33**	**33**	**32**
97-98	**Activities of households as employers and for own use**	**0**	**0**	**0**	**0**	**0**	**0**	**0**	**0**
05-39	**INDUSTRY INCLUDING ENERGY**	**573**	**592**	**531**	**512**	**530**	**525**	**518**	**527**
45-99	**TOTAL SERVICES**	**1 355**	**1 393**	**1 407**	**1 401**	**1 428**	**1 442**	**1 434**	**1 459**
45-82	**BUSINESS SECTOR SERVICES**	**858**	**889**	**898**	**888**	**915**	**934**	**926**	**940**
45-82x	**BUSINESS SECTOR SERVICES excluding real estate**	**836**	**869**	**879**	**867**	**891**	**910**	**903**	**918**
05-82x	**NON-AGRICULTURE BUSINESS SECTOR excluding real estate**	..	..	..	..	..	..	..	..

.. Not available

Note: Detailed metadata at: http://metalinks.oecd.org/stan/20170410/1c43.
Information on data for Israel: http://oe.cd/israel-disclaimer.

Disclaimer: http://oe.cd/disclaimer

Table 6. Labour costs (compensation of employees), current prices

ISIC Rev. 4

Million EUR

		2007	2008	2009	2010	2011	2012	2013	2014
	TOTAL	**22 300**	**24 256**	**24 064**	**24 975**	**26 112**	**26 928**	**27 481**	**28 605**
01-03	**AGRICULTURE, FORESTRY AND FISHING**	**592**	**591**	**557**	**551**	**586**	**582**	**618**	**613**
05-09	**MINING AND QUARRYING**	**113**	**121**	**117**	**111**	**124**	**120**	**116**	**119**
10-33	**MANUFACTURING**	**5 352**	**5 973**	**5 250**	**5 414**	**5 842**	**6 164**	**6 292**	**6 658**
10-12	Food products, beverages and tobacco	445	506	483	485	485	501	473	491
13-14	Textiles and wearing apparel	281	262	224	216	214	215	210	225
15	Leather and related products	106	105	98	92	102	113	111	122
16	Wood, wood and cork products	208	197	179	180	187	163	172	194
17	Paper and paper products	112	121	119	124	115	119	116	120
18	Printing and reproduction of recorded media	106	109	111	105	96	101	98	97
19-23	Chemical, rubber, plastics, non-metallic products	827	955	869	870	955	976	953	1 012
20	Chemicals and chemical products	137	172	140	138	152	160	152	158
21	Pharmaceutical products	42	43	45	43	45	49	40	46
22-23	Rubber, plastic, non-metallic mineral products	578	660	605	613	679	684	671	717
24	Basic metals	500	515	410	429	457	469	474	496
25	Metal products, except machinery and equipment	503	578	506	519	577	621	625	682
26-28	Machinery and equipment	1 072	1 220	1 007	1 054	1 146	1 193	1 312	1 382
26	Computer, electronic and optical products	202	253	262	248	230	225	238	229
27	Electrical equipment	360	358	313	327	362	369	419	459
28	Machinery and equipment n.e.c.	510	610	432	479	554	600	655	694
29-30	Transport equipment	704	863	754	830	985	1 140	1 196	1 270
29	Motor vehicles, trailers and semi-trailers	657	805	705	779	920	1 071	1 134	1 203
30	Other transport equipment	46	58	48	51	64	68	62	67
31-33	Furniture; repair, installation of machinery and equipment	489	542	490	510	523	552	550	567
31-32	Furniture, other manufacturing	241	247	236	246	250	264	254	280
33	Repair and installation of machinery and equipment	248	295	254	263	273	288	297	286
35-39	**ELECTRICITY, GAS, WATER AND WASTE MANAGEMENT**	**734**	**708**	**728**	**755**	**791**	**795**	**819**	**829**
35	Electricity, gas, steam and air conditioning supply	477	443	443	470	472	478	477	501
36-39	Water supply; sewerage, waste, remediation activities	257	265	285	285	319	317	342	328
41-43	**CONSTRUCTION**	**1 227**	**1 428**	**1 376**	**1 423**	**1 403**	**1 373**	**1 343**	**1 332**
45-56	Distribution; transportation, accommodation, food service	5 823	5 873	5 747	6 003	6 337	6 448	6 396	6 759
45-47	**Wholesale and retail trade; motor vehicle and motorcycle repairs**	**4 089**	**3 847**	**3 748**	**3 937**	**4 180**	**4 266**	**4 145**	**4 429**
49-53	**Transportation and storage**	**1 358**	**1 653**	**1 609**	**1 640**	**1 677**	**1 665**	**1 722**	**1 772**
55-56	**Accommodation and food service activities**	**376**	**374**	**390**	**426**	**480**	**517**	**528**	**557**
58-63	**Information and communication**	**758**	**913**	**905**	**946**	**1 095**	**1 121**	**1 174**	**1 226**
58-60	Publishing, audiovisual and broadcasting activities	167	186	174	167	183	160	151	164
61	Telecommunications	232	258	277	279	297	309	323	353
62-63	IT and other information services	359	469	454	500	615	651	700	709
64-66	**Financial and insurance activities**	**820**	**829**	**806**	**792**	**845**	**912**	**862**	**930**
68	**Real estate activities**	**174**	**217**	**213**	**280**	**317**	**320**	**288**	**275**
69-82	**Professional, scientific, technical, admin., support activities**	**1 492**	**1 764**	**1 974**	**1 991**	**2 118**	**2 248**	**2 397**	**2 352**
69-75	Professional, scientific and technical activities	983	1 118	1 295	1 254	1 289	1 448	1 619	1 514
69-71	Legal, accounting activities; mgt consultancy; engineering	632	740	906	852	870	978	1 166	1 047
73-75	Advertising, market research; other prof., scientific, tech.	219	255	284	298	317	375	345	359
77-82	Administrative and support service activities	509	647	680	737	829	800	779	837
84-88	**Public administration, defence; social security; education; health**	**4 773**	**5 405**	**5 910**	**6 230**	**6 168**	**6 350**	**6 677**	**6 989**
84	**Public administration, defence; compulsory social security**	**2 238**	**2 572**	**2 801**	**2 953**	**2 797**	**2 822**	**2 890**	**3 018**
85	**Education**	**1 396**	**1 547**	**1 702**	**1 779**	**1 804**	**1 878**	**2 067**	**2 196**
86-88	**Human health and social work activities**	**1 139**	**1 286**	**1 406**	**1 497**	**1 567**	**1 650**	**1 720**	**1 776**
90-99	**Arts, entertainment, household goods repairs, other**	**443**	**433**	**481**	**480**	**486**	**497**	**499**	**523**
90-93	**Arts, entertainment and recreation**	**210**	**226**	**251**	**254**	**272**	**285**	**276**	**309**
94-96	**Other service activities**	**233**	**207**	**230**	**226**	**214**	**212**	**224**	**214**
97-98	**Activities of households as employers and for own use**	**0**	**0**	**0**	**0**	**0**	**0**	**0**	**0**
05-39	INDUSTRY INCLUDING ENERGY	6 198	6 802	6 095	6 280	6 757	7 079	7 226	7 606
45-99	**TOTAL SERVICES**	**14 284**	**15 435**	**16 036**	**16 721**	**17 367**	**17 895**	**18 294**	**19 054**
45-82	**BUSINESS SECTOR SERVICES**	**9 068**	**9 597**	**9 646**	**10 011**	**10 712**	**11 048**	**11 117**	**11 542**
45-82x	**BUSINESS SECTOR SERVICES excluding real estate**	**8 893**	**9 380**	**9 432**	**9 731**	**10 395**	**10 728**	**10 829**	**11 267**
05-82x	**NON-AGRICULTURE BUSINESS SECTOR excluding real estate**	..	..	..	..	..	..	..	..

.. Not available

Note: Detailed metadata at: http://metalinks.oecd.org/stan/20170410/1c43.

Information on data for Israel: http://oe.cd/israel-disclaimer.

Disclaimer: http://oe.cd/disclaimer

SLOVENIA

Table 1. Production (gross output), current prices

ISIC Rev. 4

Million EUR

		2007	2008	2009	2010	2011	2012	2013	2014
	TOTAL	**70 426**	**75 928**	**68 358**	**70 391**	**71 776**	**69 436**	**68 681**	**70 935**
01-03	**AGRICULTURE, FORESTRY AND FISHING**	**1 509**	**1 551**	**1 411**	**1 446**	**1 623**	**1 538**	**1 560**	**1 704**
05-09	**MINING AND QUARRYING**	**296**	**305**	**294**	**295**	**295**	**286**	**274**	**278**
10-33	**MANUFACTURING**	**23 411**	**23 731**	**19 042**	**21 083**	**22 502**	**22 037**	**21 887**	**22 946**
10-12	Food products, beverages and tobacco	1 844	1 891	1 739	1 719	1 844	1 803	1 792	1 842
13-14	Textiles and wearing apparel	825	750	567	493	553	533	461	449
15	Leather and related products	326	283	226	260	285	242	249	280
16	Wood, wood and cork products	840	744	605	661	718	710	701	746
17	Paper and paper products	727	681	651	698	713	674	680	727
18	Printing and reproduction of recorded media	455	485	432	397	415	400	395	399
19-23	Chemical, rubber, plastics, non-metallic products	5 267	5 399	4 542	5 153	5 282	5 240	5 511	5 686
20	Chemicals and chemical products	1 362	1 292	1 094	1 306	1 399	1 421	1 412	1 447
21	Pharmaceutical products	1 409	1 541	1 409	1 541	1 660	1 758	1 912	1 961
22-23	Rubber, plastic, non-metallic mineral products	2 489	2 555	2 032	2 302	2 220	2 059	2 185	2 275
24	Basic metals	1 694	1 651	825	1 208	1 500	1 451	1 423	1 545
25	Metal products, except machinery and equipment	3 100	3 225	2 407	2 696	2 978	2 902	2 960	3 050
26-28	Machinery and equipment	4 320	4 546	3 507	3 904	4 196	4 145	4 045	4 170
26	Computer, electronic and optical products	697	698	523	595	607	613	582	610
27	Electrical equipment	2 131	2 179	1 717	2 050	2 148	2 129	2 110	2 174
28	Machinery and equipment n.e.c.	1 492	1 669	1 267	1 259	1 441	1 404	1 352	1 387
29-30	Transport equipment	2 786	2 788	2 518	2 864	2 840	2 721	2 367	2 698
29	Motor vehicles, trailers and semi-trailers	2 641	2 627	2 433	2 775	2 763	2 639	2 291	2 627
30	Other transport equipment	146	161	86	89	77	82	75	72
31-33	Furniture; repair, installation of machinery and equipment	1 228	1 288	1 025	1 031	1 177	1 217	1 303	1 353
31-32	Furniture, other manufacturing	881	913	715	698	718	645	639	679
33	Repair and installation of machinery and equipment	347	374	310	333	459	572	664	674
35-39	**ELECTRICITY, GAS, WATER AND WASTE MANAGEMENT**	**2 310**	**2 618**	**2 639**	**2 909**	**3 179**	**3 139**	**3 210**	**3 103**
35	Electricity, gas, steam and air conditioning supply	1 552	1 778	1 890	1 959	2 129	2 107	2 161	2 011
36-39	Water supply; sewerage, waste, remediation activities	759	840	749	950	1 050	1 032	1 049	1 091
41-43	**CONSTRUCTION**	**8 733**	**9 830**	**8 240**	**7 084**	**6 101**	**5 654**	**5 285**	**5 535**
45-56	Distribution; transportation, accommodation, food service	12 830	14 310	13 053	13 273	13 877	13 516	13 558	13 898
45-47	**Wholesale and retail trade; motor vehicle and motorcycle repairs**	**7 295**	**8 110**	**7 533**	**7 377**	**7 503**	**7 241**	**7 257**	**7 275**
49-53	**Transportation and storage**	**4 117**	**4 672**	**4 059**	**4 433**	**4 854**	**4 792**	**4 786**	**5 053**
55-56	**Accommodation and food service activities**	**1 418**	**1 528**	**1 462**	**1 464**	**1 519**	**1 484**	**1 514**	**1 570**
58-63	**Information and communication**	**2 625**	**2 944**	**2 855**	**2 900**	**2 841**	**2 871**	**2 808**	**2 870**
58-60	Publishing, audiovisual and broadcasting activities	663	711	669	653	648	651	581	593
61	Telecommunications	1 238	1 387	1 331	1 332	1 287	1 282	1 275	1 262
62-63	IT and other information services	724	846	855	914	906	938	952	1 015
64-66	**Financial and insurance activities**	**2 431**	**2 554**	**2 647**	**2 798**	**2 748**	**2 355**	**2 352**	**2 453**
68	**Real estate activities**	**2 702**	**2 976**	**3 124**	**3 007**	**2 964**	**2 786**	**2 667**	**2 624**
69-82	**Professional, scientific, technical, admin., support activities**	**5 183**	**5 864**	**5 428**	**5 657**	**5 619**	**5 450**	**5 455**	**5 953**
69-75	Professional, scientific and technical activities	3 784	4 359	4 056	4 216	4 167	4 020	4 030	4 348
69-71	Legal, accounting activities; mgt consultancy; engineering	2 488	2 892	2 679	2 805	2 684	2 533	2 524	2 834
73-75	Advertising, market research; other prof., scientific, tech.	953	1 060	974	972	997	955	954	948
77-82	Administrative and support service activities	1 399	1 505	1 372	1 441	1 451	1 430	1 426	1 604
84-88	**Public administration, defence; social security; education; health**	**6 838**	**7 587**	**7 972**	**8 182**	**8 256**	**8 077**	**7 927**	**7 875**
84	**Public administration, defence; compulsory social security**	**2 650**	**2 939**	**3 066**	**3 152**	**3 122**	**2 991**	**2 966**	**2 891**
85	**Education**	**2 094**	**2 294**	**2 389**	**2 463**	**2 491**	**2 428**	**2 352**	**2 347**
86-88	**Human health and social work activities**	**2 094**	**2 354**	**2 517**	**2 568**	**2 643**	**2 658**	**2 610**	**2 637**
90-99	**Arts, entertainment, household goods repairs, other**	**1 559**	**1 658**	**1 654**	**1 757**	**1 770**	**1 726**	**1 697**	**1 696**
90-93	**Arts, entertainment and recreation**	**849**	**901**	**900**	**965**	**970**	**962**	**948**	**938**
94-96	**Other service activities**	**689**	**734**	**729**	**766**	**773**	**737**	**722**	**730**
97-98	**Activities of households as employers and for own use**	**21**	**23**	**24**	**26**	**27**	**27**	**27**	**28**
05-39	INDUSTRY INCLUDING ENERGY	26 017	26 654	21 975	24 287	25 977	25 462	25 371	26 326
45-99	TOTAL SERVICES	34 167	37 892	36 733	37 574	38 074	36 781	36 464	37 369
45-82	BUSINESS SECTOR SERVICES	25 770	28 648	27 107	27 635	28 048	26 979	26 840	27 798
45-82x	BUSINESS SECTOR SERVICES excluding real estate	23 068	25 672	23 982	24 628	25 084	24 193	24 173	25 174
05-82x	NON-AGRICULTURE BUSINESS SECTOR excluding real estate	..	..	..	..	..	..	..	..

.. Not available

Note: Detailed metadata at: http://metalinks.oecd.org/stan/20170410/1c43.
Information on data for Israel: http://oe.cd/israel-disclaimer.

Disclaimer: http://oe.cd/disclaimer

Table 2. Value added, current prices

ISIC Rev. 4

Million EUR

		2007	2008	2009	2010	2011	2012	2013	2014
	TOTAL	**30 809**	**33 230**	**31 638**	**31 583**	**32 106**	**31 226**	**30 972**	**32 231**
01-03	**AGRICULTURE, FORESTRY AND FISHING**	**659**	**628**	**599**	**626**	**734**	**647**	**653**	**779**
05-09	**MINING AND QUARRYING**	**146**	**147**	**145**	**139**	**146**	**144**	**126**	**129**
10-33	**MANUFACTURING**	**7 183**	**7 292**	**6 188**	**6 367**	**6 730**	**6 754**	**6 954**	**7 430**
10-12	Food products, beverages and tobacco	508	473	505	464	458	455	466	493
13-14	Textiles and wearing apparel	314	299	224	190	188	186	167	178
15	Leather and related products	81	69	67	59	80	65	67	75
16	Wood, wood and cork products	273	243	202	203	220	221	219	247
17	Paper and paper products	180	158	192	148	154	156	166	185
18	Printing and reproduction of recorded media	173	178	153	140	144	139	135	136
19-23	Chemical, rubber, plastics, non-metallic products	1 920	1 876	1 710	1 800	1 881	1 859	1 999	2 117
20	Chemicals and chemical products	334	313	301	331	366	361	374	405
21	Pharmaceutical products	802	790	747	782	815	824	895	918
22-23	Rubber, plastic, non-metallic mineral products	782	772	661	687	700	673	729	793
24	Basic metals	377	377	191	238	292	274	282	346
25	Metal products, except machinery and equipment	934	1 031	809	842	911	923	971	1 025
26-28	Machinery and equipment	1 395	1 477	1 201	1 288	1 324	1 352	1 360	1 421
26	Computer, electronic and optical products	292	296	228	246	231	240	238	243
27	Electrical equipment	641	655	536	619	628	663	664	688
28	Machinery and equipment n.e.c.	462	526	437	423	465	449	458	489
29-30	Transport equipment	529	586	503	562	590	615	581	617
29	Motor vehicles, trailers and semi-trailers	492	542	482	537	569	591	553	594
30	Other transport equipment	38	44	21	25	21	24	28	22
31-33	Furniture; repair, installation of machinery and equipment	499	523	430	435	487	509	542	590
31-32	Furniture, other manufacturing	331	342	275	269	264	242	249	271
33	Repair and installation of machinery and equipment	169	182	155	166	223	267	293	320
35-39	**ELECTRICITY, GAS, WATER AND WASTE MANAGEMENT**	**1 047**	**1 144**	**1 134**	**1 145**	**1 166**	**1 187**	**1 267**	**1 251**
35	Electricity, gas, steam and air conditioning supply	718	797	803	835	851	882	947	916
36-39	Water supply; sewerage, waste, remediation activities	329	347	330	309	314	305	320	335
41-43	**CONSTRUCTION**	**2 454**	**2 764**	**2 464**	**2 015**	**1 885**	**1 817**	**1 655**	**1 837**
45-56	Distribution; transportation, accommodation, food service	6 241	6 842	6 343	6 300	6 441	6 229	6 269	6 506
45-47	**Wholesale and retail trade; motor vehicle and motorcycle repairs**	**3 802**	**4 225**	**3 939**	**3 863**	**3 894**	**3 708**	**3 744**	**3 828**
49-53	**Transportation and storage**	**1 738**	**1 877**	**1 704**	**1 747**	**1 829**	**1 828**	**1 825**	**1 953**
55-56	**Accommodation and food service activities**	**700**	**740**	**701**	**689**	**718**	**693**	**700**	**725**
58-63	**Information and communication**	**1 234**	**1 333**	**1 236**	**1 286**	**1 314**	**1 335**	**1 301**	**1 351**
58-60	Publishing, audiovisual and broadcasting activities	261	275	251	248	251	258	220	227
61	Telecommunications	568	590	512	531	543	543	531	525
62-63	IT and other information services	405	468	473	508	519	534	544	599
64-66	**Financial and insurance activities**	**1 428**	**1 603**	**1 673**	**1 697**	**1 649**	**1 353**	**1 247**	**1 297**
68	**Real estate activities**	**2 171**	**2 408**	**2 636**	**2 537**	**2 469**	**2 334**	**2 250**	**2 217**
69-82	**Professional, scientific, technical, admin., support activities**	**2 705**	**3 016**	**2 871**	**2 990**	**3 021**	**2 962**	**2 982**	**3 191**
69-75	Professional, scientific and technical activities	1 896	2 185	2 101	2 153	2 179	2 130	2 171	2 251
69-71	Legal, accounting activities; mgt consultancy; engineering	1 183	1 374	1 325	1 369	1 343	1 264	1 284	1 350
73-75	Advertising, market research; other prof., scientific, tech.	482	543	508	496	520	492	498	506
77-82	Administrative and support service activities	809	831	769	837	842	831	812	939
84-88	**Public administration, defence; social security; education; health**	**4 723**	**5 185**	**5 478**	**5 611**	**5 666**	**5 602**	**5 419**	**5 378**
84	**Public administration, defence; compulsory social security**	**1 748**	**1 929**	**2 031**	**2 083**	**2 080**	**2 042**	**1 958**	**1 927**
85	**Education**	**1 635**	**1 750**	**1 824**	**1 881**	**1 914**	**1 868**	**1 802**	**1 792**
86-88	**Human health and social work activities**	**1 341**	**1 505**	**1 624**	**1 647**	**1 673**	**1 693**	**1 659**	**1 658**
90-99	**Arts, entertainment, household goods repairs, other**	**817**	**869**	**872**	**870**	**885**	**862**	**851**	**865**
90-93	**Arts, entertainment and recreation**	**457**	**485**	**485**	**504**	**494**	**480**	**473**	**482**
94-96	**Other service activities**	**340**	**361**	**363**	**340**	**364**	**355**	**350**	**355**
97-98	**Activities of households as employers and for own use**	**21**	**23**	**24**	**26**	**27**	**27**	**27**	**28**
05-39	**INDUSTRY INCLUDING ENERGY**	**8 376**	**8 582**	**7 467**	**7 651**	**8 042**	**8 086**	**8 348**	**8 810**
45-99	**TOTAL SERVICES**	**19 320**	**21 255**	**21 109**	**21 291**	**21 445**	**20 676**	**20 317**	**20 805**
45-82	**BUSINESS SECTOR SERVICES**	**13 779**	**15 202**	**14 759**	**14 810**	**14 894**	**14 212**	**14 048**	**14 562**
45-82x	**BUSINESS SECTOR SERVICES excluding real estate**	**11 608**	**12 794**	**12 122**	**12 272**	**12 425**	**11 878**	**11 798**	**12 345**
05-82x	**NON-AGRICULTURE BUSINESS SECTOR excluding real estate**	..	..	..	..	..	..	..	..

.. Not available

Note: Detailed metadata at: http://metalinks.oecd.org/stan/20170410/1c43.

Information on data for Israel: http://oe.cd/israel-disclaimer.

Disclaimer: http://oe.cd/disclaimer

SLOVENIA

Table 3. Value added, volumes

ISIC Rev. 4

Million 2010 EUR

		2007	2008	2009	2010	2011	2012	2013	2014
	TOTAL	32 689	33 643	31 171	31 583	31 687	30 943	30 707	31 889
01-03	AGRICULTURE, FORESTRY AND FISHING	676	680	616	626	668	613	609	706
05-09	MINING AND QUARRYING	141	142	136	139	140	136	126	128
10-33	MANUFACTURING	7 051	7 062	5 934	6 367	6 546	6 338	6 310	6 643
10-12	Food products, beverages and tobacco	564	497	466	464	485	462	462	473
13-14	Textiles and wearing apparel	314	296	223	190	177	166	141	138
15	Leather and related products	78	71	59	59	61	51	52	57
16	Wood, wood and cork products	279	235	185	203	220	210	190	198
17	Paper and paper products	164	146	150	148	146	144	142	152
18	Printing and reproduction of recorded media	157	163	147	140	146	137	133	134
19-23	Chemical, rubber, plastics, non-metallic products	1 875	1 866	1 632	1 800	1 825	1 766	1 846	1 915
20	Chemicals and chemical products	345	330	285	331	341	329	330	341
21	Pharmaceutical products	717	743	724	782	838	868	939	946
22-23	Rubber, plastic, non-metallic mineral products	825	800	621	687	646	575	588	632
24	Basic metals	242	250	195	238	240	235	241	270
25	Metal products, except machinery and equipment	898	895	773	842	871	853	857	905
26-28	Machinery and equipment	1 399	1 485	1 155	1 288	1 343	1 298	1 277	1 340
26	Computer, electronic and optical products	263	291	223	246	258	257	260	273
27	Electrical equipment	658	651	515	619	619	607	584	616
28	Machinery and equipment n.e.c.	479	542	417	423	466	435	435	452
29-30	Transport equipment	527	587	511	562	542	528	460	503
29	Motor vehicles, trailers and semi-trailers	493	548	490	537	521	508	438	484
30	Other transport equipment	31	36	21	25	20	20	22	18
31-33	Furniture; repair, installation of machinery and equipment	560	567	434	435	490	488	517	562
31-32	Furniture, other manufacturing	384	379	278	269	266	227	231	251
33	Repair and installation of machinery and equipment	178	189	156	166	224	261	287	311
35-39	ELECTRICITY, GAS, WATER AND WASTE MANAGEMENT	1 096	1 173	1 114	1 145	1 148	1 156	1 188	1 197
35	Electricity, gas, steam and air conditioning supply	791	819	792	835	813	828	860	885
36-39	Water supply; sewerage, waste, remediation activities	309	354	322	309	335	327	326	308
41-43	CONSTRUCTION	2 717	2 846	2 464	2 015	1 812	1 673	1 526	1 667
45-56	Distribution; transportation, accommodation, food service	6 597	6 827	6 223	6 300	6 408	6 146	6 143	6 359
45-47	Wholesale and retail trade; motor vehicle and motorcycle repairs	4 144	4 320	3 951	3 863	3 933	3 756	3 751	3 901
49-53	Transportation and storage	1 667	1 751	1 598	1 747	1 765	1 715	1 707	1 756
55-56	Accommodation and food service activities	802	766	682	689	710	674	684	702
58-63	Information and communication	1 171	1 301	1 244	1 286	1 287	1 283	1 293	1 336
58-60	Publishing, audiovisual and broadcasting activities	277	289	253	248	247	242	218	215
61	Telecommunications	474	539	517	531	529	514	526	516
62-63	IT and other information services	424	475	474	508	511	527	550	607
64-66	Financial and insurance activities	1 630	1 690	1 706	1 697	1 632	1 561	1 530	1 509
68	Real estate activities	2 357	2 501	2 496	2 537	2 527	2 536	2 549	2 586
69-82	Professional, scientific, technical, admin., support activities	2 858	3 006	2 829	2 990	3 009	2 956	2 961	3 216
69-75	Professional, scientific and technical activities	1 987	2 168	2 056	2 153	2 170	2 140	2 173	2 283
69-71	Legal, accounting activities; mgt consultancy; engineering	1 203	1 327	1 280	1 369	1 355	1 303	1 342	1 429
73-75	Advertising, market research; other prof., scientific, tech.	533	567	504	496	504	480	459	474
77-82	Administrative and support service activities	873	838	773	837	839	816	789	931
84-88	Public administration, defence; social security; education; health	5 452	5 465	5 546	5 611	5 629	5 696	5 635	5 643
84	Public administration, defence; compulsory social security	1 930	1 973	2 038	2 083	2 070	2 065	2 015	1 995
85	Education	1 889	1 854	1 872	1 881	1 896	1 921	1 931	1 933
86-88	Human health and social work activities	1 636	1 641	1 637	1 647	1 662	1 710	1 690	1 715
90-99	Arts, entertainment, household goods repairs, other	908	911	881	870	883	859	854	868
90-93	Arts, entertainment and recreation	524	522	497	504	501	488	489	498
94-96	Other service activities	360	364	358	340	356	344	339	344
97-98	Activities of households as employers and for own use	24	25	25	26	26	26	26	26
05-39	INDUSTRY INCLUDING ENERGY	8 299	8 383	7 184	7 651	7 833	7 629	7 622	7 968
45-99	TOTAL SERVICES	20 970	21 724	20 923	21 291	21 374	21 036	20 967	21 543
45-82	BUSINESS SECTOR SERVICES	14 615	15 337	14 498	14 810	14 863	14 480	14 477	15 031
45-82x	BUSINESS SECTOR SERVICES excluding real estate	12 252	12 830	12 001	12 272	12 335	11 946	11 931	12 441
05-82x	NON-AGRICULTURE BUSINESS SECTOR excluding real estate	..	..	..	..	..	..	..	..

.. Not available

Note: Detailed metadata at: http://metalinks.oecd.org/stan/20170410/1c43.

Information on data for Israel: http://oe.cd/israel-disclaimer.

Disclaimer: http://oe.cd/disclaimer

Table 4. Gross fixed capital formation, current prices

ISIC Rev. 4

Million EUR

		2007	2008	2009	2010	2011	2012	2013	2014
	TOTAL	**10 108**	**11 230**	**8 806**	**7 727**	**7 451**	**6 934**	**7 175**	**7 316**
01-03	**AGRICULTURE, FORESTRY AND FISHING**	**250**	**293**	**271**	**203**	**223**	**230**	**238**	**276**
05-09	**MINING AND QUARRYING**	**45**	**57**	**37**	**57**	**41**	**39**	**41**	**10**
10-33	**MANUFACTURING**	**1 861**	**1 988**	**1 497**	**1 442**	**1 653**	**1 559**	**1 624**	**1 714**
10-12	Food products, beverages and tobacco	110	131	112	118	123	97	71	100
13-14	Textiles and wearing apparel	34	42	34	17	32	24	15	22
15	Leather and related products	10	7	5	16	13	10	4	8
16	Wood, wood and cork products	103	62	43	56	56	63	41	42
17	Paper and paper products	50	55	37	35	71	46	39	32
18	Printing and reproduction of recorded media	52	75	55	31	29	25	22	21
19-23	Chemical, rubber, plastics, non-metallic products	510	617	415	399	478	442	480	516
20	Chemicals and chemical products	104	139	65	95	102	..	..	..
21	Pharmaceutical products	195	217	177	139	185	..	..	..
22-23	Rubber, plastic, non-metallic mineral products	210	261	170	165	191	..	..	..
24	Basic metals	150	139	163	92	124	88	107	109
25	Metal products, except machinery and equipment	211	268	162	206	201	191	167	235
26-28	Machinery and equipment	328	321	250	237	277	278	324	326
26	Computer, electronic and optical products	53	51	46	47	23	20	21	26
27	Electrical equipment	162	139	119	128	152	164	231	198
28	Machinery and equipment n.e.c.	114	131	85	62	101	94	72	102
29-30	Transport equipment	208	177	161	167	127	205	295	240
29	Motor vehicles, trailers and semi-trailers	183	164	156	153	116	201	289	236
30	Other transport equipment	24	13	5	13	11	5	5	4
31-33	Furniture; repair, installation of machinery and equipment	94	95	61	69	123	89	60	63
31-32	Furniture, other manufacturing	65	65	48	46	61	51	40	38
33	Repair and installation of machinery and equipment	29	30	12	23	62	38	21	25
35-39	**ELECTRICITY, GAS, WATER AND WASTE MANAGEMENT**	**667**	**678**	**647**	**526**	**600**	**621**	**1 008**	**649**
35	Electricity, gas, steam and air conditioning supply	493	509	445	459	547	574	972	605
36-39	Water supply; sewerage, waste, remediation activities	174	168	202	68	54	47	36	44
41-43	**CONSTRUCTION**	**419**	**448**	**323**	**228**	**130**	**144**	**122**	**152**
45-56	Distribution; transportation, accommodation, food service	2 370	2 670	1 632	1 227	1 200	876	849	907
45-47	**Wholesale and retail trade; motor vehicle and motorcycle repairs**	**783**	**924**	**555**	**515**	**530**	**413**	**361**	**363**
49-53	**Transportation and storage**	**1 320**	**1 435**	**782**	**515**	**522**	**374**	**394**	**455**
55-56	**Accommodation and food service activities**	**267**	**311**	**295**	**196**	**148**	**88**	**94**	**89**
58-63	**Information and communication**	**418**	**502**	**322**	**271**	**277**	**300**	**271**	**306**
58-60	Publishing, audiovisual and broadcasting activities	43	42	43	48	37	43	55	27
61	Telecommunications	326	401	205	155	162	191	180	230
62-63	IT and other information services	48	59	74	69	79	66	36	49
64-66	**Financial and insurance activities**	**314**	**275**	**241**	**241**	**281**	**278**	**170**	**176**
68	**Real estate activities**	**1 682**	**1 956**	**1 545**	**1 267**	**1 127**	**944**	**871**	**840**
69-82	**Professional, scientific, technical, admin., support activities**	**400**	**501**	**440**	**409**	**470**	**470**	**440**	**412**
69-75	Professional, scientific and technical activities	338	446	391	347	415	426	402	362
69-71	Legal, accounting activities; mgt consultancy; engineering	247	345	301	231	242	194	208	225
73-75	Advertising, market research; other prof., scientific, tech.	43	37	36	47	34	50	26	23
77-82	Administrative and support service activities	62	55	49	62	55	44	39	51
84-88	**Public administration, defence; social security; education; health**	**1 465**	**1 691**	**1 688**	**1 714**	**1 309**	**1 316**	**1 454**	**1 797**
84	**Public administration, defence; compulsory social security**	**1 063**	**1 096**	**1 124**	**1 235**	**854**	**846**	**1 032**	**1 324**
85	**Education**	**240**	**309**	**271**	**290**	**270**	**249**	**272**	**315**
86-88	**Human health and social work activities**	**162**	**286**	**292**	**190**	**185**	**221**	**149**	**158**
90-99	**Arts, entertainment, household goods repairs, other**	**218**	**173**	**165**	**142**	**142**	**157**	**88**	**77**
90-93	**Arts, entertainment and recreation**	**176**	**130**	**131**	**108**	**111**	**131**	**68**	**58**
94-96	**Other service activities**	**42**	**43**	**34**	**34**	**31**	**26**	**20**	**19**
97-98	**Activities of households as employers and for own use**	**0**	**0**	**0**	**0**	**0**	**0**	**0**	**0**
05-39	**INDUSTRY INCLUDING ENERGY**	**2 573**	**2 722**	**2 181**	**2 025**	**2 294**	**2 219**	**2 673**	**2 373**
45-99	**TOTAL SERVICES**	**6 866**	**7 767**	**6 032**	**5 270**	**4 804**	**4 340**	**4 142**	**4 515**
45-82	**BUSINESS SECTOR SERVICES**	**5 184**	**5 904**	**4 179**	**3 414**	**3 354**	**2 867**	**2 601**	**2 641**
45-82x	**BUSINESS SECTOR SERVICES excluding real estate**	**3 502**	**3 948**	**2 635**	**2 147**	**2 227**	**1 923**	**1 730**	**1 801**
05-82x	**NON-AGRICULTURE BUSINESS SECTOR excluding real estate**	..	..	..	..	..	..	..	..

.. Not available

Note: Detailed metadata at: http://metalinks.oecd.org/stan/20170410/1c43.

Information on data for Israel: http://oe.cd/israel-disclaimer.

Disclaimer: http://oe.cd/disclaimer

SLOVENIA

Table 5. Number of persons engaged, total employment

ISIC Rev. 4

Thousands

		2007	2008	2009	2010	2011	2012	2013	2014
	TOTAL	**976**	**1 001**	**983**	**962**	**946**	**937**	**927**	**931**
01-03	**AGRICULTURE, FORESTRY AND FISHING**	**85**	**83**	**82**	**80**	**78**	**77**	**77**	**77**
05-09	**MINING AND QUARRYING**	**4**	**4**	**3**	**3**	**3**	**3**	**3**	**3**
10-33	**MANUFACTURING**	**232**	**230**	**208**	**196**	**195**	**192**	**188**	**188**
10-12	Food products, beverages and tobacco	18	17	17	16	16	16	16	16
13-14	Textiles and wearing apparel	19	18	15	11	10	9	8	7
15	Leather and related products	5	5	4	4	4	4	3	4
16	Wood, wood and cork products	13	12	10	10	10	9	9	9
17	Paper and paper products	6	5	5	5	4	4	4	4
18	Printing and reproduction of recorded media	6	6	6	5	5	5	4	4
19-23	Chemical, rubber, plastics, non-metallic products	38	38	35	34	35	34	35	35
20	Chemicals and chemical products	8	8	7	7	7	7	7	7
21	Pharmaceutical products	6	6	6	6	7	7	7	8
22-23	Rubber, plastic, non-metallic mineral products	24	24	22	21	21	21	21	21
24	Basic metals	10	10	9	8	7	7	8	8
25	Metal products, except machinery and equipment	35	36	33	31	32	32	31	31
26-28	Machinery and equipment	46	47	42	40	40	39	38	37
26	Computer, electronic and optical products	9	9	8	8	7	6	6	7
27	Electrical equipment	21	21	19	19	19	19	18	18
28	Machinery and equipment n.e.c.	16	17	15	14	14	14	13	13
29-30	Transport equipment	15	16	14	14	14	14	14	15
29	Motor vehicles, trailers and semi-trailers	14	14	13	13	13	13	13	14
30	Other transport equipment	2	2	1	1	1	1	1	1
31-33	Furniture; repair, installation of machinery and equipment	22	22	20	19	20	19	19	19
31-32	Furniture, other manufacturing	15	15	14	13	12	10	10	9
33	Repair and installation of machinery and equipment	7	7	6	6	9	9	9	10
35-39	**ELECTRICITY, GAS, WATER AND WASTE MANAGEMENT**	**17**	**17**	**17**	**18**	**18**	**19**	**19**	**19**
35	Electricity, gas, steam and air conditioning supply	8	8	8	8	9	9	9	9
36-39	Water supply; sewerage, waste, remediation activities	9	9	9	10	10	10	10	10
41-43	**CONSTRUCTION**	**82**	**92**	**91**	**83**	**73**	**68**	**63**	**62**
45-56	Distribution; transportation, accommodation, food service	204	212	212	207	202	200	197	197
45-47	**Wholesale and retail trade; motor vehicle and motorcycle repairs**	**118**	**123**	**123**	**121**	**119**	**117**	**115**	**115**
49-53	**Transportation and storage**	**52**	**54**	**53**	**52**	**49**	**48**	**47**	**48**
55-56	**Accommodation and food service activities**	**34**	**35**	**35**	**35**	**34**	**34**	**34**	**35**
58-63	**Information and communication**	**23**	**24**	**25**	**25**	**25**	**26**	**26**	**27**
58-60	Publishing, audiovisual and broadcasting activities	8	8	8	8	8	8	7	7
61	Telecommunications	5	5	5	5	5	5	5	5
62-63	IT and other information services	10	11	12	12	13	13	14	14
64-66	**Financial and insurance activities**	**24**	**25**	**26**	**25**	**25**	**24**	**24**	**23**
68	**Real estate activities**	**5**	**5**	**6**	**6**	**5**	**5**	**5**	**5**
69-82	**Professional, scientific, technical, admin., support activities**	**108**	**111**	**110**	**113**	**114**	**115**	**115**	**118**
69-75	Professional, scientific and technical activities	59	63	65	68	69	70	73	72
69-71	Legal, accounting activities; mgt consultancy; engineering	34	37	39	40	41	41	43	43
73-75	Advertising, market research; other prof., scientific, tech.	20	22	21	22	22	23	24	22
77-82	Administrative and support service activities	50	48	45	45	45	44	41	46
84-88	**Public administration, defence; social security; education; health**	**163**	**166**	**170**	**173**	**175**	**177**	**176**	**176**
84	**Public administration, defence; compulsory social security**	**52**	**52**	**53**	**53**	**53**	**52**	**50**	**50**
85	**Education**	**61**	**62**	**63**	**65**	**67**	**67**	**68**	**68**
86-88	**Human health and social work activities**	**51**	**52**	**54**	**55**	**56**	**57**	**58**	**58**
90-99	**Arts, entertainment, household goods repairs, other**	**30**	**32**	**33**	**33**	**33**	**33**	**35**	**36**
90-93	**Arts, entertainment and recreation**	**13**	**13**	**14**	**14**	**14**	**14**	**16**	**17**
94-96	**Other service activities**	**16**	**17**	**17**	**17**	**17**	**17**	**17**	**18**
97-98	**Activities of households as employers and for own use**	**2**	**2**	**2**	**2**	**2**	**2**	**2**	**2**
05-39	**INDUSTRY INCLUDING ENERGY**	**252**	**251**	**229**	**217**	**216**	**214**	**209**	**210**
45-99	**TOTAL SERVICES**	**557**	**575**	**581**	**582**	**579**	**579**	**577**	**581**
45-82	**BUSINESS SECTOR SERVICES**	**364**	**377**	**378**	**376**	**371**	**369**	**367**	**369**
45-82x	**BUSINESS SECTOR SERVICES excluding real estate**	**359**	**372**	**373**	**371**	**366**	**364**	**361**	**364**
05-82x	**NON-AGRICULTURE BUSINESS SECTOR excluding real estate**	..	..	..	..	..	..	..	..

.. Not available

Note: Detailed metadata at: http://metalinks.oecd.org/stan/20170410/1c43.

Information on data for Israel: http://oe.cd/israel-disclaimer.

Disclaimer: http://oe.cd/disclaimer

SLOVENIA

Table 6. Labour costs (compensation of employees), current prices

ISIC Rev. 4

Million EUR

		2007	2008	2009	2010	2011	2012	2013	2014
	TOTAL	**17 212**	**18 956**	**18 790**	**19 018**	**18 921**	**18 487**	**18 073**	**18 390**
01-03	**AGRICULTURE, FORESTRY AND FISHING**	**122**	**125**	**123**	**118**	**111**	**110**	**107**	**108**
05-09	**MINING AND QUARRYING**	**103**	**111**	**105**	**99**	**98**	**99**	**91**	**94**
10-33	**MANUFACTURING**	**4 235**	**4 423**	**4 013**	**4 083**	**4 179**	**4 212**	**4 204**	**4 366**
10-12	Food products, beverages and tobacco	330	314	309	310	300	300	292	296
13-14	Textiles and wearing apparel	251	234	199	162	146	139	124	111
15	Leather and related products	67	68	56	57	62	60	56	59
16	Wood, wood and cork products	184	169	146	151	156	151	146	151
17	Paper and paper products	110	100	107	105	100	99	100	104
18	Printing and reproduction of recorded media	106	114	100	92	93	86	84	83
19-23	Chemical, rubber, plastics, non-metallic products	904	955	897	941	963	961	992	1 041
20	Chemicals and chemical products	182	184	168	180	187	185	181	182
21	Pharmaceutical products	270	294	299	295	301	321	341	371
22-23	Rubber, plastic, non-metallic mineral products	450	474	428	464	474	454	469	487
24	Basic metals	202	211	170	182	179	185	191	201
25	Metal products, except machinery and equipment	577	645	575	588	628	628	638	666
26-28	Machinery and equipment	879	942	854	864	884	891	878	888
26	Computer, electronic and optical products	181	188	171	159	148	147	147	149
27	Electrical equipment	387	405	367	402	409	413	400	412
28	Machinery and equipment n.e.c.	311	348	317	302	327	331	331	327
29-30	Transport equipment	298	323	287	307	314	333	319	361
29	Motor vehicles, trailers and semi-trailers	269	288	264	290	301	319	306	346
30	Other transport equipment	29	35	23	16	13	15	14	15
31-33	Furniture; repair, installation of machinery and equipment	327	347	313	326	353	378	383	403
31-32	Furniture, other manufacturing	219	234	207	205	196	171	164	161
33	Repair and installation of machinery and equipment	107	114	106	121	157	207	220	242
35-39	**ELECTRICITY, GAS, WATER AND WASTE MANAGEMENT**	**420**	**459**	**481**	**501**	**515**	**522**	**538**	**550**
35	Electricity, gas, steam and air conditioning supply	234	252	267	276	282	288	299	306
36-39	Water supply; sewerage, waste, remediation activities	186	207	213	225	233	234	239	244
41-43	**CONSTRUCTION**	**1 209**	**1 472**	**1 393**	**1 304**	**1 137**	**1 030**	**966**	**986**
45-56	Distribution; transportation, accommodation, food service	3 585	4 004	3 960	4 013	3 950	3 863	3 820	3 896
45-47	**Wholesale and retail trade; motor vehicle and motorcycle repairs**	**2 218**	**2 468**	**2 430**	**2 472**	**2 454**	**2 395**	**2 364**	**2 383**
49-53	**Transportation and storage**	**935**	**1 063**	**1 048**	**1 053**	**1 005**	**996**	**988**	**1 035**
55-56	**Accommodation and food service activities**	**432**	**473**	**482**	**488**	**490**	**472**	**467**	**478**
58-63	**Information and communication**	**625**	**715**	**738**	**747**	**731**	**741**	**736**	**747**
58-60	Publishing, audiovisual and broadcasting activities	188	204	210	207	201	201	183	174
61	Telecommunications	166	188	195	191	183	190	190	195
62-63	IT and other information services	271	322	334	349	347	349	362	378
64-66	**Financial and insurance activities**	**776**	**833**	**842**	**834**	**807**	**787**	**759**	**775**
68	**Real estate activities**	**117**	**135**	**121**	**127**	**121**	**116**	**111**	**112**
69-82	**Professional, scientific, technical, admin., support activities**	**1 756**	**1 935**	**1 934**	**2 001**	**2 076**	**1 948**	**1 889**	**1 976**
69-75	Professional, scientific and technical activities	1 052	1 201	1 242	1 276	1 342	1 253	1 234	1 215
69-71	Legal, accounting activities; mgt consultancy; engineering	667	776	809	831	861	798	788	782
73-75	Advertising, market research; other prof., scientific, tech.	252	275	274	275	292	253	243	238
77-82	Administrative and support service activities	704	734	692	724	733	695	656	761
84-88	**Public administration, defence; social security; education; health**	**3 785**	**4 219**	**4 536**	**4 641**	**4 666**	**4 546**	**4 355**	**4 284**
84	**Public administration, defence; compulsory social security**	**1 308**	**1 471**	**1 553**	**1 572**	**1 555**	**1 485**	**1 386**	**1 351**
85	**Education**	**1 424**	**1 547**	**1 639**	**1 692**	**1 717**	**1 663**	**1 590**	**1 571**
86-88	**Human health and social work activities**	**1 053**	**1 201**	**1 344**	**1 377**	**1 394**	**1 398**	**1 379**	**1 363**
90-99	**Arts, entertainment, household goods repairs, other**	**479**	**525**	**544**	**550**	**530**	**514**	**497**	**497**
90-93	**Arts, entertainment and recreation**	**279**	**307**	**319**	**325**	**306**	**297**	**281**	**276**
94-96	**Other service activities**	**179**	**196**	**200**	**200**	**197**	**190**	**188**	**192**
97-98	**Activities of households as employers and for own use**	**21**	**23**	**24**	**26**	**27**	**27**	**27**	**28**
05-39	**INDUSTRY INCLUDING ENERGY**	**4 759**	**4 992**	**4 599**	**4 683**	**4 792**	**4 832**	**4 833**	**5 009**
45-99	**TOTAL SERVICES**	**11 122**	**12 366**	**12 675**	**12 913**	**12 881**	**12 514**	**12 167**	**12 287**
45-82	**BUSINESS SECTOR SERVICES**	**6 859**	**7 622**	**7 595**	**7 721**	**7 685**	**7 454**	**7 315**	**7 506**
45-82x	**BUSINESS SECTOR SERVICES excluding real estate**	**6 742**	**7 487**	**7 474**	**7 594**	**7 563**	**7 338**	**7 204**	**7 394**
05-82x	**NON-AGRICULTURE BUSINESS SECTOR excluding real estate**	..	..	..	..	..	..	..	..

.. Not available

Note: Detailed metadata at: http://metalinks.oecd.org/stan/20170410/1c43.

Information on data for Israel: http://oe.cd/israel-disclaimer.

Disclaimer: http://oe.cd/disclaimer

SPAIN

Table 1. Production (gross output), current prices

ISIC Rev. 4

Million EUR

		2007	2008	2009	2010	2011	2012	2013	2014
	TOTAL	**2 215 596**	**2 252 545**	**2 053 895**	**2 038 315**	**2 033 198**	**1 965 826**	**1 923 235**	**1 961 416**
01-03	**AGRICULTURE, FORESTRY AND FISHING**	**46 512**	**46 116**	**42 223**	**44 916**	**45 815**	**45 807**	**49 559**	**46 040**
05-09	**MINING AND QUARRYING**	**9 739**	**9 633**	**8 076**	**8 325**	**8 083**	**7 498**	**6 244**	**5 944**
10-33	**MANUFACTURING**	**594 134**	**600 557**	**480 947**	**519 887**	**549 837**	**534 343**	**523 738**	**536 242**
10-12	Food products, beverages and tobacco	115 556	125 453	116 640	121 486	132 237	133 575	133 196	136 948
13-14	Textiles and wearing apparel	19 373	17 287	14 787	14 805	15 832	14 219	14 108	13 630
15	Leather and related products	5 748	5 604	4 600	5 283	6 067	5 282	5 684	6 334
16	Wood, wood and cork products	12 241	10 785	7 823	7 427	7 177	6 300	5 766	6 093
17	Paper and paper products	12 805	12 746	10 641	12 028	13 009	12 361	12 240	11 529
18	Printing and reproduction of recorded media	12 806	12 054	10 988	10 967	10 012	8 532	8 119	8 198
19-23	Chemical, rubber, plastics, non-metallic products	147 959	154 975	115 580	130 204	143 749	147 556	141 782	139 921
20	Chemicals and chemical products	42 923	47 093	37 805	45 182	49 768	50 640	48 352	49 170
21	Pharmaceutical products	13 573	14 582	14 280	14 268	13 906	14 034	14 871	14 866
22-23	Rubber, plastic, non-metallic mineral products	57 174	52 572	38 595	38 399	38 378	33 937	33 089	33 517
24	Basic metals	49 167	48 617	31 728	43 591	46 758	43 540	40 587	41 095
25	Metal products, except machinery and equipment	46 380	44 436	32 192	32 692	32 359	28 952	27 426	28 672
26-28	Machinery and equipment	65 290	65 457	48 732	50 085	50 800	49 163	46 717	48 630
26	Computer, electronic and optical products	12 312	11 814	8 646	9 531	8 417	7 475	7 065	6 959
27	Electrical equipment	25 311	25 338	18 950	19 686	18 933	17 564	15 475	16 114
28	Machinery and equipment n.e.c.	27 667	28 305	21 136	20 868	23 450	24 124	24 177	25 557
29-30	Transport equipment	75 654	72 003	59 633	64 521	66 572	61 021	65 936	71 811
29	Motor vehicles, trailers and semi-trailers	61 427	53 518	43 268	48 684	50 826	45 785	49 631	54 679
30	Other transport equipment	14 227	18 485	16 365	15 837	15 746	15 236	16 305	17 132
31-33	Furniture; repair, installation of machinery and equipment	31 155	31 140	27 603	26 798	25 265	23 842	22 177	23 381
31-32	Furniture, other manufacturing	21 175	20 112	16 522	15 244	14 179	13 218	12 089	12 584
33	Repair and installation of machinery and equipment	9 980	11 028	11 081	11 554	11 086	10 624	10 088	10 797
35-39	**ELECTRICITY, GAS, WATER AND WASTE MANAGEMENT**	**83 066**	**99 442**	**90 500**	**105 597**	**102 961**	**107 264**	**111 831**	**112 574**
35	Electricity, gas, steam and air conditioning supply	61 848	77 332	69 078	80 612	77 695	82 460	86 969	88 182
36-39	Water supply; sewerage, waste, remediation activities	21 218	22 110	21 422	24 985	25 266	24 804	24 862	24 392
41-43	**CONSTRUCTION**	**371 031**	**328 204**	**281 543**	**213 668**	**176 656**	**147 747**	**132 271**	**136 024**
45-56	Distribution; transportation, accommodation, food service	427 605	439 440	413 580	419 166	423 093	413 447	403 576	413 162
45-47	**Wholesale and retail trade; motor vehicle and motorcycle repairs**	**206 567**	**210 613**	**199 410**	**201 160**	**202 005**	**196 921**	**194 905**	**197 658**
49-53	**Transportation and storage**	**105 210**	**110 870**	**102 555**	**106 903**	**108 771**	**106 202**	**102 146**	**107 120**
55-56	**Accommodation and food service activities**	**115 828**	**117 957**	**111 615**	**111 103**	**112 317**	**110 324**	**106 525**	**108 384**
58-63	**Information and communication**	**89 830**	**92 655**	**90 661**	**89 949**	**89 480**	**86 264**	**82 748**	**82 937**
58-60	Publishing, audiovisual and broadcasting activities	26 220	26 383	24 683	24 325	23 365	20 881	19 122	19 408
61	Telecommunications	40 747	41 609	41 561	40 645	39 176	37 286	34 910	33 194
62-63	IT and other information services	22 863	24 663	24 417	24 979	26 939	28 097	28 716	30 335
64-66	**Financial and insurance activities**	**82 233**	**86 719**	**85 289**	**71 782**	**69 860**	**69 138**	**64 164**	**66 800**
68	**Real estate activities**	**106 993**	**114 307**	**120 169**	**122 430**	**125 924**	**128 898**	**128 678**	**128 617**
69-82	**Professional, scientific, technical, admin., support activities**	**128 775**	**135 205**	**129 368**	**128 417**	**127 741**	**122 217**	**121 430**	**130 911**
69-75	Professional, scientific and technical activities	75 769	80 276	78 156	76 724	75 852	72 236	71 026	77 572
69-71	Legal, accounting activities; mgt consultancy; engineering	54 136	56 922	55 588	53 978	53 422	51 114	50 287	55 715
73-75	Advertising, market research; other prof., scientific, tech.	16 826	18 045	16 877	16 890	16 357	14 906	14 448	15 218
77-82	Administrative and support service activities	53 006	54 929	51 212	51 693	51 889	49 981	50 404	53 339
84-88	**Public administration, defence; social security; education; health**	**217 734**	**237 726**	**248 665**	**250 300**	**249 843**	**242 161**	**240 079**	**241 811**
84	**Public administration, defence; compulsory social security**	**78 512**	**85 549**	**88 943**	**89 526**	**89 137**	**84 858**	**84 532**	**83 946**
85	**Education**	**57 820**	**62 312**	**65 167**	**65 885**	**65 227**	**63 932**	**63 503**	**63 922**
86-88	**Human health and social work activities**	**81 402**	**89 865**	**94 555**	**94 889**	**95 479**	**93 371**	**92 044**	**93 943**
90-99	**Arts, entertainment, household goods repairs, other**	**57 944**	**62 541**	**62 874**	**63 878**	**63 905**	**61 042**	**58 917**	**60 354**
90-93	**Arts, entertainment and recreation**	**29 422**	**32 475**	**32 672**	**32 741**	**32 575**	**30 464**	**28 998**	**29 845**
94-96	**Other service activities**	**19 430**	**20 532**	**20 410**	**20 842**	**21 203**	**21 213**	**20 873**	**21 394**
97-98	**Activities of households as employers and for own use**	**9 092**	**9 534**	**9 792**	**10 295**	**10 127**	**9 365**	**9 046**	**9 115**
05-39	**INDUSTRY INCLUDING ENERGY**	**686 939**	**709 632**	**579 523**	**633 809**	**660 881**	**649 105**	**641 813**	**654 760**
45-99	**TOTAL SERVICES**	**1 111 114**	**1 168 593**	**1 150 606**	**1 145 922**	**1 149 846**	**1 123 167**	**1 099 592**	**1 124 592**
45-82	**BUSINESS SECTOR SERVICES**	**835 436**	**868 326**	**839 067**	**831 744**	**836 098**	**819 964**	**800 596**	**822 427**
45-82x	**BUSINESS SECTOR SERVICES excluding real estate**	**728 443**	**754 019**	**718 898**	**709 314**	**710 174**	**691 066**	**671 918**	**693 810**
05-82x	**NON-AGRICULTURE BUSINESS SECTOR excluding real estate**	..	..	..	..	..	..	..	..

.. Not available

Note: Detailed metadata at: http://metalinks.oecd.org/stan/20170410/1c43.

Information on data for Israel: http://oe.cd/israel-disclaimer.

Disclaimer: http://oe.cd/disclaimer

SPAIN

Table 2. Value added, current prices

ISIC Rev. 4

Million EUR

		2007	2008	2009	2010	2011	2012	2013	2014
	TOTAL	**972 855**	**1 025 672**	**1 006 122**	**989 913**	**983 721**	**954 026**	**935 655**	**943 779**
01-03	**AGRICULTURE, FORESTRY AND FISHING**	**26 376**	**25 561**	**23 549**	**25 253**	**24 391**	**24 019**	**25 749**	**23 560**
05-09	**MINING AND QUARRYING**	**4 094**	**4 058**	**3 311**	**3 478**	**3 518**	**3 212**	**2 638**	**2 398**
10-33	**MANUFACTURING**	**145 643**	**148 740**	**132 507**	**131 436**	**132 447**	**126 036**	**125 681**	**130 050**
10-12	Food products, beverages and tobacco	24 954	26 204	26 260	26 805	28 007	27 673	27 237	27 793
13-14	Textiles and wearing apparel	5 246	5 318	4 657	4 466	4 780	4 267	4 047	3 853
15	Leather and related products	1 555	1 619	1 426	1 449	1 693	1 466	1 615	1 763
16	Wood, wood and cork products	3 308	3 271	2 442	2 270	2 067	1 866	1 755	1 746
17	Paper and paper products	3 384	3 340	3 046	3 317	3 380	3 208	3 099	2 698
18	Printing and reproduction of recorded media	4 817	4 815	4 311	4 401	4 077	3 501	3 281	3 269
19-23	Chemical, rubber, plastics, non-metallic products	34 112	34 522	29 597	29 250	29 512	27 383	26 950	27 762
20	Chemicals and chemical products	9 468	9 863	9 150	10 211	10 876	9 953	9 517	9 905
21	Pharmaceutical products	6 233	6 751	6 394	5 117	4 654	4 879	5 778	6 540
22-23	Rubber, plastic, non-metallic mineral products	15 753	16 103	12 844	12 091	11 456	10 275	10 238	10 489
24	Basic metals	7 497	6 914	5 405	6 811	6 690	6 636	6 404	7 129
25	Metal products, except machinery and equipment	14 448	14 888	11 949	11 237	10 773	9 628	9 413	9 746
26-28	Machinery and equipment	18 181	19 380	17 193	16 634	16 356	16 492	16 576	17 318
26	Computer, electronic and optical products	3 615	3 870	3 567	3 334	3 377	3 308	3 266	3 051
27	Electrical equipment	6 143	6 484	5 510	5 402	4 650	4 392	4 327	4 532
28	Machinery and equipment n.e.c.	8 423	9 026	8 116	7 898	8 329	8 792	8 983	9 735
29-30	Transport equipment	16 448	16 039	14 425	13 681	14 454	13 368	15 187	16 573
29	Motor vehicles, trailers and semi-trailers	11 865	10 649	9 210	8 932	8 544	7 533	8 641	10 047
30	Other transport equipment	4 583	5 390	5 215	4 749	5 910	5 835	6 546	6 526
31-33	Furniture; repair, installation of machinery and equipment	11 693	12 430	11 796	11 115	10 658	10 548	10 117	10 400
31-32	Furniture, other manufacturing	7 165	7 364	6 401	5 683	5 424	5 471	5 004	5 091
33	Repair and installation of machinery and equipment	4 528	5 066	5 395	5 432	5 234	5 077	5 113	5 309
35-39	**ELECTRICITY, GAS, WATER AND WASTE MANAGEMENT**	**27 168**	**31 072**	**31 647**	**35 064**	**35 686**	**36 320**	**35 625**	**33 530**
35	Electricity, gas, steam and air conditioning supply	19 285	22 773	23 220	25 533	25 701	26 361	25 334	23 772
36-39	Water supply; sewerage, waste, remediation activities	7 883	8 299	8 427	9 531	9 985	9 959	10 291	9 758
41-43	**CONSTRUCTION**	**109 192**	**113 190**	**106 503**	**87 526**	**73 980**	**63 521**	**53 948**	**53 524**
45-56	Distribution; transportation, accommodation, food service	214 838	224 635	220 893	222 593	225 464	222 077	216 619	219 194
45-47	**Wholesale and retail trade; motor vehicle and motorcycle repairs**	**111 304**	**116 592**	**113 834**	**114 537**	**115 838**	**114 374**	**112 839**	**112 743**
49-53	**Transportation and storage**	**40 606**	**42 221**	**41 817**	**43 573**	**44 458**	**43 244**	**42 097**	**43 991**
55-56	**Accommodation and food service activities**	**62 928**	**65 822**	**65 242**	**64 483**	**65 168**	**64 459**	**61 683**	**62 460**
58-63	**Information and communication**	**42 582**	**44 071**	**44 637**	**43 430**	**42 726**	**41 972**	**41 285**	**40 445**
58-60	Publishing, audiovisual and broadcasting activities	9 443	9 314	9 270	9 499	8 977	8 218	7 602	7 692
61	Telecommunications	20 107	20 595	20 754	19 914	19 055	18 611	17 772	16 355
62-63	IT and other information services	13 032	14 162	14 613	14 017	14 694	15 143	15 911	16 398
64-66	**Financial and insurance activities**	**51 678**	**55 125**	**57 216**	**43 936**	**40 895**	**39 870**	**35 183**	**37 910**
68	**Real estate activities**	**86 701**	**91 968**	**89 901**	**100 489**	**106 819**	**110 666**	**113 229**	**112 596**
69-82	**Professional, scientific, technical, admin., support activities**	**69 727**	**74 609**	**73 116**	**70 971**	**72 678**	**69 502**	**69 200**	**73 768**
69-75	Professional, scientific and technical activities	38 828	42 512	43 256	41 097	41 968	40 464	40 458	43 612
69-71	Legal, accounting activities; mgt consultancy; engineering	28 326	31 131	31 784	29 378	29 872	28 756	29 061	31 744
73-75	Advertising, market research; other prof., scientific, tech.	7 393	7 969	7 869	7 900	8 080	7 553	7 165	7 441
77-82	Administrative and support service activities	30 899	32 097	29 860	29 874	30 710	29 038	28 742	30 156
84-88	**Public administration, defence; social security; education; health**	**158 626**	**173 798**	**183 092**	**185 094**	**184 169**	**176 785**	**177 503**	**177 669**
84	**Public administration, defence; compulsory social security**	**55 835**	**61 109**	**64 470**	**65 581**	**65 051**	**61 573**	**62 621**	**62 170**
85	**Education**	**50 087**	**53 895**	**56 630**	**56 863**	**56 650**	**55 369**	**55 493**	**55 763**
86-88	**Human health and social work activities**	**52 704**	**58 794**	**61 992**	**62 650**	**62 468**	**59 843**	**59 389**	**59 736**
90-99	**Arts, entertainment, household goods repairs, other**	**36 230**	**38 845**	**39 750**	**40 643**	**40 948**	**40 046**	**38 995**	**39 135**
90-93	**Arts, entertainment and recreation**	**15 753**	**17 169**	**17 519**	**17 684**	**17 702**	**17 162**	**16 608**	**16 547**
94-96	**Other service activities**	**11 385**	**12 142**	**12 439**	**12 664**	**13 119**	**13 519**	**13 341**	**13 473**
97-98	**Activities of households as employers and for own use**	**9 092**	**9 534**	**9 792**	**10 295**	**10 127**	**9 365**	**9 046**	**9 115**
05-39	**INDUSTRY INCLUDING ENERGY**	**176 905**	**183 870**	**167 465**	**169 978**	**171 651**	**165 568**	**163 944**	**165 978**
45-99	**TOTAL SERVICES**	**660 382**	**703 051**	**708 605**	**707 156**	**713 699**	**700 918**	**692 014**	**700 717**
45-82	**BUSINESS SECTOR SERVICES**	**465 526**	**490 408**	**485 763**	**481 419**	**488 582**	**484 087**	**475 516**	**483 913**
45-82x	**BUSINESS SECTOR SERVICES excluding real estate**	**378 825**	**398 440**	**395 862**	**380 930**	**381 763**	**373 421**	**362 287**	**371 317**
05-82x	**NON-AGRICULTURE BUSINESS SECTOR excluding real estate**	..	..	..	..	..	..	..	..

.. Not available

Note: Detailed metadata at: http://metalinks.oecd.org/stan/20170410/1c43.

Information on data for Israel: http://oe.cd/israel-disclaimer.

Disclaimer: http://oe.cd/disclaimer

SPAIN

Table 3. Value added, volumes

ISIC Rev. 4

Million 2010 EUR

		2007	2008	2009	2010	2011	2012	2013	2014
	TOTAL	**1 010 811**	**1 024 343**	**989 810**	**989 913**	**984 159**	**956 227**	**942 134**	**953 792**
01-03	**AGRICULTURE, FORESTRY AND FISHING**	**26 371**	**25 656**	**24 724**	**25 253**	**26 373**	**23 821**	**27 051**	**26 625**
05-09	**MINING AND QUARRYING**	**3 813**	**3 938**	**3 178**	**3 478**	**3 641**	**3 352**	**2 726**	**2 473**
10-33	**MANUFACTURING**	**150 688**	**147 531**	**131 433**	**131 436**	**129 720**	**122 971**	**122 708**	**126 564**
10-12	Food products, beverages and tobacco	26 022	26 115	25 928	26 805	24 872	23 605	22 102	21 906
13-14	Textiles and wearing apparel	..	..	..	..	..	..	..	..
15	Leather and related products	..	..	..	..	..	..	..	..
16	Wood, wood and cork products	3 380	3 236	2 409	2 270	2 075	1 857	1 736	1 709
17	Paper and paper products	3 496	3 346	3 067	3 317	3 078	3 135	3 252	2 906
18	Printing and reproduction of recorded media	4 850	4 705	4 218	4 401	4 090	3 441	3 112	3 122
19-23	Chemical, rubber, plastics, non-metallic products	35 265	34 164	29 920	29 250	28 871	26 364	26 779	27 822
20	Chemicals and chemical products	10 306	9 897	9 178	10 211	10 131	9 001	8 636	8 988
21	Pharmaceutical products	6 192	6 677	6 313	5 117	5 123	5 803	7 185	7 832
22-23	Rubber, plastic, non-metallic mineral products	16 043	15 678	12 474	12 091	11 507	10 478	10 349	10 565
24	Basic metals	7 922	6 950	5 680	6 811	6 679	8 376	10 199	12 734
25	Metal products, except machinery and equipment	15 387	14 911	11 775	11 237	11 102	9 712	9 151	9 432
26-28	Machinery and equipment	18 504	18 976	16 939	16 634	16 727	16 548	16 148	16 541
26	Computer, electronic and optical products	3 595	3 761	3 479	3 334	3 569	3 563	3 645	3 520
27	Electrical equipment	6 059	6 131	5 381	5 402	4 649	4 303	4 007	4 105
28	Machinery and equipment n.e.c.	8 847	9 082	8 080	7 898	8 509	8 690	8 519	8 908
29-30	Transport equipment	16 443	15 532	13 787	13 681	15 270	14 073	15 741	17 032
29	Motor vehicles, trailers and semi-trailers	11 725	10 259	8 764	8 932	9 145	8 049	8 956	10 385
30	Other transport equipment	4 685	5 271	5 027	4 749	6 125	6 012	6 769	6 632
31-33	Furniture; repair, installation of machinery and equipment	12 388	12 607	11 649	11 115	10 569	10 190	9 598	9 777
31-32	Furniture, other manufacturing	7 446	7 408	6 290	5 683	5 478	5 426	4 884	4 911
33	Repair and installation of machinery and equipment	4 921	5 185	5 356	5 432	5 091	4 769	4 707	4 855
35-39	**ELECTRICITY, GAS, WATER AND WASTE MANAGEMENT**	**29 449**	**31 059**	**29 677**	**35 064**	**36 250**	**35 052**	**29 608**	**29 021**
35	Electricity, gas, steam and air conditioning supply	20 841	22 336	21 265	25 533	26 372	25 574	20 543	20 684
36-39	Water supply; sewerage, waste, remediation activities	8 640	8 750	8 445	9 531	9 878	9 481	9 048	8 274
41-43	**CONSTRUCTION**	**110 553**	**110 786**	**102 405**	**87 526**	**76 317**	**69 610**	**62 273**	**61 503**
45-56	Distribution; transportation, accommodation, food service	227 675	227 535	219 216	222 593	222 302	218 176	214 526	218 474
45-47	**Wholesale and retail trade; motor vehicle and motorcycle repairs**	**115 402**	**115 813**	**112 260**	**114 537**	**113 351**	**111 098**	**112 010**	**114 701**
49-53	**Transportation and storage**	**44 357**	**43 894**	**41 565**	**43 573**	**44 279**	**43 273**	**40 999**	**42 696**
55-56	**Accommodation and food service activities**	**67 995**	**67 882**	**65 411**	**64 483**	**64 672**	**63 806**	**61 450**	**60 985**
58-63	**Information and communication**	**40 528**	**41 540**	**41 787**	**43 430**	**43 358**	**44 036**	**45 485**	**48 099**
58-60	Publishing, audiovisual and broadcasting activities	9 701	9 300	9 104	9 499	8 830	7 712	6 651	6 690
61	Telecommunications	17 258	18 082	18 271	19 914	19 946	21 557	23 495	26 275
62-63	IT and other information services	13 762	14 283	14 527	14 017	14 582	14 846	15 668	15 890
64-66	**Financial and insurance activities**	**46 880**	**48 401**	**45 425**	**43 936**	**42 892**	**40 400**	**37 536**	**36 199**
68	**Real estate activities**	**93 148**	**95 356**	**98 566**	**100 489**	**103 343**	**105 784**	**107 186**	**107 557**
69-82	**Professional, scientific, technical, admin., support activities**	**73 441**	**74 749**	**71 987**	**70 971**	**72 615**	**69 838**	**69 317**	**74 352**
69-75	Professional, scientific and technical activities	40 995	42 886	42 769	41 097	42 266	41 576	41 681	45 236
69-71	Legal, accounting activities; mgt consultancy; engineering	29 585	31 113	31 311	29 378	30 122	29 178	29 595	32 485
73-75	Advertising, market research; other prof., scientific, tech.	8 168	8 353	7 911	7 900	7 990	8 028	7 622	8 069
77-82	Administrative and support service activities	32 426	31 850	29 229	29 874	30 349	28 280	27 675	29 192
84-88	**Public administration, defence; social security; education; health**	**168 150**	**176 576**	**180 692**	**185 094**	**186 767**	**183 457**	**183 658**	**182 766**
84	**Public administration, defence; compulsory social security**	**58 461**	**61 806**	**63 768**	**65 581**	**65 853**	**64 665**	**65 405**	**66 067**
85	**Education**	**53 118**	**54 802**	**55 777**	**56 863**	**57 879**	**56 771**	**56 070**	**55 795**
86-88	**Human health and social work activities**	**56 572**	**59 970**	**61 147**	**62 650**	**63 035**	**62 020**	**62 199**	**60 917**
90-99	**Arts, entertainment, household goods repairs, other**	**38 662**	**39 822**	**40 087**	**40 643**	**40 581**	**39 297**	**39 204**	**39 194**
90-93	**Arts, entertainment and recreation**	**16 767**	**17 397**	**17 520**	**17 684**	**17 663**	**16 826**	**17 460**	**17 371**
94-96	**Other service activities**	**12 057**	**12 494**	**12 573**	**12 664**	**12 972**	**13 423**	**13 157**	**13 238**
97-98	**Activities of households as employers and for own use**	**9 839**	**9 928**	**9 992**	**10 295**	**9 946**	**9 049**	**8 592**	**8 586**
05-39	**INDUSTRY INCLUDING ENERGY**	**183 765**	**182 279**	**164 043**	**169 978**	**169 611**	**161 361**	**155 017**	**157 851**
45-99	**TOTAL SERVICES**	**689 385**	**704 981**	**698 271**	**707 156**	**711 858**	**701 177**	**697 063**	**706 787**
45-82	**BUSINESS SECTOR SERVICES**	**482 322**	**488 440**	**477 482**	**481 419**	**484 510**	**478 412**	**474 250**	**484 747**
45-82x	**BUSINESS SECTOR SERVICES excluding real estate**	**388 719**	**392 670**	**378 776**	**380 930**	**381 167**	**372 509**	**366 843**	**377 104**
05-82x	**NON-AGRICULTURE BUSINESS SECTOR excluding real estate**	..	..	..	..	..	..	..	..

.. Not available

Note: Detailed metadata at: http://metalinks.oecd.org/stan/20170410/1c43.
Information on data for Israel: http://oe.cd/israel-disclaimer.

Disclaimer: http://oe.cd/disclaimer

Table 4. Gross fixed capital formation, current prices

ISIC Rev. 4

Million EUR

		2007	2008	2009	2010	2011	2012	2013	2014
	TOTAL	**335 552**	**326 064**	**262 499**	**248 987**	**229 884**	**205 839**	**192 371**	**198 335**
01-03	**AGRICULTURE, FORESTRY AND FISHING**	**3 732**	**4 632**	**4 936**	**4 499**	**4 491**	**4 277**	**4 126**	**3 926**
05-09	**MINING AND QUARRYING**	**654**	**696**	**1 158**	**1 493**	**753**	**987**	**789**	**1 244**
10-33	**MANUFACTURING**	**24 608**	**26 655**	**18 926**	**18 416**	**17 826**	**19 859**	**19 723**	**19 031**
10-12	Food products, beverages and tobacco	..	..	..	..	..	..	..	..
13-14	Textiles and wearing apparel	..	..	..	..	..	..	..	..
15	Leather and related products	..	..	..	..	..	..	..	..
16	Wood, wood and cork products	..	..	..	..	..	..	..	..
17	Paper and paper products	..	..	..	..	..	..	..	..
18	Printing and reproduction of recorded media	..	..	..	..	..	..	..	..
19-23	Chemical, rubber, plastics, non-metallic products	..	..	..	..	..	..	..	..
20	Chemicals and chemical products	..	..	..	..	..	..	..	..
21	Pharmaceutical products	..	..	..	..	..	..	..	..
22-23	Rubber, plastic, non-metallic mineral products	..	..	..	..	..	..	..	..
24	Basic metals	..	..	..	..	..	..	..	..
25	Metal products, except machinery and equipment	..	..	..	..	..	..	..	..
26-28	Machinery and equipment	..	..	..	..	..	..	..	..
26	Computer, electronic and optical products	..	..	..	..	..	..	..	..
27	Electrical equipment	..	..	..	..	..	..	..	..
28	Machinery and equipment n.e.c.	..	..	..	..	..	..	..	..
29-30	Transport equipment	..	..	..	..	..	..	..	..
29	Motor vehicles, trailers and semi-trailers	..	..	..	..	..	..	..	..
30	Other transport equipment	..	..	..	..	..	..	..	..
31-33	Furniture; repair, installation of machinery and equipment	..	..	..	..	..	..	..	..
31-32	Furniture, other manufacturing	..	..	..	..	..	..	..	..
33	Repair and installation of machinery and equipment	..	..	..	..	..	..	..	..
35-39	**ELECTRICITY, GAS, WATER AND WASTE MANAGEMENT**	**12 567**	**13 912**	**22 864**	**20 291**	**22 010**	**22 935**	**24 724**	**21 233**
35	Electricity, gas, steam and air conditioning supply	7 336	9 128	18 634	14 032	18 310	20 650	21 953	18 801
36-39	Water supply; sewerage, waste, remediation activities	5 231	4 784	4 231	6 259	3 700	2 284	2 771	2 432
41-43	**CONSTRUCTION**	**50 205**	**42 358**	**15 287**	**13 923**	**13 216**	**7 450**	**7 107**	**12 443**
45-56	Distribution; transportation, accommodation, food service	43 766	44 304	32 162	37 608	38 065	38 191	33 685	33 023
45-47	**Wholesale and retail trade; motor vehicle and motorcycle repairs**	**17 958**	**17 532**	**11 796**	**15 033**	**16 019**	**17 900**	**18 388**	**17 299**
49-53	**Transportation and storage**	**21 164**	**22 924**	**17 864**	**19 710**	**19 385**	**16 604**	**11 890**	**12 593**
55-56	**Accommodation and food service activities**	**4 643**	**3 849**	**2 502**	**2 866**	**2 662**	**3 687**	**3 407**	**3 131**
58-63	**Information and communication**	**10 117**	**10 049**	**8 165**	**9 906**	**10 513**	**11 163**	**8 821**	**9 459**
58-60	Publishing, audiovisual and broadcasting activities	..	..	..	..	..	..	..	..
61	Telecommunications	..	..	..	..	..	..	..	..
62-63	IT and other information services	..	..	..	..	..	..	..	..
64-66	**Financial and insurance activities**	**3 546**	**8 426**	**9 655**	**7 478**	**10 628**	**6 086**	**4 846**	**2 984**
68	**Real estate activities**	**112 156**	**99 486**	**75 667**	**67 900**	**56 102**	**51 744**	**43 536**	**46 437**
69-82	**Professional, scientific, technical, admin., support activities**	**15 806**	**14 158**	**9 556**	**11 057**	**11 481**	**10 952**	**12 730**	**16 875**
69-75	Professional, scientific and technical activities	5 622	5 787	4 635	8 406	8 607	8 255	8 321	9 431
69-71	Legal, accounting activities; mgt consultancy; engineering	..	..	..	..	..	..	..	..
73-75	Advertising, market research; other prof., scientific, tech.	..	..	..	..	..	..	..	..
77-82	Administrative and support service activities	10 185	8 371	4 922	2 650	2 874	2 697	4 409	7 444
84-88	**Public administration, defence; social security; education; health**	**47 425**	**49 971**	**53 316**	**47 614**	**39 680**	**27 365**	**26 949**	**26 117**
84	**Public administration, defence; compulsory social security**	**30 311**	**32 340**	**35 422**	**31 751**	**24 448**	**15 192**	**12 166**	**11 768**
85	**Education**	**9 114**	**9 498**	**9 621**	**8 664**	**7 680**	**6 045**	**8 009**	**7 570**
86-88	**Human health and social work activities**	**8 000**	**8 134**	**8 274**	**7 199**	**7 553**	**6 128**	**6 774**	**6 779**
90-99	**Arts, entertainment, household goods repairs, other**	**10 971**	**11 416**	**10 805**	**8 801**	**5 117**	**4 829**	**5 335**	**5 562**
90-93	**Arts, entertainment and recreation**	**9 302**	**9 683**	**9 584**	**7 997**	**4 297**	**3 685**	**4 096**	**4 184**
94-96	**Other service activities**	**1 668**	**1 733**	**1 221**	**804**	**821**	**1 144**	**1 239**	**1 378**
97-98	**Activities of households as employers and for own use**	**0**	**0**	**0**	**0**	**0**	**0**	**0**	**0**
05-39	**INDUSTRY INCLUDING ENERGY**	**37 828**	**41 263**	**42 948**	**40 200**	**40 590**	**43 781**	**45 236**	**41 508**
45-99	**TOTAL SERVICES**	**243 787**	**237 810**	**199 327**	**190 364**	**171 587**	**150 331**	**135 902**	**140 457**
45-82	**BUSINESS SECTOR SERVICES**	**185 391**	**176 423**	**135 206**	**133 950**	**126 790**	**118 137**	**103 618**	**108 778**
45-82x	**BUSINESS SECTOR SERVICES excluding real estate**	**73 235**	**76 937**	**59 539**	**66 049**	**70 688**	**66 392**	**60 082**	**62 341**
05-82x	**NON-AGRICULTURE BUSINESS SECTOR excluding real estate**	..	..	..	..	..	..	..	..

.. Not available

Note: Detailed metadata at: http://metalinks.oecd.org/stan/20170410/1c43.

Information on data for Israel: http://oe.cd/israel-disclaimer.

Disclaimer: http://oe.cd/disclaimer

Table 5. Number of persons engaged, total employment

ISIC Rev. 4

Thousands

		2007	2008	2009	2010	2011	2012	2013	2014
	TOTAL	**21 285**	**21 324**	**19 987**	**19 640**	**19 113**	**18 343**	**17 862**	**18 022**
01-03	**AGRICULTURE, FORESTRY AND FISHING**	**854**	**820**	**781**	**794**	**760**	**738**	**729**	**731**
05-09	**MINING AND QUARRYING**	**54**	**52**	**45**	**44**	**39**	**34**	**31**	**30**
10-33	**MANUFACTURING**	**2 781**	**2 758**	**2 408**	**2 311**	**2 217**	**2 063**	**1 964**	**1 945**
10-12	Food products, beverages and tobacco	456	475	450	443	445	432	418	422
13-14	Textiles and wearing apparel	172	158	133	128	122	110	104	100
15	Leather and related products	52	47	38	39	44	41	43	47
16	Wood, wood and cork products	111	111	87	76	71	62	55	53
17	Paper and paper products	54	53	49	47	47	45	44	41
18	Printing and reproduction of recorded media	108	106	96	95	79	73	66	65
19-23	Chemical, rubber, plastics, non-metallic products	488	476	406	389	363	339	324	317
20	Chemicals and chemical products	118	118	107	107	97	95	94	93
21	Pharmaceutical products	43	43	41	43	41	41	41	43
22-23	Rubber, plastic, non-metallic mineral products	319	307	249	230	216	194	180	173
24	Basic metals	109	106	96	98	93	86	79	77
25	Metal products, except machinery and equipment	372	371	294	279	262	230	217	210
26-28	Machinery and equipment	308	301	266	256	251	237	226	221
26	Computer, electronic and optical products	61	56	52	50	51	48	46	41
27	Electrical equipment	92	90	78	77	68	61	54	55
28	Machinery and equipment n.e.c.	156	155	136	129	133	129	126	126
29-30	Transport equipment	236	230	207	203	200	192	187	192
29	Motor vehicles, trailers and semi-trailers	181	173	152	148	147	140	137	141
30	Other transport equipment	56	57	55	55	53	51	50	51
31-33	Furniture; repair, installation of machinery and equipment	315	322	287	257	240	216	201	201
31-32	Furniture, other manufacturing	218	223	185	158	140	123	113	107
33	Repair and installation of machinery and equipment	97	99	103	99	99	93	88	94
35-39	**ELECTRICITY, GAS, WATER AND WASTE MANAGEMENT**	**183**	**183**	**187**	**204**	**209**	**207**	**205**	**203**
35	Electricity, gas, steam and air conditioning supply	53	54	56	60	60	59	58	58
36-39	Water supply; sewerage, waste, remediation activities	130	129	132	145	149	148	147	146
41-43	**CONSTRUCTION**	**2 731**	**2 416**	**1 870**	**1 631**	**1 383**	**1 149**	**1 008**	**968**
45-56	Distribution; transportation, accommodation, food service	6 062	6 157	5 844	5 762	5 700	5 480	5 324	5 418
45-47	**Wholesale and retail trade; motor vehicle and motorcycle repairs**	**3 692**	**3 742**	**3 502**	**3 469**	**3 431**	**3 334**	**3 247**	**3 265**
49-53	**Transportation and storage**	**943**	**968**	**930**	**924**	**891**	**845**	**791**	**795**
55-56	**Accommodation and food service activities**	**1 427**	**1 448**	**1 412**	**1 369**	**1 378**	**1 301**	**1 287**	**1 357**
58-63	**Information and communication**	**464**	**479**	**476**	**471**	**478**	**459**	**451**	**445**
58-60	Publishing, audiovisual and broadcasting activities	178	174	168	151	149	138	128	130
61	Telecommunications	65	74	75	77	76	72	69	68
62-63	IT and other information services	221	231	233	243	254	250	253	246
64-66	**Financial and insurance activities**	**405**	**414**	**407**	**402**	**389**	**381**	**369**	**361**
68	**Real estate activities**	**216**	**230**	**203**	**194**	**188**	**184**	**174**	**188**
69-82	**Professional, scientific, technical, admin., support activities**	**2 110**	**2 267**	**2 173**	**2 163**	**2 114**	**2 064**	**2 036**	**2 119**
69-75	Professional, scientific and technical activities	981	1 025	1 004	985	958	930	909	938
69-71	Legal, accounting activities; mgt consultancy; engineering	689	721	714	697	679	660	641	666
73-75	Advertising, market research; other prof., scientific, tech.	248	257	236	232	222	213	210	212
77-82	Administrative and support service activities	1 129	1 242	1 168	1 178	1 156	1 134	1 128	1 181
84-88	**Public administration, defence; social security; education; health**	**3 729**	**3 836**	**3 899**	**3 978**	**3 985**	**3 926**	**3 904**	**3 948**
84	**Public administration, defence; compulsory social security**	**1 348**	**1 389**	**1 404**	**1 446**	**1 447**	**1 415**	**1 429**	**1 435**
85	**Education**	**1 167**	**1 198**	**1 227**	**1 223**	**1 209**	**1 224**	**1 209**	**1 220**
86-88	**Human health and social work activities**	**1 215**	**1 249**	**1 268**	**1 310**	**1 330**	**1 286**	**1 266**	**1 293**
90-99	**Arts, entertainment, household goods repairs, other**	**1 697**	**1 713**	**1 695**	**1 686**	**1 650**	**1 657**	**1 668**	**1 665**
90-93	**Arts, entertainment and recreation**	**362**	**382**	**379**	**405**	**391**	**380**	**376**	**404**
94-96	**Other service activities**	**560**	**574**	**579**	**545**	**547**	**592**	**599**	**579**
97-98	**Activities of households as employers and for own use**	**776**	**757**	**737**	**736**	**713**	**684**	**693**	**682**
05-39	**INDUSTRY INCLUDING ENERGY**	**3 018**	**2 992**	**2 640**	**2 559**	**2 466**	**2 305**	**2 200**	**2 179**
45-99	**TOTAL SERVICES**	**14 682**	**15 096**	**14 696**	**14 656**	**14 504**	**14 151**	**13 926**	**14 144**
45-82	**BUSINESS SECTOR SERVICES**	**9 256**	**9 546**	**9 102**	**8 992**	**8 869**	**8 568**	**8 354**	**8 531**
45-82x	**BUSINESS SECTOR SERVICES excluding real estate**	**9 040**	**9 317**	**8 900**	**8 798**	**8 681**	**8 384**	**8 179**	**8 343**
05-82x	**NON-AGRICULTURE BUSINESS SECTOR excluding real estate**	..	..	..	..	..	..	..	..

.. Not available

Note: Detailed metadata at: http://metalinks.oecd.org/stan/20170410/1c43.
Information on data for Israel: http://oe.cd/israel-disclaimer.

Disclaimer: http://oe.cd/disclaimer

Table 6. Labour costs (compensation of employees), current prices

ISIC Rev. 4

Million EUR

		2007	2008	2009	2010	2011	2012	2013	2014
	TOTAL	**522 556**	**559 777**	**549 173**	**541 475**	**530 986**	**498 790**	**485 315**	**491 752**
01-03	**AGRICULTURE, FORESTRY AND FISHING**	**4 551**	**4 524**	**4 509**	**4 887**	**4 930**	**4 307**	**4 320**	**4 422**
05-09	**MINING AND QUARRYING**	**1 850**	**1 900**	**1 709**	**1 672**	**1 546**	**1 344**	**1 229**	**1 212**
10-33	**MANUFACTURING**	**85 470**	**88 919**	**79 784**	**78 340**	**77 045**	**72 356**	**69 848**	**69 235**
10-12	Food products, beverages and tobacco	12 434	13 277	12 989	13 095	13 330	12 789	12 786	12 562
13-14	Textiles and wearing apparel	3 705	3 479	3 046	2 879	2 862	2 724	2 504	2 389
15	Leather and related products	1 075	1 038	911	933	1 070	854	939	1 023
16	Wood, wood and cork products	2 369	2 555	2 022	1 788	1 699	1 469	1 281	1 275
17	Paper and paper products	1 972	2 063	1 870	1 822	1 898	1 822	1 833	1 706
18	Printing and reproduction of recorded media	3 095	3 048	2 747	2 788	2 344	2 133	1 954	1 896
19-23	Chemical, rubber, plastics, non-metallic products	18 375	19 036	16 736	16 463	15 479	14 996	14 255	14 194
20	Chemicals and chemical products	5 208	5 392	5 021	5 009	4 627	4 593	4 479	4 528
21	Pharmaceutical products	2 258	2 415	2 348	2 618	2 352	2 418	2 404	2 413
22-23	Rubber, plastic, non-metallic mineral products	10 348	10 622	8 768	8 192	7 798	7 284	6 648	6 439
24	Basic metals	4 490	4 745	4 180	4 379	4 490	4 088	3 781	3 638
25	Metal products, except machinery and equipment	10 275	10 853	8 766	8 451	8 134	7 200	6 769	6 582
26-28	Machinery and equipment	11 088	11 539	10 347	10 067	10 199	9 802	9 412	9 281
26	Computer, electronic and optical products	2 105	2 089	1 966	1 921	1 986	1 891	1 860	1 648
27	Electrical equipment	3 371	3 543	3 177	3 116	2 826	2 633	2 357	2 344
28	Machinery and equipment n.e.c.	5 612	5 907	5 204	5 030	5 387	5 278	5 195	5 289
29-30	Transport equipment	9 060	9 394	8 759	8 788	8 908	8 524	8 770	9 048
29	Motor vehicles, trailers and semi-trailers	6 755	6 734	6 086	5 986	6 157	5 780	5 872	6 122
30	Other transport equipment	2 305	2 660	2 673	2 802	2 751	2 744	2 898	2 926
31-33	Furniture; repair, installation of machinery and equipment	7 532	7 892	7 411	6 887	6 632	5 955	5 564	5 641
31-32	Furniture, other manufacturing	4 677	4 919	4 196	3 704	3 437	2 959	2 704	2 590
33	Repair and installation of machinery and equipment	2 855	2 973	3 215	3 183	3 195	2 996	2 860	3 051
35-39	**ELECTRICITY, GAS, WATER AND WASTE MANAGEMENT**	**7 632**	**7 873**	**8 618**	**9 596**	**9 381**	**9 795**	**9 713**	**9 845**
35	Electricity, gas, steam and air conditioning supply	3 557	3 596	4 116	4 619	4 230	4 619	4 595	4 899
36-39	Water supply; sewerage, waste, remediation activities	4 075	4 277	4 502	4 977	5 151	5 176	5 118	4 946
41-43	**CONSTRUCTION**	**63 744**	**63 694**	**54 305**	**46 896**	**39 240**	**31 625**	**27 159**	**26 288**
45-56	Distribution; transportation, accommodation, food service	117 692	130 000	129 054	128 055	128 721	122 772	117 626	120 580
45-47	**Wholesale and retail trade; motor vehicle and motorcycle repairs**	**66 678**	**73 692**	**72 401**	**71 492**	**71 577**	**68 686**	**66 466**	**67 747**
49-53	**Transportation and storage**	**23 520**	**26 313**	**26 212**	**26 080**	**25 747**	**24 271**	**22 377**	**22 708**
55-56	**Accommodation and food service activities**	**27 494**	**29 995**	**30 441**	**30 483**	**31 397**	**29 815**	**28 783**	**30 125**
58-63	**Information and communication**	**20 422**	**19 776**	**20 403**	**21 086**	**21 792**	**20 752**	**20 423**	**20 504**
58-60	Publishing, audiovisual and broadcasting activities	6 688	6 606	6 603	6 383	6 644	5 884	5 491	5 686
61	Telecommunications	5 670	4 127	4 270	4 672	4 643	4 327	4 161	3 977
62-63	IT and other information services	8 064	9 043	9 530	10 031	10 505	10 541	10 771	10 841
64-66	**Financial and insurance activities**	**22 313**	**23 286**	**23 113**	**22 862**	**22 380**	**21 232**	**21 465**	**20 175**
68	**Real estate activities**	**4 354**	**5 021**	**4 187**	**4 359**	**4 314**	**4 264**	**3 938**	**4 111**
69-82	**Professional, scientific, technical, admin., support activities**	**43 288**	**49 520**	**49 051**	**48 837**	**48 985**	**47 460**	**47 035**	**50 430**
69-75	Professional, scientific and technical activities	22 680	25 720	26 163	26 248	25 996	25 123	24 702	27 130
69-71	Legal, accounting activities; mgt consultancy; engineering	15 902	18 126	18 725	18 706	18 681	17 970	17 761	20 085
73-75	Advertising, market research; other prof., scientific, tech.	5 105	5 714	5 369	5 439	5 110	4 963	4 704	4 705
77-82	Administrative and support service activities	20 608	23 800	22 888	22 589	22 989	22 337	22 333	23 300
84-88	**Public administration, defence; social security; education; health**	**126 223**	**137 689**	**146 207**	**146 555**	**144 502**	**135 882**	**136 364**	**138 077**
84	**Public administration, defence; compulsory social security**	**42 696**	**47 268**	**50 433**	**50 728**	**49 848**	**46 393**	**47 540**	**46 740**
85	**Education**	**40 553**	**43 310**	**45 933**	**45 908**	**44 913**	**43 219**	**43 045**	**43 483**
86-88	**Human health and social work activities**	**42 974**	**47 111**	**49 841**	**49 919**	**49 741**	**46 270**	**45 779**	**47 854**
90-99	**Arts, entertainment, household goods repairs, other**	**25 017**	**27 575**	**28 233**	**28 330**	**28 150**	**27 001**	**26 195**	**26 873**
90-93	**Arts, entertainment and recreation**	**9 082**	**10 606**	**10 792**	**10 862**	**10 739**	**10 021**	**9 741**	**10 517**
94-96	**Other service activities**	**6 843**	**7 435**	**7 649**	**7 173**	**7 284**	**7 615**	**7 408**	**7 241**
97-98	**Activities of households as employers and for own use**	**9 092**	**9 534**	**9 792**	**10 295**	**10 127**	**9 365**	**9 046**	**9 115**
05-39	**INDUSTRY INCLUDING ENERGY**	**94 952**	**98 692**	**90 111**	**89 608**	**87 972**	**83 495**	**80 790**	**80 292**
45-99	**TOTAL SERVICES**	**359 309**	**392 867**	**400 248**	**400 084**	**398 844**	**379 363**	**373 046**	**380 750**
45-82	**BUSINESS SECTOR SERVICES**	**208 069**	**227 603**	**225 808**	**225 199**	**226 192**	**216 480**	**210 487**	**215 800**
45-82x	**BUSINESS SECTOR SERVICES excluding real estate**	**203 715**	**222 582**	**221 621**	**220 840**	**221 878**	**212 216**	**206 549**	**211 689**
05-82x	**NON-AGRICULTURE BUSINESS SECTOR excluding real estate**	..	..	..	..	..	..	..	..

.. Not available

Note: Detailed metadata at: http://metalinks.oecd.org/stan/20170410/1c43.

Information on data for Israel: http://oe.cd/israel-disclaimer.

Disclaimer: http://oe.cd/disclaimer

SWEDEN

Table 1. Production (gross output), current prices

ISIC Rev. 4

Million SEK

		2007	2008	2009	2010	2011	2012	2013	2014
	TOTAL	**6 045 315**	**6 299 764**	**5 909 592**	**6 338 289**	**6 656 883**	**6 687 827**	**6 710 108**	**6 961 693**
01-03	**AGRICULTURE, FORESTRY AND FISHING**	**83 897**	**90 900**	**84 444**	**93 801**	**98 880**	**95 527**	**94 197**	**95 962**
05-09	**MINING AND QUARRYING**	**30 731**	**35 716**	**24 183**	**46 030**	**49 927**	**45 437**	**40 766**	**39 027**
10-33	**MANUFACTURING**	**1 860 340**	**1 883 112**	**1 566 764**	**1 744 471**	**1 833 340**	**1 756 508**	**1 688 472**	**1 731 717**
10-12	Food products, beverages and tobacco	134 954	146 602	145 782	145 470	151 449	153 519	156 532	156 307
13-14	Textiles and wearing apparel	11 718	11 047	9 620	9 842	9 548	9 218	9 350	..
15	Leather and related products	1 687	1 446	1 249	1 394	1 428	1 236	1 324	..
16	Wood, wood and cork products	95 538	86 390	77 193	85 757	85 255	78 930	75 402	84 326
17	Paper and paper products	125 160	127 061	119 550	130 146	131 933	125 830	121 811	126 999
18	Printing and reproduction of recorded media	26 783	27 815	25 058	24 688	23 833	22 566	20 475	20 323
19-23	Chemical, rubber, plastics, non-metallic products	309 840	340 637	316 372	343 053	361 734	373 666	340 497	353 189
20	Chemicals and chemical products	..	..	..	..	..	73 669	72 963	..
21	Pharmaceutical products	..	..	..	..	..	84 948	76 471	..
22-23	Rubber, plastic, non-metallic mineral products	78 597	80 420	69 564	79 852	87 599	84 542	83 122	85 005
24	Basic metals	169 645	161 289	104 096	145 241	156 604	136 455	122 746	124 508
25	Metal products, except machinery and equipment	130 650	135 856	106 790	117 066	124 351	126 530	123 390	125 520
26-28	Machinery and equipment	442 598	454 181	369 751	405 305	415 504	399 245	381 029	381 408
26	Computer, electronic and optical products	163 610	170 112	156 835	167 147	144 429	135 884	140 495	143 345
27	Electrical equipment	64 658	66 704	59 507	59 905	63 344	62 010	62 976	62 057
28	Machinery and equipment n.e.c.	214 330	217 365	153 409	178 253	207 731	201 351	177 558	176 006
29-30	Transport equipment	323 374	301 344	204 804	251 783	287 831	251 717	263 183	274 209
29	Motor vehicles, trailers and semi-trailers	288 318	264 931	166 372	213 859	250 277	214 622	222 835	233 007
30	Other transport equipment	35 056	36 413	38 432	37 924	37 554	37 095	40 348	41 202
31-33	Furniture; repair, installation of machinery and equipment	88 393	89 444	86 499	84 726	83 850	77 596	72 733	73 928
31-32	Furniture, other manufacturing	55 764	55 081	52 753	53 276	54 179	51 162	46 935	48 105
33	Repair and installation of machinery and equipment	32 629	34 363	33 746	31 450	29 671	26 434	25 798	25 823
35-39	**ELECTRICITY, GAS, WATER AND WASTE MANAGEMENT**	**155 980**	**178 290**	**174 579**	**197 673**	**198 068**	**202 905**	**199 215**	**196 384**
35	Electricity, gas, steam and air conditioning supply	108 742	128 909	127 809	146 324	139 488	141 837	138 766	133 134
36-39	Water supply; sewerage, waste, remediation activities	47 238	49 381	46 770	51 349	58 580	61 068	60 449	63 250
41-43	**CONSTRUCTION**	**380 767**	**387 139**	**355 904**	**381 074**	**394 863**	**390 867**	**392 933**	**424 344**
45-56	Distribution; transportation, accommodation, food service	1 033 894	1 108 586	1 051 586	1 124 945	1 183 796	1 202 125	1 209 550	1 248 281
45-47	**Wholesale and retail trade; motor vehicle and motorcycle repairs**	**485 475**	**523 794**	**498 668**	**538 698**	**567 010**	**571 671**	**574 015**	**599 153**
49-53	**Transportation and storage**	**453 573**	**482 922**	**451 725**	**477 356**	**500 122**	**508 033**	**506 342**	**513 240**
55-56	**Accommodation and food service activities**	**94 846**	**101 870**	**101 193**	**108 891**	**116 664**	**122 421**	**129 193**	**135 888**
58-63	**Information and communication**	**329 263**	**343 503**	**338 157**	**350 165**	**372 586**	**384 646**	**388 078**	**411 707**
58-60	Publishing, audiovisual and broadcasting activities	96 053	99 070	98 221	101 030	103 668	107 896	107 960	108 601
61	Telecommunications	101 520	103 458	105 279	107 061	107 739	111 885	110 456	115 909
62-63	IT and other information services	131 690	140 975	134 657	142 074	161 179	164 865	169 662	187 197
64-66	**Financial and insurance activities**	**168 997**	**176 311**	**193 082**	**190 898**	**199 809**	**209 260**	**218 225**	**238 310**
68	**Real estate activities**	**452 836**	**472 799**	**489 820**	**499 620**	**530 069**	**536 134**	**551 887**	**570 894**
69-82	**Professional, scientific, technical, admin., support activities**	**534 174**	**560 217**	**539 505**	**580 049**	**619 782**	**650 445**	**668 604**	**701 060**
69-75	Professional, scientific and technical activities	368 358	382 351	369 306	396 248	417 300	440 704	457 444	483 381
69-71	Legal, accounting activities; mgt consultancy; engineering	194 831	212 620	210 203	222 200	239 204	258 355	263 789	281 078
73-75	Advertising, market research; other prof., scientific, tech.	80 057	84 840	79 590	84 572	90 894	92 882	93 644	98 686
77-82	Administrative and support service activities	165 816	177 866	170 199	183 801	202 482	209 741	211 160	217 679
84-88	**Public administration, defence; social security; education; health**	**865 069**	**906 000**	**931 976**	**961 750**	**1 000 215**	**1 032 750**	**1 070 156**	**1 112 086**
84	**Public administration, defence; compulsory social security**	**243 017**	**248 812**	**252 740**	**263 206**	**270 754**	**280 902**	**288 400**	**297 013**
85	**Education**	**228 363**	**238 986**	**243 494**	**250 101**	**257 820**	**263 055**	**270 811**	**278 857**
86-88	**Human health and social work activities**	**393 689**	**418 202**	**435 742**	**448 443**	**471 641**	**488 793**	**510 945**	**536 216**
90-99	**Arts, entertainment, household goods repairs, other**	**149 367**	**157 191**	**159 592**	**167 813**	**175 548**	**181 223**	**188 025**	**191 921**
90-93	**Arts, entertainment and recreation**	**78 401**	**81 879**	**83 581**	**87 011**	**90 573**	**94 564**	**98 994**	**99 896**
94-96	**Other service activities**	**70 046**	**74 294**	**74 968**	**79 726**	**83 825**	**85 402**	**87 528**	**90 258**
97-98	**Activities of households as employers and for own use**	**920**	**1 018**	**1 043**	**1 076**	**1 150**	**1 257**	**1 503**	**1 767**
05-39	INDUSTRY INCLUDING ENERGY	2 047 051	2 097 118	1 765 526	1 988 174	2 081 335	2 004 850	1 928 453	1 967 128
45-99	TOTAL SERVICES	3 533 600	3 724 607	3 703 718	3 875 240	4 081 805	4 196 583	4 294 525	4 474 259
45-82	BUSINESS SECTOR SERVICES	2 519 164	2 661 416	2 612 150	2 745 677	2 906 042	2 982 610	3 036 344	3 170 252
45-82x	BUSINESS SECTOR SERVICES excluding real estate	2 066 328	2 188 617	2 122 330	2 246 057	2 375 973	2 446 476	2 484 457	2 599 358
05-82x	NON-AGRICULTURE BUSINESS SECTOR excluding real estate	..	..	..	..	..	..	..	..

.. Not available

Note: Detailed metadata at: http://metalinks.oecd.org/stan/20170410/1c43.

Information on data for Israel: http://oe.cd/israel-disclaimer.

Disclaimer: http://oe.cd/disclaimer

SWEDEN

Table 2. Value added, current prices

ISIC Rev. 4

Million SEK

		2007	2008	2009	2010	2011	2012	2013	2014
	TOTAL	**2 907 813**	**2 992 009**	**2 887 785**	**3 094 787**	**3 222 931**	**3 253 975**	**3 333 436**	**3 486 881**
01-03	**AGRICULTURE, FORESTRY AND FISHING**	**46 108**	**47 981**	**42 602**	**50 271**	**52 549**	**48 384**	**46 230**	**46 804**
05-09	**MINING AND QUARRYING**	**17 949**	**21 590**	**11 087**	**28 187**	**27 938**	**23 477**	**18 448**	**17 227**
10-33	**MANUFACTURING**	**597 176**	**570 497**	**499 889**	**575 259**	**588 552**	**559 308**	**560 002**	**575 210**
10-12	Food products, beverages and tobacco	36 717	36 413	37 941	39 347	40 476	38 980	41 352	41 307
13-14	Textiles and wearing apparel	4 436	4 251	3 722	3 897	3 646	3 563	3 627	..
15	Leather and related products	496	442	426	347	444	382	378	..
16	Wood, wood and cork products	27 187	19 422	18 586	19 972	16 998	16 376	17 551	20 297
17	Paper and paper products	34 812	31 442	31 452	33 526	34 266	32 837	31 159	34 523
18	Printing and reproduction of recorded media	10 922	10 690	9 757	8 037	8 225	7 744	6 704	6 816
19-23	Chemical, rubber, plastics, non-metallic products	106 902	103 881	118 894	117 733	119 497	115 008	112 375	108 957
20	Chemicals and chemical products	..	..	..	..	..	27 184	29 005	..
21	Pharmaceutical products	..	..	..	..	..	50 736	45 871	..
22-23	Rubber, plastic, non-metallic mineral products	28 005	26 902	23 022	26 706	30 611	30 608	28 617	28 078
24	Basic metals	40 549	33 040	14 784	25 078	26 476	23 809	25 438	27 877
25	Metal products, except machinery and equipment	51 931	52 377	40 723	46 840	47 243	49 594	49 722	50 172
26-28	Machinery and equipment	170 826	167 342	136 967	167 145	177 577	165 846	166 156	167 131
26	Computer, electronic and optical products	76 618	75 455	70 619	79 513	77 503	73 304	79 784	84 903
27	Electrical equipment	22 593	22 608	18 765	18 874	22 662	19 935	19 638	17 639
28	Machinery and equipment n.e.c.	71 615	69 279	47 583	68 758	77 412	72 607	66 734	64 589
29-30	Transport equipment	76 633	76 420	53 798	81 543	81 602	73 242	76 008	83 297
29	Motor vehicles, trailers and semi-trailers	60 726	60 246	34 227	62 872	62 681	54 911	56 161	61 890
30	Other transport equipment	15 907	16 174	19 571	18 671	18 921	18 331	19 847	21 407
31-33	Furniture; repair, installation of machinery and equipment	35 765	34 777	32 839	31 794	32 102	31 927	29 532	30 748
31-32	Furniture, other manufacturing	22 265	21 632	20 531	20 305	20 810	20 274	18 699	19 867
33	Repair and installation of machinery and equipment	13 500	13 145	12 308	11 489	11 292	11 653	10 833	10 881
35-39	**ELECTRICITY, GAS, WATER AND WASTE MANAGEMENT**	**84 967**	**101 651**	**99 026**	**109 544**	**107 830**	**111 357**	**109 042**	**111 403**
35	Electricity, gas, steam and air conditioning supply	66 535	83 152	81 654	91 326	87 314	89 593	86 441	87 586
36-39	Water supply; sewerage, waste, remediation activities	18 432	18 499	17 372	18 218	20 516	21 764	22 601	23 817
41-43	**CONSTRUCTION**	**181 522**	**182 019**	**167 276**	**182 358**	**185 821**	**180 787**	**181 899**	**193 821**
45-56	Distribution; transportation, accommodation, food service	523 293	545 473	525 958	559 064	579 218	596 004	599 528	630 159
45-47	**Wholesale and retail trade; motor vehicle and motorcycle repairs**	**306 682**	**319 076**	**315 223**	**340 589**	**350 006**	**352 366**	**355 757**	**379 740**
49-53	**Transportation and storage**	**173 608**	**181 637**	**168 376**	**173 544**	**179 695**	**189 389**	**186 247**	**189 760**
55-56	**Accommodation and food service activities**	**43 003**	**44 760**	**42 359**	**44 931**	**49 517**	**54 249**	**57 524**	**60 659**
58-63	**Information and communication**	**149 866**	**159 531**	**156 107**	**166 347**	**176 233**	**181 801**	**186 801**	**198 966**
58-60	Publishing, audiovisual and broadcasting activities	40 780	42 916	40 065	42 557	43 753	46 161	46 249	47 822
61	Telecommunications	34 552	34 417	36 075	39 650	39 841	40 506	40 672	43 280
62-63	IT and other information services	74 534	82 198	79 967	84 140	92 639	95 134	99 880	107 864
64-66	**Financial and insurance activities**	**104 040**	**106 417**	**126 786**	**120 104**	**131 575**	**140 297**	**151 752**	**161 047**
68	**Real estate activities**	**249 052**	**267 458**	**264 004**	**256 087**	**275 367**	**275 591**	**290 967**	**309 368**
69-82	**Professional, scientific, technical, admin., support activities**	**284 376**	**291 192**	**282 157**	**310 639**	**333 757**	**344 370**	**365 226**	**386 307**
69-75	Professional, scientific and technical activities	199 371	199 075	190 926	210 770	223 716	231 849	251 273	264 456
69-71	Legal, accounting activities; mgt consultancy; engineering	111 912	121 044	119 702	125 593	138 308	145 692	153 485	162 461
73-75	Advertising, market research; other prof., scientific, tech.	29 611	30 711	29 449	31 503	33 074	32 922	35 766	36 557
77-82	Administrative and support service activities	85 005	92 117	91 231	99 869	110 041	112 521	113 953	121 851
84-88	**Public administration, defence; social security; education; health**	**587 823**	**611 815**	**626 512**	**646 294**	**669 327**	**693 972**	**720 469**	**750 297**
84	**Public administration, defence; compulsory social security**	**144 043**	**144 673**	**145 898**	**151 644**	**153 483**	**161 066**	**166 123**	**171 445**
85	**Education**	**155 730**	**162 243**	**166 667**	**170 247**	**176 642**	**181 011**	**186 321**	**193 348**
86-88	**Human health and social work activities**	**288 050**	**304 899**	**313 947**	**324 403**	**339 202**	**351 895**	**368 025**	**385 504**
90-99	**Arts, entertainment, household goods repairs, other**	**81 641**	**86 385**	**86 381**	**90 633**	**94 764**	**98 627**	**103 072**	**106 272**
90-93	**Arts, entertainment and recreation**	**37 687**	**39 390**	**38 790**	**40 007**	**41 567**	**43 900**	**46 890**	**47 335**
94-96	**Other service activities**	**43 034**	**45 977**	**46 548**	**49 550**	**52 047**	**53 470**	**54 679**	**57 170**
97-98	**Activities of households as employers and for own use**	**920**	**1 018**	**1 043**	**1 076**	**1 150**	**1 257**	**1 503**	**1 767**
05-39	**INDUSTRY INCLUDING ENERGY**	**700 092**	**693 738**	**610 002**	**712 990**	**724 320**	**694 142**	**687 492**	**703 840**
45-99	**TOTAL SERVICES**	**1 980 091**	**2 068 271**	**2 067 905**	**2 149 168**	**2 260 241**	**2 330 662**	**2 417 815**	**2 542 416**
45-82	**BUSINESS SECTOR SERVICES**	**1 310 627**	**1 370 071**	**1 355 012**	**1 412 241**	**1 496 150**	**1 538 063**	**1 594 274**	**1 685 847**
45-82x	**BUSINESS SECTOR SERVICES excluding real estate**	**1 061 575**	**1 102 613**	**1 091 008**	**1 156 154**	**1 220 783**	**1 262 472**	**1 303 307**	**1 376 479**
05-82x	**NON-AGRICULTURE BUSINESS SECTOR excluding real estate**	..	..	..	..	..	..	..	..

.. Not available

Note: Detailed metadata at: http://metalinks.oecd.org/stan/20170410/1c43.

Information on data for Israel: http://oe.cd/israel-disclaimer.

Disclaimer: http://oe.cd/disclaimer

SWEDEN

Table 3. Value added, volumes

ISIC Rev. 4

Million 2010 SEK

		2007	2008	2009	2010	2011	2012	2013	2014
	TOTAL	**3 100 391**	**3 091 199**	**2 913 193**	**3 094 787**	**3 185 944**	**3 182 030**	**3 224 732**	**3 310 548**
01-03	**AGRICULTURE, FORESTRY AND FISHING**	**55 722**	**54 914**	**53 358**	**50 271**	**50 229**	**50 721**	**50 440**	**51 349**
05-09	**MINING AND QUARRYING**	**28 654**	**25 939**	**20 919**	**28 187**	**24 472**	**23 809**	**21 258**	**20 035**
10-33	**MANUFACTURING**	**600 359**	**582 829**	**468 437**	**575 259**	**603 579**	**559 797**	**555 903**	**553 211**
10-12	Food products, beverages and tobacco	37 699	34 665	32 458	39 347	37 776	34 547	34 123	34 065
13-14	Textiles and wearing apparel	..	..	..	..	..	..	..	..
15	Leather and related products	..	..	..	..	..	..	..	..
16	Wood, wood and cork products	22 522	22 228	21 064	19 972	19 648	18 002	16 960	17 327
17	Paper and paper products	31 193	31 586	28 771	33 526	32 838	34 291	33 516	32 488
18	Printing and reproduction of recorded media	9 985	9 558	9 224	8 037	7 751	7 399	5 969	5 962
19-23	Chemical, rubber, plastics, non-metallic products	110 120	109 468	110 184	117 733	131 373	121 699	119 398	111 407
20	Chemicals and chemical products	..	..	..	..	..	..	..	..
21	Pharmaceutical products	..	..	..	..	..	..	..	..
22-23	Rubber, plastic, non-metallic mineral products	29 546	29 067	21 892	26 706	30 251	28 656	24 537	23 631
24	Basic metals	40 158	34 814	12 008	25 078	26 628	24 614	26 596	27 761
25	Metal products, except machinery and equipment	58 950	55 914	39 303	46 840	47 353	46 032	46 183	46 609
26-28	Machinery and equipment	162 962	160 281	127 361	167 145	181 941	169 607	168 610	167 012
26	Computer, electronic and optical products	61 702	64 301	63 914	79 513	80 050	79 027	87 479	93 373
27	Electrical equipment	23 493	22 363	16 839	18 874	22 921	19 540	18 675	16 508
28	Machinery and equipment n.e.c.	83 914	78 114	46 169	68 758	78 970	71 110	63 341	58 908
29-30	Transport equipment	88 319	88 387	53 730	81 543	82 238	69 761	73 008	77 162
29	Motor vehicles, trailers and semi-trailers	66 331	67 045	33 684	62 872	63 123	52 376	54 734	58 421
30	Other transport equipment	21 355	20 556	20 573	18 671	19 114	17 388	18 278	18 776
31-33	Furniture; repair, installation of machinery and equipment	38 390	35 667	31 780	31 794	31 722	29 623	27 175	28 329
31-32	Furniture, other manufacturing	23 524	22 030	20 085	20 305	20 778	19 002	17 388	18 658
33	Repair and installation of machinery and equipment	14 877	13 640	11 689	11 489	10 943	10 609	9 775	9 673
35-39	**ELECTRICITY, GAS, WATER AND WASTE MANAGEMENT**	**115 594**	**111 516**	**110 005**	**109 544**	**111 086**	**125 217**	**121 667**	**126 418**
35	Electricity, gas, steam and air conditioning supply	95 626	92 355	88 284	91 326	92 092	104 907	97 655	102 018
36-39	Water supply; sewerage, waste, remediation activities	20 725	19 913	22 377	18 218	18 994	20 445	23 297	23 705
41-43	**CONSTRUCTION**	**208 068**	**194 551**	**175 962**	**182 358**	**178 214**	**167 647**	**161 413**	**165 984**
45-56	Distribution; transportation, accommodation, food service	562 205	559 514	532 633	559 064	581 967	593 248	610 520	635 767
45-47	**Wholesale and retail trade; motor vehicle and motorcycle repairs**	**333 222**	**329 768**	**321 115**	**340 589**	**350 741**	**357 303**	**371 859**	**394 679**
49-53	**Transportation and storage**	**182 357**	**182 023**	**167 106**	**173 544**	**184 313**	**187 957**	**188 586**	**189 655**
55-56	**Accommodation and food service activities**	**46 470**	**47 543**	**44 411**	**44 931**	**46 913**	**47 981**	**50 072**	**51 729**
58-63	**Information and communication**	**146 812**	**155 834**	**154 635**	**166 347**	**176 145**	**183 097**	**187 645**	**201 196**
58-60	Publishing, audiovisual and broadcasting activities	45 391	45 964	41 290	42 557	43 263	45 809	45 438	46 914
61	Telecommunications	29 814	31 860	35 203	39 650	39 372	40 949	41 283	45 600
62-63	IT and other information services	72 534	78 689	78 233	84 140	93 510	96 320	100 937	108 754
64-66	**Financial and insurance activities**	**115 888**	**114 976**	**118 999**	**120 104**	**130 674**	**130 302**	**139 480**	**142 759**
68	**Real estate activities**	**261 392**	**277 531**	**268 198**	**256 087**	**264 711**	**275 169**	**286 657**	**301 568**
69-82	**Professional, scientific, technical, admin., support activities**	**300 155**	**297 982**	**287 549**	**310 639**	**327 755**	**332 171**	**348 111**	**364 619**
69-75	Professional, scientific and technical activities	208 828	201 247	192 994	210 770	219 205	224 119	240 576	250 171
69-71	Legal, accounting activities; mgt consultancy; engineering	120 393	123 258	121 708	125 593	135 146	140 866	147 111	152 102
73-75	Advertising, market research; other prof., scientific, tech.	28 419	29 934	30 514	31 503	31 648	30 625	31 049	32 061
77-82	Administrative and support service activities	91 187	96 743	94 610	99 869	108 550	108 039	107 559	114 448
84-88	**Public administration, defence; social security; education; health**	**624 957**	**630 213**	**639 682**	**646 294**	**645 109**	**647 371**	**646 609**	**652 635**
84	**Public administration, defence; compulsory social security**	**156 565**	**152 303**	**148 430**	**151 644**	**148 741**	**153 269**	**155 318**	**157 329**
85	**Education**	**162 854**	**163 894**	**170 002**	**170 247**	**171 302**	**169 567**	**167 946**	**168 601**
86-88	**Human health and social work activities**	**305 864**	**314 222**	**321 254**	**324 403**	**325 066**	**324 552**	**323 409**	**326 780**
90-99	**Arts, entertainment, household goods repairs, other**	**88 370**	**90 349**	**87 933**	**90 633**	**92 003**	**92 726**	**93 908**	**95 020**
90-93	**Arts, entertainment and recreation**	**40 259**	**40 687**	**39 228**	**40 007**	**40 328**	**41 153**	**42 785**	**42 016**
94-96	**Other service activities**	**47 060**	**48 559**	**47 629**	**49 550**	**50 565**	**50 390**	**49 731**	**51 379**
97-98	**Activities of households as employers and for own use**	**1 025**	**1 090**	**1 071**	**1 076**	**1 110**	**1 182**	**1 385**	**1 617**
05-39	INDUSTRY INCLUDING ENERGY	743 343	719 838	597 891	712 990	739 137	708 797	699 032	699 525
45-99	TOTAL SERVICES	2 099 081	2 126 620	2 089 586	2 149 168	2 218 364	2 253 968	2 312 207	2 390 854
45-82	BUSINESS SECTOR SERVICES	1 385 866	1 406 173	1 362 143	1 412 241	1 481 252	1 514 106	1 572 955	1 646 267
45-82x	BUSINESS SECTOR SERVICES excluding real estate	1 124 873	1 128 930	1 094 214	1 156 154	1 216 541	1 238 768	1 286 137	1 344 528
05-82x	NON-AGRICULTURE BUSINESS SECTOR excluding real estate	..	..	..	..	..	..	..	..

.. Not available

Note: Detailed metadata at: http://metalinks.oecd.org/stan/20170410/1c43.

Information on data for Israel: http://oe.cd/israel-disclaimer.

Disclaimer: http://oe.cd/disclaimer

SWEDEN

Table 4. Gross fixed capital formation, current prices

ISIC Rev. 4

Million SEK

		2007	2008	2009	2010	2011	2012	2013	2014
	TOTAL	**787 626**	**823 864**	**733 903**	**783 315**	**829 735**	**834 180**	**842 148**	**907 443**
01-03	**AGRICULTURE, FORESTRY AND FISHING**	**15 774**	**17 890**	**16 744**	**18 409**	**19 116**	**16 743**	**14 768**	**15 298**
05-09	**MINING AND QUARRYING**	**8 641**	**9 521**	**6 832**	**6 322**	**10 495**	**13 379**	**11 417**	**9 578**
10-33	**MANUFACTURING**	**158 177**	**163 282**	**145 349**	**149 812**	**159 504**	**151 926**	**157 051**	**178 707**
10-12	Food products, beverages and tobacco	7 175	6 330	6 129	6 477	6 377	6 483	6 706	..
13-14	Textiles and wearing apparel	505	829	405	359	378	319	387	..
15	Leather and related products	65	40	19	63	34	25	24	..
16	Wood, wood and cork products	4 852	5 635	3 703	4 498	4 690	3 365	2 511	..
17	Paper and paper products	10 311	10 908	8 366	7 825	9 158	8 804	9 444	..
18	Printing and reproduction of recorded media	1 898	1 668	1 465	1 529	1 801	1 355	927	..
19-23	Chemical, rubber, plastics, non-metallic products	27 844	27 947	26 183	23 763	29 130	27 669	29 250	..
20	Chemicals and chemical products	..	..	..	..	..	12 597	13 469	..
21	Pharmaceutical products	..	..	..	..	..	6 294	6 229	..
22-23	Rubber, plastic, non-metallic mineral products	4 819	5 019	3 921	4 597	5 008	6 682	6 462	..
24	Basic metals	8 823	10 143	7 595	8 568	10 326	7 000	7 604	..
25	Metal products, except machinery and equipment	8 782	9 213	7 546	7 078	8 471	7 696	7 482	..
26-28	Machinery and equipment	55 426	58 253	53 820	57 299	58 152	56 201	54 930	..
26	Computer, electronic and optical products	38 459	41 455	36 212	38 220	38 728	36 075	34 998	..
27	Electrical equipment	4 439	4 586	4 108	4 595	3 854	4 786	4 473	..
28	Machinery and equipment n.e.c.	12 528	12 212	13 500	14 484	15 570	15 340	15 459	..
29-30	Transport equipment	26 579	26 871	24 944	27 247	25 857	28 601	33 556	..
29	Motor vehicles, trailers and semi-trailers	21 597	21 656	18 515	20 270	18 268	22 143	24 057	..
30	Other transport equipment	4 982	5 215	6 429	6 977	7 589	6 458	9 499	..
31-33	Furniture; repair, installation of machinery and equipment	5 917	5 445	5 174	5 106	5 130	4 408	4 230	..
31-32	Furniture, other manufacturing	3 804	3 422	3 004	3 178	3 484	2 810	3 044	..
33	Repair and installation of machinery and equipment	2 113	2 023	2 170	1 928	1 646	1 598	1 186	..
35-39	**ELECTRICITY, GAS, WATER AND WASTE MANAGEMENT**	**49 909**	**51 989**	**49 923**	**48 516**	**45 868**	**54 141**	**57 105**	**63 518**
35	Electricity, gas, steam and air conditioning supply	40 486	40 783	38 644	38 950	33 110	41 552	43 640	48 362
36-39	Water supply; sewerage, waste, remediation activities	9 423	11 206	11 279	9 566	12 758	12 589	13 465	15 156
41-43	**CONSTRUCTION**	**19 688**	**25 610**	**18 413**	**23 571**	**25 431**	**24 267**	**24 293**	**22 337**
45-56	Distribution; transportation, accommodation, food service	121 735	136 888	120 673	122 102	126 572	136 134	128 975	133 384
45-47	**Wholesale and retail trade; motor vehicle and motorcycle repairs**	**46 888**	**51 911**	**42 224**	**45 208**	**45 911**	**47 481**	**49 521**	**48 123**
49-53	**Transportation and storage**	**68 620**	**78 536**	**72 656**	**71 275**	**74 623**	**81 916**	**72 676**	**78 208**
55-56	**Accommodation and food service activities**	**6 227**	**6 441**	**5 793**	**5 619**	**6 038**	**6 737**	**6 778**	**7 053**
58-63	**Information and communication**	**36 733**	**39 453**	**34 893**	**34 397**	**38 159**	**45 057**	**46 662**	**48 870**
58-60	Publishing, audiovisual and broadcasting activities	7 847	8 213	7 689	7 828	8 603	9 894	10 354	10 654
61	Telecommunications	16 190	16 213	14 786	13 253	13 315	16 528	15 869	17 405
62-63	IT and other information services	12 696	15 027	12 418	13 316	16 241	18 635	20 439	20 811
64-66	**Financial and insurance activities**	**20 097**	**19 302**	**19 491**	**21 625**	**26 987**	**22 020**	**19 757**	**19 058**
68	**Real estate activities**	**205 100**	**199 606**	**171 924**	**191 638**	**204 044**	**195 723**	**201 848**	**228 166**
69-82	**Professional, scientific, technical, admin., support activities**	**65 363**	**70 706**	**61 181**	**71 590**	**75 195**	**74 093**	**70 865**	**78 686**
69-75	Professional, scientific and technical activities	49 810	52 592	48 091	54 245	56 406	56 156	57 338	60 376
69-71	Legal, accounting activities; mgt consultancy; engineering	16 353	17 689	13 438	15 518	16 944	16 114	18 031	17 697
73-75	Advertising, market research; other prof., scientific, tech.	3 194	3 809	2 868	3 082	3 232	2 873	4 346	4 736
77-82	Administrative and support service activities	15 553	18 114	13 090	17 345	18 789	17 937	13 527	18 310
84-88	**Public administration, defence; social security; education; health**	**71 578**	**73 920**	**73 439**	**79 681**	**82 827**	**84 179**	**90 507**	**89 258**
84	**Public administration, defence; compulsory social security**	**42 637**	**41 861**	**41 281**	**44 918**	**44 479**	**47 185**	**52 742**	**44 839**
85	**Education**	**13 247**	**13 945**	**13 739**	**14 263**	**15 443**	**14 842**	**15 244**	**20 008**
86-88	**Human health and social work activities**	**15 694**	**18 114**	**18 419**	**20 500**	**22 905**	**22 152**	**22 521**	**24 411**
90-99	**Arts, entertainment, household goods repairs, other**	**14 831**	**15 697**	**15 041**	**15 652**	**15 537**	**16 518**	**18 900**	**20 583**
90-93	**Arts, entertainment and recreation**	**11 007**	**11 124**	**10 981**	**11 128**	**11 570**	**12 045**	**13 773**	**15 162**
94-96	**Other service activities**	**3 824**	**4 573**	**4 060**	**4 524**	**3 967**	**4 473**	**5 127**	**5 421**
97-98	**Activities of households as employers and for own use**	**0**	**0**	**0**	**0**	**0**	**0**	**0**	**0**
05-39	**INDUSTRY INCLUDING ENERGY**	**216 727**	**224 792**	**202 104**	**204 650**	**215 867**	**219 446**	**225 573**	**251 803**
45-99	**TOTAL SERVICES**	**535 437**	**555 572**	**496 642**	**536 685**	**569 321**	**573 724**	**577 514**	**618 005**
45-82	**BUSINESS SECTOR SERVICES**	**449 028**	**465 955**	**408 162**	**441 352**	**470 957**	**473 027**	**468 107**	**508 164**
45-82x	**BUSINESS SECTOR SERVICES excluding real estate**	**243 928**	**266 349**	**236 238**	**249 714**	**266 913**	**277 304**	**266 259**	**279 998**
05-82x	**NON-AGRICULTURE BUSINESS SECTOR excluding real estate**	..	..	..	..	..	..	..	..

.. Not available

Note: Detailed metadata at: http://metalinks.oecd.org/stan/20170410/1c43.
Information on data for Israel: http://oe.cd/israel-disclaimer.

Disclaimer: http://oe.cd/disclaimer

SWEDEN

Table 5. Number of persons engaged, total employment

ISIC Rev. 4

Thousands

		2007	2008	2009	2010	2011	2012	2013	2014
	TOTAL	**4 524**	**4 565**	**4 455**	**4 498**	**4 594**	**4 627**	**4 672**	**4 737**
01-03	**AGRICULTURE, FORESTRY AND FISHING**	**91**	**93**	**92**	**97**	**106**	**108**	**109**	**108**
05-09	**MINING AND QUARRYING**	**8**	**9**	**8**	**8**	**9**	**9**	**9**	**9**
10-33	**MANUFACTURING**	**682**	**683**	**617**	**607**	**614**	**603**	**590**	**583**
10-12	Food products, beverages and tobacco	58	58	57	56	56	56	55	55
13-14	Textiles and wearing apparel	10	10	9	8	8	7	7	..
15	Leather and related products	1	1	1	1	1	1	1	..
16	Wood, wood and cork products	40	40	35	36	35	33	31	31
17	Paper and paper products	35	34	32	31	30	30	29	28
18	Printing and reproduction of recorded media	20	20	18	17	16	15	14	14
19-23	Chemical, rubber, plastics, non-metallic products	85	83	76	76	76	75	73	71
20	Chemicals and chemical products	..	..	..	..	..	18	18	..
21	Pharmaceutical products	..	..	..	..	..	13	12	..
22-23	Rubber, plastic, non-metallic mineral products	43	43	38	40	41	41	40	38
24	Basic metals	36	37	32	33	34	33	31	31
25	Metal products, except machinery and equipment	85	87	78	75	77	78	76	76
26-28	Machinery and equipment	165	168	153	149	151	150	148	145
26	Computer, electronic and optical products	42	44	44	42	42	43	43	43
27	Electrical equipment	30	30	28	27	27	27	27	27
28	Machinery and equipment n.e.c.	94	94	81	80	82	80	78	75
29-30	Transport equipment	94	92	76	75	80	76	77	78
29	Motor vehicles, trailers and semi-trailers	79	77	60	60	65	61	62	63
30	Other transport equipment	15	15	16	15	15	15	15	15
31-33	Furniture; repair, installation of machinery and equipment	54	55	51	49	51	50	47	47
31-32	Furniture, other manufacturing	33	33	31	30	31	30	28	28
33	Repair and installation of machinery and equipment	21	22	20	19	20	20	19	19
35-39	**ELECTRICITY, GAS, WATER AND WASTE MANAGEMENT**	**50**	**51**	**52**	**51**	**53**	**54**	**56**	**57**
35	Electricity, gas, steam and air conditioning supply	27	28	29	28	28	28	29	29
36-39	Water supply; sewerage, waste, remediation activities	23	23	23	23	25	26	27	28
41-43	**CONSTRUCTION**	**277**	**296**	**295**	**301**	**316**	**321**	**324**	**332**
45-56	Distribution; transportation, accommodation, food service	920	931	923	941	956	960	973	984
45-47	**Wholesale and retail trade; motor vehicle and motorcycle repairs**	**536**	**536**	**536**	**544**	**551**	**550**	**552**	**560**
49-53	**Transportation and storage**	**251**	**256**	**245**	**249**	**252**	**250**	**251**	**248**
55-56	**Accommodation and food service activities**	**133**	**139**	**142**	**148**	**153**	**160**	**170**	**176**
58-63	**Information and communication**	**167**	**173**	**169**	**167**	**168**	**171**	**173**	**176**
58-60	Publishing, audiovisual and broadcasting activities	54	56	55	53	53	53	54	54
61	Telecommunications	26	25	24	22	21	21	21	22
62-63	IT and other information services	87	92	90	92	94	97	98	100
64-66	**Financial and insurance activities**	**93**	**97**	**94**	**94**	**96**	**96**	**96**	**96**
68	**Real estate activities**	**71**	**70**	**70**	**69**	**72**	**72**	**75**	**76**
69-82	**Professional, scientific, technical, admin., support activities**	**478**	**495**	**482**	**503**	**527**	**543**	**553**	**564**
69-75	Professional, scientific and technical activities	270	277	277	285	291	302	309	315
69-71	Legal, accounting activities; mgt consultancy; engineering	166	171	173	177	185	196	200	205
73-75	Advertising, market research; other prof., scientific, tech.	60	61	58	59	58	58	59	59
77-82	Administrative and support service activities	208	218	205	218	236	241	244	249
84-88	**Public administration, defence; social security; education; health**	**1 470**	**1 452**	**1 439**	**1 443**	**1 463**	**1 470**	**1 484**	**1 517**
84	**Public administration, defence; compulsory social security**	**274**	**255**	**243**	**249**	**244**	**249**	**255**	**259**
85	**Education**	**452**	**451**	**455**	**455**	**466**	**469**	**467**	**478**
86-88	**Human health and social work activities**	**744**	**746**	**742**	**739**	**754**	**752**	**763**	**780**
90-99	**Arts, entertainment, household goods repairs, other**	**218**	**214**	**215**	**218**	**215**	**220**	**231**	**234**
90-93	**Arts, entertainment and recreation**	**102**	**100**	**99**	**100**	**99**	**105**	**107**	**105**
94-96	**Other service activities**	**114**	**111**	**113**	**115**	**113**	**112**	**120**	**125**
97-98	**Activities of households as employers and for own use**	**2**	**3**	**3**	**3**	**3**	**3**	**4**	**4**
05-39	**INDUSTRY INCLUDING ENERGY**	740	743	677	666	676	666	655	649
45-99	**TOTAL SERVICES**	**3 416**	**3 433**	**3 391**	**3 434**	**3 496**	**3 532**	**3 584**	**3 648**
45-82	**BUSINESS SECTOR SERVICES**	**1 729**	**1 766**	**1 737**	**1 774**	**1 818**	**1 842**	**1 869**	**1 896**
45-82x	**BUSINESS SECTOR SERVICES excluding real estate**	**1 658**	**1 696**	**1 667**	**1 705**	**1 746**	**1 770**	**1 794**	**1 820**
05-82x	**NON-AGRICULTURE BUSINESS SECTOR excluding real estate**	..	..	..	..	..	..	..	..

.. Not available

Note: Detailed metadata at: http://metalinks.oecd.org/stan/20170410/1c43.
Information on data for Israel: http://oe.cd/israel-disclaimer.

Disclaimer: http://oe.cd/disclaimer

SWEDEN

Table 6. Labour costs (compensation of employees), current prices

ISIC Rev. 4

Million SEK

		2007	2008	2009	2010	2011	2012	2013	2014
	TOTAL	1 479 068	1 552 003	1 552 248	1 600 603	1 692 809	1 760 363	1 813 304	1 882 976
01-03	AGRICULTURE, FORESTRY AND FISHING	14 256	15 252	15 826	16 580	17 036	16 930	17 607	18 281
05-09	MINING AND QUARRYING	3 463	3 677	3 615	3 984	4 488	4 657	4 846	5 112
10-33	MANUFACTURING	265 249	274 384	254 972	254 720	267 648	270 870	269 706	273 967
10-12	Food products, beverages and tobacco	19 570	20 185	20 781	20 600	21 193	21 262	21 481	22 065
13-14	Textiles and wearing apparel	2 605	2 645	2 412	2 332	2 310	2 261	2 330	..
15	Leather and related products	356	335	272	299	295	271	278	..
16	Wood, wood and cork products	12 482	12 864	11 768	11 930	12 277	12 040	11 352	12 074
17	Paper and paper products	15 403	15 622	15 234	14 969	15 477	15 743	15 326	15 347
18	Printing and reproduction of recorded media	7 065	7 464	6 981	6 762	6 595	6 493	6 169	6 088
19-23	Chemical, rubber, plastics, non-metallic products	36 261	36 016	34 145	34 849	36 509	37 576	36 809	36 445
20	Chemicals and chemical products	..	..	..	..	..	9 896	9 974	..
21	Pharmaceutical products	..	..	..	..	..	9 071	8 577	..
22-23	Rubber, plastic, non-metallic mineral products	15 900	15 935	14 692	15 556	17 074	17 119	16 801	17 056
24	Basic metals	14 436	15 039	13 298	14 254	15 403	15 149	14 693	14 955
25	Metal products, except machinery and equipment	29 336	31 122	27 507	26 636	28 831	29 799	29 850	30 210
26-28	Machinery and equipment	69 696	71 513	67 225	66 801	70 272	71 960	72 075	72 642
26	Computer, electronic and optical products	21 622	22 623	22 939	22 877	22 933	24 226	24 483	24 746
27	Electrical equipment	12 013	11 883	11 667	11 415	12 106	12 441	12 221	12 761
28	Machinery and equipment n.e.c.	36 061	37 007	32 619	32 509	35 233	35 293	35 371	35 135
29-30	Transport equipment	39 119	41 818	35 974	36 549	38 883	38 796	40 395	42 416
29	Motor vehicles, trailers and semi-trailers	32 280	34 554	28 308	28 887	31 137	30 543	31 969	33 513
30	Other transport equipment	6 839	7 264	7 666	7 662	7 746	8 253	8 426	8 903
31-33	Furniture; repair, installation of machinery and equipment	18 920	19 761	19 375	18 739	19 603	19 520	18 948	19 048
31-32	Furniture, other manufacturing	11 032	11 483	11 363	11 401	11 768	11 498	11 089	11 328
33	Repair and installation of machinery and equipment	7 888	8 278	8 012	7 338	7 835	8 022	7 859	7 720
35-39	ELECTRICITY, GAS, WATER AND WASTE MANAGEMENT	19 950	21 087	22 122	22 810	24 467	25 453	26 614	27 737
35	Electricity, gas, steam and air conditioning supply	12 638	13 661	14 574	14 972	15 579	16 044	16 688	17 072
36-39	Water supply; sewerage, waste, remediation activities	7 312	7 426	7 548	7 838	8 888	9 409	9 926	10 665
41-43	CONSTRUCTION	94 558	103 790	103 065	107 565	116 495	122 088	125 705	131 806
45-56	Distribution; transportation, accommodation, food service	289 514	304 042	305 245	317 083	336 447	349 904	360 469	373 972
45-47	Wholesale and retail trade; motor vehicle and motorcycle repairs	179 497	187 418	189 199	195 866	207 239	216 117	223 330	232 863
49-53	Transportation and storage	82 911	86 793	85 905	89 004	94 185	95 851	96 427	97 941
55-56	Accommodation and food service activities	27 106	29 831	30 141	32 213	35 023	37 936	40 712	43 168
58-63	Information and communication	78 570	83 391	84 353	85 680	91 484	95 669	98 320	104 982
58-60	Publishing, audiovisual and broadcasting activities	21 027	22 451	22 799	22 751	23 441	24 106	24 880	25 146
61	Telecommunications	11 432	11 623	11 756	11 313	11 418	12 114	12 466	13 633
62-63	IT and other information services	46 111	49 317	49 798	51 616	56 625	59 449	60 974	66 203
64-66	Financial and insurance activities	49 519	50 362	50 719	52 417	53 886	54 887	57 215	56 504
68	Real estate activities	22 497	23 259	23 321	24 133	25 703	26 810	28 279	29 254
69-82	Professional, scientific, technical, admin., support activities	158 968	171 483	175 179	185 201	203 599	215 624	224 007	234 014
69-75	Professional, scientific and technical activities	100 989	108 509	113 562	119 160	129 386	138 647	145 246	151 553
69-71	Legal, accounting activities; mgt consultancy; engineering	63 166	68 140	71 855	75 574	82 873	91 329	95 421	100 010
73-75	Advertising, market research; other prof., scientific, tech.	16 954	17 836	17 745	18 350	19 613	19 976	20 563	21 415
77-82	Administrative and support service activities	57 979	62 974	61 617	66 041	74 213	76 977	78 761	82 461
84-88	Public administration, defence; social security; education; health	431 811	448 461	459 243	474 022	492 830	515 960	535 877	560 162
84	Public administration, defence; compulsory social security	92 905	93 146	93 179	97 859	99 407	105 115	109 376	113 286
85	Education	115 624	120 581	124 325	127 013	131 740	136 785	140 520	146 705
86-88	Human health and social work activities	223 282	234 734	241 739	249 150	261 683	274 060	285 981	300 171
90-99	Arts, entertainment, household goods repairs, other	50 713	52 815	54 588	56 408	58 726	61 511	64 659	67 185
90-93	Arts, entertainment and recreation	21 500	22 358	23 079	23 441	24 398	25 901	27 011	27 863
94-96	Other service activities	28 416	29 560	30 581	32 007	33 295	34 491	36 331	37 782
97-98	Activities of households as employers and for own use	797	897	928	960	1 033	1 119	1 316	1 539
05-39	INDUSTRY INCLUDING ENERGY	288 662	299 148	280 709	281 514	296 603	300 980	301 166	306 816
45-99	TOTAL SERVICES	1 081 592	1 133 813	1 152 648	1 194 944	1 262 675	1 320 365	1 368 826	1 426 073
45-82	BUSINESS SECTOR SERVICES	599 068	632 537	638 817	664 514	711 119	742 894	768 290	798 726
45-82x	BUSINESS SECTOR SERVICES excluding real estate	576 571	609 278	615 496	640 381	685 416	716 084	740 011	769 472
05-82x	NON-AGRICULTURE BUSINESS SECTOR excluding real estate	..	..	..	..	..	..	..	..

.. Not available

Note: Detailed metadata at: http://metalinks.oecd.org/stan/20170410/1c43.

Information on data for Israel: http://oe.cd/israel-disclaimer.

Disclaimer: http://oe.cd/disclaimer

ORGANISATION FOR ECONOMIC CO-OPERATION AND DEVELOPMENT

The OECD is a unique forum where governments work together to address the economic, social and environmental challenges of globalisation. The OECD is also at the forefront of efforts to understand and to help governments respond to new developments and concerns, such as corporate governance, the information economy and the challenges of an ageing population. The Organisation provides a setting where governments can compare policy experiences, seek answers to common problems, identify good practice and work to co-ordinate domestic and international policies.

The OECD member countries are: Australia, Austria, Belgium, Canada, Chile, the Czech Republic, Denmark, Estonia, Finland, France, Germany, Greece, Hungary, Iceland, Ireland, Israel, Italy, Japan, Korea, Latvia, Luxembourg, Mexico, the Netherlands, New Zealand, Norway, Poland, Portugal, the Slovak Republic, Slovenia, Spain, Sweden, Switzerland, Turkey, the United Kingdom and the United States. The European Union takes part in the work of the OECD.

OECD Publishing disseminates widely the results of the Organisation's statistics gathering and research on economic, social and environmental issues, as well as the conventions, guidelines and standards agreed by its members.

OECD PUBLISHING, 2, rue André-Pascal, 75775 PARIS CEDEX 16
(01 2017 09 1 P) ISBN 978-92-64-27443-3 – 2017

www.ingramcontent.com/pod-product-compliance
Lightning Source LLC
Chambersburg PA
CBHW061222240926
51846CB00006B/1317
* 9 7 8 9 2 6 4 2 7 4 4 3 3 *